UNDERSTANDING ZOOLOGY

By

Dr. P.R. Yadav

Lecturer

Dept. of Zoology

D.A.V. College

Muzaffarnagar (U.P.)

(India)

DISCOVERY PUBLISHING HOUSE PVT. LTD.

NEW DELHI-110 002

First Published-2010
Reprinted - 2014
ISBN 978-81-8356-522-6

Published by:
DISCOVERY PUBLISHING HOUSE PVT. LTD.
4831/24, Ansari Road, Prahlad Street
Darya Ganj, New Delhi-110002 (India)
Phone: 23279245 • Fax: 91-11-23253475
E-mail: parul.wasan@gmail.com
info@discoverypublishinggroup.com
Website: www.discoverypublishinggroup.com

Printed at:
Infinity Imaging Systems
Delhi

Preface

The present title "Understanding Zoology" has been written for those students interested in careers in diverse fields of biological sciences. It provides a structured approach to learning by covering all the important topics in a uniform, systematic format. The book has been comprehensively designed incorporating recent advances in this fast moving field. It also provides accessible information on zoology in compact form for undergraduate students in biology and related life sciences. It is intelligible to the educated layman, though it deals with some complex ideas. It is an adequate text for all the requirements of students in this area. In addition, busy lecturers who require a quick reference compendium will find it useful, particularly for tutional planning. Simple, yet hopefully clear figures and tables are provided throughout the book.

The over-riding goal of this book, and indeed of the whole *Understanding series*, is to present the essential information concering zoology in a compact, readily accessible form which leads itself to student learning and revision. The convergence of various approaches has generated a rich panorama of detail, the significance of which we are still attempting to unraval. The present text has been written as an introduction to this rapidly growing field.

To make the work more comprehensive and informative, the author has consulted many authoritative books, research journals, abstracts, monographs etc., so there can be no claim to originality except in the manner of treatment.

The author expresses his thanks to his friends and colleagues whose continue inspirations have initiated him to bring out this book.

The author expresses his gratitude to Mr. Wasan and staff of M/s Discovery Publishing House Pvt. Ltd. for their whole hearted co-operation in the publication of this book.

In the mean time, the author will remain sincerely responsible for any shortcomings of the book and be grateful to the readers for their suggestions and constructive criticism for the continuous betterment of the book. He takes this opportunity to appeal to the readers to send their suggestions straightaway to his Publisher.

Author

Contents

1

INTRODUCTION

The most casual survey will show us that living things are extremely diverse in size, structure, function, and behaviour. Some obvious differences exist between ourselves and our brothers, sisters, parents, and cousins; between our family and other families; between our and other racial groups.

More differences are seen between ourselves as humans and such living things as dogs, cats, horses, fishes, and other animals. Even greater differences are seen between animals and plants. In size alone, animals vary from tiny organisms that are not visible to the unaided eye to that giant of all animal life, the blue whale. Probably one of the smallest living organisms that can be classified as an animal is the spore (resting stage) of tiny protozoan parasites of insects and fish, the Microsporida.

Some of these are as small as 2 microns (1 micron equals about 1/25,000 of an inch) in diameter and weigh about 2.0×10^{-12} gram. At the other end of the scale is the largest animal that ever lived, even larger than the extinct dinosaurs. This is the blue whale, which reaches lengths in excess of 100 feet and weights of more than 115 tons. Upon converting the length of this whale into microns, we find that it is about 15,000,000 (or 1.5×10^{7}) times longer than the microsporidian spore.

As spectacular as are these differences in linear dimensions, differences in weight (a better measure of how much living material is present) are even more fantastic. If we let the weight of the microsporidian be equal to that of a cup of water, then the whale, by comparison, would be equal to more than all the water in the Carribbean Sea, or about three times the volume of water in the Mediterranean Sea.

Shape is another way in which animals differ. Consider various kinds of animals that are about 6 inches in length: a jellyfish, a starfish, an earthworm, a large clam, a small lobster, a fish, a frog, a small bird, and a large mouse. Certainly these exhibit a diversity of shapes!

BIOLOGICAL COMMUNITIES

Diverse forms of life exist in nature, not as isolated organisms, but as groups of individuals of various kinds that live together in complex communities. For example, a forest community consists of trees of many kinds, vines, shrubs, herbs, grasses, and other plants, as well as many kinds of animals ranging from microscopic, single-celled protozoans to such complex forms as worms, insects, snails, frogs, reptiles, birds, and mammals.

Just as the human body needs food to provide energy for the various activities of living, so do all other living organisms need sources of energy. How many of us have ever stopped to consider where this energy in our food came from? We can easily determine that our food consists largely of things that were once alive-things like meat, potatoes, wheat, and eggs.

We can further determine that all animals depend upon plants as a source of food, either directly or indirectly, by feeding on other animals that fed on plants. Biochemical studies have shown that green plants, in the presence of sunlight, convert carbon dioxide and water into various starches and sugars plus oxygen. By this process, called photosynthesis, part of the energy from sunlight is stored, and when these starches and sugars are recombined with oxygen (burned), the stored energy is released.

It is this process that is the source of all of the energy utilized by living organisms. A biological community consists of a large number of green plants that store energy from the sun and utilize this energy to maintain the life processes in the plant. Many animals, called herbivores or plant-feeders, and a few parasitic plants, such as the fungi, depend upon living and dead plants as a source of energy in the form of the stored starches and sugars.

Still other animals, called carnivores or flesh-feeders, feed upon the herbivores. The size and shape of the organisms making up a biological community vary greatly, as we have seen in comparing aquatic with terrestrial communities. All, however, depend upon a flow of energy from the sun-energy that is stored by green plants and utilized either directly or indirectly by animals.

Table 1.1: Diversity in Size of Animals.

Animal	Average Size	Average Weight in Grains	Weight Relative to that of Microsporidia
Microsporidian spore	2 microns	0.000,000,000,02 (= 2×10^{-12})	1.0
Ameba	500 microns	0.000,05 (= 5×10^{-5})	25,000,000 (= 25×10^{6})
Grasshopper	1.5 inches	2.2	1.100,000,000,000 (= 11×10^{11})
Pigeon	15 inches	270	135,000,000,000,000 (= 13.5×10^{13})
Fox	36 inches	4600	2,300,000,000,000,000 (=23×10^{14})
Man	68 inches	68,040 (= 150 lbs.)	34,020,000,000,000,000 (= 34×10^{15})
Gorilla	65 inches	226,800 (= 500lbs.)	113,400,000,000,000,000 (= 11.3×10^{16})
African elephant	11 feet'	6,577.200 (= 14,500 lbs.)	3,288,600,000,000,000,000 (= 32.8×10^{17})
Blue whale	100 feet	104,325,700 (= 230,000 lbs.)	52,162,850,000,000,000,000 (= 52.2×10^{18})
Shoulder			

The various means by which this energy is obtained and utilized constitutes one of the many fascinating facets of the study of zoology.

The Origin and Relationship of Animals

Probably no one will ever know exactly how and when living organisms originated on earth, but several theories have been proposed to explain their origin. Some of these theories are explored in other chapter of this book.

In any case, the available evidence indicates that both plants and animals originated many millions of years ago as small, simple organisms in the sea, and that the huge diversity of plants and animals living today are the descendants, with modifications, of these ancestral organisms.

EVOLUTION AS A PROCESS

We are all aware that offspring are never exactly like their parents. Among humans, none of us is exactly like his father or mother or any other person on earth (unless we happen to have an identical twin) in physical and functional characteristics.

This is true for most living organisms. Some of the slight difference between parents and offspring may permit the offspring to have a better chance of surviving and reproducing other individuals possessing the same slight difference. Other differences may lessen the chance of survival; some individuals are therefore less likely to reproduce their kind.

Biologists believe that just such changes as we can observe in animals from generation to generation, if we allow enough time, are sufficient to account for all the forms of life which occur on earth today as descendants of perhaps a single life form.

Geology has given us ample evidence that more than enough time has been provided since life first appeared on earth, and that, moreover, living forms have evolved along lines leading in general from the simple to the more complex. If the chance variations occurring in the history of a species allow a group of individuals to invade a new territory, a considerable advantage is usually conferred upon them.

A new territory means new sources of food, new space for population growth, and escape from old enemies and competitors. Successful invasion of a new territory also means that the inherited characteristics of the individuals will be tested by new criteria, such as changed environment, new competitors, and new enemies.

Thus, the characteristics of the group are likely to evolve in

Figure 1.1: The life cycle of a typical frog. Breeding and larval development both occur in the water, but the larvae metamorphose (change in appearance) to become adults, and the adults live mostly on land.

directions which are quite different from that of the parent stock in the old environment; that is the say, given sufficient time, the old and the new groups are likely to diverge and become quite different kinds of animals. Because of this, an extremely interesting place to look for evidence of evolution is at the threshold between two quite different environments.

Frequently one will find there some animal form which appears to be "stuck" at the threshold, as though the changes necessary to allow them to move into the new habitat have not, by chance, occurred. Actually, such animals may not be "stuck" at all, for there may be some advantage in remaining at the threshold. After all, the threshold is in itself an environment in which such forms are successful.

THE FROG: "STUCK" AT THE WATER-LAND THRESHOLD

An excellent example of an animal in this kind of situation is the frog, which is "stuck" between a fresh-water world and a dry-land world, spending part of its life in each. Frogs as larvae (tadpoles) are equipped to live in the fresh-water world and as adults are terrestrial animals.

A comparison of the tadpole with the adult frog shows us the changes which must have occurred as permanently fresh-water animals (primitive fishes) gradually acquired the abilities to live on dry land (primitive reptiles). The changes are of many kinds, involving not only changes in the structure of different organs, but also changes in the chemistry of life itself.

Modification in Body Form

The more obvious changes that occur during frog metamorphosis (change from tadpole to adult frog) are the loss of the tail by reabsorption and the appearance of limbs. These changes are correlated with a change in the kind of locomotion best suited to each of the two environments.

After all, it is difficult to swim on land and just as hard to walk in water. Preceding and accompanying these changes is a gradual change from gill respiration (breathing), like that of a fish, to lung respiration, like that of a man. Use of the lungs begins quite early during metamorphosis, as evidenced by the fact that tadpoles rise more and more frequently to the surface of the water to gulp air.

Finally, the gill clefts are closed and respiration is carried out mainly by means of the lungs, although the skin of the entire body retains some functional respiratory ability. The skin is not as efficient a respiratory organ, since it must also be adapted to resist the excessive loss of water through evaporation.

Tadpole skin is thin and delicate, while frog skin is tougher, thicker, and equipped with slime glands-all adaptations for conserving body moisture while living on land and surrounded by air.

Modificaiton in Diet

A change in diet from herbivorous (plant eating) to carnivorous (animal eating) also occurs. The digestion of plant materials requires a long, complex digestive system, while the digestion of animal tissues requires a less lengthy system and certain new enzymes (chemicals that help in the digestion of foods).

During metamorphosis the young frog stops feeding while changes occur in the structure of the digestive system. The abdomen shrinks, the intestine shortens, the stomach, liver, and pancreas increase in size, and different secreting glandular cells appear in the digestive tract. Different digestive enzymes appear in the digestive tract-ones that are related to the new kinds of foods eaten by the adult frog.

Modification in Body Function

Changes in the chemistry of the cells accompany the reabsorption of the tail and the growth of new tissues elsewhere. There is a general increase in the rate of oxygen consumption, indicating increased chemical activity associated with the extensive body remodeling that is going on. Because the adult is more active than the tadpole, increased oxygen consumption continues, supporting a higher metabolic rate.

Increased activity also results in the adult frog's requirement of a higher blood pressure. This in turn demands a better heart as well as certain changes in the protein content of the blood. An increase in the amount of blood albumin is necessary in an animal with high blood pressure, for reasons that will become clear in a later chapter. Needless to say, all these changes occur during metamorphosis.

Another interesting change in blood chemistry reflects the fact that a tadpole, obtaining its oxygen from the limited quantities available in the water, needs blood which readily takes up oxygen from the environment. The adult frog has plenty of oxygen available in the environment (air), so this factor is of less importance, and adult frog blood does not take up oxygen quite so readily,

Instead, the adult frog requires blood which will easily give up its oxygen to the active tissues of the body. Adult frog blood behaves in this way. The end product of the chemical breakdown of proteins is ammonia. Since ammonia is quite toxic, it must be rapidly eliminated from the body of the frog.

For an aquatic animal like a tadpole, this is no problem. Water is abundant and can be used in large quantities to wash away the ammonia as rapidly as it collects. Aquatic animals in general eliminate ammonia directly. A terrestrial animal, however, cannot afford the large water loss associated with this method, and, instead, converts the ammonia internally to a less toxic compound, urea.

Urea can be excreted with much less water loss, but energy is required to make it from ammonia. The adult frog pays the price in energy to avoid the loss in water, as do terrestrial animals in general. In the case of one amphibian, the South African clawed toad *(Xenopus laevis)*, metamorphosis is not accompanied by a change to predominantly terrestrial habitat; rather, the adult remains largely aquatic.

The shift from ammonia excretion to urea excretion begins but disappears again during metamorphosis. The small, oval, sucker-type mouth of the tadpole is equipped with horny jaws and teeth. In the adult it is replaced by the wide slit mouth containing a specialized tongue.

Each form of mouth is adapted, of course, to the diet of a stage in the development of the animal. In the adults, the eyes enlarge and are modified in such a way as to be retractable into the head.

At the same time the chemistry of the light-receptor cells of the retina also changes in a way that permits better vision on land. The kidney is changed from a type characteristic of lower animals to one characteristic of primitive terrestrial animals.

Changes in colouration and body shape and the appearance of sexual differentiation are other prominent features of the process of metamorphosis.

All these changes appear to be under the control of certain hormones released by endocrine glands. This is particularly true of the pituitary gland and the thyroid gland, both of which show increased activity during metamorphosis.

Thyroid hormone is a requirement for metamorphosis, and tadpoles deprived of it continue to grow without transforming into frogs. Tadpoles given early and abnormally large quantities of thyroid hormone metamorphose early, becoming miniature adult frogs.

ZOOLOGY: THE STUDY OF ANIMALS AND THEIR EVOLUTION

It is obvious that in the evolution of the frog, during which its ancestors moved from fresh water to a terrestrial habitat, extensive changes in body form and chemistry occurred. These changes must, therefore, have occurred slowly, a tiny bit at a time. Yet the frog, in its life cycle, reviews much of the process for us in a period of a few days.

It is easy to see that we cannot understand the significance of many of these changes until we know more about the processes of life in general. We must consider the various aspects of the science one at a time; but we must never lose sight of the fact that everything we study is a part of the same science.

We can, for instance, "take the animal apart" and consider its structure and function organ by organ; but when we have finished we must try to "put the animal back together" and visualize it as the single, living organism that it is.

ZOOLOGY AS A SCIENCE

While dictionary definitions may be taken as correct, they are, we must admit, completely cold statements of fact. Definitions of "science," "biology," or "zoology" reflect nothing of the interest and satisfaction that is to be found in the study of life, its diversity, and its mechanisms. There are aspects of life sciences-indeed all sciences-which cannot be expressed in dictionary fashion, but must be experienced to be understood.

It is hoped that in this book, which for many may be the first contact with a biological science, the reader will gain some insight into the esthetic aspects and some familiarity with the factual material.

Hundreds of men and women have devoted lifetimes to the study of living things, not simply because they had to "make a living" but because they considered it to be "fun." The student who approaches his study in this frame of mind will find the study rewarding far beyond the effort he expends.

The definition of the word "science" as given by Webster's New Collegiate Dictionary is, in part, "Accumulated knowledge systematized and formulated with reference to the discovery of general truths or the operation of general laws, especially such knowledge as relates to the physical world." The same reference defines biology as, "The science of life; the branch of knowledge which treats living organisms," and zoology as, "The branch of biology dealing with the animal kingdom ... and with animal life."

The other large branch of biology is, of course, botany, which deals with the plant kingdom and with plant life. Still other branches of biology exist. These are concerned with groups of organisms which cannot easily be classified as either plant or animal. We shall see something more of such organisms in subsequent chapters of this book.

SCIENTIFIC METHOD

If science is a body of accumulated knowledge and general laws, then quite obviously it is necessary to be certain that the data included as a part of science be thoroughly examined and tested to assure ourselves that they qualify as being generally true. Thus, the methods used to obtain this information must be chosen with equal care.

As a well-known contemporary scientist, Dr. Daniel Mazia, has pointed out, performing an experiment is actually asking a question of nature, and we must bear in mind the fact that nature answers our questions literally.

The answer we get will depend upon how the question is asked. If we ask a stupid question, we can depend upon receiving a stupid answer! In attempts to form intelligent questions and to provide a more or less standard approach to science and research, the scientific method has evolved. This method in practice has proved to be a productive and reliable way in which to attack scientific problems of all kinds and to obtain trustworthy results. The first step of the scientific method is best carried out with the feet on the desk.

The scientist who has a question to ask must think of ways of asking it so that meaningful answers will be obtained. One problem arises from the fact that nature will answer questions only with a "yes" or "no" (or sometimes with a "perhaps").

A scientist cannot ask, for example, "How does a starfish open a clam shell so as to eat the clam within?" Rather, he must ask such questions as, "Can the starfish force open the shell by the strength of its own muscles?" or "Does the starfish inject some poison which kills the clam and causes it to fall open by itself?" or other questions that can be answered with a "yes" or a "no."

There is no single experiment by which one can answer the question, "Which of these methods does the starfish use?" The scientist must test each possibility with a separate experiment or series of experiments. Therefore, after formulating the question, his first job is to pose a possible answer; his second job is to test to see if that answer is the correct one.

Each possible answer to the question is called a hypothesis, and upon it an experiment is designed. The investigator could set up experiments to test the strength of the muscles of the starfish and the clam to see which is capable of the greater effort.

He could also closely observe a starfish feeding on a clam and try, by careful measurement, to determine whether any such tug-of-war seems to be involved. He could test extracts of parts of the starfish's feeding apparatus to see if there is any substance which appears to be poisonous to clams, and then, by subsequent experiments, attempt to determine whether or not such a substance, if it exists, is actually used by the starfish to enforce the cooperation of his prey.

If our scientist does not happen to know that a starfish can turn its stomach inside out and insert it into very tiny crevices between the edges of the clam shell and then digest the clam within its own shell, he may be led far astray in his interpretation of what he observes.

We are used to thinking of digestion as a process which occurs within the "eater" rather than within the prey. Nature is not so limited in its "thinking." Virtually everything which is remotely possible actually occurs somewhere within the plant or animal kingdom. This illustrates the need for almost uninhibited imagination as a characteristic of our scientist as he sits, feet on the desk, considering hypotheses which are possible answers to a question he wishes to ask of nature.

When a hypothesis has been tested and retested by experiments with a number of different kinds of starfish and a number of different kinds of clams, it may well be found that in all cases the hypothesis has proved to be correct. Our scientist may now feel that it is safe to state, as a theory, his belief that all starfish gain entrance into clamshells in this same way.

He may do this even though there are still some kinds of starfish and clams which have not been tested. In other words, a theory is only a statement or probable fact based upon a body of experimental evidence that is not necessarily exhaustive in scope.

It is difficult to draw any precise line between the concepts of theory and law. Scientific theories are elevated to the status of laws when the probability of their universal truth is so great that virtually no doubt remains. Despite the care exercised in stating observations as laws, occasionally a law is found to be, after all, incorrect and must be replaced or modified in order to explain new experimental evidence.

As Einstein once said, "Ten thousand experiments will never prove me to be correct, but at any time a single experiment may prove me to be wrong!" Thus, it is a part of the scientific method to constantly re-examine established beliefs in the light of new experiments and, when necessary, to reconstruct parts of the foundations of science.

Many times it is impossible to state the results of an experiment or the measurements of some characteristic of a group of organisms as anything more than averages. Just as each human has facial characteristics which are uniquely his own, so he has internal structures and chemistry that are as individual as his face or his fingerprints. He is, however, still a member of the human species.

There are, of course, definite limits to the amount by which an individual or the results of a given experiment can deviate from the average, and so scientific facts are often expressed as averages for a given species. In addition, a measure of the degree by which most individuals of that species deviate from this average may be given as the standard deviation.

The total observed range of deviation may also be given, and there are a number of other mathematical values used to express other aspects of the same tendency-the tendency for living things to vary one from another in all respects.

THE SUBDIVISIONS OF ZOOLOGY

Just as zoology and botany are the two main branches of biology, so zoology is subdivided into a number of specialized areas or disciplines.

Each of these areas of study broadly overlaps with other disciplines of zoology, so that no absolutely definite and limiting boundaries exist. The names given to these disciplines are as indefinite as are the geographical terms Southwest, West, Mid-west, South, and East, as applied to the United States of America.

The subdivisions or disciplines of the science of zoology are of many kinds; some are based upon interest in a particular group of animals, e.g., mammalogy, ornithology, and protozoology. Others are based upon interest in a certain type of information, e.g., physiology, biochemistry, histology, and anatomy.

Still others rest on still different bases. A list of a few common disciplines and subdisciplines, together with brief statements of definition, is given in Table elsewhere in this chapter. This list is far from being complete; furthermore, since relationships exist in all directions between these listed areas, they could easily be classified in other ways.

Each discipline 'is not a separate science but merely a different view of a common subject: animal life, its similarities and differences, and most important of all, how these similarities and differences came to be.

WHAT IS LIFE?

It is not always as easy as one might suppose to distinguish between living and non-living matter. Indeed, some forms, such as the viruses, seem to lie at the uncertain borderline between the living and the non-living. Let us consider some characteristics of living and non-living matter.

The major characteristics of living matter are:

(1) the tendency to respond to stimuli,

(2) the utilization of some source of nutrition,

(3) the tendency toward growth and development, and

(4) the ability to reproduce.

Non-living things respond to stimuli in certain relatively simple ways. Gunpowder responds to the application of a lighted match by exploding. Metals expand and contract with changing temperatures, and an electric light bulb responds by producing light when an electric current is passed through it.

These responses are not nearly so complex as the responses of a man to the stimuli of his environment or even the responses of a plant to light. Similarly, non-living things often make use of energy sources and appear to engage in a form of nutritive activity. Man-made machines

Table 1.2: Differences Between Plants and Animals.

Animals	*Plants*
Usually require complex, synthesized foods *which* are altered chemically to provide material for growth or are broken down to yield energy (heterotrophic or holozoic nutrition).	Usually are able to use simple foods from the soil and energy from sunlight to synthesize complex materials for growth (autotrophic or holophytic nutrition).
Require oxygen and produce carbon dioxide and other simple substances such as urea as waste products.	Require carbon dioxide and produce oxygen as a waste product.
Usually able to move about (locomotion) or to move body parts rapidly.	Usually unable to move about or to move body rapidly.
Usually have invariable body form and shape (definite number of arms and legs placed in definite positions).	Usually have variable body form and shape (variable number and position of branches).
Organs usually internal and growth differential in character and sharply limited in extent.	Organs often added externally and growth apical in character and not so sharply limited in extent.
Cell walls, if present, usually delicate and not containing cellulose.	Cell walls usually rigid and containing cellulose.
Usually show rapid response to stimuli.	Usually only slow response to stimuli.
Usually carbohydrates are stored in the form of glycogen.	Usually carbohydrates are stored in the form of starch.

in particular, consume fuel; but again this is a simple process, compared with the nutritive activity of a plant or animal which converts various raw materials into plant or animal tissue and into the particular compounds which are suitable as fuel for its energy-releasing processes.

The automobile cannot create its own gasoline from other substances and then proceed to use it for self-repair, growth, reproduction, and energy; but living things, in general, can carry out analogous processes. Certain non-living things display a simple form of growth.

The formation of crystals or even the accumulation of greater size in a snowball rolling down a hill are examples of growth. This is entirely growth by accretion (the adding of more material to the outside) and does not involve any reorganization or change in internal structure accompanying the total increase in size.

Growth of living things is far more than increase in total size. The growing child changes in body proportions, develops in intellectual ability as a result of growth in the complexity of his nervous system, and changes in appearance as a result of sexual maturation. Another familiar and even more striking example is the change of certain insects from larva to pupa to adult-each with a totally different appearance and a change in total size.

Probably the most reliable criterion of the life of a unit or system is the ability of that unit or system to reproduce itself. No non-living system is capable of reproduction as complex as biological reproduction.

Theoretical models of self-duplicating machines have been presented in literature, and crude examples of natural self-duplication of crystals have been presented as examples of nonliving reproducing systems. These are all on a scale of simplicity so far removed from the processes of reproduction in plants and animals that no serious comparison is warranted.

The viruses constitute a group which appears to lie on the borderline between the living and the non-living. They can sometimes be crystallized like non-living chemicals, subjected to all sorts of stresses, such as high temperatures, acids, etc., and still remain able to reproduce and continue to "live" when returned to the proper environment.

They are able to reproduce, but only with the help of the cells of a plant or animal "host" in which they live. They can, perhaps, be thought of as incomplete living things. They live only when they can borrow a part of the machinery of a higher plant or animal in which they exist as a parasite. Probably these viruses are very close to the first and simplest form of life to appear on our planet.

WHAT IS AN ANIMAL

In much the same way, it is sometimes difficult to distinguish between plants and animals. Though our criteria for this differentiation are good in the vast majority of cases, there are many examples of living things which appear to lie on the borderline between the two "kingdoms" of living things.

The general criteria on which the division between animals and plants is made are presented in tabular form in Table elsewhere in this chapter. It must be remembered that no one of these criteria can be considered as adequate alone, since exceptions exist in all cases.

Moreover, certain living things combine the characteristics of plants and animals to such an extent that they are claimed by both zoologists and botanists. Some writers have proposed the use of a third kingdom, the Protista, to include, among other organisms, those of doubtful position.

2

BIOMOLECULES

Despite their great diversity, the chemical composition and metabolic processes of all living things are remarkably similar. At one time it was believed that there was a unique substance in their chemical composition that distinguished living organisms from inanimate matter. The search for this substance proved fruitless.

Instead, biologists came to understand that it is the specific organization and precise interaction of its components that characterize life. To understand life processes, then, one must know the basic principles of chemistry, or, to bc more specific, biochemistry. For those who have never enjoyed a formal chemistry course, this chapter provide the basic definitions and concepts necessary for an understanding of biology.

CHEMICAL ELEMENTS

All matter, living and nonliving alike, is composed of chemical *elements*, substances that cannot be broken down into simpler substances by chemical reactions. The matter of the universe is composed of 92 naturally occurring elements, ranging from hydrogen, the lightest, to uranium, the heaviest.

In addition to the naturally occurring elements, about 17 elements heavier than uranium have been made by bombarding elements with subatomic particles in devices known as particle accelerators.

About 98% of an organism's mass' is composed of only six elements-oxygen, carbon, hydrogen, nitrogen, calcium, and phosphorus. Approximately 14 other elements are consistently present in living things, but in smaller quantities. Some of these, such as iodine and copper, are known as *trace elements* because they are present in such minute amounts. Table elsewhere in this chapter lists the elements that make up a living organism and explains why each is important.

Instead of writing out the name of each element, chemists use a system of abbreviations called *chemical symbols*—usually the first one or two letters of the English or Latin name of the element. For example, 0 is the symbol for oxygen, C for carbon, Cl for chlorine, N for nitrogen, and Na for sodium (its Latin name is *natrium*). Chemical symbols for the elements found in living organisms are given in Table elsewhere in this chapter.

THE ATOM

Imagine a bit of gold being divided into smaller and smaller pieces. The smallest possible particle of gold that could be obtained would be an atom of gold. The *atom* is the smallest subdivision of an element that retains the characteristic chemical properties of that element.

The subdivision of any kind of matter ultimately yields atoms. This is true no matter what physical state matter may assume-solid, liquid, or gas. Atoms are almost unimaginably small-much smaller than the tiniest particle visible under a light microscope.

By special scanning electron microscopy, with magnification as much as 5 million times, researchers have been able to photograph some of the larger atoms, such as uranium.

Atomic Structure

An atom is composed of smaller components called *subatomic particles*. For our purposes we need consider only three types-protons, neutrons, and electrons. *Protons* have a positive electric charge; *neutrons* are uncharged particles with about the same mass as protons. Protons and neutrons make up almost all the mass of an atom and are concentrated in the *atomic nucleus*.

Electrons have a negative electrical charge and an extremely small mass (only about 1/1800 of the mass of a proton). The electrons, as we will see, spin about in the space surrounding the atomic nucleus.

Each kind of element has a fixed number of protons in the atomic nucleus. This number, called the *atomic number*, is written as a subscript to the left of the chemical symbol. Thus $_1H$ and $_8O$ indicate that the hydrogen nucleus contains one proton and the oxygen nucleus has eight protons.

It is the atomic number, the number of protons in the nucleus, that determines the chemical identity of the atom. The total number of protons plus neutrons in the nucleus is termed the *mass number* and is

Table 2.1: Elements that Make Up the Human Body.

Name	*Chemical symbol*	*Approximate composition by mass (%)*	*Importance or function*
Oxygen	O	65	Required for cellular respiration; present in most organic compounds; component of water
Carbon	C	18	Backbone of organic molecules; can form four bonds with other atoms
Hydrogen	H	10	Present in most organic compounds; component of water
Nitrogen	N	3	Component of all proteins and nucleic acids
Calcium	Ca	1.5	Structural component of bones and teeth; important in muscle contraction, conduction of nerve impulses, and blood clotting
Phosphorus	P	1	Component of nucleic acids; structural component of bone; important in energy transfer
Potassium	K	0.4	Principal positive ion (cation) within cells; important in nerve function; affects muscle contraction
Sulfur	S	0.3	Component of most proteins
Sodium	Na	0.2	Principal positive ion in interstitial (tissue) fluid; important in fluid balance; essential for conduction of nerve impulses
Magnesium	Mg	0.1	Needed in blood and other body tissues
Chlorine	Cl	0.1	Principal negative ion (anion) of interstitial fluid; important in fluid balance; component of sodium chloride
Iron	Fe		Trace amount Component of hemoglobin and myoglobin; component

		of certain enzymes
Iodine	I	Trace amount Component of thyroid hormones

Other elements found in very small amounts in the body include manganese (Mn), copper (Cu), zinc (Zn), cobalt (Co), fluorine (F), molybdenum (Mo), selenium (Se), and a few others. They are called trace elements.

indicated by a superscript to the left of the chemical symbol. The common form of oxygen atom, with eight protons and eight neutrons in its nucleus, has an atomic number of 8, and a mass number of 16. It is indicated by the symbol $^{16}_{8}O$.

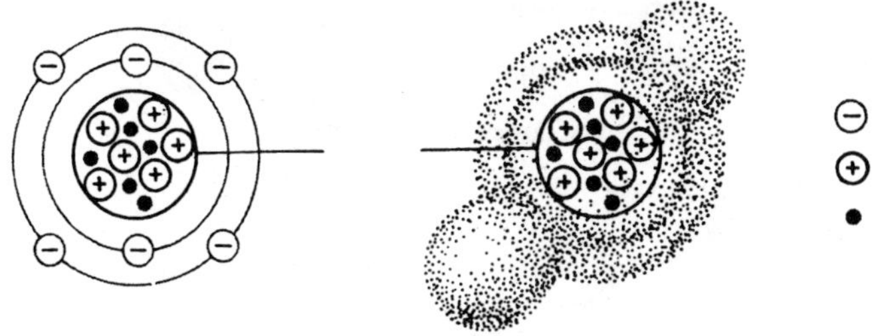

Figure 2.1: Two ways of representing an atom.

Electron Configuration

The way electrons are arranged around an atomic nucleus is referred to as the atom's *electron configuration*. Knowing the locations of electrons enables chemists to predict how atoms can combine to form different types of chemical compounds.

Because they are negatively charged, electrons are attracted to the positively charged protons in the atomic nucleus (opposite charges tend to attract). At the same time, electrons repel one another (like charges tend to repel one another).

These considerations help determine the locations of electrons. An atom may have several *energy levels*, or *electron shells*, where electrons are located. The lowest energy level is the one closest to the nucleus. Only two electrons can occupy this energy level. The second energy level can accommodate a maximum of eight electrons.

Although the third and outer shells can each contain more than eight electrons, they are most stable when only eight are present. We may consider the first shell complete when it contains two electrons, and every other shell complete when it contains eight electrons.

The atomic structures of some elements that are important in biological systems-carbon, hydrogen, oxygen, nitrogen, sodium, and chlorine—are shown in Figure elsewhere in this chapter. Although the simple diagrams, called *Bohr models*, of electron configuration shown in Figure 2-2 are helpful in understanding atomic structure, they are highly oversimplified. Within energy levels, electrons occur in characteristic regions of space, termed *orbitals*.

There may be several orbitals within a given energy level, and each orbital can contain at most two electrons. Electron orbitals may be represented by spherical, dumbbell-shaped, or more complex three-dimensional coordinates.

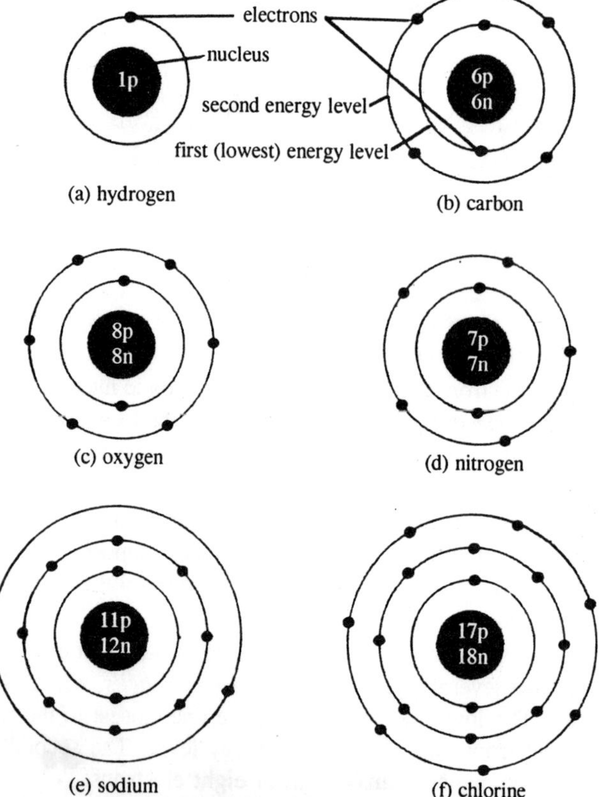

Figure 2.2: Bohr models of some biologically important atoms. (a) Hydrogen. (b) Carbon. (c) Oxygen. (d) Nitrogen. (e) Sodium. (f) Chlorine. Each circle represents an energy level, or electron shell. Electrons are represented by dots on the circles; p, proton; n, neutron.

Electrons are thought to whirl around the nucleus, now close to it, now farther away. Orbitals represent the places where electrons are most probably found. In fact, one way of illustrating an atom is to show its orbitals as electron clouds. Each occupied orbital can be represented as an electron cloud. The density of the shaded areas represents the likelihood that an electron is present at a given time.

The distance of the electrons from the atomic nucleus depends upon their respective energy levels. The specific orbital that an electron occupies is determined by the total energy of the system and the number of electrons available to the atom.

An electron can be moved to an orbital farther from the nucleus by providing it with more energy, or an electron can give up energy and sink back to a lower energy level in an orbital nearer the central nucleus. Energy is required to move a negatively charged electron further away from the positively charged nucleus.

When energy is added to the system, an electron can jump from one level to the next, but it cannot stop in the space in between. To move an electron from one level to the next, the atom must absorb a discrete packet of energy known as a quantum, which contains just the right amount of energy needed for the transition-no more and no less. The term "quantum jump" is used in everyday language to indicate a sudden discontinuous move from one level to another.

CHEMICAL COMPOUNDS

Two or more atoms may combine chemically to form a *molecule*. When two atoms of oxygen combine, a molecule of oxygen is formed. Different kinds of atoms can combine, forming *chemical compounds*. A chemical compound is a substance that consists of two or more different elements combined in a fixed ratio. Water is a chemical compound consisting of two atoms of hydrogen combined with one atom of oxygen.

What Are Formulas?

A *chemical formula* is a shorthand method for describing the chemical composition of a molecule. Chemical symbols are used to indicate the types of atoms in the molecule, and subscript numbers are used to indicate the number of each type of atom present.

The chemical formula for molecular oxygen, O_2, tells us that this molecule consists of two atoms of oxygen. The chemical formula for water, H_2O, indicates that each molecule consists of two atoms of hydrogen and one atom of oxygen. (Note that when a single atom of one type is present, it is not necessary to write 1; one does not write H_2O_1.)

Another type of formula is the *structural formula*, which shows not only the types and numbers of atoms in a molecule but also their arrangement. In any type of chemical compound the atoms are always arranged in the same way. From the chemical formula for water, H_2O, you could only guess whether the atoms were arranged H—H—O or H—H. The structural formula, H—O—H, settles the matter, indicating Mat the two hydrogen atoms are attached to the oxygen atom.

In water this arrangement is the only one chemically possible. However, there are other substances that consist of the same atoms yet have different chemical properties due to alternative arrangements. Such compounds are known as *structural isomers*. The sugars glucose and fructose are examples.

Chemical Equations

During any moment in the life of an organism, be it an earthworm or a pine tree, many complex, highly organized chemical reactions are taking place. The chemical reactions that occur between atoms and moleculesfor instance, between methane (natural gas) and oxygen-can be described on paper by means of chemical equations:

$$\underset{\text{Methane}}{CH_4} + \underset{\text{Oxygen}}{2O_2} \rightarrow \underset{\text{Carbon dioxide}}{CO_2} + \underset{\text{Water}}{2H_2O}$$

In a *chemical equation* the *reactants* (the substances that participate in the reaction) are written on the left side of the equation and the *products* (the substances formed by the reaction) are written on the right side. The arrow means *yields* and indicates the direction in which the reaction tends to proceed. The number preceding a chemical symbol or formula indicates the number of atoms or molecules reacting.

Thus $2O_2$ means two molecules of oxygen and $2H_2O$ means two molecules of water. The absence of a number indicates that only one atom or molecule is present.

In some cases the reaction will proceed in the reverse direction as well as forward; at *equilibrium* a certain amount of the product continuously breaks up to form the reactants, and the rate of the forward reaction equals the rate of the reverse action. Reversible reactions are indicated by double arrows:

$$\underset{\text{Nitrogen}}{N_2} + \underset{\text{Hydrogen}}{3H_2} \rightleftarrows \underset{\text{Ammonia}}{2NH_3}$$

HOW ATOMS COMBINE: CHEMICAL BONDS

The chemical properties of an element are determined primarily by the number and arrangement of electrons in the *outermost* energy level (electron shell). In a few elements, called the *noble gases*, the outermost shell is filled. These elements are chemically inert, meaning that they will not readily combine with other elements. Two such elements are helium with two electrons (a complete inner shell) and neon with ten electrons (a complete inner shell of two and a complete second shell of eight).

The electrons in the outermost energy level of an atom are referred to as *valence electrons*. When the outer shell of an atom contains fewer than eight electrons, the atom tends to lose, gain, or share electrons to achieve an outer shell of eight (zero or two in the case of the lightest elements).

The elements in a given compound are always present in a certain proportion by mass. This reflects the fact that atoms are attached to each other by chemical bonds in a precise way to form the compound. A *chemical bond* is the attractive force that holds two atoms together.

Each bond represents a certain amount of potential chemical energy. The atoms of each element form a specific number of bonds with the atoms of other elements-a number dictated by the number of valence electrons. The two principal types of chemical bonds are covalent bonds and ionic bonds.

Covalent Bonds

Covalent bonds involve the sharing of electrons between atoms. The more precise definition of a *molecule* is a combination of two or more atoms joined by covalent chemical bonds. A simple example of a covalent bond is the one joining two hydrogen atoms in a molecule of hydrogen gas, H_2.

Each atom of hydrogen has one electron, but two electrons are required to complete the first energy level. Each hydrogen atom has the same capacity to attract electrons, so one does not donate an electron to the other.

Instead, the two hydrogen atoms share their single electrons so that each of the two electrons is attracted simultaneously to the two protons in the two hydrogen nuclei. The two electrons are thus under the influence of *both* atomic nuclei, and they join the two atoms together.

The carbon atom has four electrons in its outer energy level. These four electrons are available for covalent bonding. When one carbon and four hydrogen atoms share electrons a molecule of methane (CH_4) is formed:

```
   H
   |
H—C—H
   |
   H
```

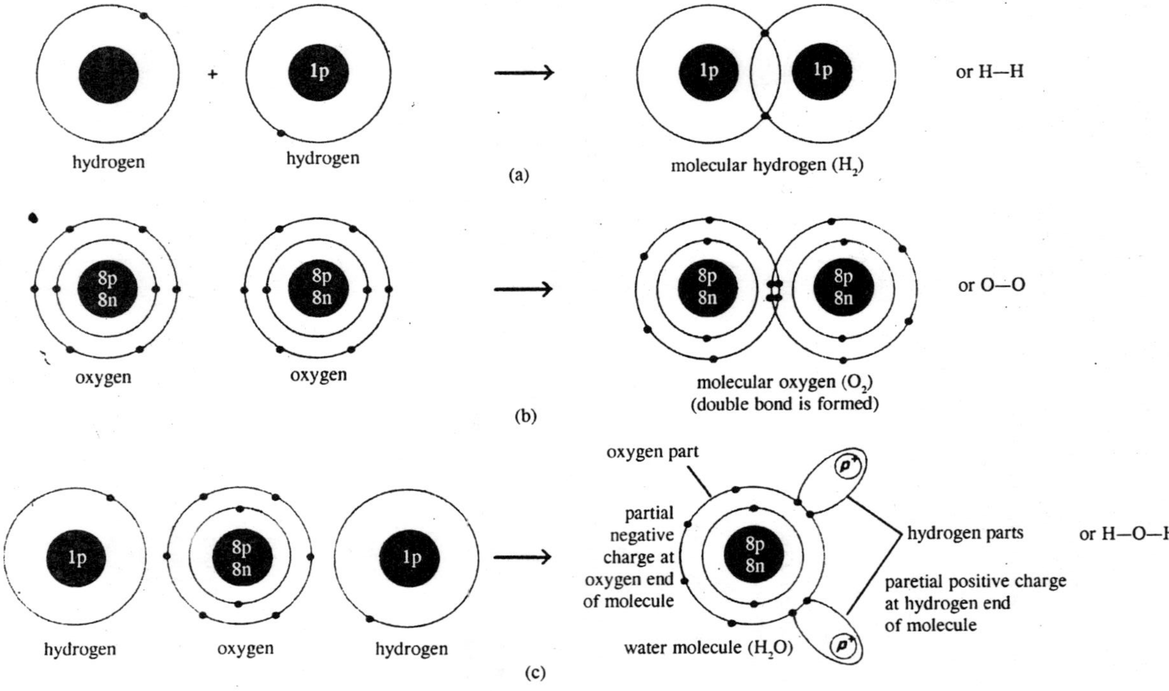

Figure 2.3: Formation of covalent compounds.

Each atom shares its outer-level electrons with the others, thereby completing the first energy level of each hydrogen atom and the energy level of the carbon atom. When one electron pair is shared between two atoms, the covalent bond is referred to as a single bond.

The nitrogen atom has five electrons in its outer shell. When a nitrogen atom shares electrons with three hydrogen atoms, a molecule of ammong, NH_3, is formed:

```
H—N—H
  |
  H
```

Two oxygen atoms may achieve stability by forming covalent bonds with one another. Each oxygen atom has six electrons in its outer shell. To become stable, the two atoms share two pairs of electrons, forming molecular oxygen.

When two pairs of electrons are shared in this way, the covalent bond is referred to as a *double bond*. Some atoms form tr-iple bonds with one another, sharing three pairs of electrons.

Table 2.2: Some Biologiclly Important Ions.

Name	*Formula*	*Charge*	
Sodium	Na^+	1 +	
Potassium	K^+	1 +	
Hydrogen	H^+	1 +	
Magnesium	Mg^{2+}	2 +	
Calcium	Ca^{2+}	2 +	
Iron	Fe^{2+} or Fe^{3+}	2 +	[iron(II)1 or 3+ [iron(III)1
Ammonium	NH_4^+	1 +	
Chloride	Cl	1 –	
Iodide	I^-	1 –	
Carbonate	CO_3^2	2 –	
Bicarbonate	HCO_3^-	1 –	
Phosphate	PO_4^{3-}	3 –	
Acetate	CH_3OOO^-	1 –	
Sulfate	SO_4^2	2 –	
Hydroxide	OH^-	1 –	
Nitrate	NO_3	1 –	
Nitrite	NO_2^-	1 –	

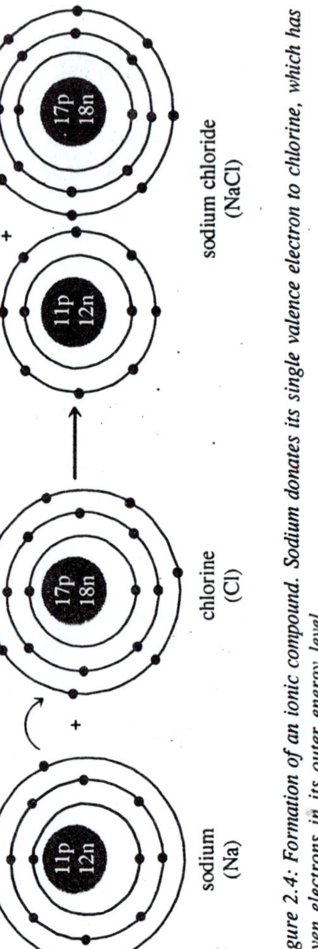

Figure 2.4: Formation of an ionic compound. Sodium donates its single valence electron to chlorine, which has seven electrons in its outer energy level.

Electronegativity is a measure of an atom's attraction for the electrons in chemical bonds. A covalent bond between atoms of different electronegativities is known as a *polar covalent bond*.

The polarity of compounds is very important in understanding the structure of biological membranes and their properties. Covalent bonds have many degrees of polarity, from *nonpolar*, in which the electrons are exactly shared (as in the hydrogen molecule), to those in which the electrons are *much* closer to one atom than to the other.

Ionic Bonds

One extreme of polarity is the ionic bond, in which electrons are pulled completely from one atom to the other. The number of protons in the nucleus remains unchanged, so the loss or gain of electrons produces an atom with a net positive or negative charge.

Such electrically charged atoms are termed *ions*. Atoms with one, two, or three electrons in the outer shell generally donate electrons to other atoms.

These atoms, then, become positively charged because of the excess of protons in the nucleus. For example, sodium has one valence electron. It tends to donate this electron, becoming a sodium ion (Na^+) with a one plus charge. Calcium tends to lose its two valence electrons to become a calcium ion (Ca^{2+}) with a two plus charge. Positively charged ions are termed *cations*.

Atoms with five, six, or seven electrons in their outer shell tend to *gain* electrons from other atoms and become negatively charged anions (e.g., Cl^-, chloride ion). Charged particles, both anions and cations, play many important roles in biological systems, such as the transmission of nerve impulses and the contraction of muscles.

An *ionic bond* is the force of electrical attraction between two oppositely charged ions. When held together by ionic bonds, oppositely charged ions form an ionic compound. Sodium chloride is a good example of an ionic compound. A sodium atom, with atomic number 11, has two electrons in its inner shell, eight in the second, and one in the third shell.

A sodium atom cannot fill its third shell by obtaining seven electrons from other atoms because it would then have a vast excess of negative charge. Instead, it gives up the single electron in its third shell to some electron acceptor, leaving the second shell as the complete outer shell. A chlorine atom, atomic number 17, has two electrons in its inner shell, eight in the second, and seven in the third shell.

The chlorine atom achieves a complete outer shell not by losing the seven electrons in its third shell (for it would then have a vast positive charge) but by accepting an electron from an electron donor, such as sodium, to complete its third shell.

When an electron donor, such as sodium, meets an electron acceptor, such as chlorine, the electron may be transferred completely from the donor to the acceptor. The sodium ion now has 11 protons in its nucleus and ten electrons around the nucleus, giving it a net charge of 1^+. The chlorine ion has 17 protons in its nucleus and 18 electrons around the nucleus, so it has a net charge of 1^-.

These ions attract each other as a result of their opposite charges.

They are held together by this electrical attraction to form sodium chloride (NaCl), common table salt. This transfer of one or more electrons from one atom to another and the binding together of two ions of opposite charge (the ionic bond) results in the formation of an ionic compound. Ionic bonds occur between electron donors and electron acceptors.

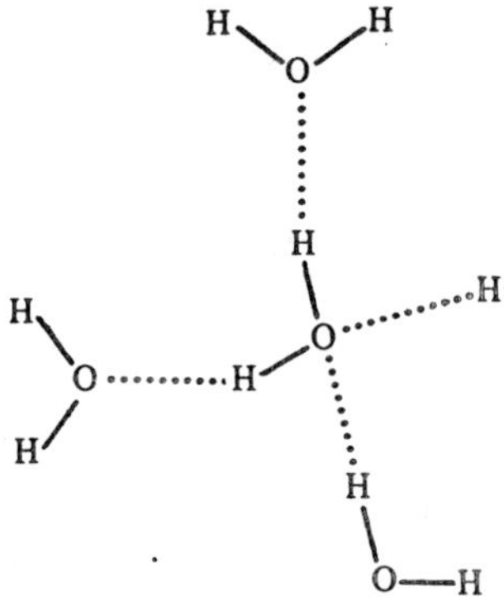

Figure 2.5: Hydrogen bonding of water molecules. Each water molecule tends to form hydrogen bonds with four neighboring water molecules.

Whether an ionic compound is in solid form or is dissolved in water, its constituent particles (ions) do not share electrons. Because of this, the term *molecule* does not adequately explain the properties of ionic compounds such as NaCl. Chemists simply refer to them as compounds.

Hydrogen Bonds

Another type of bond that is important in biological systems is the *hydrogen bond*. This type of bond is formed when a hydrogen atom is attracted to two other atoms, one of which is usually oxygen or nitrogen. Hydrogen bonds tend to form between a hydrogen atom covalently bonded to oxygen or nitrogen and some other electronegative atom, usually oxygen or nitrogen.

The atoms involved may be in two parts of the same molecule or in two molecules. When hydrogen is combined with an electronegative atom, such as oxygen, it has a partial positive charge because its electron is positioned closer to the oxygen atom. Hydrogen bonds are weak and are readily formed and broken.

They have a specific length and orientation, which is very important in their role in helping to determine the three-dimensional structure of large molecules, such as nucleic acids and proteins. Though relatively weak individually, the large numbers of hydrogen bonds that occur in the double helix of DNA and in the alpha helix of proteins are together very effective.

OXIDATION-REDUCTION

Rusting-the combination of iron with oxygen-is a familiar example of oxidation and reduction:

$$4Fe + 3O_2 \rightarrow 2Fe_2O_3$$

Oxidation is a chemical process in which a substance loses electrons. In rusting, iron is changing from its metallic state to its iron(III) (Fe^{3+}) state. We say it is being oxidized:

$$4Fe \rightarrow 4Fe^{3+} + 12e^-$$

The e^- stands for electron. At the same time, oxygen is changing from its molecular state to its charged state:

$$3O_2 + 12e^- \rightarrow 6CO_2$$

Oxygen accepts the electrons removed from the iron and is said to be reduced. *Reduction* is a chemical process in which a substance gains electrons. An oxidation cannot take place without a reduction because electrons have to go somewhere; free electrons are not usually found in nature. Some substance must accept the electrons that are lost. Oxidation-reduction reactions are sometimes called *redox reactions*.

Electrons are not easy to remove from covalent compounds unless an entire atom is removed. In living cells oxidation almost always involves the removal of a hydrogen atom from a compound. Reduction often involves a gain in hydrogen atoms. As will be discussed in later chapters, redox reactions are an essential part of photosynthesis, cellular respiration, and other aspects of metabolism.

INORGANIC COMPOUNDS

Chemical compounds can be divided into two broad groups-inorganic and organic. *Inorganic compounds* are relatively small, simple substances. *Organic compounds* are usually large and complex and always contain carbon. Among the biologically important groups of inorganic compounds are water, simple acids and bases, and salts.

Organisms depend upon appropriate amounts of these substances for fluid balance, acid-base balance, and many cell activities, such as transporting materials through cell membranes.

Water

Water is an essential ingredient of life. It accounts for about 80% of the weight of an average active cell. In fact, the human body is about 70% water by weight. Many organisms make their homes in lakes, rivers, or the sea, and the cells of terrestrial organisms are bathed in body fluids composed largely of water.

Polar Properties

The physical and chemical properties of water permit life to exist on our planet. Water molecules are *polar*; that is, they bear a partial positive and a partial negative charge. The water molecules in liquid water and in ice are held together in part by hydrogen bonds.

The hydrogen atom of one water molecule, with its partial positive charge, is attracted to the oxygen atom of a neighboring water molecule, with its partial negative charge, forming a hydrogen bond. Each water molecule can form hydrogen bonds with a maximum of four neighboring water molecules.

Properties as a Solvent

Because its molecules are polar, water is an excellent *solvent*, a liquid capable of dissolving many polar substances. For example, the ions of a salt, such as sodium chloride, are held together by strong ionic bonds; in fact, they form a crystal lattice.

Considerable energy is required to pull the positively and negatively charged ions apart. However, when the sodium chloride is placed in water, the strong electrical attractions between the polar water molecules and Na^+ and Cl^- ions result in the formation of stable dissociated Na^+ and Cl^- ions.

$$\underset{\text{Sodium chloride}}{NaCl} \xrightarrow{\text{In } H_2O} \underset{\text{sodium ion}}{Na^+} + \underset{\text{Chloride ion}}{Cl^-}$$

Because of its solvent properties and its tendency to cause the ionization of compounds in solution, water is important in facilitating chemical reactions.

Cohesive and Adhesive Forces

Water exhibits both cohesive and adhesive forces. Water molecules have a very strong tendency to stick to each other; that is, they are *cohesive*. This is due to the hydrogen bonds among the molecules. Water molecules also stick to many other kinds of substances (i.e., those substances that have charged groups of atoms or molecules on their surfaces).

These *adhesive* forces explain how water makes things wet. Water has a high degree of surface tension because of the cohesiveness of its molecules; its molecules have a much greater attraction for other water molecules than for molecules in the air. Thus water molecules at the surface crowd together, producing a strong layer as they are pulled downward by the attraction of other water molecules beneath them.

Adhesive4id cohesive forces account for the tendency, termed *capillary action*, of water to rise in very fine tubes. Capillary action plays some part in the rise of water through the stems of plants to their leaves.

Temperature Stabilization

Other properties are responsible for water's ability to minimize temperature changes. Water has a high specific heat. *Specific heat* is the amount of heat required to raise the temperature of 1 gram of water 1°C. The high specific heat of water is due to its hydrogen bonds.

For the temperature of a substance to be raised, heat energy must be added to make its molecules move faster-to increase the kinetic energy of the molecules. Before water molecules can move freely, some of the hydrogen bonds holding the water molecules together must be broken.

Thus a great deal of the heat energy added to water is used up in breaking the hydrogen bonds, and only a part of this energy is available to speed the motion of the water molecules (increase the temperature of the water).

Because so much heat input (or heat loss) is required to raise (or lower) the temperature of water, the oceans and other large bodies of water have relatively constant temperatures. Thus the aquatic environment provides the multitude of organisms that inhabit it with a relatively constant environmental temperature.

The water within all organisms, even those that live on land, contributes to a relatively constant internal temperature. This is important because metabolic reactions can take place only within a relatively narrow temperature range.

Because its molecules are held together by hydrogen bonds, water also has a high heat of vaporization, another property that helps stabilize temperature. More than 500 calories are required to change 1 gram of liquid water into 1 gram of water vapor.

A calorie is a unit of heat energy (defined as 4.184 joules). Because of the heat of vaporization, we can rid ourselves of excess heat by the evaporation of sweat. And plants can remain cool in the midday heat by evaporating water from their surface.

Although most substances become more and more dense as the temperature decreases, water reaches its maximum density at 4°C and then begins to expand again as the temperature decreases. Hydrogen bonds become more rigid and ordered, and ice floats upon the denser cold water.

This important property of water explains why lakes and ponds freeze from the surface down rather than from the bottom up. The sheet of ice that forms at the pond surface insulates the water below from the wintry chill so that it is less likely to freeze. Further, organisms that inhabit northern lakes and ponds are able to carry on their life activities despite the frigid winter.

Acids and Bases

An *acid* is a compound that ionizes in solution to yield hydrogen ions (H^+)[1] and an anion. An acid is a proton *donor.* Acids turn blue litmus paper red and have a sour taste. Hydrochloric acid (HC1) and sulfuric acid (H_2SO_4) are examples of inorganic acids.

The strength of an acid depends upon the degree to which it ionizes in water. Thus HCl is a very strong acid because most of its molecules dissociate, producing hydrogen and chloride ions.

$$\underset{\text{hydrochloric acid}}{HCl} \xrightarrow{\text{in } H_2O} \underset{\text{Hydrogen ion}}{H^+} + \underset{\text{Chloride ion}}{Cl^-}$$

A base is defined as a proton *acceptor.* Most bases are substances that yield a hydroxide ion (OH^-) and a cation when dissolved in water. Bases turn red litmus paper blue and feel slippery to the touch. Sodium hydroxide (NaOH) and aqueous ammonia (NH_4OH) are inorganic bases.

$$\underset{\text{hydrochloric acid}}{HCl} \xrightarrow{\text{in } H_2O} \underset{\text{Hydrogen ion}}{H^+} + \underset{\text{Chloride ion}}{Cl^-}$$

Since the concentration of hydrogen or hydroxide ions is usually small, it is convenient to express the degree of acidity or alkalinity in a solution in terms of pH, formally defined as the logarithm of the reciprocal of the hydrogen ion concentration, log ($1/[H^+]$). The pH scale is logarithmic, extending from 0, the pH of a strong acid, such as HCl, to 14, the pH of a strong base, such as NaOH.

The pH of pure water is 7. Even though water does ionize slightly, the concentrations of H^+ ions and OH^- ions are exactly equal. Solutions with a pH of less than 7 are acidic and contain e H^+ ions than OH^- ions.

Solutions with a pH greater than 7 are alkaline, or basic, and contain more OH^- ions than H^+ ions. Because the scale is logarithmic, a solution with a pH of 6 has a hydrogen ion concentration that is ten

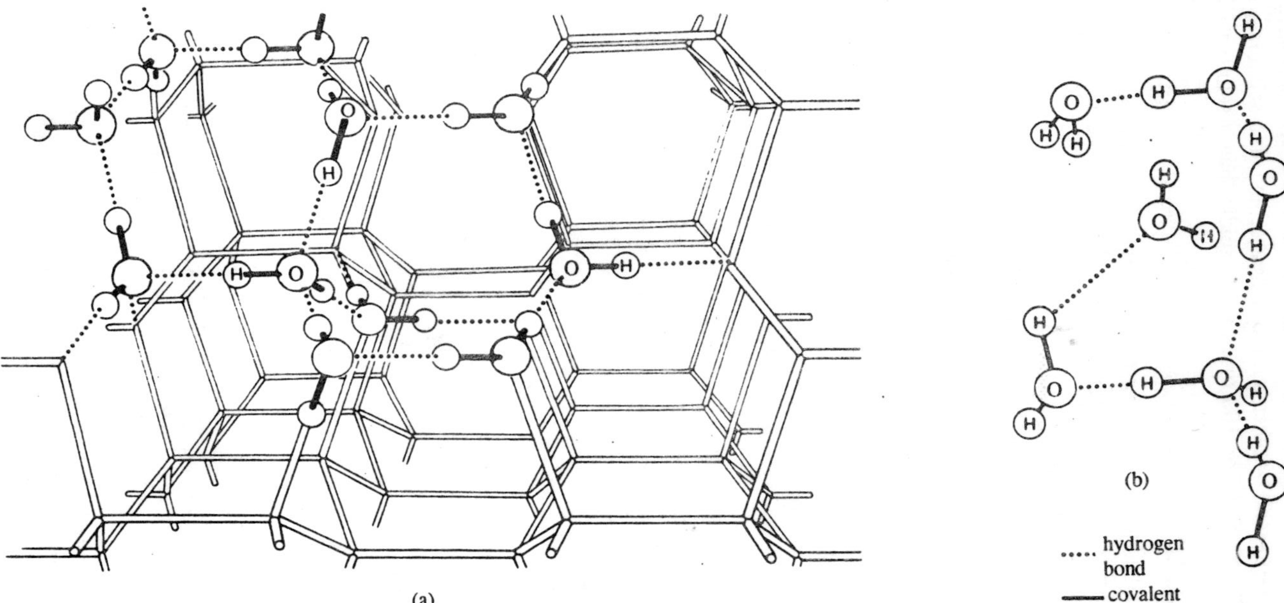

Figure 2.6: The hydrogen bonding in ice compared with that in liquid water. (a) Note the regular, evenly distanced hydrogen bonds in the superstructure of ice. (b) When ice melts, the hydrogen bonds occur less consistently and are of unequal length, and the crystal structure collapses.

times greater than a solution with a pH of 7 and is much more acidic. A pH of 5 represents another tenfold increase, and so a solution with a pH of 4 is 10 × 10 or 100 times more acidic than a solution with a pH of 6.

The contents of most animal and plant cells are neither strongly acidic nor alkaline but are an essentially neutral mixture of acidic and basic substances. Life is not compatible with any considerable change in the pH of the cell.

Salts

When an acid and a base are mixed together, the H^+ of the acid unites with the OH^- of the base to form a molecule of water. The remainder of the acid (anion) combines with the remainder of the base (cation) to form a *salt*. This type of reaction is called acid-base neutralization. Hydrochloric acid reacts with sodium hydroxide to form water and sodium chloride:

$$\underset{\text{hydrochloric acid}}{HCl} + \underset{\text{Sodium hydroxide}}{NaOH} \rightarrow \underset{\text{Water}}{H_2O} + \underset{\text{Sodium chloride}}{NaCl}$$

A *salt* can be defined as a compound in which the hydrogen atom of an acid is replaced by some other cation. A salt contains a cation other than H^+ and an anion other than OH^-. Sodium chloride, NaCl, is a compound in which the hydrogen ion of HCl has been replaced by the cation, Na^+.

When a salt, an acid, or a base is dissolved in water, its constituent ions separate. Because these charged particles can conduct an electric current, these substances are called *electrolytes*. Sugars, alcohols, and

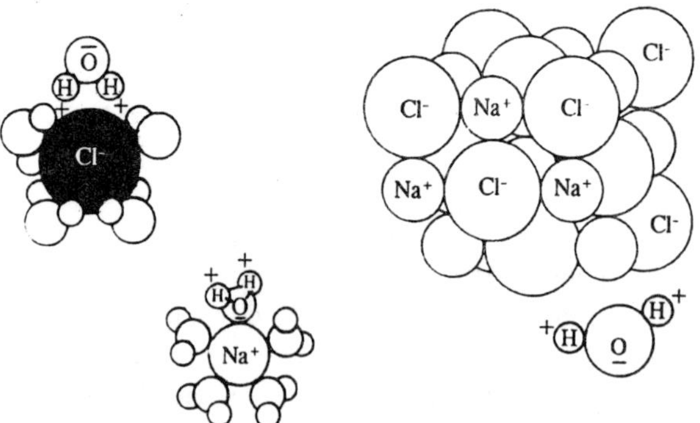

Figure 2.7: The crystal lattice of a salt like NaCl is held together by the strong ionic bonds between the Na^+ and Cl^- ions, and considerable energy is required to pull the ions apart.

many other substances do not ionize when dissolved in water; they do not conduct an electrical current and are termed *nonelectrolytes*.

The cells and extracellular fluids (such as blood) of plants and animals contain a variety of dissolved salts. They are a source of many important mineral ions. Such ions are essential for fluid balance, acidbase balance, nerve and muscle function in animals, blood clotting, bone formation, and many other aspects of body function.

Although the concentration of salts in the cells and body fluids of plants and animals is small, these salts are of great importance for normal cell function. The concentrations of the respective cations and anions are kept remarkably constant under normal conditions. Any marked change results in impaired cellular functions and ultimately in death.

Buffers

Many homeostatic mechanisms operate to maintain appropriate pH levels. For example, the pH of human blood is about 7.4 and must be maintained within very narrow limits. Should the blood become too acidic, coma and death may result. Excessive alkalinity can result in overexcitability of the nervous system and even convulsions.

A *buffer* is a substance or combination of substances that resists changes in pH when acids or bases are added. The buffer either accepts or donates hydrogen ions. A buffer consists of a weak acid and a salt of that acid, or a weak base and a salt of the base.

One of the most common buffering systems and one that is important in human blood is carbonic acid and the bicarbonate ion. Bicarbonate ions are formed in the body as follows:

$$\underset{\text{Carbon dioxide}}{CO_2} + \underset{\text{Water}}{H_2O} \rightleftarrows \underset{\text{Carbonic acid}}{H_2CO_3} \rightleftarrows H^+ + \underset{\text{Bicarbonate ion}}{HCO_3^-}$$

As indicated by the arrows, the reactions are reversible. When excess hydrogen ions are present in blood or other body fluids, bicarbonate ions combine with them to form carbonic acid, a weak acid.

$$H^+ + HCO_3^- \rightleftarrows \underset{\text{Carbon acid}}{H_2CO_3}$$

In this way a strong acid can be converted to a weak acid. The carbonic acid is unstable and quickly breaks down into carbon dioxide and water.

Buffers also work to reduce pH when excessive numbers of hydroxide ions are present. A buffer may release hydrogen ions, which combine with the hydroxide ions to form water.

$$OH^- + 2H^+ + CO_3^- \rightleftarrows HCO_3 + H_2O$$

THE CHEMISTRY OF LIFE: ORGANIC COMPOUNDS

In a way, the chemistry of the carbon atom is the chemistry of life itself. With four electrons in its outer energy level, the carbon atom can share electrons with other atoms, forming four covalent bonds. This ability of carbon atoms yields an immense variety of *organic compounds*, complex compounds that contain carbon.

Organic compounds are the main structural components of cells and tissues, the participants in and regulators of thousands of metabolic reactions, and the fuel molecules of living systems.

In all organic compounds the main chain of atoms that makes up the principal axis of the molecule consists of carbon atoms. Thus carbon atoms share electrons with other carbon atoms to form chains of varying lengths.

These chains may be unbranched or branched, or the carbon atoms may join to form rings. Adjacent carbon atoms may form single bonds, or by sharing additional pairs of electrons, they may form double (—C=C—) or triple (—C=—C—) bonds.

In this chapter we discuss some of the major groups of organic compounds that are important in living organisms, including carbohydrates, lipids, proteins, and nucleic acids.

CARBOHYDRATES

Familiar to us as sugars and starches, *carbohydrates* serve as fuel molecules and are also important structural components, especially in plant cells. Carbohydrates contain carbon, hydrogen, and oxygen atoms in a ratio of approximately one carbon to two hydrogens to one oxygen $(CH_2O)_n$. The term carbohydrate, meaning "hydrate (water) of carbon," stems from the 2 to 1 ratio of hydrogen to oxygen, the same ratio found in water (H_2O). Carbohydrates may be classified as monosaccharides, disaccharide, or polysaccharides.

Monosaccharides

Monosaccharides are simple sugars that usually contain from three to six carbon atoms. *Glucose* (also called dextrose) and *fructose* are examples of monosaccharides. Each is composed of a single *hexose* unit (consists of six carbon atoms) with the formula $C_6H_{12}O_6$. Recall that such compounds as glucose and fructose, which have identical molecular formulas but different arrangements of atoms, are termed *isomers*. Because of their different arrangement of atoms, the two sugars have different chemical properties.

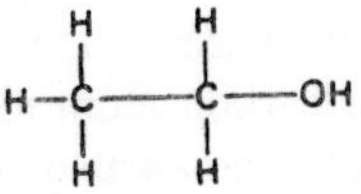

ethyl alcohol
(a)

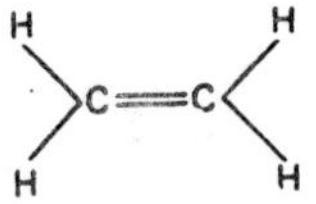

ethylene
(b)

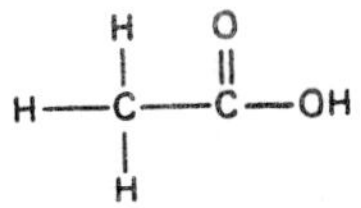

acetic acid
(c)

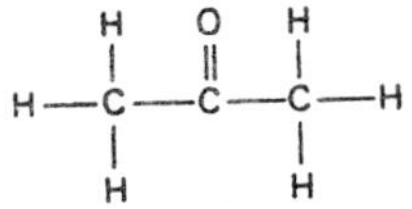

acetone
(d)

Figure 2.8: Some simple organic compounds. Note that each carbon atom has four covalent bonds. (a) Ethyl alcohol, the type of alcohol used in alcoholic beverages. (b) Ethylene, a raw material used in making polyethylene plastic. Note the double bond. (c) Acetic acid, an organic acid found in vinegar. (d) Acetone, used as a fingernail polish remover, but also important in fat metabolism.

Glucose, often referred to as blood sugar, is the most abundant hexose in the bodies of humans and other animals. Its concentration is kept at a homeostatic level in the blood, and glucose is utilized by the cells as a fuel molecule. The *pentoses* (five-carbon sugars) ribose and deoxyribose are components of nucleotides and nucleic acids.

The "stick" formulas in Figure elsewhere in this chapter give a clear but somewhat unrealistic picture of the structures of some common monosaccharides. Actually, molecules are not the simple two-dimensional structures depicted on a printed page.

In fact, the properties of each compound depend in part on its three-dimensional structure. Molecules of glucose and other monosaccharides in solution exist mainly as rings.

In some compounds certain atoms can be arranged in more than one position in space around the carbon atom to which they are bonded. Such stereoisomers differ from one another only in some geometric or three-dimensional way. There are two ring forms of glucose, for instance, that differ only in the orientation of an -OH group.

Disaccharides

A *disaccharide* (two sugars) is a carbohydrate that can be degraded into two monosaccharide units. The disaccharide *maltose* (malt sugar) consists of two chemically combined glucose units. *Sucrose*, the sugar we use to sweeten our foods, consists of a glucose unit combined with a fructose unit. *Lactose* (the sugar present in milk) is composed of one molecule of glucose and one of galactose, another hexose monosaccharide.

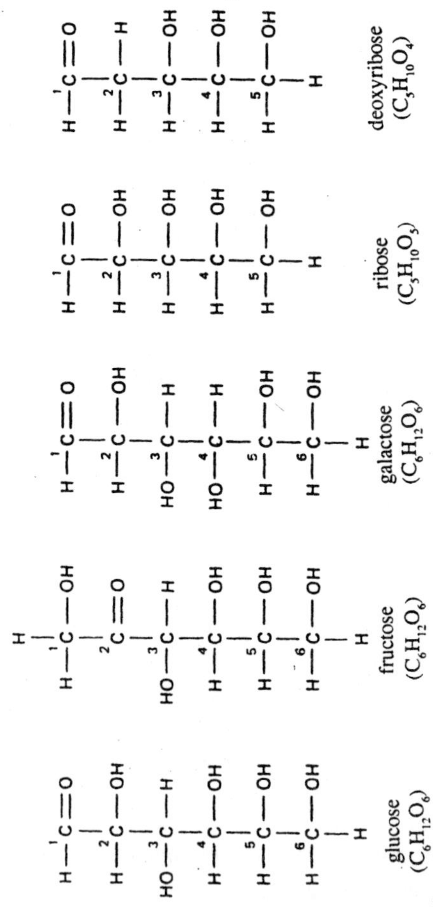

glucose ($C_6H_{12}O_6$)

fructose ($C_6H_{12}O_6$)

galactose ($C_6H_{12}O_6$)

ribose ($C_5H_{10}O_5$)

deoxyribose ($C_5H_{10}O_4$)

Figure 2.9: Structural formulas of some important monosaccharides (simple sugars). The monosaccharides are represented here as straight chains, called stick formulas. Although it is convenient to show monosaccharides in this form, they are more accurately depicted as ring structures.

The covalent bond that joins two monosaccharide units is called a *glycosidic bond.*

During digestion maltose is cleaved (degraded) to form two molecules of glucose:

Maltose + Water → Glucose + Glucose

Similarly, sucrose is cleaved during digestion to form glucose and fructose:

Sucrose + Water → Glucose + Fructose

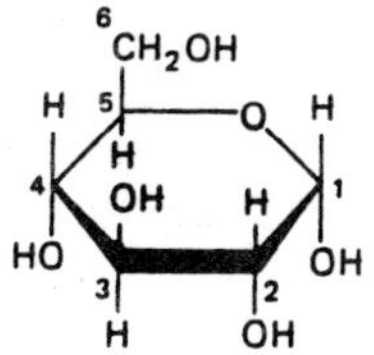

glucose

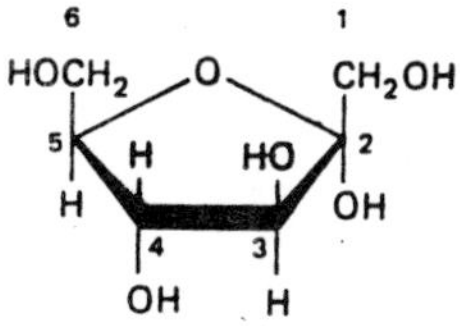

fructose

Figure 2.10: Two monosaccharides, glucose and fructose, drawn to represent their ring structures. At each angle in the ring is a carbon atom; its presence is understood by convention.

Structural formulas for the compounds in these reactions are shown in Figure elsewhere in this chapter. Because water is added during the cleavage of a disaccharide, this type of reaction is called a *hydrolysis* reaction.

Polysaccharides

The most abundant carbohydrates are *polysaccharides*, such as starches, glycogen, or celluloses. A polysaccharide is a single long chain, or a branched chain, consisting of repeating units of a simple sugar, usually glucose.

The precise number of sugar units varies, but typically, thousands of units may be present in a single molecule of a polysaccharide. Because they are composed of different stereoisomers of glucose, or because the glucose units are arranged differently, these polysaccharides have very different properties.

Starch is the typical storage form of carbohydrate in plants, whereas *glycogen* (sometimes referred to as animal starch) is the form in which

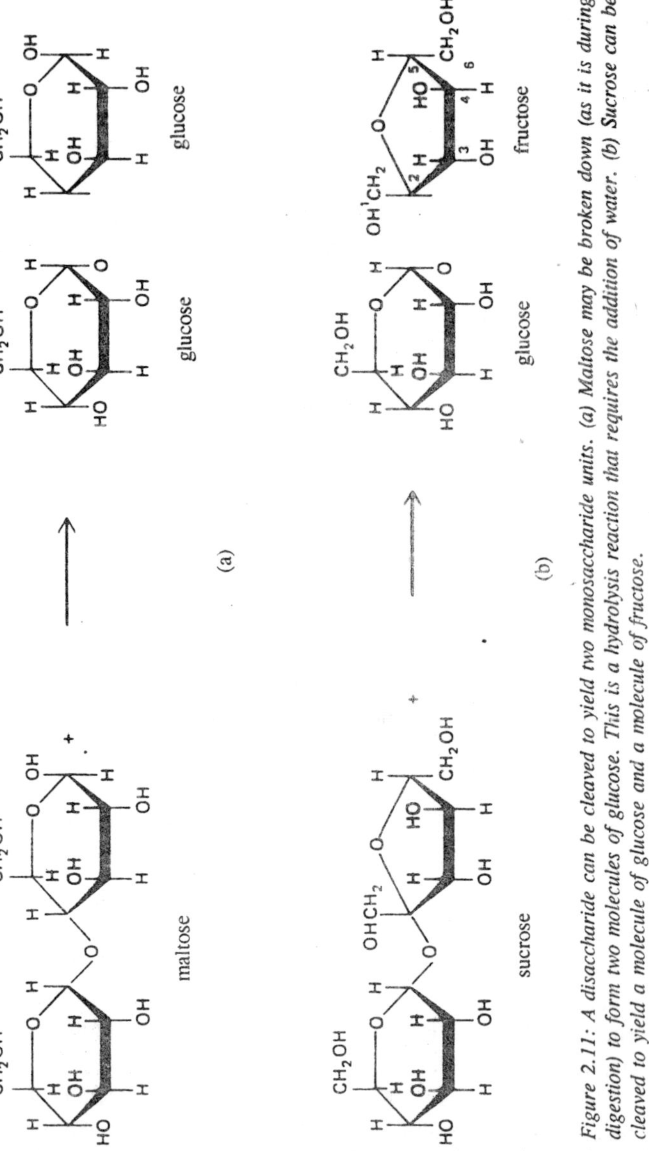

Figure 2.11: A disaccharide can be cleaved to yield two monosaccharide units. (a) Maltose may be broken down (as it is during digestion) to form two molecules of glucose. This is a hydrolysis reaction that requires the addition of water. (b) Sucrose can be cleaved to yield a molecule of glucose and a molecule of fructose.

glucose is stored in animal tissues. Glycogen is a highly branched polysaccharide, more water-soluble than plant starch. Glucose cannot be stored as such because its small, readily soluble molecules would leak out of the cells. The larger, less soluble starch and glycogen molecules do not readily pass through the cell membrane. Thus, instead of storing

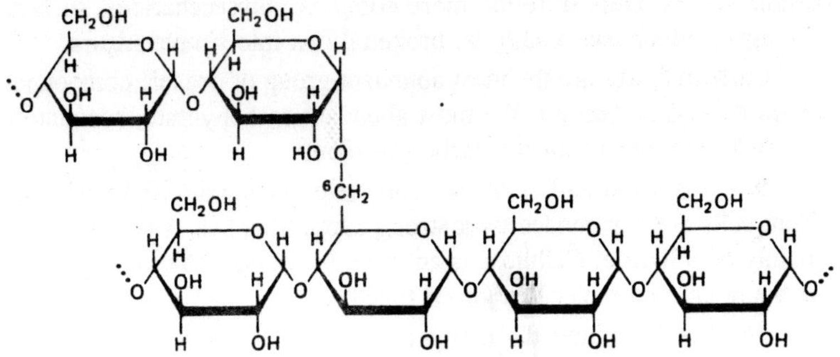

glycogen or starch
(a)

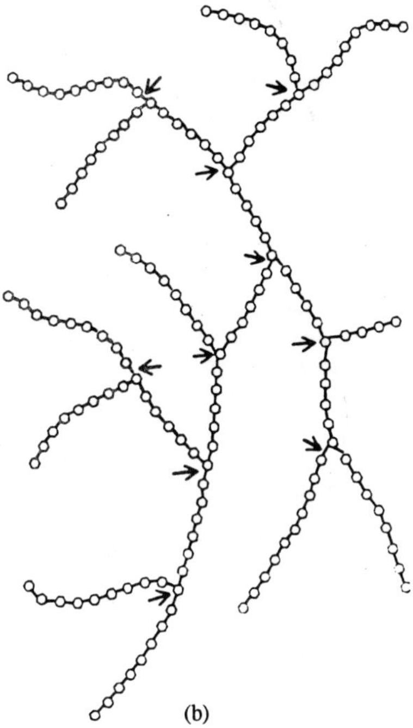

(b)

Figure 2.12: Molecular structure of glycogen or starch. (a) These molecules are branched polysaccharides composed of glucose molecules joined by glycosidic bonds. At the branch points there are bonds between carbon-6 of a glycogen in the straight chain and carbon-1 of the glucose in the branching chain. Glycogen is more highly branched than starch. (b) Diagrammatic representation of starch or glucose. The arrows represent the branch points.

simple sugars, cells store the more complex polysaccharides, such as glycogen, which can readily be broken down into simple sugars.

Carbohydrates are the most abundant group of organic compounds on earth, and *cellulose* is the most abundant carbohydrate, accounting for 50% or more of all the carbon in plants.

Wood is about half cellulose, and cotton is at least 90% cellulose. Plant cells are surrounded by a strong supporting cell. wall consisting mainly of cellulose. Cellulose is an insoluble polysaccharide composed of many glucose molecules joined together.

The bonds joining these sugar units are different from those in starch and are not split by the enzyme that cleaves the bonds in starch.

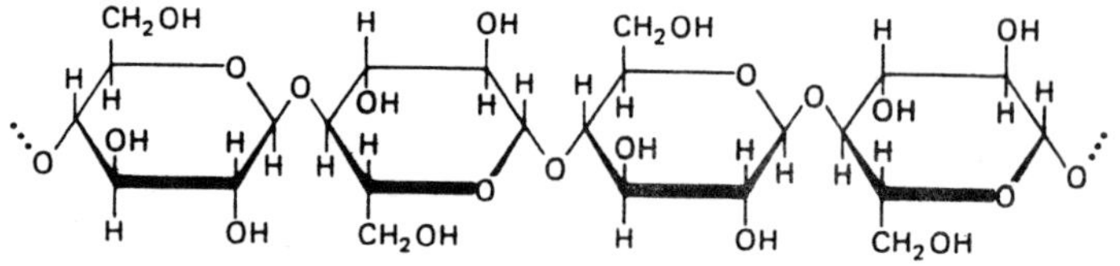

cellulose

(a)

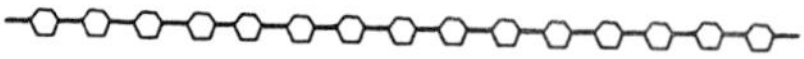

(b)

Figure 2.13: The structure of cellulose. (a) The cellulose molecule is an unbranched polysaccharide composed of approximately 10,000 glucose units joined by glycosidic bonds. (b) A more diagrammatic representation of cellulose structure. Each hexagon represents a glucose molecule bound by a glycosidic bond to the adjacent glucose molecule.

The amino sugars glucosamine and galactosamine are modified carbohydrates, compounds in which a hydroxide group (-OH) of a monosaccharide is replaced by an amino group ($-NH_2$; see the section on proteins). Glucosamine is the molecular unit found in chitin; galactosamine is found in cartilage. Chitin, a tough modified polysaccharide, is the main component of the external skeletons of insects, crayfish, and other arthropod animals.

LIPIDS

Lipids are a heterogeneous group of compounds that have a greasy or oily consistency and are relatively insoluble in water. Like carbohydrates, lipids are composed of carbon, hydrogen, and oxygen atoms, but they have relatively less oxygen in proportion to the carbon and hydrogen than carbohydrates do.

Among the groups of lipids especially significant biologically are the neutral fats, phospholipids, steroids, carotenoids (red and yellow plant pigments), and waxes. Lipids are important biological fuels; they serve as structural components of cell membranes, and some are essential hormones. Glycolipids, lipids that contain watersoluble carbohydrate components, are important in interactions among cells.

Neutral Fats

The most abundant group of lipids in living things is the *neutral fats*. These compounds yield more than twice as much energy per gram as do carbohydrates and are an economical form for the storage of fuel energy. Carbohydrates and proteins can be transformed by enzymes into fats and stored within the cells of adipose tissue.

A neutral fat consists of glycerol joined to one, two, or three molecules of a fatty acid. *Glycerol* is a three-carbon alcohol' that contains three -OH groups. A *fatty acid* is a long, straight chain of carbon atoms with a carboxyl group (-OOOH) at one end.

About 30 varieties of fatty acids are commonly found in animal lipids. They typically have an even number of carbon atoms. For example, butyric acid, present in rancid butter, has four carbon atoms, and oleic acid, the most widely distributed fatty acid in nature, has 18 carbon atoms.

Saturated fatty acids contain the maximum possible hydrogen atoms, while *unsaturated fatty acids* contain carbon atoms that are doubly bonded with one another and are not fully saturated with hydrogens.

Fatty acids with several double bonds are called polyunsaturated fatty acids. Fats containing unsaturated fatty acids are the oils, and most of them are liquid at room temperature. Saturated fats are solids; butter and animal fat are examples. At least two fatty acids (linoleic and linolenic) are *essential nutrients*, which must be included in the diet.

When a glycerol molecule combines chemically with one fatty acid, a *monoacylglycerol* (sometimes called monoglyceride) is formed. When two fatty acids combine with a glycerol, a *diacylglycerol* (or diglyceride) is formed, and when three fatty acids combine with one glycerol molecule, a *triacylglycerol* (or triglyceride) is formed. In combining with glycerol, the carboxyl end of the fatty acid attaches to one of the -OH groups.

This is a dehydration reaction in which H^+ and OH^-, the equivalent of water, is split off. During digestion, on the other hand, the neutral fats may be hydrolyzed to produce fatty acids and glycerol.

Phospholipids

Phospholipids are important constituents of the cell membranes of plants and animals. A phospholipid consists of a glycerol molecule attached to one or two fatty acids, but the glycerol is also bonded to phosphorus, which is part of an organic base. Phospholipids also usually contain nitrogen. (Note that phosphorus and nitrogen are absent from neutral fats.)

The two ends of the phospholipid molecule differ physically as well as chemically. The fatty acid portion of the molecule is *hydrophobic* (water-hating) and is not soluble in water. However, the portion composed of glycerol and the organic base is ionized and readily watersoluble. This end of the molecule is said to be *hydrophilic* (waterloving).

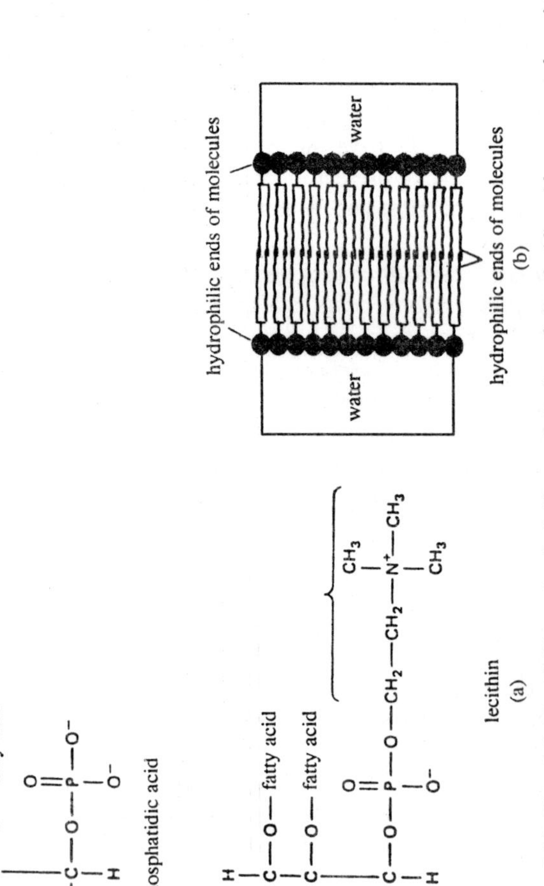

Figure 2.14: Phospholipids. (a) Many phospholipids are derivatives of phosphatidic acid, a compound consisting of glycerol chemically combined with two fatty acids and a phosphate group. Lecithin is a phospholipid found in cell membranes. It forms when phosphatidic acid combines with the compound choline. (b) A lipid bilayer, such as is found in cell membranes.

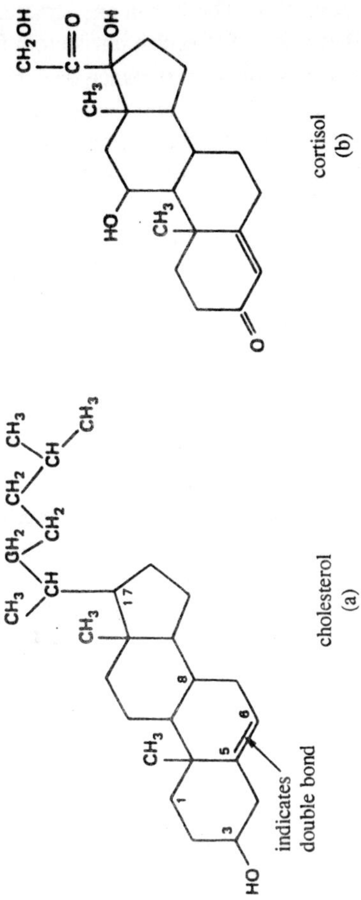

indicates double bond

cholesterol
(a)

cortisol
(b)

Figure 2.15: Steroids. All steroids have the basic skeleton of four interlocking rings of carbon atoms. Note that a carbon atom is present at each point in each ring. Each of the first three rings contains six carbon atoms, and the fourth ring contains five. For simplicity, hydrogen atoms have not been drawn within the ring structures.

The polarity of these lipid molecules causes them to take up a certain configuration in the presence of water, with their hydrophilic water-soluble heads facing outward toward the surrounding water. The hydrophobic tails face in the opposite direction.

The cell membrane is a lipid bilayer composed of two layers of phospholipid molecules with their hydrophobic tails meeting in the middle and their hydrophilic heads oriented toward the outside and inside surfaces of the cell membrane.

Steroids

Although steroids are classified as lipids, their structure is quite different from other lipids. A *steroid* molecule contains carbon atoms arranged in four interlocking rings; three of the rings contain six carbon atoms and the fourth contains five. The length and structure of the side chains that extend from these rings distinguish one steroid from another.

Among the steroids of biological importance are cholesterol, bile salts, the male and female sex hormones, and the hormones secreted by the adrenal cortex. Cholesterol is a structural component of animal cell membranes. Steroid hormones regulate certain aspects of metabolism in a variety of animals, including vertebrates, insects, and crabs.

PROTEINS

Proteins serve as important structural components of cells and tissues, so growth and repair, as well as maintenance of the organism, depend upon an adequate supply of these compounds. Some proteins serve as *enzymes*, catalysts that regulate the thousands of different chemical reactions that take place in a living system.

The protein constituents of a cell are the clue to its life-style. Each cell type has characteristic types, distributions, and amounts of protein that determine what the cell looks like and how it functions.

A muscle cell is different from other cell types by virtue of its large content of the contractile proteins myosin and actin, which are largely responsible for its appearance as well as its ability to contract. The protein hemoglobin, found in red blood cells, is responsible for the specialized function of oxygen transport.

Most proteins are species-specific; that is, they vary slightly in each species, so the protein complement (as determined by the instructions in the genes) is also mainly responsible for differences among species. Thus the types and distributions of proteins in the cells of a dog vary somewhat from those in the cells of a fox or a coyote.

The degree of difference in the proteins of two species is thought to depend upon evolutionary relationships. Organisms less closely related by evolution have proteins that differ more markedly than those of closely related forms. Some proteins differ slightly even among individuals of the same species, so each individual is biochemically unique. Only genetically identical organisms—identical twins or members of closely inbred strains of organisms—have identical proteins.

Amino Acid Structure

A basic knowledge of protein chemistry is essential for understanding nutrition as well as other aspects of metabolism. Proteins are composed of carbon, hydrogen, oxygen, nitrogen, and usually sulfur. Atoms of these elements are arranged into molecular subunits called *amino acids*. All of the more than 20 kinds of amino acids commonly found in

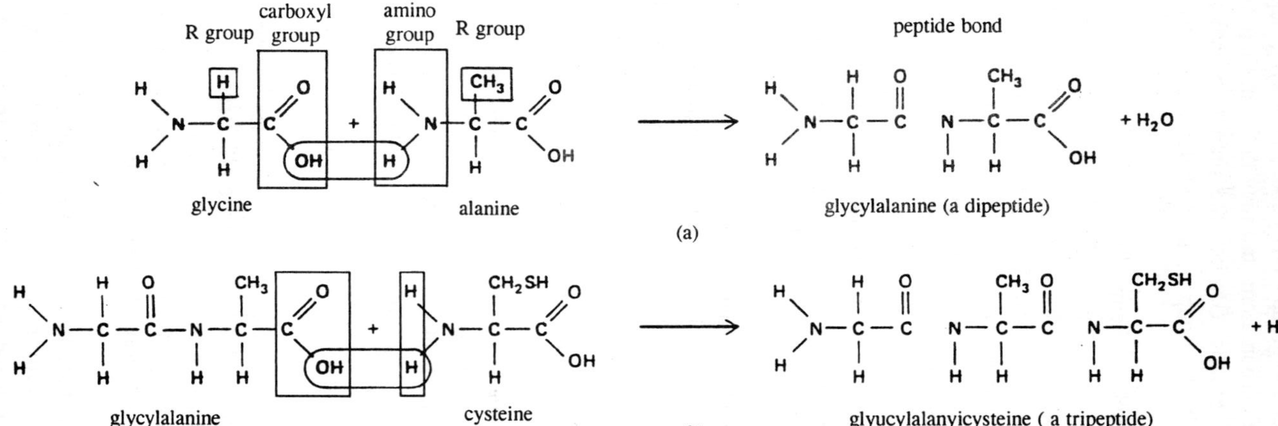

Figure 2.16: (a) Formation of a dipeptide. Two amino acids combine chemically to form a dipeptide. Water is produced as a by-product during this reaction. (b) A third amino acid is added to the dipeptide to form a chain of three amino acids (a tripeptide or small polypeptide). The bond between two amino acids is a peptide bond.

proteins contain an amino group (-NH_2) and a carboxyl group (-OOOH) bonded to the same carbon atom, but they differ in their side chains, abbreviated as "R" groups. *Glycine*, the simplest amino acid, has a hydrogen atom as its R group or side chain; alanine has a methyl (-CH_3) group.

Amino acids combine chemically with one another by bonding the carboxyl carbon of one molecule to the amino nitrogen of another. This covalent bond linking two amino acids is referred to as a *peptide bond*. When two amino acids combine, a *dipeptide* is formed; a longer chain of amino acids is a *polypeptide*.

Each protein may contain hundreds of amino,acids joined in a specific linear order. An almost infinite variety of protein molecules is possible. It should be clear that the various proteins differ from one another in the number, types, and arrangement of amino acids that they contain. The 20 types of amino acids found in biologic proteins may be thought of as letters of a protein alphabet. Each protein is a word made up of amino acid letters.

With some exceptions, plants can synthesize all their needed amino acids from simpler substances. The cells of humans and animals in general can manufacture some, but not all, of the various kinds of biologically significant amino acids if the proper raw materials are available.

Those that animals cannot synthesize but must obtain in the diet are known as *essential amino acids*. Animals differ in their biosynthetic capacities; what is an essential amino acid for one species may not be essential in the diet of another.

Protein Structure-Levels of Organization

Several levels of organization can be distinguished in the protein molecule. The sequence of amino acids in a polypeptide chain constitutes its *primary structure*. This sequence, as we shall see later, is specified by the instructions in a gene.

The *secondary structure* of protein molecules involves the coiling of the peptide chain into a helix or some other regular conformation (shape). Peptide chains ordinarily do not lie out flat or coil randomly, but undergo coiling to yield a specific three-dimensional structure. A common secondary structure in protein molecules is known as the a-helix.

This involves the formation of spiral coils of the polypeptide chain. The a-helix is a very uniform geometric structure with 3.6 amino acids occupying each turn of the helix. The helical structure is determined and maintained by the formation of hydrogen bonds between amino acids in successive turns of the spiral coil.

The *tertiary structure* of a protein molecule involves the folding of the a-helix upon itself, folds that impart a specific overall structure to the protein molecule. Hydrogen bonds between one part of the peptide chain and another part help hold the folds in place.

Disulfide bonds (—S—S—) between certain amino acids and other covalent bonds may also be important in maintaining the tertiary structure of many proteins. The biological activity of the protein depends in large part on the specific tertiary structure of the molecule, held together by these bonds.

When a protein is heated or treated with any of a number of chemicals, the tertiary structure becomes disordered and the coiled peptide chains unfold to give a more random conformation. This unfolding is accompanied by a loss of the biological activity of the protein, for example, its ability to act as an enzyme. This change is termed *denaturation* of the protein.

Proteins composed of two or more subunits have a *quaternary structure*. This refers to the combination of two or more like or unlike peptide chain subunits, each with its own primary, secondary, and tertiary structures, to form the biologically active protein molecule. Hemoglobin, the protein in red blood cells that is responsible for oxygen transport, consists of 574 amino acids arranged in four polypeptide chainstwo identical a and two identical 0 chains. Its chemical formula is $C_{3032}H_{4816}O_{872}N_{780}S_8Fe_4$.

NUCLEIC ACIDS AND NUCLEOTIDES

Nucleic acids, like proteins, are large, complex molecules. They were first isolated by Friedrich Miescher in 1870 from the nuclei of pus cells, and their name stems from the fact that they are acidic and were first identified in nuclei.

There are two classes of nucleic acids, *ribonucleic acids* (RNA) and *deoxyribonucleic acids* (DNA); the different kinds of RNA and DNA vary in some of their structural components and in their metabolic functions.

DNA contains the instructions for making all the proteins needed by the organism and constitutes the genes themselves, the hereditary material of the cell. The various kinds of RNA function in the process of protein synthesis.

Nucleic acids are composed of ***nucleotides***, molecular units that consist of (1) a five-carbon sugar, either ribose or deoxyribose, (2) a phosphate group, and (3) a nitrogenous base that may be either a double-ringed purine or a single-ringed pyrimidine. DNA contains the purines adenine (A) and guanine (G), and the pyrimidines cytosine (C) and thymine (T), together with the sugar deoxyribose and phosphate. RNA contains the purines adenine and guanine and the pyrimidines cytosine and uracil (U), together with the sugar ribose and phosphate.

The molecules of nucleic acids are made of linear chains of nucleotides, each attached to the next by bonds between the sugar molecule of one and the phosphate group of the next.

As we will see in our discussion of the genetic code, the specific information of the nucleic acid is coded in the unique sequence of the four kinds of nucleotides present in the chain.

Besides the importance of nucleotides as subunits of nucleic acids, a number of them serve other vital functions in living cells. *Adenosine triphosphate* (ATP), composed of adenine, ribose, and three phosphates, is of major importance as the energy currency of all cells.

The two terminal phosphate groups are joined to the nucleotide by special "energy-rich" bonds, indicated by the -P symbol. These are energyrich bonds in the sense that much free energy is released when the bonds are hydrolyzed.

The biologically useful energy of these bonds can be transferred to other molecules. Most of the chemical energy of the cell is stored in these high energy phosphate bonds of ATP, ready to be released when the phosphate group is transferred to another molecule.

A nucleotide may be converted by enzymes called cyclases to a cyclic form. ATP, for example, is converted to cyclic adenosine monophosphate (*cyclic AMP*) by the enzyme adenylate cyclase. Cyclic nucleotides play important roles in mediating the effects of hormones and in regulating various aspects of cellular function.

Cells contain several dinucleotides that are of great importance in metabolic processes. For example, nicotinamide adenine dinucleotide (NAD^+) is very important as a primary electron and hydrogen acceptor and donor in biological oxidations and reductions within cells.

3

Cell Organization

A number of features within the cytoplasm and nucleus of the cell are visible by means of the optical microscope. The resolving power of that instrument, however, is such that one cannot see these structures in detail. Let us pretend, then, that an ideal cell has been placed under the electron microscope. The vast increase in resolving power becomes apparent when one compares the electron micrographwith the optical micrograph.

THE CELL MEMBRANE

The *cell membrane* (sometimes called the plasma membrane) is a triple-layered structure composed of a double layer of fat molecules sandwiched between two layers of protein molecules.

All substances which enter or leave the cell must pass through the cell membrane. In many cases this movement is in response to the natural tendency for substances to diffuse along their own concentration gradients.

Such passage through a membrane is spoken of as passive *transport*. In such cases the membrane functions only to permit the passage of certain kinds of molecules and to block the passage of certain other kinds. This selectiveness of the membrane is a characteristic of all living (and of many nonliving) membranes and is spoken of as semipermeability.

In addition to such passive transport, however, the living cell membrane is capable of actually "pumping" some substances against their own concentration gradients-that is, in a direction opposite to that in which they would be expected to diffuse. This process is spoken of

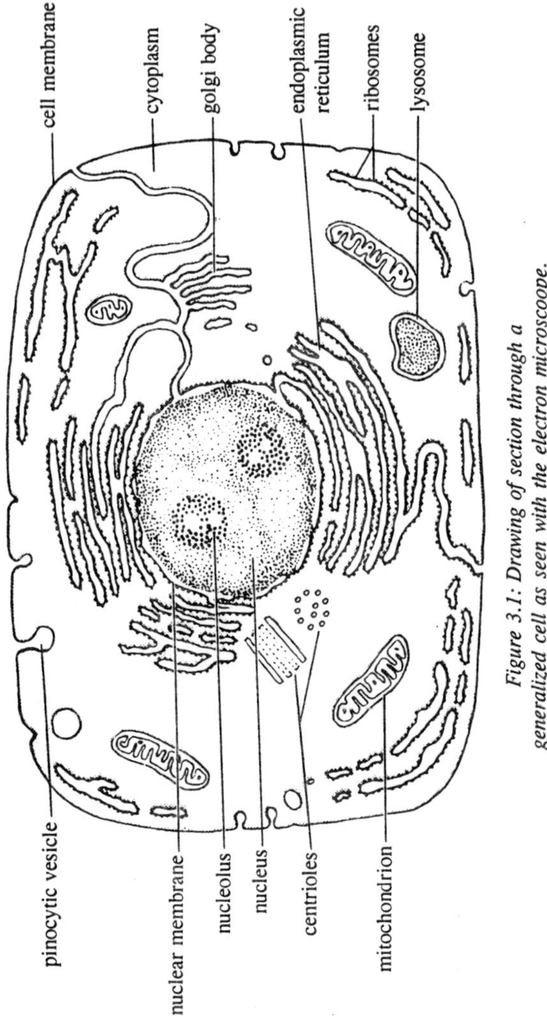

Figure 3.1: Drawing of section through a generalized cell as seen with the electron microscoope.

as active transport. The absorption of digested materials from the intestine, the elimination of selected materials in the urine, glandular activity, and many other internal processes in animals depend upon active transport. The actual mechanisms involved, situated within the membrane concerned, are complex and imperfectly understood.

The exact substances excluded or allowed to pass passively through the membrane and the exact substances actively transported by cell membranes vary from cell type to cell type and, in fact, from time to time within the same cell.

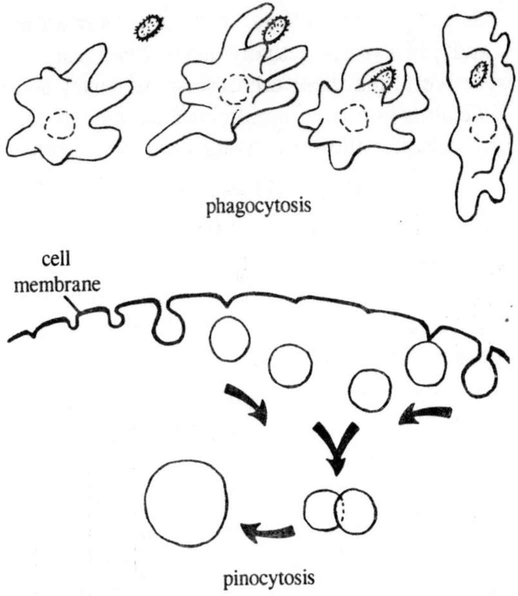

Figure 3.2: Phagocytosis and Pinocytosis

The fact of selectivity, however, is always present. There is some evidence which suggests that perhaps not all of the membrane area of a given cell is alike in its specific selectivity. Other evidence suggests that special enzymes at the surface of some cells may control its permeability.

In addition to active and passive transport of substances through the cell membrane, certain cells have developed other methods for the ingestion of particles or substances from the environment. The single-celled *Amoeba* is capable of engulfing other minute organisms, upon which it feeds, by literally flowing around its prey so as to surround it on all sides.

The engulfed material is thus enclosed in a vacuole within the Amoeba in which it can be digested and from which it can be absorbed into the surrounding cytoplasm. The walls of the vacuole are composed of a part of the former cell membrane.

A number of cell types, including some of the white blood cells of higher animals, are also capable of this process of phagocytosis. Certain cells, especially those lining the intestine and the kidney tubules, have been observed to take in through the cell membrane small quantities of liquid material as tiny droplets.

This process, called pinocytosis, has an outward appearance similar to that of phagocytosis but differs from it in a number of ways. Phagocytosis and pinocytosis actually mean "cell eating" and "cell drinking" respectively, but these are descriptive terms and should not be taken as indicating the true significance of the processes. Figure elsewhere in this chapter illustrates phagocytosis and pinocytosis.

MITOCHONDRIA AND LYSOSOMES

In the cytoplasm of cells are a number of rodshaped bodies called mitochondria. With the optical microscope they are seen only as rods without detailed structure, but with the electron microscope they are revealed as relatively complex structures.

There is a limiting membrane which appears to be much like the cell membrane -four-layered and composed of protein and lipid portions. The electron microscope also shows that the innermost layer of the mitochondrial membrane is thrown into internal folds called cristae.

These increase the internal surface area and partially divide the internal space of the mitochondrion. The remaining space inside is filled with a liquid matrix. Individual mitochondria vary widely in size from time to time, and it has been shown that the permeability of the mitochondrial membrane varies as the structure is expanded or contracted in size.

The total number of mitochondria per cell varies widely (50 to 50,000) in different cell types. They are particularly abundant in cells that are actively synthesizing substances or that are growing and dividing rapidly. Virtually all of the processes of glycolysis or biological oxidation (Section 2.26) involve the attachment or detachment of phosphate groups, and the energy released is stored by forming high energy phosphate bonds on such compounds as ATP.

The transfer of these phosphate groups requires the presence of phosphorylating enzymes. Within the cell it has been shown that phosphorylating enzymes as well as other enzymes associated with biological oxidation reactions occur almost exclusively in the mitochondria.

Individual cells obtain their energy by these means, so we are led to the conclusion that the mitochondria are the sites of energy metabolism within the cell. They are often spoken of collectively as the "powerhouse of the cell." It is believed that the enzymes are located in the inner layer of the mitochondrial membrane and are arranged there in the proper order of their activity.

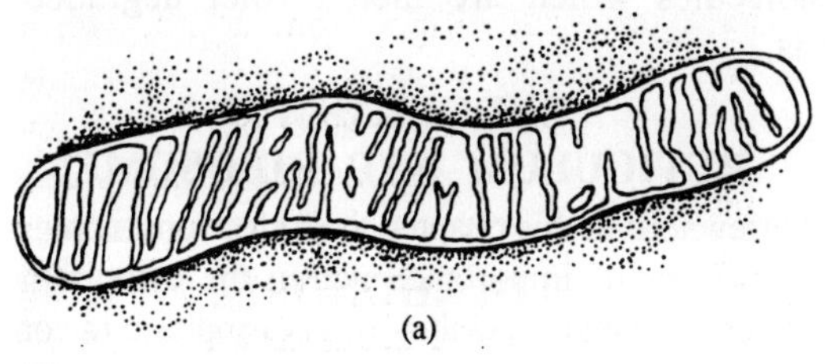

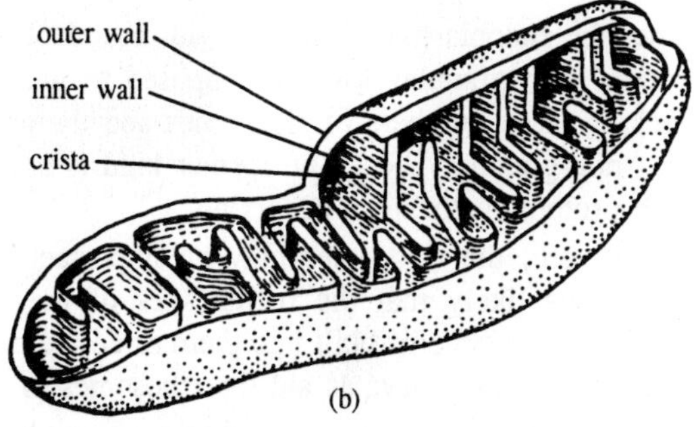

Figure 3.3: A. Line drawing of a section through a mitochondrion. B. A three-dimensional view of the same structure.

The breakdown of carbohydrates, fats, and proteins are long, successive chains of enzymecontrolled reactions. The first stages of these reactions occur outside the mitochondria and the products (pyruvic acid, fatty acids, and amino acids) pass into the mitochondria.

There, enzymes arranged in proper order become a sort of assembly line. Molecules are passed along from site to site, as if they were on conveyor belts, each enzyme directing another stage of the breakdown and, at some sites, tapping a part of the stored energy.

At each energy-yielding step the energy is transferred to some energy-storing compound like ATP, and, finally, the ultimate products, carbon dioxide and water, leave the end of the conveyor. The carbon dioxide and water produced leave the mitochondria and the cell by passive transport, and the ATP diffuses to other parts of the cell, where its stored energy is used to drive synthetic processes, cell movements, and so forth.

The l*ysosomes* are other mitochondria-like, rod-shaped structures of the cytoplasm. They lack the internal cristae of mitochondria, and the enzyme systems which they enclose are different from those of the mitochondria. It is believed that the lysosomes are internal digestive systems of the cell-that they break down complex molecules to yield the simpler molecules which are then further degraded within the mitochondria.

ENDOPLASMIC RETICULUM AND RIBOSOMES

Figure elsewhere in this chapter is an electron micrograph showing two other structures of importance within the cytoplasm of the cell. These are the endoplasmic reticulum or ergastoplasm (a complex system of membranes) and the *ribosomes* (tiny granules apparently adhering to the membranes of the endoplasmic reticulum).

Sometimes the endoplasmic reticulum with abundant ribosomes is called a "rough" or "granular ER," as opposed to the endoplasmic reticulum lacking large numbers of ribosomes and therefore called a "smooth" or "non-granular ER." The former kind is associated with cells in which protein synthesis is occurring.

As we shall see, the ribosomes play an important role in such syntheses. It seems likely that the membranes of the endoplasmic reticulum have enzyme systems built into them as do the mitochondrial membranes and that these enzymes aid the ribosomes in some way.

Ribosomes can operate in protein synthesis without being attached to the endoplasmic reticulum, but such attachment may serve to organize them in a "factory assembly-line" sequence and, therefore, increase the efficiency of synthesis. Smooth ER is often associated with cells in which fat or steroid syntheses are occurring, and it is probable that the enzymes involved in these syntheses are also incorporated into the membranes comprising the endoplasmic reticulum.

Besides serving as surface areas on which synthetic processes can be organized, the endoplasmic reticulum provides channels for the transport of materials about the cell and probably contributes to the structural framework of the cell.

The channels of the endoplasmic reticulum open through both the cell membrane and the nuclear membrane; in fact it appears that both membranes are continuous with those of the endoplasmic reticulum and not unlike it in structure.

GOLGI APPARATUS

A similar set of interconnected channels, lacking ribosomes, is the *Golgi apparatus*. The function is not completely understood, but it is present in abundance in glandular cellscells which specialize in the production of certain cellular secretions-and it waxes and wanes as the glandular output of these cells waxes and wanes.

It seems certain that the Golgi apparatus plays some role in such glandular activities, and some authorities believe that it serves as a sort of staging ground—a place where materials are collected, concentrated, and stored in readiness for the manufacture of large quantities of the specific cell secretory product.

The fact that the Golgi apparatus stains with fat-staining chemicals and that its appearance is changed by changes in the fat content of animal diets suggests also that it plays some role in fat metabolism.

CHROMOSOMES AND DNA

It has been established for a number of years that the nucleus contains deoxyribonucleic acid (DNA) and that the similar substance, ribonucleic acid (RNA) occurs in both the nucleus and the cytoplasm.

It has also been recognized for some time that DNA is associated with the inheritance of characteristics from generation to generation, and that it in some way constitutes the "*blueprints*" which are carried by the male and female gametes. Consequently, a great deal of research has been concentrated on these substances in an effort to learn precisely how they function in the cell.

When a cell is about to divide to form two daughter cells, the DNA portion of the nucleus becomes concentrated into a number of variously-shaped bodies known as *chromosomes*. The number of chromosomes and the characteristic shape of each are constant features of every cell of any given kind of organism.

A major part of the preparation for cell division consists of the duplication of each individual chromosome. During the actual division of the cell, each daughter cell receives one complete set of chromosomes.

Electron microscopy has shown that between successive cell divisions, a stage in the life of a cell known as the interphase, the chromosomes do not actually disappear but merely change in form so that they are no longer distinguishable by means of the ordinary optical microscope.

During interphase the electron microscope shows that the expanded chromosome is composed of a fine axial filament having pairs of small swellings called chromomeres at more or less regular intervals. Sometimes, in addition, there is a pair of "lampbrush loops" attached to each chromomere. Each lampbrush loop pair has a characteristic shape and appearance; they occur along the axial filament in a partitular order which is unique for each specific chromosome.

A particular chromosome, when it is condensed in preparation for cell division, is recognizable on the basis of its shape and size. That

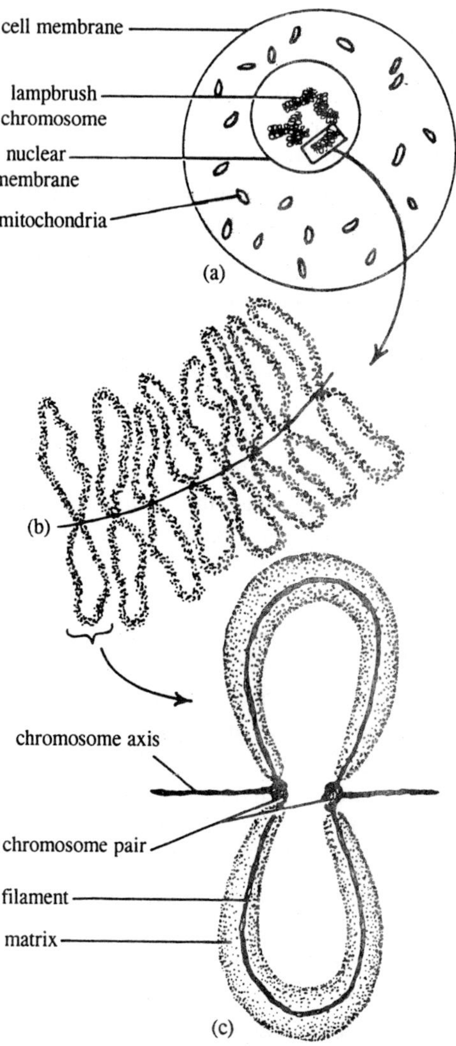

Figure 3.4: Line drawing of lampbrush chromosomes.

same chromosome, when it is expanded during interphase, may be recognizable on the basis of its complement of lampbrush loops. In general, the same specific chromosome from a cell of another individual of the same kind of animal will have the same, identifiable characteristics.

This uniformity of appearance is not surprising when we recall that the chromosomes and their contained DNA are the "blueprints" which are duplicated with each cell division and which are passed from parents to offspring in animal reproduction.

A unit of inheritable characteristics is called a *gene*. It may be that each lampbrush loop represents a gene, but this is by no means certain. At any rate it seems clear that the overall mechanism of cell inheritance and cell specificity is based upon a "one gene: one enzyme: one reaction" sequence.

In other words, one unit of inheritance (gene) directs the formation of some one, specific enzyme, and this enzyme functions by controlling one step in some chemical sequence within the cell. It may appear on first consideration that the number of specific inheritable characteristics of an animal would require a prohibitively large array of enzymes to account for them all, and that this large number could not all be present simultaneously within a single cell.

It must be remembered, though, that biological reactions are long series of connected and branched reactions. Just as a single dam or canal near the headwaters of a stream can influence the flow of water in all the rest of the stream, so a single enzyme acting near the beginning of a series of chemical reactions might influence the direction and the end products of all succeeding reactions.

DNA, RNA, AND PROTEIN SYNTHESIS

The DNA is known to be the chemical "code" by which the inherited characteristics are passed on from generation to generation. This encoded message is duplicated during each interphase, so that at the time of the next cell division each daughter cell can receive an exact copy. Each cell, then, uses its copy of the code as directions for the synthesis of specific enzymes.

These, in turn, direct the chemistry of the cell so as to produce the characteristics that we recognize as inheritable traits. Enzymes are protein molecules, and protein synthesis occurs in the cytoplasm, not in the nucleus.

The DNA code, therefore, must be transmitted from the chromosomes, where it is stored, to the cytoplasmic sites of protein synthesis, where it is used. This comes about through the formation of *messenger RNA* molecules in the nucleus and the subsequent movement of these molecules out to the cytoplasm.

It will be recalled that RNA is chemically much like DNA, and that there is a specificity of attachment of purines and pyrimidines in each. In DNA adenine is always associated with thymine, and guanine is always associated with cytosine. RNA is the same, except that uracil replaces thymine.

Thus, in the RNA molecule adenine is always associated with uracil, and guanine is always associated with cytosine. In some way that is not completely understood, the parts of RNA molecules are assembled in the nucleus, using the DNA there as a "model" or "template" for this construction, so that the RNA molecules are like the DNA molecules in every particular except for the substitution of uracil for thymine.

Most important of all, the sequence of purines and pyrimidines in the molecule is duplicated. The finished RNA molecule, now called messenger RNA, moves out of the nucleus and becomes attached to the ribosome RNA on the endoplasmic reticulum.

Molecules of RNA in the cytoplasm of the cell are called *transfer RNA*. Apparently a specific transfer RNA molecule exists for each of the 20 amino acids that occur in protoplasm. All these amino acids are available to the cell, and each becomes attached to its specific transfer RNA molecule.

Now, the transfer RNA molecules are attracted to the messenger RNA molecules, and they line up in the same sequence (adenine with uracil and guanine with cytosine), so that the pattern of purine and pyrimidine molecules is again reproduced in the transfer RNA sequence.

This brings the attached amino acids together in a particular sequence, peptide bonds are formed, and a completed protein molecule is produced. This molecule finally splits away and moves to other parts of the cell, where it acts as an enzyme or as a part of the structural protein of the cell.

The exact order of amino acids in this protein determines its chemical characteristics, and it is this order of amino acids that has been dictated by the order of purines and pyrimidines in the DNA of the chromosomes.

Because of the certainty that the chromosome DNA is a chemical "code," it has been of enormous interest to scientists to attempt to decode the information contained. A considerable amount of progress has been made in that direction. As implied in the preceding paragraph, the code probably lies in the exact sequence of purines and pyrimidines in the DNA molecule.

Starting on this assumption, we can reason that a single purine or pyrimidine cannot stand for a single amino acid in the protein molecule to be assembled. There are 20 amino acids to be considered and only

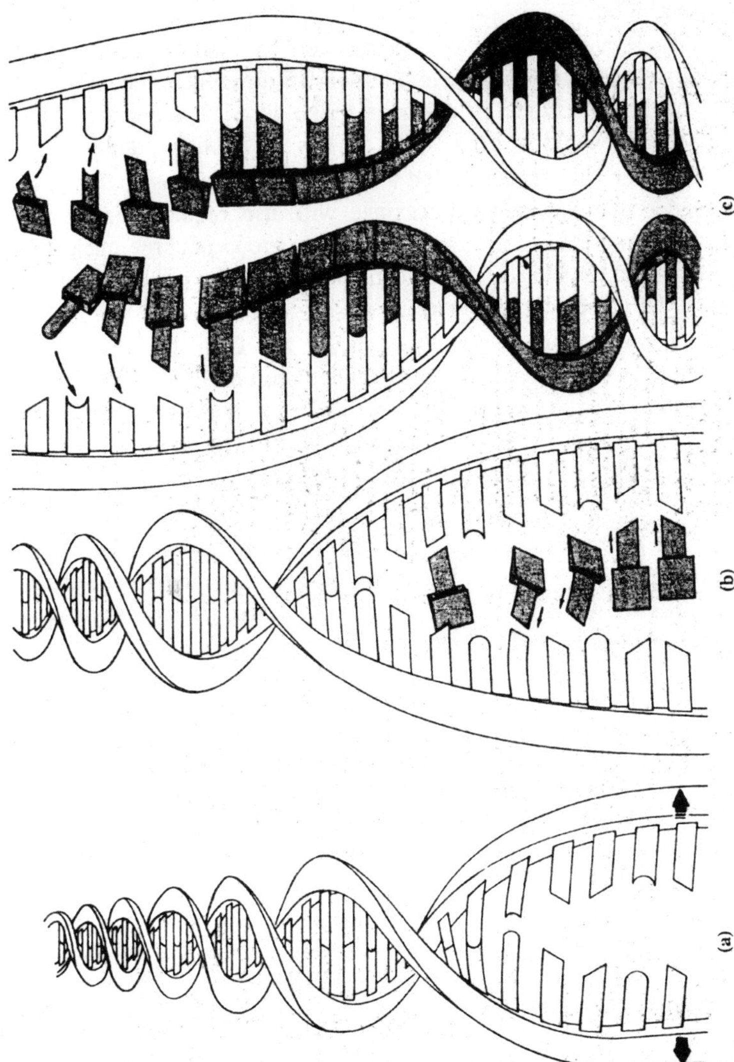

Figure 3.5: DNA replication. A. The DNA double helix unwinds atone end and the nitrogenous bases separate. B. Other nucleotides in the medium are attracted toward the unattached nitrogen bases and (C) become attached in specific locations to form duplicate chains. Frown the four resulting nucleotide chains two duplicate double helices are formed.

four different purines or pyrimidines. This would be like writing 20 different words with an alphabet of only four letters-obviously an impossibility.

If a sequence of two nucleotides were to stand for a single amino acid, we could still only have $4 \times 4 = 16$ different combinations and so could only encode 16 different amino acids. A sequence of three nucleotides would give us $4 \times 4 \times 4 = 64$ possible combinations.

At first this appears to be too many combinations, but when we consider that the encoded message will also require "commas" to separate one amino acid designation (one group of three nucleotides) from the next amino acid designation, the number of possible combinations turns out to be exactly correct.

If, for instance, we allow A, B, C, and D to stand for our four nucleotides, the sequence in a molecule of chromosome DNA might be something like this: (ABABCACDB). The message occurs in triplets and calls for amino acids 1, 2, and 3 in that sequence:

ABA	BCA	CDB	nucleotide sequence
1	2	3	amino acid sequence

All other possible sequences of three in this mesage must be meaningless combinations. It must be impossible to interpret the message as A BAB CAC DB. That is, BAB and CAC must not have any meaning in terms of any of the 20 amino acids.

When such meaningless combinations are deducted from our potential 64 combinations, there are 20 combinations remaining-exactly enough to encode the 20 amino acids.

It is now possible to make synthetic DNA of known nucleotide content and, using this, to synthesize proteins from amino acids in the test tube. By synthesizing simple DNA codes and then determining what protein results from using that DNA, a part of the real DNA code of living cells has been determined.

Much work remains before it will be possible to read hereditary messages, but we can look forward confidently to the solution of this problem in the next few years.

CENTRIOLES

The process of cell division involves the function of still another cytoplasmic structure, the centriole. *Centrioles* are permanent, self-reproducing structures, generally seen as a pair of short, rod-like bodies lying at right angles to each other. Each centriole when seen with the electron microscope is revealed as a short cylinder composed of a

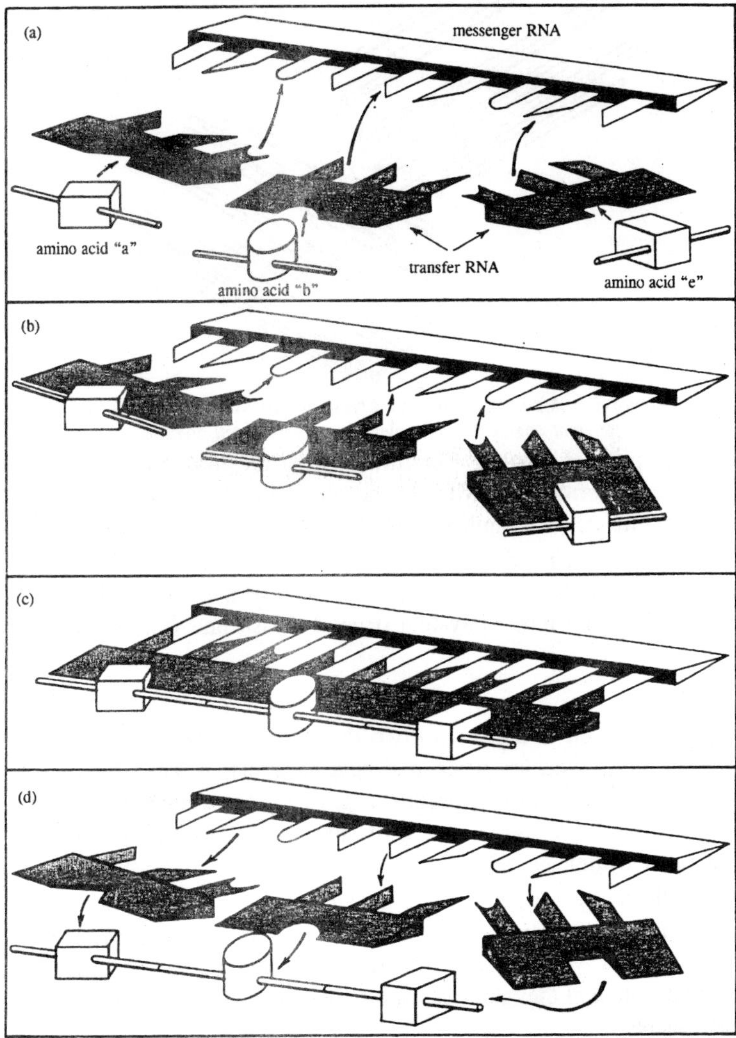

Figure 3.6: Protein synthesis: Messenger RNA is formed on the DNA template in the nucleus in a manner presumably similar to that of DNA replication. Messenger RNA then passes into the cytoplasm where it serves as a template for the attachment of transfer RNA molecules.

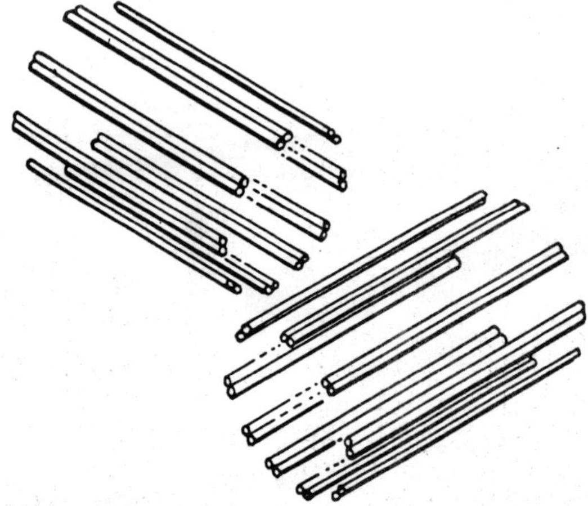

Figure 3.7: A pair of centrioles. Characteristically the centrioles lie at right angles to each other except during cell division.

series of parallel tubules. Commonly there are nine groups of three tubules each forming the walls of the centriole. The whole structure is about 0.4 micron in length and about 0.15 micron in diameter.

Remarkably similar structures are found in the base of each flagellum or cilium. Thus far centrioles have not been seen in plant cells, but it seems likely that some equivalent structure exists and will be identified in time.

MITOSIS

The division of a cell into two daughter cells is not a haphazard process such as occurs when one cuts an apple in half. Rather, the ordinary cell division that occurs in growth and development of new cells consists of a precise series of steps involving changes in many structures within the cell.

Collectively these processes are known as mitosis. When a cell is not actually undergoing division it is said to be in interphase. During interphase, as we have seen, the chromosomes are in such a diffuse, swollen state that they are not visible by means of the ordinary optical microscope.

During interphase each chromosome (known as a monad) is duplicated so that a second, identical chromosome comes to lie alongside it. The original chromosome together with its newly formed duplicate is termed a dyad.

Each chromosome contains the DNA "blueprints" of inheritance, and the duplication of chromosomes must also involve the duplication of the DNA helix as well. While we cannot see the process of duplication of the DNA molecule, many recent experiments and speculations make the following sequence of events seem likely.

The DNA is visualized as being composed of two parallel chains of deoxyribose and phosphate molecules and cross-connected by "ladder rungs" of purines and pyrimidines. During duplication (or replication as it is often called) of the DNA molecule, the purines and pyrimidines become disconnected from each other, as in sawing the rungs of a ladder in half.

The helix untwists so that the two halves of the ladder can move farther apart. In the surrounding protoplasm are individual, unattached nucleotide molecules of all kinds. These, because of the specific affinities of adenine to thymine and guanine to cytosine, are attracted to each of the halves of the separated "ladder" and become attached.

Thus, where a molecule of adenine has been separated from its old thymine partner, it now acquires a new thymine partner, and simultaneously its old thymine partner acquires a new adenine partner. The new, duplicate DNA molecules each twist, forming the characteristic spiral or helix.

This process of separation, duplication, and reformation of the helix occurs progressively, beginning at one end of the DNA molecule and progressing to the opposite end, so that at any one time it only involves a portion of the entire molecule.

The stimulus which begins the process, the power that drives it, and the factors which control and direct it remain as mysteries to be solved by future research biologists. In any case, the DNA replication occurs before or during the duplication of the entire chromosome, so that the resulting dyad consists of two monads identical not only in appearance but in DNA content.

Such duplications have occurred almost simultaneously in all the chromosomes, so that there are actually twice the normal number of chromosomes present-enough to provide each of the two cells resulting from mitosis with a complete set.

Once the duplication of chromosomes is completed, the cell may begin the sequence of changes known as mitosis. Many of these changes are readily visible with the ordinary optical microscope. Although these changes represent one continuous, complete process, they are usually divided into four phases for convenience in study and discussion. These are prophase, metaphase, anaphase, and telophase.

Prophase begins when the first visible signs of mitosis occur in the cell. Several different changes appear simultaneously.

(1) The diffuse chromatin material of the dyads condenses so that the individual chromosomes become visible. The double nature of the dyads at this time is readily visible in certain types of cells.

(2) The two centrioles migrate to opposite sides of the nucleus. Between the two centrioles forms a spindle composed of thread-like fibers. One fiber from each centriole attaches to a definite point (the centromere) of one monad of each dyad, and a fiber from the other centriole attaches to the centromere of the other monad of each dyad.

(3) The nuclear membrane disappears, and the nucleoplasm and cytoplasm intermix.

Metaphase begins when the dyads are lined up equidistant from the *poles* (centriole positions) along the *equatorial* plane of the cell. The paired chromosomes are arranged in such a way that the attached spindle fibers lead directly to the centrioles.

For ease in discussion the cell is spoken of as having poles where the centrioles are located in cell division, and as having an equatorial plane where the chromosomes lie in metaphase and along which the actual division will occur in telophase.

Anaphase is the phase in which the individual monads of each dyad are separated and move toward the opposite poles. During this time the attached spindle fibers appear to shorten and to pull the monads apart and toward the poles, though many investigators doubt that such active contraction really occurs.

It may well be that the spindle fibers merely control the direction of the chromosome movement, while protoplasmic currents or other invisible processes provide the motive power. In any case, one half of each dyad (one monad) moves toward each of the opposite poles of the cell, resulting in two clusters of chromosomes, each composed of identical numbers and kinds of monads.

Telophase is the final phase of the process of mitosis. Again, several simultaneous changes occur.

(1) The spindle fibers making up the spindle disappear.
(2) The individual chromosomes lose their compactness and again take on the diffuse appearance characteristic of interphase.
(3) The nuclear membranes form around each of the two clusters of chromosomes.
(4) The cell membrane of the original single cell constricts around the cell equator until the cytoplasm of the original cell is

physically divided into two parts, each containing one of the two newly created nuclei.

(5) Each centriole reproduces itself to form a pair of centrioles. These remain together just outside the nuclear membrane.

Many facets of mitosis remain unknown. The fundamental mechanics of chromosomal and DNA duplication, spindle formation and function, and nuclear membrane degeneration and regeneration are but a few of the aspects that are, as yet, incompletely understood.

In any case, at the end of telophase each daughter cell has half the cytoplasm of the mother cell, one paired centriole, and a complete set of the chromosomes characteristic of all of the cells of the particular kind of animal from which it came.

CELL MOTILITY, IRRITABILITY, AND CONDUCTIVITY

One of the most universal properties of living cells is the ability to move. In every cell some kind of motion occurs. Viruses are the only organisms in which motion has not been commonly observed, and, as we have seen, these lie on the borderline between the living and the non-living and are in many other ways non-typical cells.

In some cases cellular movements are confined to internal currents in the cytoplasm. In other cases special organelles called cilia or flagella serve as tiny "oars" to move the cell about or to move the medium past the cell.

Finally, certain kinds of cells of multicellular animals have become specialized to produce movement of the entire organism (skeletal muscles) or of certain organs within it (cardiac muscle of the heart and visceral or smooth muscle of the digestive tract and other organs).

To do this muscle cells have capitalized upon other nearly universal properties of cells, those of irritability and conductivity. These properties make the muscles capable of responding to stimuli.

Nerve cells are specialized as irritable and conductive structures. They respond easily to stimuli of various kinds and conduct the resulting nerve impulses rapidly to other parts of the body. As a result motility can be made purposeful and controllable.

Cilia and Flagella

Cilia and flagella are tiny, hair-like structures extending from the surface of certain cells. Certain protozoans are equipped with either cilia or flagella which they use as locomotor organs, whipping them about in certain ways so as to propel themselves through the water.

Cilia and flagella differ from each other in length and in the numbers commonly associated with a single cell, but they are remarkably alike in their internal structure and presumably in the mechanisms which power and control them.

Cilia are very small and a single ciliated protozoan cell commonly has large numbers of them more or less evenly spaced over the entire cell surface. Some fixed tissue cells of higher animals also have cilia. These are always cells of the lining tissue of a tubular organ, such as the tubules of the human lung.

In such cases only the part of the cell surface which is exposed to the lumen of the tubular organ is covered with cilia. The cilia act to move materials along through the lumen (cavity) of the tube.

Flagella are often up to 50 times as long as cilia but are of about the same diameter. Typically, only one to four flagella per cell are seen. They also exhibit various kinds of characteristic motions designed to carry the cell through its environmental medium, or in some cases to move the medium past the cell.

Since there is little difference between the internal structure of cilia and flagella, we can discuss both kinds of organelles together. Not only are they much alike among the Protozoa, but such organelles remain virtually alike wherever they occur throughout the animal kingdom.

Such differences as do exist are correlated with differences in the functions to which they are adapted, rather than with differences in the evolutionary position of the animal.

Typically, cilia and flagella are encased in a membrane which is an extension of the surface membrane of the cell; they typically contain a definite number of longitudinally oriented fibers in a characteristic arrangement.

These fibers include two central axial filaments surrounded by nine peripheral filaments. The axial filaments are round, while the peripheral filaments appear as double filaments in cross-section. Frequently the axial filaments extend beyond the peripheral filaments or even beyond the membranous sheath.

There is some indication that there may be minute fibers interconnecting these various filaments. All the filaments end at the cell surface, where they contact a structure known as the *basal* granule or basal body. This basal granule, which is believed to be derived from the centriole of the cell, also contains nine peripheral filaments somewhat like those of the shaft of the cilium or flagellum.

Note that the structure as described thus far bears a remarkable resemblance to that of the centriole itself. The functions of centrioles and of basal bodies apparently overlap in many cells. The basal body associated with the flagellar tail of a sperm cell (male gamete) arises by modification of one of the centrioles of the developing sperm cell.

One feature of the cilium or flagellum which is not shared by the basal body or centriole is the pair of axial filaments. Certain cells are known which have cilia similarly lacking axial filaments, and in such cases the cilium does not function in cell movement, but rather in the conduction of impulses.

The light-sensitive portion (retina) of the eyes of vertebrate animals is composed of cells with modified cilia of this sort which conduct impulses originating in photo-chemical reactions in the eye. It seems reasonable to suppose that the axial filaments are necessary for the motility of the cilium or flagellum.

Possibly the membranous sheath of the cilium plays a role in impulse conduction. In some cases (e.g., *Paramecium)* the basal granules of the cilia are interconnected by a fibrillar network. Undoubtedly this functions in the coordination of ciliary activity in these forms.

In all cases the basal granule is also connected with deeper parts of the cell, perhaps even the nucleus, by striated rootlets and other fibrillar structures. The precise roles played by these are not known, but their existence is not surprising.

Even though cilia and flagella have self-duplicating basal bodies and even though the motion of these organelles seems to be an intrinsic ability, it is obvious that they must be dependent upon the rest of the cell for sources of energy and structural materials with which to carry out these functions.

Groups of cilia are sometimes modified and combined with each other to form specialized mobile cell organelles. The undulating membrane of certain protozoans (e.g., *Trypanosoma)* is composed of a flagellum fused to the cell to produce a membrane-like structure.

A wavelike motion of this undulating membrane proceeds from one end of the organism to the other, propelling it through the medium. In other cases groups of cilia combine to form stiff, spike-like *cirri* which can be used as "legs" for movement along solid surfaces.

In some multicellular animals there are flagellated cells called *flame cells* which serve as simple excretory organs. These cells are fixed in position, and the movement of the flagella propels waste materials out of the body.

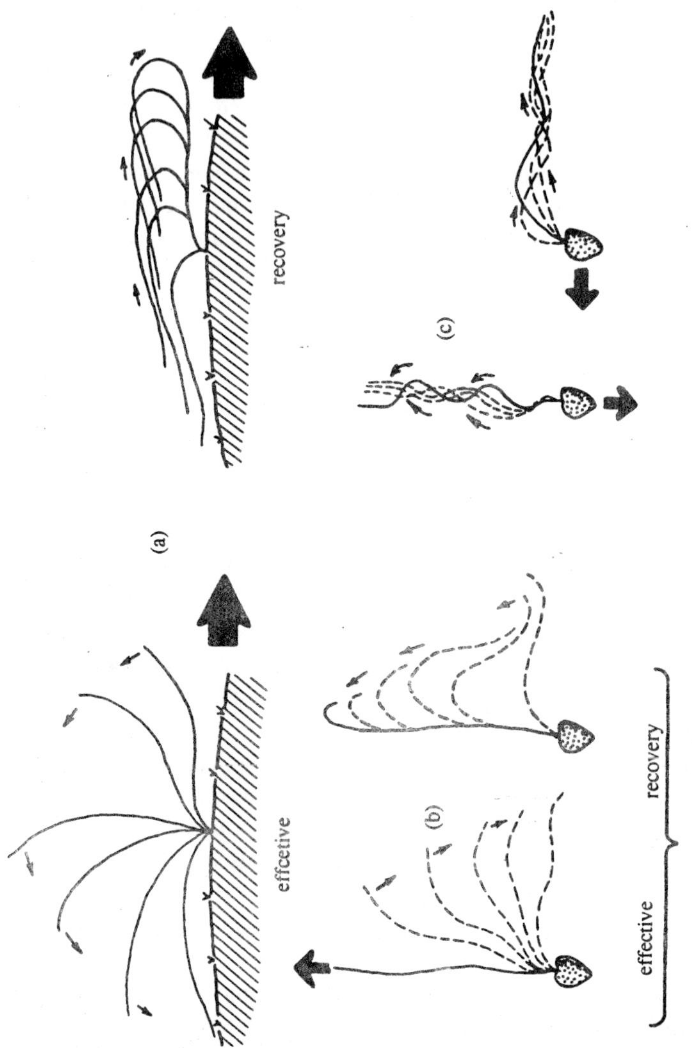

Figure 3.8: A. Cilium; effective and recovery strokes. B. Flagellum; effective and recovery strokes. C. Other types of flagellar action. Heavy arrows indicate the direction in which the organism is moving.

Just as a human while swimming under water must stroke with an extended arm and then bring the arm forward again in a flexed position, so cilia stroke backward and then return forward in a relaxed and less forceful manner.

Some cilia exhibit less difference between the effective and the recovery strokes, while other cilia have even more complex movements involving rotations something like those of an oar in the hands of a boatman.

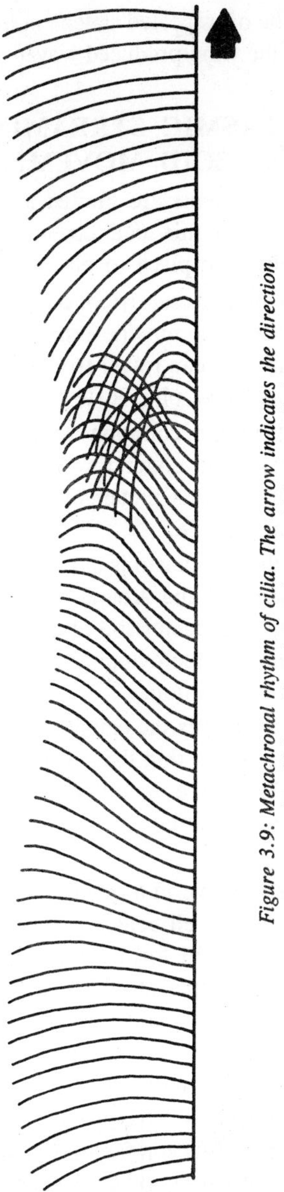

Figure 3.9: Metachronal rhythm of cilia. The arrow indicates the direction in which a ciliated organism would be propelled.

The cilia on the surface of a protozoan are coordinated with each other, as are all the cilia on the inner surface of a tubular organ of higher animals. The ciliary beat is propagated in a wavelike motion over the entire surface. The oft-repeated statement that this metachronal rhythm of cilia looks like the wind-produced waves over a field of grain cannot be improved upon.

CYTOPLASMIC STREAMING AND AMEBOID MOVEMENT

In some cases cell movements are limited to internal currents in the cytoplasm which serve to mix cell contents and to aid in the transportation of materials from place to place within the cell.

In other cases such as in *Amoeba,* cytoplasmic currents are directed and coordinated in such a way as to provide a mechanism for locomotion-a means whereby the entire cell can travel from place to place and can engage in other activities such as phagocytosis.

If one places a leaf of the common water plant *Elodea* on a microscope slide for observation under low magnification, it will be seen that each cell of the leaf is a rectangular, box-shaped structure containing a large, central vacuole.

Around this vacuole the cytoplasm is slowly flowing, carrying the other cellular inclusions around and around the central vacuole. This kind of internal streaming is characteristic of plant cells in general. In animal cells similar currents in the cytoplasm exist, but they are less obvious and less uniform in direction.

In either case they serve to mix the cell contents, so that substances are carried from place to place within the cell in less time than would be required if diffusion alone were operating. *Amoeba* is an organism in which similar cytoplasmic streaming is used by the animal in moving from place to place.

As the animal begins to move in a given direction, the cytoplasm simply begins to flow from the cell center in the given direction, and as a result an extension of the cell forms. Such an extension is called a *pseudopod.* Of course the cytoplasm which forms this pseudopod is drawn from the rest of the cell, so as the pseudopod grows in volume the remainder of the cell shrinks by a corresponding amount.

The movement of *Amoeba* is made possible by another interesting property of cytoplasm, the ability to change itself from a semi-solid gel to a liquid sol and vice versa. This is a familiar property of protoplasm in general and of certain substances other than protoplasm. Common gelatin desserts, for example, are prepared as liquids and then "set" as semi-solids.

Warming or stirring the gel will result in liquefying it again, and subsequent chilling will return it to the gelled state. The rapid change from sol to gel to sol again that occurs in living protoplasm is a similar phenomenon but occurs more rapidly, is less extreme, and does not require changes in temperature or mechanical stirring. *Amoeba* depends upon this ability for locomotion and phagocytosis.

Imagine an oblong mass of material which is semi-solid near its surface but liquid in its internal portion. Suppose that this inner, liquid part develops a current flowing toward the right, and suppose that as each bit of liquid reaches the extreme right-hand end of the mass it is suddenly converted into a semi-solid gel.

Suppose that at the same time an equal amount of gel at the left-hand end of the mass is converted into sol and added to the flowing internal portion. This does not tell us how *Amoeba* drives and directs the process, but it is an accurate picture of the process itself as it occurs.

Since sol-gel changes can be produced by changes in pressure, some theories of ameboid movement assume internal pressure changes are responsible. None of the theories offered to date seems completely acceptable, so the actual mechanisms involved remain unsolved.

Amoeba uses similar mechanisms in some of its feeding behaviour. Naturally some substances which are dissolved in the medium can be absorbed by diffusion through the cell membrane, but other, particulate masses of food material (such as other protozoans) can be taken in only by physical engulfment.

This is the process of phagocytosis. Certain cells of higher organisms retain the ability to move about and to engage in phagocytosis. For example, some human white blood cells and some tissue cells (macrophages) engage in both kinds of activity.

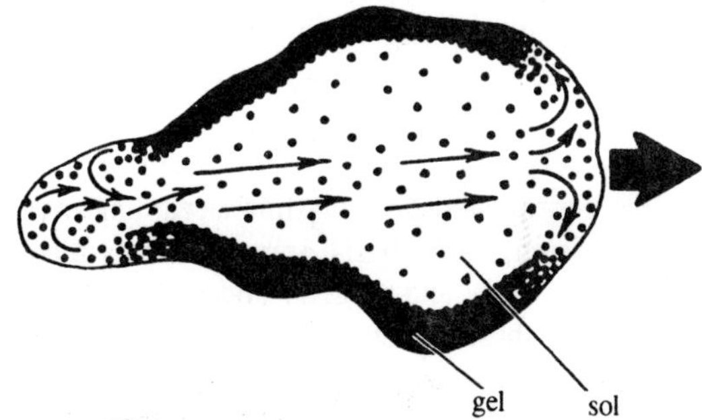

Figure 3.10: The locomotion of Amoeba. Protoplasm is changing from gel to sol at the left and from sol to gel at the right. As a result the organism is moving from left to right.

A more complex type of protoplasmic streaming occurs in the members of a group of organisms known to zoologists as Mycetozoa (moldanimals) and to botanists as Myxomycetes (slime molds). As the dual name suggests, these are organisms which are difficult to classify either as animals or as plants (molds or fungi), since they display characteristics of each.

At one stage of the life cycle they exist as individual, unicellular, ameboid animals but during another stage, numbers of these organisms coalesce to form larger masses of protoplasm. In this form they produce spore-containing fruiting bodies of the type which is typical of the molds or fungi.

They have sometimes been referred to as the "Social Amoebae" (John Tyler Bonner). In the aggregated form protoplasmic streaming is complicated by the fact that many streams are simultaneously present and are moving in different directions.

Moreover, if a bit of the aggregated slime mold is divided in such a way that two masses are connected by a narrow protoplasmic strand, the flow within this strand is seen to proceed in one direction for a while and then reverse its direction for another short period of time.

This ebb and flow continues rhythmically and periodically so long as the connecting strand is maintained. While the protoplasmic streaming in slime molds appears to be more complex than in *Amoeba,* there is no reason to believe that the fundamental mechanisms producing it are different.

In some species of slime molds the aggregated cells behave as though they were tissue cells of a multicellular organism. They assort themselves into special regions of the mass and there perform special functions. The entire "super-organism" acquires a definite head and tail region and moves about in an oriented fashion.

Locomotion is still due to the streaming movements of the individual cells. Centrioles are capable of reproducing themselves and do so following each cell division. In an entirely similar manner basal gametes reproduce themselves.

Just as centrioles serve as centers for the organization of the spindle fibers and the coordinated protoplasmic streaming movements associated with cell division, so do basal granules act as focal points for the formation of new cilia and flagella and for the coordinated movements carried out by these structures.

It seems reasonable to suppose that there is some fundamental principle involving the centrioles, basal granules, cilia and flagella,

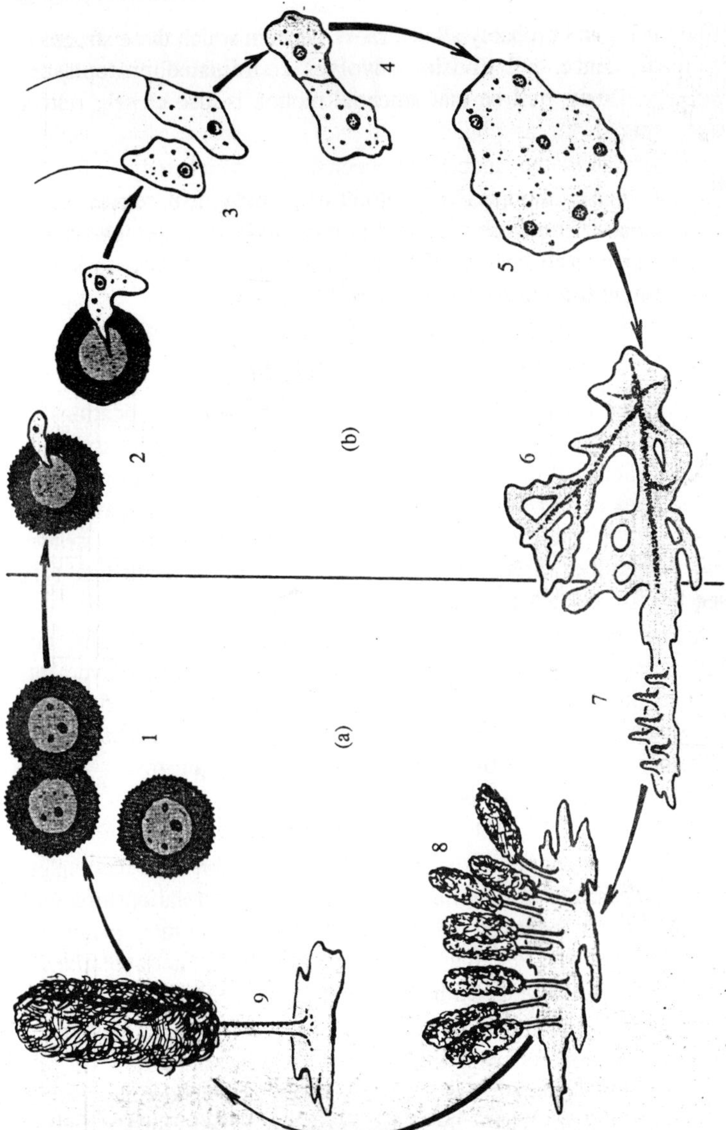

Figure 3.11: The life cycle of a typical slime mold: (A) plant-like portion and (B) animal-like portion of the cycle. (1) Spores. (2) Spores germinating. (3) Flagellar and ameboid single-cell phase. (4) Ameboid cells joining. (5) Small plasmodium formed by nuclear divisions of fused ameboid cells. (6) Plasmodium growing and moving in ameboid fashion. (7) The formation of a sporangium with fungus-like fruiting bodies. (8) Mature sporangium. (9) Single sporangium producing spores.

spindle fibers, and probably all cell movements in which these structures participate. Since cell division involves coordinated protoplasmic streaming, it may well be that ameboid motion is also closely related in some way.

Unfortunately the underlying mechanisms which may unify and explain all these examples of protoplasmic movement remain to be elucidated. Much research activity continues to be directed toward this problem, and it will be surprising if it does not yield itself to logical explanation within the next few years.

STRIATED MUSCLE CELLS AND CONTRACTILITY

In higher organisms, in addition to specialized applications of ameboid, ciliary, and flagellar movements, one encounters essentially new kinds of cellular mechanisms used for locomotion and other purposes. Such cells exhibit strong contractile abilities and are associated with each other to compose muscle of three general types: skeletal or striated muscle, smooth or visceral muscle, and a somewhat intermediate type called cardiac or heart muscle.

Just as there is a considerable amount of evidence indicating that protoplasmic streaming and ciliary, flagellar, and spindle movements are related in some fundamental way, so there is reason to believe that muscle contraction is also related. Probably it has arisen as an evolutionary refinement of the more primitive mechanisms.

From all that is known of the process of evolution, it will be strange indeed if this did not prove to be the case. At this time, however, understanding of the mechanisms of motion is so incomplete that it is impossible to determine just what the interrelationships may be. It is generally believed that flagellar motion is the most primitive, with ciliary, ameboid, and muscular movements being later evolutionary developments in that approximate order.

Most of the studies of muscle to date have concentrated upon striated muscle, and relatively little is known of visceral muscle. Current research employing the electron microscope and other modern techniques can be expected to clarify these issues in the not-too-distant future. Some inferences are possible now, however, when one considers the internal structure of a striated muscle cell.

A single cell of striated muscle is a multinucleate structure filled with longitudinally-oriented fibers of two sizes-relatively short, thick "A" rods and longer, thinner "I" rods. These are interdigitated with each other, as shown. The "I" rods are interrupted at their mid points by a "Z" membrane (or "Z" disc, as it is sometimes called). This membrane partitions the whole cell at intervals. Each unit of the cell, from "Z" membrane to "Z" membrane, is called a sarcomere.

Groups of muscle cells are bound to each other side by side with connective tissue cells to form muscle *fibers*, and the fibers are similarly bound together in larger bundles called fasciculi. Fasciculi form still larger bundles and so on until the whole skeletal muscle is formed. This structure is familiar to anyone who has ever eaten a rather dry roast and noticed that it comes apart in coarse strings which can easily be subdivided into smaller and smaller fibers.

The "A" rods are composed of a protein called myosin, and the "I" rods are composed of another protein called actin. These two proteins are capable of combining to form a more complex protein called actinomyosin.

When skeletal muscle contracts the "A" and "I" rods slide farther together, presumably as a result of this chemical combination taking place. Energy is required to re-separate the two proteins, and ATP is the source of this energy. Re-separation allows the "A" and "I" rods to slide apart again (muscle relaxes).

IRRITABILITY AND CONDUCTIVITY OF CELLS

By irritability we mean the property of responding in some way to a stimulus, and by conductivity we mean the ability to transmit an impulse originating from a stimulus to parts of the cell or the organism remote from the site of the stimulus. Both terms involve the concept of *stimulation,* and it is important that we understand just what is meant by that word as well.

A *stimulus* is any change in the environment which is of sufficient magnitude and which occurs in a sufficiently short period of time to be effective in producing some response from an irritable cell or organism. An electrical current of very low intensity flowing through one's body would be a change in environment but not of sufficient magnitude to be noticed; that is, one would not respond to it, so it would not be a stimulus.

A current of greater intensity is a decidedly effective stimulus. Actually, if one is speaking of ordinary household alternating current, it is 240 stimuli every second, since common 60-cycle current turns on and off 120 times in each second, and each *change* is a stimulus.

In the past 15 to 20 years it is likely that each of us has changed

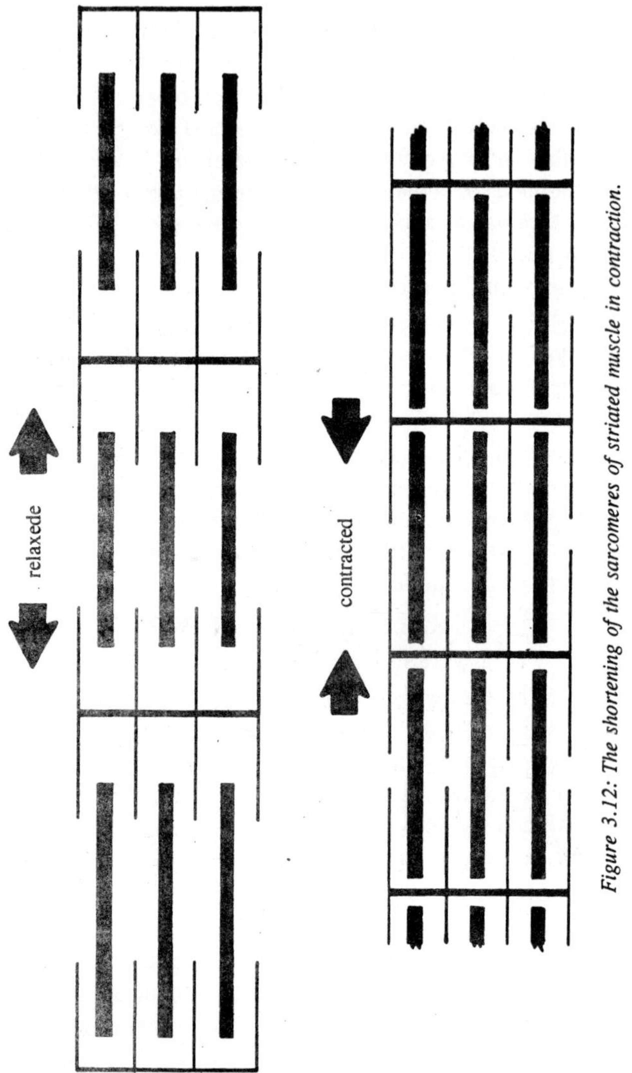

Figure 3.12: The shortening of the sarcomeres of striated muscle in contraction.

considerably in weight. If that change in weight took place in a matter of a second or two it is quite certain that it would be a stimulus; we would each react to it in some way.

There is, then, adequate magnitude of change, but the change ordinarily does not take place in a sufficiently short time to be an effective stimulus. If these limitations of magnitude and duration werenot involved, we would constantly be reacting, since probably no single environmental factor is completely unchanging at any time. There are many kinds or *modalities* of stimulus (e.g., temperature, pressure, electrical current), and there is value in being able to distinguish between these modalities.

Certain cells have become modified so that they are relatively insensitive to all but one kind of stimulus. There are, for example, cells which respond readily to changes in temperature but not to other modalities.

This selective sensitivity is usually the result of the anatomical position of the cell and its own structural characteristics. Such cells serve in animal bodies as *sensory receptors*, and are connected to sensory nerves which carry impulses toward the central nervous system whenever the sensory receptor cells are stimulated. Thus, the sensory cells are specialists in irritability, and the connecting nerve cells are specialists in conductivity.

4

CONTINUITY OF SPECIES

REPRODUCTIVE PROCESSES

From the standpoint of the individual and the cells making up the individual, survival is the important thing in life. From the standpoint of the species, however, individual survival is not biologically important unless that individual reproduces.

Even if individuals could survive for centuries, the species would eventually become extinct if at least some individuals did not produce young. Once reproduction has occurred, the new individuals must undergo developmental stages until they, too, reach the stage in their life cycle when reproduction is possible.

The Repproductive Cycle

Reproduction is the formation of new individuals from a part or parts of old individuals. Biologists often define reproduction as the maintenance of a species from generation to generation. Two types of reproduction are generally recognized: asexual or vegetative reproduction, and sexual reproduction.

Asexual reproduction involves only one parent and no egg or sperm. The result of asexual reproduction is a new individual having the same characteristics of the parent and is often similar to the growth of a limb on a tree. Of course the limb would have to drop off, develop its own root system, and live as a separate individual for our simile to be complete.

Sexual reproduction involves the union of two different cells, usually an egg and a sperm, to form a new individual. This process, as we shall see in Chapter 5, often permits the new individuals to differ from either of the parents. Variations exist among the different animals as to how the processes of asexual and sexual reproduction are accomplished. Some of these variations are indicated in the following sections.

ASEXUAL REPRODUCTION

Asexual reproduction occurs when new individuals are produced by only one "parent," without gametes being involved and without the fusion of gametic nuclei. Asexual reproduction is common in many plants and in the lower groups of animals. Several different types of asexual reproduction are known.

Binary fission is common in protozoans. It involves the division of one individual into two almost equal parts and the subsequent growth of the two smaller individuals into adult size. In some cases mitotic spindles similar to those seen in mitosis form during the splitting of the nuclei.

Binary fission is termed *transverse* when, as in the paramecium, the division cuts across the cell body, and longitudinal when, as in the *Euglena,* it extends the length of the cell body. Many protozoans undergo various types of multiple fission (known by such terms as sporulation, sporogyny, and schizogony) in which the nucleus divides a few to many times, and the cytoplasm then fragments and associates with the individual nuclei, thus producing many small individuals simultaneously.

Budding occurs when a new individual arises as a small outgrowth of another. Budding occurs in some protozoans, hydra, sponges, and others. The buds may separate, forming separate free-living individuals or may remain attached forming colonies of morphologically interconnected individuals.

Fragmentation of one individual into parts, each of which grows into a new individual, is another type of asexual reproduction.

This type is common in many sponges, some flatworms, and other primitive animals. Some sponges constrict at the base of arms; the arms then fall off, attach, and develop as new sponges. This differs from multiple fission (of a single cell), since it involves multicellular fragments of metazoan animals.

REGENERATION

Related to the asexual processes of budding and fragmentation is the ability of organisms to regenerate parts lost by accident. Studies

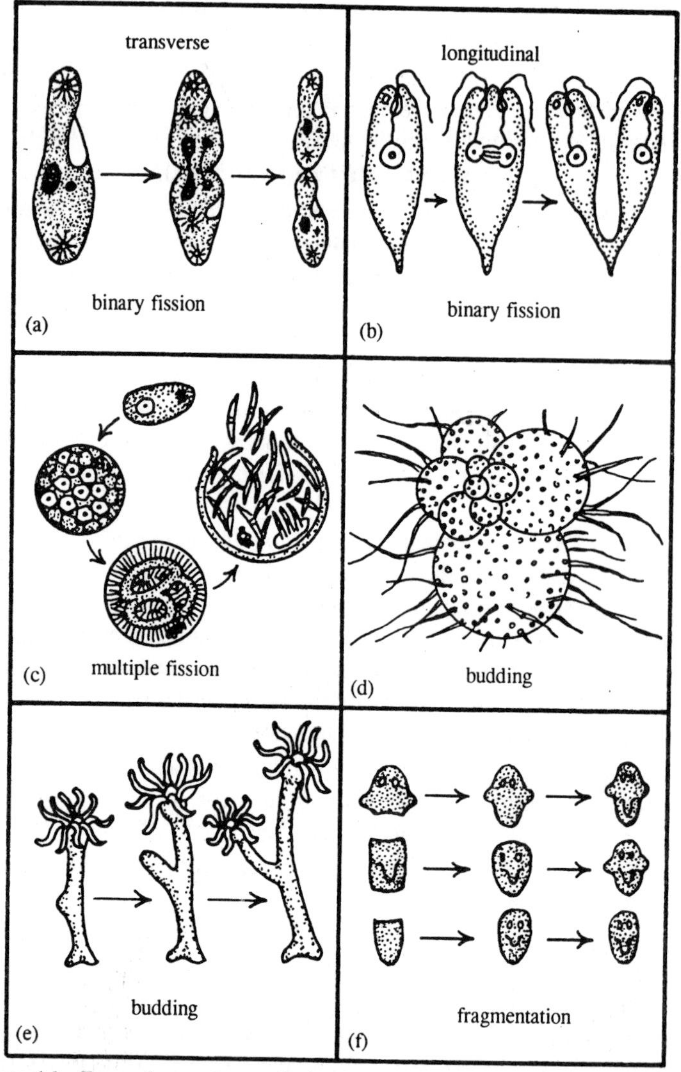

Figure 4.1: Types of asexual reproduction in the animal kingdom. A and B. Fission in protozoans. C. Multiple fission in protozoan. D. Budding in a protozoan. E. Budding in a hydra. F. Fragmentation in a planarium.

made with some large plant and animal cells show that even parts of cells can be regenerated. The single-celled marine alga known as Mermaid's-cap *(Acetabularia)* reaches lengths of 50 mm. The protozoan, *Stentor,* reaches lengths of four mm. In both, parts as small as 1/100 of the total size have been known to regenerate new individuals, so long as certain necessary parts (usually part of the macronucleus in *Stentor)* of the cell are present.

Regeneration in multicellular animals varies, being most pronounced in the sponges and less developed in higher groups. Even in these higher animals, regenerative ability is most marked in the larval, embryonic, and young stages and least likely to occur in older individuals.

A classic experiment with sponges consists of forcing a living sponge through a silk mesh, placing clumps of cells in two or three separate containers. Each group reorganizes itself as a new sponge. Some of the many regeneration experiments involving hydra are reported anywhere else in this chapter.

Some animals have the ability under stress to easily lose some body part. Various crustaceans can lose appendages by this process of autotomy, constricting their muscles so that few body fluids are lost in the process. Some lizards and some salamanders have a similar ability to cast off the tail. Parts lost in this manner are regenerated.

SEXUAL REPRODUCTION

When the production of a new individual results from the fusion of nuclear materials from two different cells (gametes), the result is known as sexual *reproduction*. The basic function of sexual reproduction is simple; it offers a means by which the offspring can differ from the parents. Such variations in the offspring make for many slightly different individuals, thus increasing the probability of survival of the species.

Gamete Foramation

We have already seen that the fertilized egg from which each individual develops is the ancestor, through a series of mitotic divisions, of every cell of which he is composed. We have seen further that each cell contains a characteristic number of chromosomes which is maintained without change through successive mitotic divisions.

Furthermore, all individuals of the same kind have an identical number of chromosomes in each of the cells of their bodies. A fertilized egg results from the fusion of nuclear material in the unfertilized egg with the nuclear material of the spermatozoan.

If the egg (ovum) and the spermatozoan each had the same number of chromosomes found in the other cells of the body producing them, the fertilized egg would have double the number characteristic of the cells of the parents. Furthermore, the number of chromosomes per cell would double with each successive generation.

Such a situation is not possible, if for no other reason than that the chromosome volume would soon exceed the volume of the whole cell. Such a progressive increase in chromosome number does not occur. Rather, the offspring have the same number of chromosomes in each cell as do their parents and other members of the same species.

Since both the ovum and the spermatozoan do contain chromosomes, some reduction of chromosome number must occur in the formation of the unfertilized ovum and the spermatozoan.

It seems logical that, for the fertilization process to be efficient, each gamete (ovum or spermato-zoan) must contain only half the number characteristic of the species, so that any two gametes that come together during fertilization will restore the original number. Such is the case.

To see how such a reduction comes about so that each fertilized egg contains the proper number and kind of chromosomes, let us assume a hypothetical animal, the spermatozoa of which each contain three different chromosomes, A, B, and C.

These three chromosomes may all be identical in size and shape, or they may differ greatly in these same features. In any case, however, many experiments have been performed that demonstrate conclusively that the chromosomes and their contained DNA materials (Section 3.6) are not identical and that all three are necessary for the spermatozoan to be successful in fertilization.

The mature ovum will also contain only three chromosomes, identical in size and shape with the three found in the spermatozoan. For identification purposes we will label these chromosomes A′, B′, and C′. As a result of fertilization, the zygote, as the fertilized egg is called, would contain six chromosomes, A, A′, B, B′, C, and C′. Each of the cells in the new individual, derived from a subsequent series of mitotic divisions, will contain an identical set of six chromosomes.

Since the cells of different species of animals contain different characteristic numbers of chromosomes, and not always six as in our example, it is convenient to represent the number of chromosomes in one gamete of any given species by the letter N or the words "haploid number."

Since fertilization doubles this number, the chromosome number of all of the body cells would be 2N, or the diploid number. The diploid cell has 2N chromosomes because it contains homologous pairs of chromosomes. In our example, chromosome A from the sperm is homologous with chromosome A′ from the ovum, B with B′, and C with C′.

By definition the haploid number of chromosomes always includes

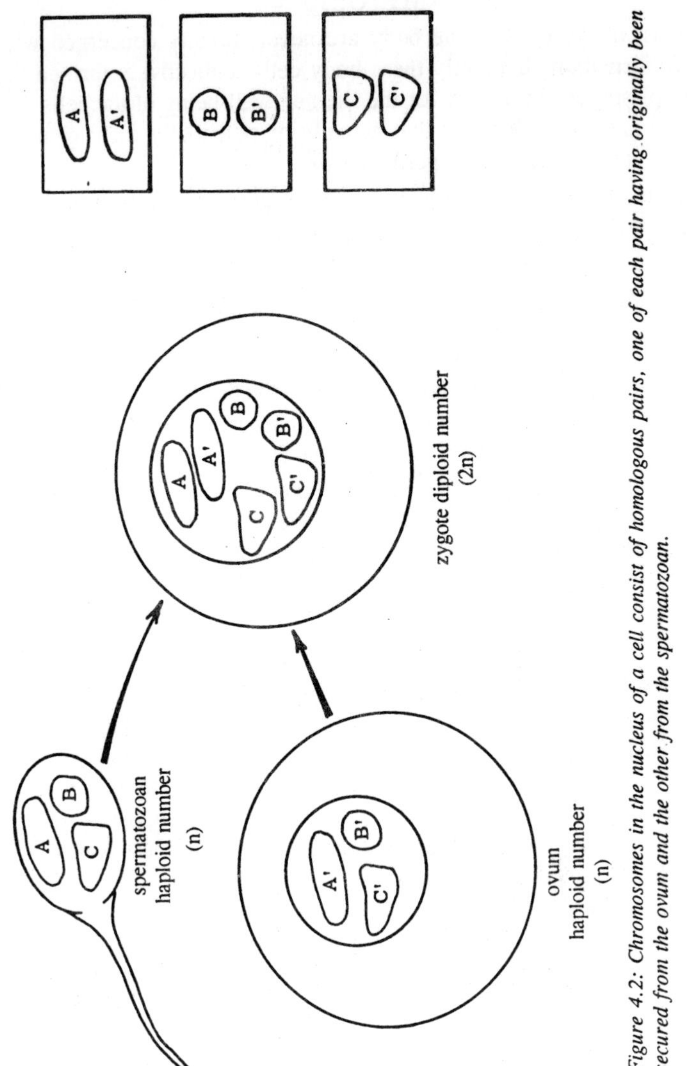

Figure 4.2: Chromosomes in the nucleus of a cell consist of homologous pairs, one of each pair having originally been secured from the ovum and the other from the spermatozoan.

one member of each of the homologous pairs. If a gamete contained chromosomes A, A′, and B, it would not be normal and would not contain the haploid number.

Obviously then, some special process, differing from mitosis, must exist to insure that each gamete will receive one member of each homologous pair of chromosomes present in the diploid cells characteristic of the species. Such a process is termed meiosis.

MEIOSIS

Most of the cells in the body are never directly concerned with gamete formation. Indirectly these body cells, collectively termed the somatoplasm, are necessary for the life and well-being of the cells that do form gametes. The cells that actually or potentially form gametes are collectively termed the germ plasm.

Cells of both the somatoplasm and the germ plasm each have the diploid number of chromosomes, and both kinds of cells potentially can or actually do reproduce themselves by ordinary cell division or mitosis.

In sexually mature individuals the germ plasm is generally found restricted to the region of the gonads (ovaries in females, testes in males). In the formation of mature gametes, some of the cells in the germ plasm undergo a special type of cell division termed meiosis, in which the diploid number (2N) of chromosomes is reduced to the haploid number (N) consisting of one chromosome from each homologous pair.

Like mitosis, meiosis is a continuous process which for convenience is divided into four phases: prophase, metaphase, anaphase, and telophase. Many of the activities in each of these phases are identical with those of the same phases of mitosis, but a few important differences exist. Furthermore, the complete process of meiosis consists of two successive divisions, the first and second meiotic division.

Prophase of the First Meiotic Division

As in mitosis, several simultaneous processes occur during prophase of the first meiotic division. (1) The centrioles separate and move to the opposite poles of the cell, and associated fibers set up the spindle. (2) The nuclear membrane disappears. (3) The chromatin material of the chromosome condenses, forming distinct chromosomes. Notice that all of these steps occur in mitosis.

The following are the key steps of meiosis that make it different from mitosis. (4) Synapsis occurs; that is, the homologous chromosomes come to lie side by side. In terms of our hypothetical animal having chromosomes A, A′, B, B′, C, and C′, this means that A would synapse with A′, B with B′, and C with C′. (5) *Tetrad formation* occurs.

Some variation exists between various species of animals as to whether each chromosome (all six in our example) is duplicated during the interphase or only after synapsis occurs. In any case, each member of the homologous pair has either already duplicated, thus forming a dyad, or duplicates shortly after synapsis. The result of dyad formation and synapsis is that two dyads (four monads) are fused together as a tetrad. A tetrad, in our example, would consist of chromosomes A and its duplicate A as well as A′ and its duplicate A′. (6) Spindle fibers attach to the chromomeres of monads in the tetrad in such a way that both members of one dyad (for example, A and A) are attached to spindle fibers leading to one pole and both members of the other dyad (A′ and A′) to the opposite pole of the cell.

Metaphase of the First Meiotic Division

The tetrads align in the equatorial plane in such a way that one dyad is on one side and the other dyad is on the opposite side (AA on one side, A′A′ on the opposite side).

Anaphase of the First Meiotic Division

The tetrads are separated into the component dyads (AA from A′A′), and these move toward opposite poles of the cell.

Telophase of the First Meiotic Division

The cell membrane constricts along the equatorial plane of the cell, dividing it into two daughter cells. However, unlike mitosis, the spindle fibers do not completely disappear, the nuclear membrane does not reappear, and the chromosomes do not become diffuse. Instead of returning to an interphase condition, both cells almost immediately begin the second meiotic division.

Prophase of the Second Meiotic Division

Occurring as it does almost immediately after the first meiotic division, many of the preliminaries have already occurred. The centrioles of each cell duplicate and reorganize a spindle, and the fibers are attached to the chromomeres of the monads in such a way that one monad of each dyad is attached to a spindle fiber leading to one pole and the other monad to the opposite pole of the cell.

Metaphase of the Second Meiotic Division

The dyads are aligned on the equatorial plane of the cell so that one monad is on one side and the other monad is on the opposite side. For example, in the cell receiving dyad AA, one A is opposite its duplicate A. In the other cell, A′ would be opposite A′.

Anaphase of the Second Meiotic Division

The dyads separate into the component monads, and these move toward opposite poles of the cell.

Telophase of the Second Meiotic Division

The cell membrane constricts, dividing the cell into two cells. As in mitosis, the nucleus, centriole, and chromosomes return to the interphase condition.

As a result of these two meiotic divisions, we have four cells, each containing a haploid number of chromosomes. In other words, each cell contains one member of each homologous pair that existed in the diploid germ plasm that underwent meiosis.

In terms of our hypothetical animal, each would contain three chromosomes, A, B, and C. Of course we could have either A or A′, B or B′, and C or C′; but for the present, we are concerned only with the fact that each contains one member of each homologous pair.

GAMETOGENESIS

Gametogenesis is the process of forming mature gametes (ova and spermatozoa) from germ plasm cells. As shown in Table elsewhere in this chapter, gametogenesis involves meiosis, but it also involves other processes as well.

Slight variations occur and differing names for the specific stages are applied, depending upon whether the gametes being produced are spermatozoa or ova. For this reason we will consider spermatogenesis and oogenesis separately.

SPERMATOGENESIS

Sperm cells or spermatozoa are produced in the reproductive glands (gonads) of the male. Testes, the male gonads, differ somewhat in structure in different animals, but the functional processes to be described are quite similar in all. The testes (singular = testis) contain many tiny seminiferous tubules, the walls of which are composed of undifferentiated *germ* cells called spermatogonia.

These spermatogonia divide mitotically to give rise to more and more identical germ cells with chromosomes of the number, size, and shape characteristic of all the other cells of the body. During the reproductive life of the individual, some spermatogonia fail to divide mitotically, and instead grow into larger cells called primary spermatocytes. Each primary spermatocyte divides to give rise to two secondary spermatocytes.

This division is called the first meiotic division. Each secondary spermatocyte again divides to give rise to two spermatids, and this division is called the second meiotic division. The spermatid alters progressively in shape and appearance, losing much of its cytoplasm and growing a flagellum or tail until it becomes a typical mature spermatazoan.

In this final metamorphosis the various cell organelles are distributed in a characteristic manner. The Golgi apparatus forms a cap over the

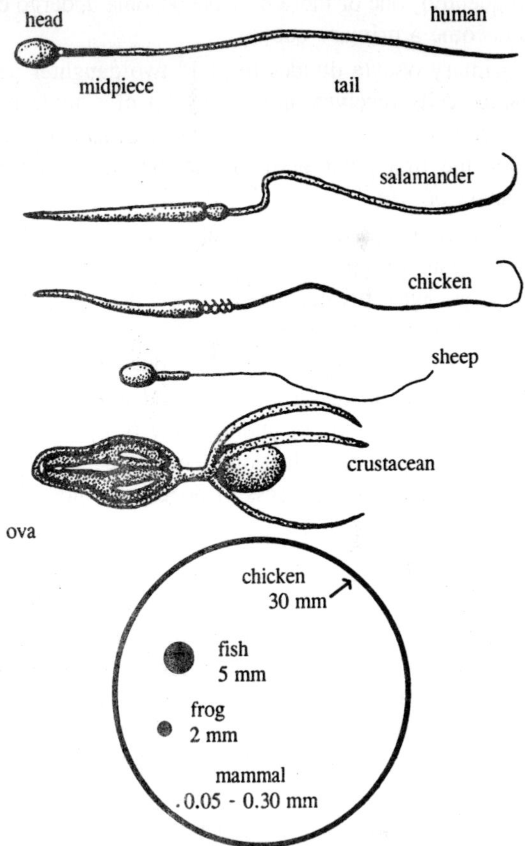

Figure 4.3: Variations in the size and shape of gametes.

head end of the nucleus, and the mitochondria move into the base of the tail. For each primitive spermatogonium which begins the process of spermatogenesis, four mature spermatozoa are produced (as a result of two generations of cell division). These vary greatly in size and shape in different animal species, but each contains a haploid number of chromosomes.

OOGENESIS

The reproductive glands (gonads) of the female are the ovaries. The ovaries contain undifferentiated sex cells called oogonia, which in early life divide mitotically to produce more and more similar oogonia, each with the same number of chromosomes as the other body cells. During the reproductive life of the individual at fairly regular intervals (annually or more frequently), one or more of these oogonia undergo considerable growth to become a primary oocyte.

Each primary oocyte divides to yield two daughter cells. One of these daughter cells receives only a tiny bit of cytoplasm, while the bulk of the cytoplasm goes to the other daughter cell. The little daughter cell is called the first polar body, while the larger one is given the name secondary oocyte.

This is the first meiotic division and is identical to that occurring in spermatogenesis, except for the unequal division of cytoplasm. The secondary oocyte again divides unequally to give rise to a second polar body and an ootid. This is the second meiotic division and is again like that of spermatogenesis, except for the unequal division of cytoplasm.

The ootid, by a process of growth and maturation becomes an ovum. The polar bodies do not undergo any further development and play no active role in reproduction. Therefore, for each primitive oogonium which begins the process of oogenesis only a single mature ovum results.

Reproductive Systems

In general terms, reproduction results in a cyclic shift from a diploid to a haploid phase and back to a diploid phase. Asexual reproduction can occur in either of these phases. In advanced animals, the gametes are the only remnants of the haploid generation, and these rarely reproduce asexually.

In fact, in primitive multicellular animals, permanent gamete-producing organs are usually absent. During the reproductive season certain cells become modified as gametogonia. In many, the gametes are released from the parent only by the rupture of the parental body wall.

In higher invertebrates and in the vertebrates specialized organ systems for the production, storage, and transport of gametes are usually present, at least in adults. The names and functions of the structures are shown in Table elsewhere in this chapter.

When male organs are in one individual and female organs in a second individual, the species is said to be dioecious, but when one individual contains both, it is termed a monoecious species. Some animals change the type of gamete produced during the course of the life of the individual. Such species are termed protandrous.

Normally, larval individuals do not produce gametes; however,

Table 4.1: Organs Present in a Reproductive System.

	Male	*female*
Gonad	Testis (pl. testes)	Ovary (pl. ovaries)
Gamete	Spennatozoan (pl. spermatozoa)	Ovrmr (pl. ova)
Ducts	Vas eferens (pl, vasa eflerentia) Vas deferens (pl. vasa deferentia)	Oviduct + uterus
Accessory glands	Sperm-activating glands	Albumen, yolk, shell
Spenn storage	Seminal vesicle	Seminal receptacle
Terminal organs (for transport or deposition)	Penis	Vagina + ovipositor

among certain animals such as the tiger salamander (Chordata: Amphibia), larval individuals become sexually mature and reproduce, a condition known as neotony. In fact, certain anthropologists have proposed the concept that man is the result of neotony, and the "adult" features characterizing the other higher primates (head shape, body shape) are never developed.

VARIATIONS IN REPRODUCTIVE CYCLES

It is now generally concluded that most organisms now living have some type of sexual reproduction. This is true of viruses, bacteria, protozoans, multicellular animals, and most plants. The few exceptions including blue-green algae, the common ameba, and certain higher plants appear to be recent descendants from forms that did not have such mechanisms.

Bisexual reproduction involving gametogenesis and fertilization (the union of two gametes from different individuals) appears to be the primitive pattern. It occurs widely in both lower and higher types of plants and animals.

Normally, gametogenesis produces two types of gametes that differ markedly in size-a large, usually non-motile macrogamete (ovum) and a small, usually motile, microgamete (sperm). Sometimes, however, there is little difference in size and structure, in which case the gametes are termed isogametes.

Often these differ widely in size, shape, and organization. In some organisms there appears to be little or no difference in structure or appearance between the gametes.

Some biologists prefer to emphasize the differences between protozoans (and similar unicellular organisms) and higher organisms by utilizing a special vocabulary to apply to sexual reproduction, wherein the whole individual (instead of just one germ cell of a multicellular individual) undergoes gametogenesis. In the paramecium, for example, bisexual reproduction is termed conjugation.

Basically, in conjugation the whole cell of each of the two original individuals is an ovum, and most of the excess nuclear material produced by meiosis is reabsorbed into the cell and not eliminated as polar bodies.

The reabsorbed material is altered in the process so that it is no longer genetic, but a mechanism for conserving chemical materials. Two haploid sets of chromosomes, however, are retained, one of which migrates to the second individual involved in the conjugation (the spermatozoan), and the second of which remains as the nuclear content of the "ovum". Still other terms have been coined to indicate other "types" of sexual reproduction in protozoans.

Among organisms included in this book as animals there is a wide variety of reproductive cycles. Perhaps at one extreme is the protozoan *Chlamydomonas,* in which the haploid phase is dominant.

The major part of the life cycle of this organism is spent as a motile isogamete that normally reproduces asexually by longitudinal binary fission. Occasionally, two isogametes fuse, restoring the diploid number of chromosomes, but thc resulting zygote almost immediately undergoes meiosis, producing four haploid offspring.

Most animals have a dominant diploid phase in which the sexes are separate. Especially in the lower invertebrates but even among the tunicates (Phylum Chordata), both males and females may also reproduce asexually, often by budding. Most higher invertebrates and all vertebrates have lost the asexual portion of the reproductive cycle.

Some insects, such as the bees, are sexually dimorphic as to the haploid-diploid phases. In the bees the males are of the haploid phase, while females (queens and workers) are diploid. Similarly, among certain moths the females are of the haploid phase while the males are diploid.

PATTERNS OF DEVELOPMENT

We have seen that in ordinary cell division (mitosis) two cells result from the division of the protoplasmic materials of the parent cell. Thus, there is a protoplasmic continuity from cell generation to cell generation. In a similar way there is protoplasmic continuity, through the gametes, from generation to generation of individuals.

The union of an ovum with a spermatozoan, a process known as fertilization, results in the formation of a zygote. In gross appearance, the zygote looks quite similar to the unfertilized egg. For this tiny spherical structure to develop into a large, adult multicellular animal, several processes, sometimes acting simultaneously, must occur. These are:

Cell Division and Cell Growth

Obviously the single-celled zygote must undergo repeated cell division to form the multitude of cells making up a large, complex adult animal. Cell division alone does not result in an increase in size. Size increase results from growth of the individual cells.

In most animals a series of cell divisions occurs just after fertilization in which there is little or no growth. Such cell divisions are known as cleavage. Cleavage divisions result in the formation of a ball of cells, little if any larger than the zygote, that is known as a blastula. Depending upon the type of egg produced by the animal, the blastula is more or less hollow.

Morphogenesis

After cleavage has divided the zygote into a number of cells and the gastrula is formed, a series of mass movements of cells and foldings of parts of the developing embryo occurs, thus forming, at first, the broad outlines of the adult structural pattern and, later, the details of the adult structure.

The first major morphogenetic process is the formation of a gastrula from the blastula stage. The gastrula usually involves a change from the spherical symmetry of the zygote to a bilateral structure in which indications of the top, bottom, and sides as well as front and back ends of the future adult organism can be seen.

Further morphogenesis occurs when details of the adult are more clearly established by organogenesis or organ and organ system formation.

Differentiation

Continuous cell division and growth is simultaneous with morphogenesis and the process of differentiation. The latter causes cells to develop into the various types of tissues such as muscle, skeletal, and blood.

The sequence and interaction of these processes is controlled by various inducers and organizers and results in protoplasmic continuity from generation to generation.

Types of OVA

The eggs produced by the various kinds of animals are not uniform. Some are large, some are small, some have a firm shell of calcium or other non-living material, and some are surrounded only by a cell membrane.

One of the major factors controlling the size of the egg is the amount of stored food (yolk materials) present. The amount of yolk present also influences the patterns of cell division occurring during cleavage and, to a lesser extent, influences patterns of gastrula formation and organogenesis.

The following three types of ova are defined primarily on the basis of the amount of yolk present.

Isolecithal Ova

Eggs of this type are generally small and contain a relatively little yolk that ordinarily is distributed uniformly throughout the ovum. Usually eggs of the starfish are of this type.

Telolecithal Ova

Eggs of this type generally are larger and have the yolk materials concentrated in the lower part of the egg. The top portion, with its concentration of protoplasmic material and the nucleus is known as the animal hemisphere.

The lower portion, predominantly yolk, is the vegetal hemisphere. Telolecithal eggs vary greatly in the amount of yolk present. Some, such as the frog egg, have only about 50 per cent yolk; but others, such as the bird egg, have as much as 95 per cent yolk, so that the cytoplasm and nucleus form only a small plate on top of the yolk.

Note that the bird egg is surrounded by additional stored food materials in the form of albumen, and the whole egg is surrounded by a calcareous shell.

Centrolecithal Ova

In eggs of this type, the yolk accumulates in the center of the egg and is surrounded by a thin layer of cytoplasm. The egg nucleus is in the center of the ovum. Such ova are characteristic of many insects.

Types of Cleavage

Once a mature egg is fertilized, it normally undergoes a number of cell divisions that do not materially increase the size of the zygote but divide the cytoplasm and yolk materials among the resulting cells. In general, isolecithal eggs divide completely, giving rise to daughter cells of equal size. In such eggs cleavage is said to be holoblastic and equal. In telolecithal eggs, such as that of the frog, cleavage is complete (the entire egg is subdivided) but unequal (the resulting cells are of unequal size).

The inequality is due to the interference of yolk material with the formation of cleavage planes. In such eggs cleavage is said to beholoblastic and unequal. In extremely telolecithal eggs, such as that of the bird, there may be so much yolk present that the cleavage is incomplete.

In such cases the cytoplasm of the animal pole subdivides, but the cleavage furrows do not penetrate through the yolk portion of the egg. Such cleavage is said to be meroblastic. These groups are not always distinct, for some isolecithal eggs do cleave unequally, usually because of factors other than the amount of yolk present.

The general tendency seen in cleavage is that the more evenly distributed the yolk material, or the smaller the amount of yolk material present, the more likely is equal cleavage to occur.

Three major types of holoblastic cleavage are known: radial, bilateral, and spiral. The type of cleavage depends in part upon the original egg type (yolk distribution) and in part upon the relationship of the animal. Radial cleavage is typical of eggs of the isolecithal type. It is holoblastic (complete) and equal.

The first two cleavages are vertical and at right angles to each other. The third cleavage is horizontal and occurs at the equator, so that all eight cells produced up to this time are of equal size. The fourth cleavage is again vertical and double, so that each of the four cells in each hemisphere is again divided.

The fifth cleavage is horizontal and double-one above and one below the plane of the third cleavage. This type of sequence continues, always resulting in cells of equal sizes in all parts.

Bilateral cleavage is the type seen in the frog. It is like radial cleavage in all respects, except that the resulting cells are unequal due to the fact that the egg is somewhat telolecithal.

In spiral cleavage the first two cleavages are like those of the frog-vertical and unequal, and usually cleavage is holoblastic. Unlike the typical bilateral cleavage of the frog, however, the spindles resulting in the third cleavage are not oriented exactly in a vertical direction; they are tipped to one side, so that the resulting daughter cells do not lie immediately above and below each other but tend to alternate with each other in position.

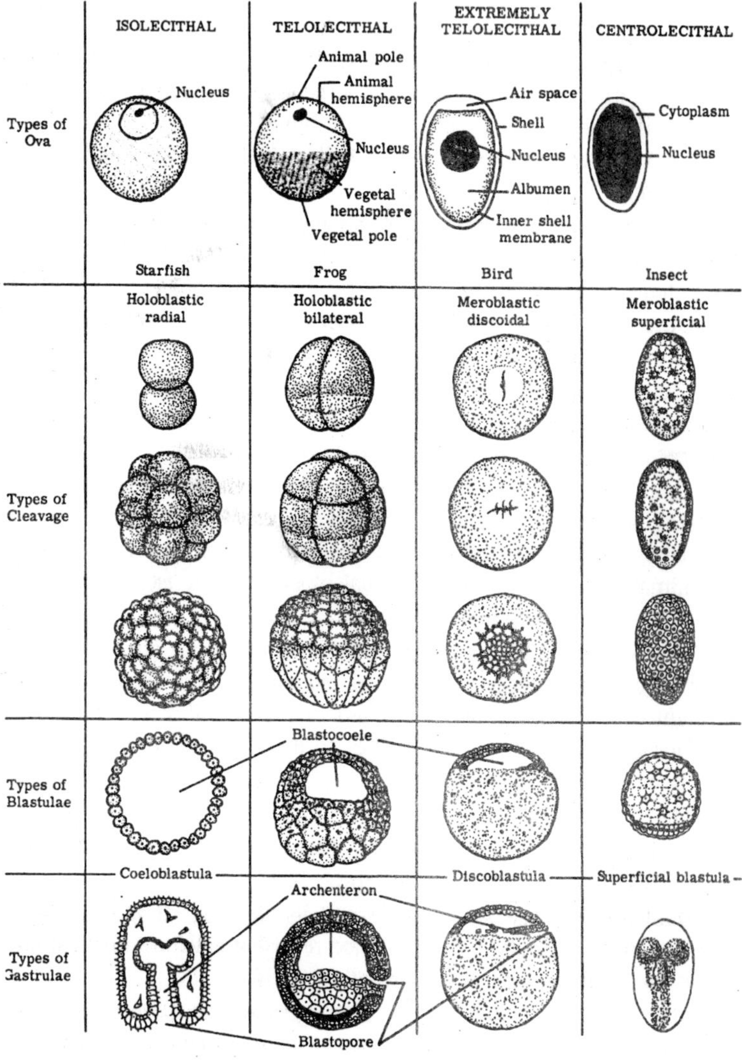

Figure 4.4: Early embryological stages of four different animals, showing differences in types of ova, cleavage, and blastula and gastnila stages.

This tendency persists in subsequent divisions-the spindles being alternately tipped in the clockwise and in the counter-clockwise direction as viewed from above.

Some eggs are so extremely telolecithal, as we have seen, that only a small disc of material on one side constitutes an animal hemisphere. In such cases cleavage is *meroblastic* (incomplete), involving as it does only this disc of cytoplasmic material. In such cases, cleavage is said to be of discoidal type. This is really only an extreme case of bilateral cleavage.

Finally, in centrolecithal eggs, the nucleus which lies in the central mass of cytoplasm divides several times without cell walls forming to divide the cytoplasm. These nuclei migrate through the cytoplasmic connection to the outer, cortical layer of cytoplasm.

This layer develops cleavage furrows which do not penetrate into the underlying yolk material; each incompletely separated cell so formed receives a daughter nucleus. This is spoken of as *superficial* cleavage. There are still other kinds of cleavage known, but they involve relatively few kinds of animals and are unimportant to our discussion.

TYPES OF BLASTULA

In the frog, cleavage results in the formation of a blastula with an internal fluid-filled space called the *blastocoele*. Such a blastula is called a coeloblastula. Some blastulas lack the clearly defined blastocoele and are given different names.

Where a single layer of cells is present, as in the frog, but these cells are elongated and there is no blastocoele, the blastula is called a *stereoblastula*. Where more than a single layer of cells exists the structure is called a morula.

Where the blastocoele is obliterated by a compression of the animal and vegetal poles toward each other, the blastula is given the name placula. The names discoblastula and *superficial* blastula refer to the structures resulting respectively from discoidal and superficial cleavage.

Figure elsewhere in this chapter reviews in tabular form the relationships between some of the types of eggs, cleavages, and blastulas. It also indicates some of the animals in which these various types are found. Note that the cleavage type and the type of resulting blastula are dependent upon the original egg-type, rather than upon the phylogenetic position of the animal concerned.

That is, there is no fundamental difference between the various cleavage and blastula types; they are all variations on the same theme resulting from different amounts and distribution patterns of yolk material and perhaps from other minor variations.

Types of Gastrulation

Following the formation of the blastula, the results of the first major morphogenetic processes are seen in the formation of the gastrula. This process results in giving the embryo a wall that is two cells in thickness. The internal cavity so formed is the archenteron or future gut of the animal.

In the frog egg gastrulation depended primarily upon the process of epiboly: an outgrowth of the vegetal hemisphere by rapidly proliferating animal hemisphere cells which, as they advance, are turned or rolled under themselves like an advancing wave of water.

The outer layer of cells, called *ectoderm*, give rise to the skin and some associated structures of the animal, while the inner layer, called endoderm, forms the lining of the adult intestinal tract. Because blastulae differ it is to be expected that the process of gastnilation will differ as will the appearance of the resulting gastrula.

Again, however, all are essentially alike, and with the events of frog gastrulation in mind they are easy to understand. Three other processes are responsible for gastrulation in other egg types: invagination, ingression, and *delamination*. The blastula of the starfish becomes flattened at the vegetal pole and sinks inward.

This is exactly comparable to pushing in the side of a tennis ball and is known as invagination. The placula type of blastula can be thought of as one in which the flattening of the vegetal hemisphere which initiates invagination is extreme. In such a blastula a secondary downward curving of the edges of the placula results in a gastrula of similar appearance.

In certain other animals, notably those with blastulae having large blastocoeles, there is an active inward migration of cells. Sometimes this is restricted to vegetal hemisphere cells (unipolar ingression), and sometimes cells from various sites on the surface of the blastula migrate inward (apolar ingression).

In the latter case a stereogastrula often results. This is one in which no archenteron cavity is formed as such; rather, the entire original blastocoele is filled with cells, and the archenteron or primitive gut forms later by splitting this internal cell mass. Finally, in some blastulae a second layer of cells is formed by tangential cleavages of the original surface layer.

This type is known as delamination. In the case of stereoblastulae, of course, the inner cells are already present, so no gastrulation as such is necessary.

In the extremely telolecithal eggs which show discoidal cleavage, the events are really quite similar to those in the frog. This statement is an oversimplification, but that point of view will still be adequate to our purpose, and the differences will soon become evident to the student who pursues his study of embryology in more advanced textbooks on the subject.

Among the birds no archenteron is formed; rather, there is an inturning of the cells of the discoblastula at a point which is homologous to the blastopore. Subsequently these cells organize as a sheet which grows completely around the yolk mass to form what is known as the yolk sac. The gastrula then consists of a double cell layer lying on top of the relatively large yolk mass.

ORGANIZATION

In some of the primitive animals, such as the hydra and related jellyfish, the morphogenesis that formed the gastrula has completed most of the adult body form. A hydra, for example, consists of only two layers of cells, the skin or ectoderm and the inner gut lining or endoderm.

Adults of the more advanced multicellular animals, however, have many more structures present than merely a skin and a gut. Such major organ systems as skeleton, muscles, circulatory system, nervous system, sense organs, gonads, and kidneys must be developed by additional morphogenic processes.

Of course, two layers of cells are not adequate to form all these structures, so that much additional cell division and growth must occur. Furthermore, cells making the muscle system, for example, are different from cells found in the skeletal system. Thus, differentiation must occur to produce the proper types of cells in the places where needed.

One source that produces most of the additional cells required in the complex organ systems is a new layer of cells, the mesoderm. This third germ layer arises in various ways, depending somewhat on the type of gastrula.

The specific germ layers giving rise to the various tissues and organs are shown in Table elsewhere in this chapter. Organogenesis is the development of the various adult structures through the processes of cell division, growth, cell differentiation, and morphogenesis. Organogenesis in the frog is covered in detail in other chapter of this book.

Table 4.2: Germ Layers from Which the Various Tissues and Organs Most Generally Arise.

Ectoderm

Epidermis of the skin; skin glands, hair, feathers, and fingernails; all nervous tissue; receptor cells in sense organs; and epidermis of the mouth, nose, and anus.

Mesoderm

All muscles; connective tissues including skeleton, blood, heart, and other organs of the circulatory system; gonads; kidneys; and linings of cavities in the body.

Endoderm

Epidermis lining gut, trachea, lungs, and urinary bladder; liver; pancreas; and thyroid gland.

THE CONTROL OF EMBRYOLOGICAL PROCESSES

Formerly it was thought that a given germ layer always gave rise to a specific type of tissue or organ. More recent studies have shown that much variation can occur in the fate of specific cells in a given germ layer.

Experiments involving transplanting cells from one germ layer to another demonstrate that the exact location of a given cell in the developing embryo is much more important than its germ layer origin. For example, ectodermal cells transplanted to regions of developing mesodermal muscles or bones will differentiate into muscle or bone.

Of course location alone does not explain why cells differentiate into skin in one region, into muscle in another, and into blood cells in still a third region. Various studies made by experimental embryologists, endocrinologists, and biochemists have shown some of the mechanisms involved.

Hans Spemann showed experimentally that in frogs and other amphibians there is a special region of cells at the upper lip of the developing gastrula that apparently releases various hormone-like secretions. These influence and control the developing embryo.

Spemann termed these cells the organizer, and both he and later researchers performed many experiments involving transplanting the cells involving the organizer region. For example, embryos from which the organizer cells have been removed do not develop properly, and certain organs and organ systems never develop.

An organizer transplanted from one early embryo to another of the same age results in both organizers attempting to control the developing embryo. Each organizer influences enough surrounding cells that two head regions form, resulting in a sort of Siamese twin.

The organizer maintains control over many major morphogenetic processes; specific. tissue differentiation and organ formations are often controlled by induction from surrounding cells. It is possible to grow isolated cells from the organs of an animal such as a rat in isolated tissue cultures.

When cells from the kidney of a rat are grown in tissue cultures, these cells become generalized, much as do the primitive embryonic cells. However, if a few cells of connective tissue from the kidney are added to the tissue culture, the generalized cells differentiate, tending to become like their ancestral cells in the kidney. Apparently the connective tissue cells release some biochemical that induces differentiation. Such induction is widespread in embryonic development.

Organogenesis in an embryo, then, is the result of the interaction of biochemical controls and the physical location of given cells.

One remarkable property of differentiated cells is the ability of most kinds to "recognize" each other and remain together or, if experimentally separated from each other, to reconvene and reorganize into the original association.

Despite specialization, the cells of some of the lower animals retain the ability to move about individually like amebae and thus lend themselves well to this type of experimentation. If a living sponge is passed through a fine sieve to separate its component cells and these cells are allowed to settle in a haphazard way on the bottom of a dish of sea water, the cells will "crawl" together, reassociate by cell type, and build a number of smaller but structurally accurate whole sponges.

In most cases, the cells of higher organisms are unable to move about independently; but if medium containing isolated cells is stirred frequently, thus making for frequent random contact between separated cells, cells of the same type will tend to stick together and ultimately reorganize recognizable replicas of the tissue from which they were originally separated.

The recognition signals by which cells "know" each other must be embodied in the protein configurations of the cell membrane in some way. Undoubtedly, similar mechanisms are involved in the "recognition" of foreign cells such as bacteria or the blood cells of a different species or blood type.

PATTERN OF INHERITANCE

You are not a duplicate of your mother or a carbon copy of your father, or even an exact mixture of the characteristics of them both. Just how were the distinctive plans for the immensely complicated machinery of your body drawn up and expressed?

What mechanisms of inheritance determine whether you are male or female, tall or short, lightor dark-skinned, whether you have type A or type O blood, whether you have normal vision or are colourblind, and countless other of your characteristics?

The Father of Genetics

The roots of much modern biology extend into the 19th century, and genetics is no exception. The foundation of our modern knowledge of genetics was laid at that time by an obscure Austrian monk, Gregor Mendel, who lived in the town of Briinn, Austria, which is now Brno, Czechoslovakia. "Natural philosophy," as biology was called in the 19th century, was usually not a profession but a hobby; only clergymen, physicians, wealthy people, or others with some leisure time were able to pursue it.

But Mendel was no dilettante. The monastery also functioned somewhat as a modern agricultural research station does, and the breeding of improved varieties of cattle, crop plants, and even honeybees was part of its mission.

Mendel was active in the natural history society of Brunn and presented his findings in a series of research reports, which were published in the society's journal. His findings were revolutionary; despite this, they were almost universally ignored.

Whatever the reasons for the neglect, Mendel did not gain the recognition rightly due him for more than 30 years, when biologists first rediscovered these principles and then rediscovered his papers during a prepublication literature search.

Mendel worked with garden peas, which exist in a number of distinct varieties differing in such characteristics as height, flower colour, seed coat colour, and seed coat texture. Pea plants also are normally selffertilized, so simple surgery of the male flower parts makes the plant incapable of being fertilized at all except by artificial means.

In this way, the crossing of varieties can be closely controlled: The emasculated flower can no longer fertilize itself and cannot be fertilized naturally by an unknown plant, and thus "illegitimate" offspring cannot occur.

Mendel's Laws

Mendel's breeding experiments led him to certain conclusions about the mechanisms of heredity, which later scholars restated as *Mendel's laws of inheritance*.

1. Heredity is transmitted by unit factors (now called genes), which exist in pairs.
2. When gametes are formed, the two genes of each pair separate from one another, and each gamete receives only one gene of each pair. This is known as the *law of segregation*.
3. When two alternative forms of the same gene are present in an individual, only one of the alternatives is usually expressed. This concept is known as the *law of dominance*.
4. If one considers two or more independent characteristics in a cross, such as flower colour and seed coat texture, each characteristic is inherited without relation to other traits. All possible combinations of independent characteristics thus will occur in the gametes. This is the *law of independent assortment*.

INTRODUCING GENES

Mendel did not think in terms of genes, although his observations were to lead to the formulation of this concept. As we have discussed, a gene may be defined as a region of DNA containing the information necessary to manufacture a specific polypeptide (or in some cases just a particular type of RNA).

This concept can be illustrated with a common genetic abnormality, albinism. One kind of *albino* is a person or animal who lacks the genetic information to produce the body pigment melanin. This pigment is the protein responsible for most of the colour of hair, skin, and eyes. Without it an organism would appear completely unpigmented, with white hair and perhaps pink eyes, through which hemoglobin of the blood would show unmasked.

In this kind of albinism it has been shown that all that is lacking is the ability to make *tyrosinase*, an enzyme needed to make melanin from the amino acid tyrosine. Without that enzyme no pigment can be formed. But what is meant by a lack of tyrosinase? It is possible, by immunological techniques, to demonstrate that many tyrosinase-negative persons have at least a version of the tyrosinase enzyme.

However, it is not a correct version and is not functional. These albinos lack the genetic information needed to produce functional tyrosinase.

How Genes Behave

Recall that two members of a pair of chromosomes are said to be homologous. They have genes for similar traits arranged in similar order. The gene for each trait occurs at a particular point in the chromosome called a *locus* (plural, loci).

In guinea pigs, for example, if one chromosome of a pair contains a gene for coat colour, so will the other chromosome of the pair. Genes governing variations of the same trait that occupy corresponding loci on homologous chromosomes are known as *alleles*.

The term allele emphasizes that there are two or more alternative forms of the gene at a specific locus in homologous chromosomes. Each of these forms can be assigned a letter as its symbol. It is customary to designate the dominant gene, the one that expresses itself, with a capital letter, and the recessive allele (the gene that does not express itself in the presence of a dominant allele) with a lowercase letter. Thus, the letter *B* could be used for black coat colour and the letter *b* for brown when specifying the alleles that determine coat colour in guinea pigs.

A Monohybrid Cross

The usage of genetic terms and some of the basic principles of genetics can be illustrated by considering a simple *monohybrid cross*, that is, a cross between two individuals that differ with respect to a single characteristic.

The mating of a genetically pure brown male guinea pig with a genetically pure black female guinea pig is illustrated in Figure elsewhere in this chapter. During meiosis in the spermatocytes in the male, the two *bb* alleles separate, so each sperm has only one *b* allele.

In the formation of ova in the female, the *BB* alleles separate, so each ovum has only one *B* allele. The fertilization of this egg by a b-bearing sperm results in an animal with the alleles *Bb,* that is with one allele for brown coat and one allele for black coat. What colour would you expect this animal to be?

Suppose that two black guinea pigs each having alleles for both brown and black coat colour were crossed. Half of the gametes of each would have alleles for black coat colour, and the other half would have alleles for brown coat colour.

The chance that two alleles for brown coat colour would meet

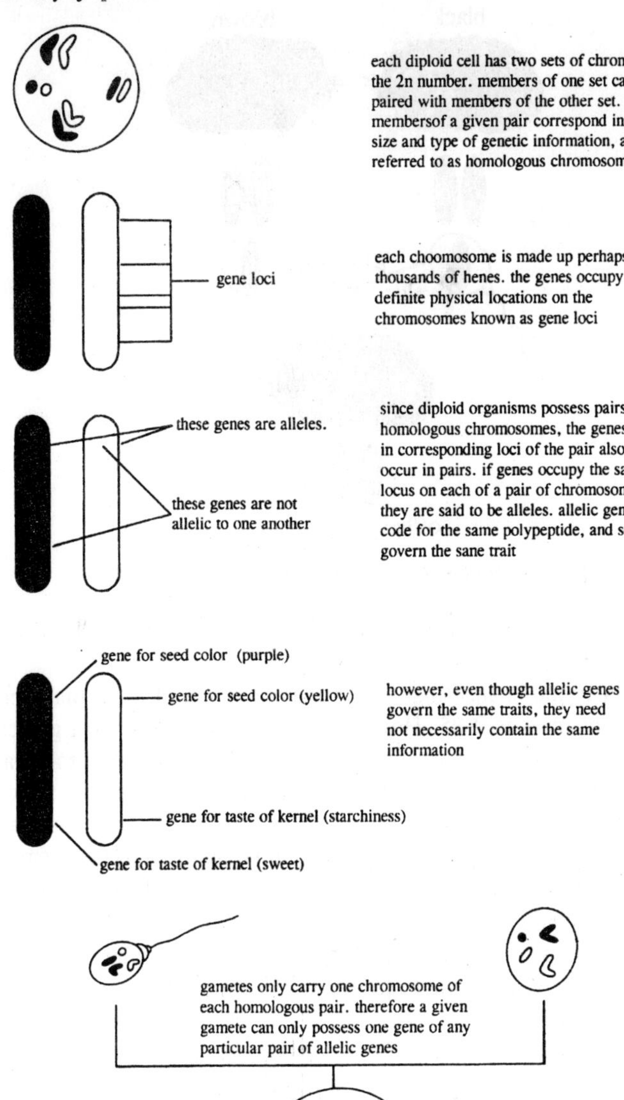

when the gametes combine to form a zygote, it, and the resulting embryo, will have homologous pairs of chromosomes,but ot each pair, one member will be maternal in origin, and one paternal in origin. each pair will bear allelic genes.

Figure 4.5: Homologous chromosomes and alleles.

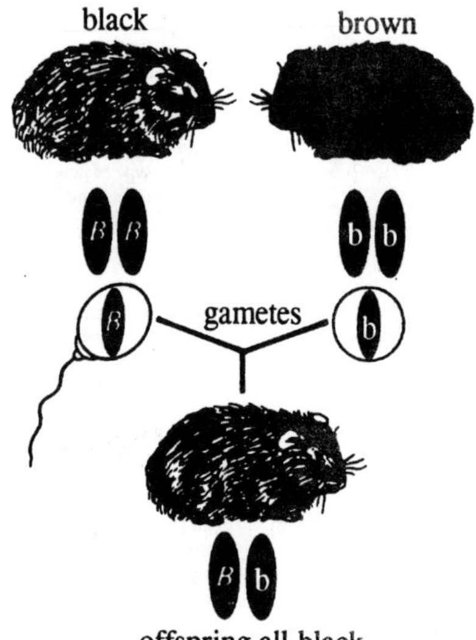

Figure 4.6: When a genetically pure black guinea pig is mated with a brown guinea pig, all the offspring are black.

would be the product of their frequencies of occurrence, that is, 0.50 × 0.50 = 0.25.

Similarly the chance that two gametes with alleles for black coat colour might meet is 0.25. However, since black and brown gametes can meet each other in two ways (brown from the mother and black from the father or black from the mother and brown from the father), their likelihood of meeting is 0.25 + 0.25 = 0.50. This means that if the number of offspring is great enough, three-quarters of the offspring (0.50 + 0.25) will have a black coat phenotype and about one-quarter (0.25) will have brown coats.

The probable combinations of eggs and sperm may be represented in a checkerboard or *Punnett square*, as illustrated in Figure anywhere else in this chapter. The types of eggs can be represented across the top and the types of sperm indicated along the left side.

The squares are filled in with the resulting zygote combinations, so that the letters in each square indicate the genotype of one genetic type of offspring.

The generation with which a particular genetic experiment is begun is called the *parental generation*, or $\mathbf{P_1}$. Offspring of this generation are referred to as the first filial generation, or F_1. Those resulting when two F_1 individuals are bred constitute the second filial generation, or F_2.

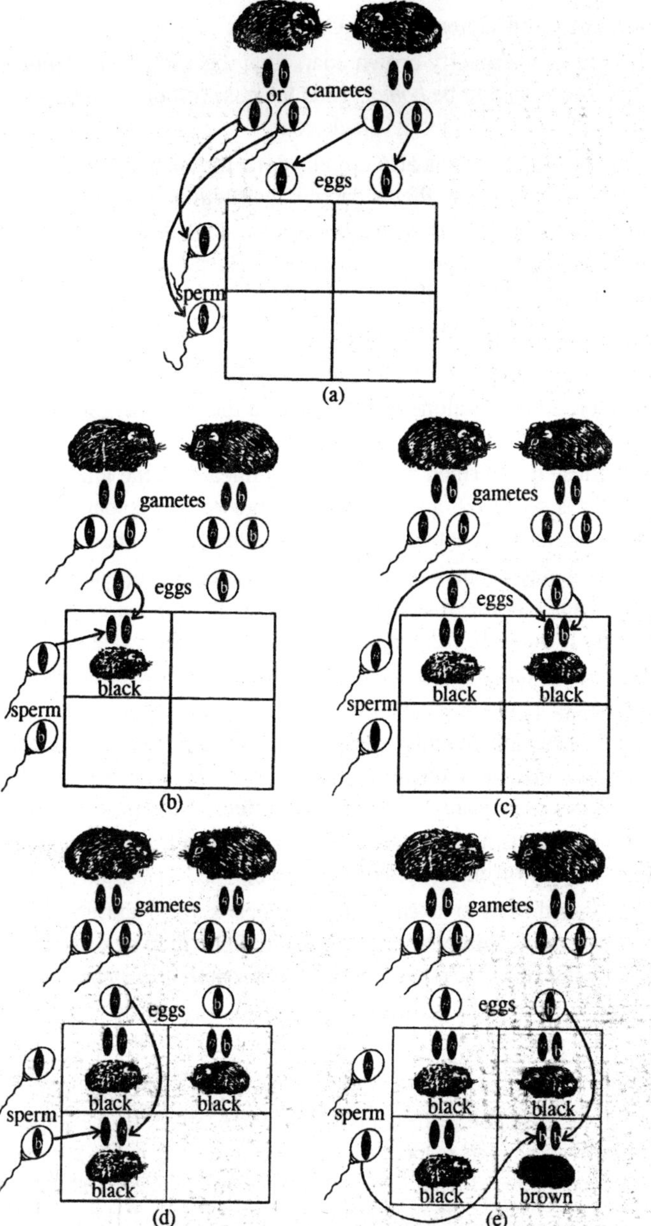

Figure 4.7: The punnett square method of predicting probable genotypes. Note that the letters in each square indicate the genotype of one genetic type of offspring.

Homozygous and Heterozygous Organisms

If both genes specify brown coat, then the alleles are identical and the organism is said to be *homozygous* for coat colour. In another guinea pig both alleles may specify black coat.

This second animal is also homozygous for coat colour. But it often happens that one of the alleles carries instructions for brown coat and the other carries instructions for black coat. In that case, the individual is said to be *heterozygous* for coat colour. Despite this, only one of the two contrasting genes will express itself.

Dominant and Recessive Genes

When one member of an allelic pair tends to dominate the other completely, so that it alone is expressed in the heterozygous condition, it is said to be *dominant*. If, however, a gene is expressed *only when* homozygous, it is termed *recessive*. In guinea pigs the allele for black coat colour is dominant, and the allele for brown coat colour is recessive. A guinea pig must have two alleles for brown coat in order to be brown.

Many genes are not clearly dominant or recessive, and when found together, tend to reach a compromise. Such traits are *incompletely dominant*. If *both* are *fully* expressed, they are said to be *codominant*. Human blood types, which we will soon discuss, provide an example of codominance.

The expression and interaction of genes can be much more complex than we are able to indicate in this brief treatment. For instance, a single gene will probably have multiple effects, a quality referred to as pleiotropy, rather than a single effect. Some genes are able to suppress the expressions of other, nonallelic genes.

This is referred to as *epistasis*. The genes thus suppressed are said to be *hypostatic*. Finally, even a dominant gene may be expressed only in certain instances, a condition called *incomplete penetrance*.

Genotype and Phenotype

An individual's genetic makeup is its *genotype*. However, the genotype is not always detectable in one who is heterozygous for the trait. So we have the term *phenotype*, which refers to the appearance of the individual with respect to a certain inherited trait. Two persons with normal skin pigmentation might very well be genetically different. One might have two alleles for normal pigmentation, while the other might have an allele for normal pigmentation and an allele for albinism without any physical evidence of the latter.

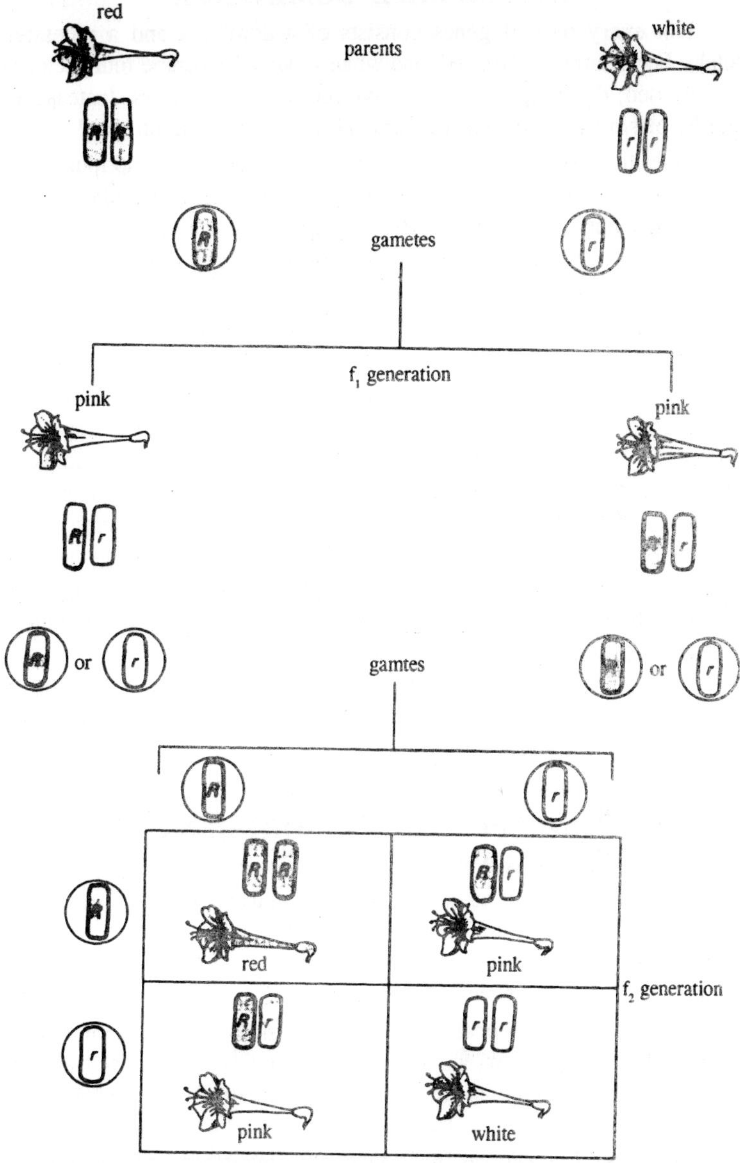

Figure 4.8: Incomplete dominance in Japanese four-o'clocks. Red is incompletely dominant to white in some types of flowers. A plant with the genotype Rr has pink flowers.

INCOMPLETE DOMINANCE

Not every pair of genes consists of a dominant and a recessive allele. For example, when red- and white-flowered Japanese four-o'clocks are crossed, the offspring do not have red or white flowers. Instead, all the F_1 offspring have pink flowers. How can we explain that?

Does this result in any way prove that Mendel's assumptions about inheritance are wrong? Quite the contrary, for when two of these pink-flowered plants are crossed, offspring appear in the ratio of one red-flowered to two pinkflowered to one white-flowered plant.

In this instance, as in other aspects of science, finding results that differ from those predicted simply prompts scientists to reexamine and modify their assumptions to account for the new exceptional results.

The pink-flowered plants are clearly the heterozygous individuals, and neither the red allele nor the white allele is completely dominant. When the heterozygote has a phenotype that is intermediate between those of its two parents, the genes are said to show incomplete dominance. In these crosses the genotypic and phenotypic ratios are identical.

Incomplete dominance is not unique to Japanese four-o'clocks. Redand white-flowered sweet pea plants also produce pink-flowered plants when crossed. In both cattle and horses, reddish coat colour is incompletely dominant to white coat colour.

The heterozygous individuals have roan-coloured coats (reddish with white spots). If you saw a white mare nursing a roan colt, what would you guess was the coat colour of the colt's father? Is there more than one possible answer?

INDEPENDENT ASSORTMENT

We now know that Mendel's law of independent assortment applies only to traits carried on nonhomologous chromosomes. If different genes are carried on the same chromosome, they will indeed tend to be inherited together. However, if they occur on *different* chromosome pairs, they will be inherited independently.

To illustrate this principle, let us consider two pairs of human traits. The ability to curl the tongue into a tube is a dominant trait; the absence of this talent is recessive. Attached or absent earlobes are recessive; free earlobes are dominant.

A mating that involves individuals differing in two traits is referred to as a dihybrid *cross*. If a man homozygous for tongue curling (CC) marries a woman without this trait (cc), all their children *(Cc)* may be expected to have this ability, since it is dominant and they are heterozygous for it. Similarly (but quite unrelated), if he has free earlobes *(EE)* and she is homozygous for attached earlobes (ee), the children will have free earlobes (Ee).

One could write the children's genotype for both sets of traits as *CcEe.* Since the two sets of traits are due to genes found on separate chromosome pairs, they will be inherited (or *assorted)* independently of each other.

Let us suppose that-improbable as it is-some of these children were to marry others who have genotypes identical to their own. For reasons of convenience, let us suppose that the total number of grandchildren produced was 16.

As you see by reference to Figure elsewhere in this chapter, four kinds of gametes are possible with respect to these genes-that is, since each gamete will have one of each pair of alleles, a total of four gametic genotypes is possible, given the genetic makeup of the F_1 generation.

If, by chance, the chromosome bearing gene *E* is sorted during meiosis into the same gamete as the chromosome bearing gene c, the resulting sperm or egg will have the genes *Ec.* Similarly, if the chromosomes bearing *e* and C are assorted together, the gamete will have the genes *eC.*

Other gametes would be *EC,* and still others would be *ec. There are no other possible combinations than* these *four.* Since allelic genes are always borne on chromosomes that are *separated* from one another in meiosis, a gamete can ordinarily have no more than *one* copy of each allele.

Since there are four possible kinds of gametes, working out a cross of that kind will require a box of 16 squares. Count the phenotypes. If you do so properly, the proportions, or ratios, of phenotypes to one another that you will predict among the offspring will fall into a 9:3:3:1 ratio.

POLYGENIC INHERITANCE

Some traits are governed in their expression by more than one pair of allelic genes known as *polygenes.* Sometimes such polygenes are located on different chromosomes and therefore assort independently. Not many such traits are known, for they are difficult to investigate. It is likely, however, that many human characteristics are inherited in this fashion and will eventually be proved to be so. One of the better-attested instances of polygenic inheritance is human skin colour.

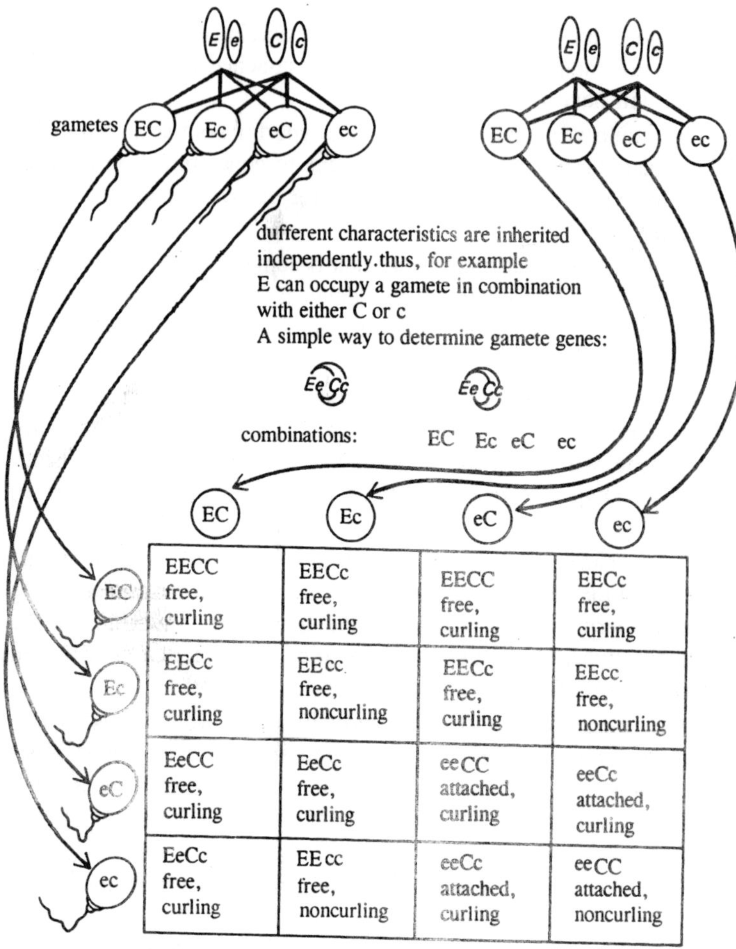

	EC	Ec	eC	ec
EC	EECC free, curling	EECc free, curling	EECC free, curling	EECc free, curling
Ec	EECc free, curling	EEcc. free, noncurling	EECc free, curling	EEcc. free, noncurling
eC	EeCC free, curling	EeCc free, curling	eeCC attached, curling	eeCc attached, curling
ec	EeCc free, curling	EEcc free, noncurling	eeCc attached, curling	eeCC attached, noncurling

Figure 4.9: Independent assortment is illustrated in this dihybrid cross. When two heterozygous individuals are crossed, the ratio of phenotypes is 9:3:3:1.

It is well known that if a person of extreme white complexion marries a person of equally extreme dark complexion, their offspring will be intermediate in colour. If that were all there was to it, it would be an obvious case of codominance. To test that assumption, let us consider the offspring of two such intermediate persons.

The assumption of simple codominance predicts a 1:2:1 ratio among their offspring. However, what we will observe instead (if their family is sufficiently large, or if we observe offspring in several such families) is a complex distribution not easily expressed by any ratio, ranging from white to very dark with the majority of intermediate colour. The explanation for this seems to be that human skin colour is governed by at least three independent allelic pairs of genes, each pair located on a different chromosome. Thus, the cross dark x white is *AABBCC x aabbcc.*

The F_1 offspring can be only *AaBbCc.* What about the F_2? We have worked out some of the genotypes of the F_2 for you in Figure anywhere else in this chapter. It is up to you to determine their phenotypes, which is not difficult. The individual with the genotype *aabbcc* would be so light that his blood would show through the skin. *AABBCC* would be very dark indeed.

Intermediate degrees of darkness can be predicted by counting the number of capital letters in each genotype. Most of us, including most who are called "blacks," would fall into one of the intermediate genotypes.

Many human traits that appear to be inheritable but have a confusing pattern of inheritance eventually may be shown to be produced by polygenes. Still others may be strongly influenced by polygenes but not entirely attributable to them. Height, body build, susceptibility to certain mental and physical diseases, and what we call "intelligence" *may* be such characteristics.

SEX-LINKED GENES

Most chromosomes occur in pairs whose members are like each other. These are called *autosomes.* However, in humans and many other animals there is a pair of chromosomes, the *sex chromosomes*, that are alike in females but different in males. Sex is chromosomally determined, and in a sense it is inherited. Two X chromosomes, as they are called, produce a female. An X and a Y chromosome produce a male.

The Y chromosome is the smallest of all chromosomes and, as far as anyone knows, in human beings contains only genes conferring male sex. Although the Y chromosome pairs with the X chromosome in meiosis, the Y and X chromosomes are not truly homologous, except for a short segment that may exist solely for purposes of meiosis.

Thus genes found on the X chromosomes have no known alleles on the Y chromosome. Therefore, in the male any allele that lies on the X-linked chromosome will be expressed whether or not such a gene is dominant or recessive in the XX female. One cannot properly refer to such an X-linked gene in the male as either homozygous or heterozygous. It must be called by a special name: *hemizygous*.

Since no important Y-linked genes are known in men, it is the X chromosomes, present in both men and women, that are meant when the term *sex linkage* is used.

The vast majority of sex-linked genes are recessive, so that in a female, they must be homozygous to be expressed. One practical consequence is that while females may carry recessive sexlinked traits, these traits usually find expression only in their sons. (A son receives his X chromosome from his mother, *never* from his father.)

In order to be expressed in a female, a recessive sex-linked trait must be present on *both* chromosomes, and so must be inherited from *both* parents. A colourblind girl, to take an example, must have a colourblind father and a mother who is at least heterozygous for colour blindness. Such a combination is unusual. Yet a colourblind boy need only have a mother who is heterozygous for the trait. His father can be normal.

Careful analysis of the foregoing will indicate that the X chromosome does not necessarily contain sex-determining genes for femaleness. They could occur on any chromosome. Sex-determining genes must, however, occur on the Y chromosome, for it is solely responsible for the difference between girls and boys.

It follows from this that the X chromosome is free to bear many genes that have nothing to do with sex, particularly since the X chromosome occurs in both sexes. In contrast, the Y chromosome is far less likely to carry any genes not directly related to sex.

Suppose for a moment that a woman who is heterozygous for both brown tooth enamel and colour blindness marries a man who also bears these traits on his single X chromosome. Admittedly, this combination is hardly likely, but comparable crosses have been made hundreds of times with fruit flies, and the results are predictable.

For our example, it is assumed that in the woman both abnormal traits occur on the same X chromosome. This will produce, as you can see from Figure elsewhere in this chapter, a female chromosomal makeup, or *karyotype*, in which only one gene for colour blindness occurs, along with only one gene for brown tooth enamel (number 1).

Since colour blindness is recessive, the phenotype does not reflect it. The *dominant* brown enamel is, however, expressed. Number 4, also female, will have brown teeth and will be colourblind. Number 2, a male, will share these shortcomings. Only number 3, a male karyotype, will be completely normal.

It should be obvious that the genes for colour blindness and brown tooth enamel in our example stay together; they are *not* independently assorted. In fact, the inheritance of multiple genes borne on a single chromosome is very much like that of a *single* gene, at least, as we shall see, if they are located close together.

The condition where genes are borne on the same chromosome is termed one of *linkage*. Linked genes tend to be inherited together'. After all, genes are just particular configurations of DNA, and we know that DNA is passed from ancestral cells to their progeny in the packages called chromosomes.

It follows that if two or more genes happen to occur in the same chromosomal package, they will tend to be handled together during meiosis and thus will tend to be inherited together.

AUTOSOMAL LINKAGE

Genes also tend to be inherited together if they occur together on a nonsex chromosome, or autosome. Let us take another example from human genetics for which there is ample evidence. Some persons secrete proteins associated with their blood type in the saliva.

The trait can be detected even before birth by an examination of the cells sloughed off the embryo in the amniotic fluid. The gene that produces this trait is dominant and is called the secretor gene; we shall call it S. The recessive allele is s.

We next introduce a serious autosomal hereditary disease involving progressive paralysis and the wasting of muscles, known as myotonic dystrophy, *m*. The dominant normal condition we shall call *M*. Since the locations, or loci, of the *Ss* and Mm genes are found on the same chromosome, they are said to be linked.

Suppose that a couple, suspecting that their unborn child may be dystrophic, consults a physician for advice. By careful investigation of the couple and their relatives the physician can deduce that their geno types and the probable genotypes of their children are as shown in Figure anywhere else in this chapter.

If these genes were independently assorted, the male, who has the genotype *SsMm,* would give rise to *four* genetically distinct kinds of gametes. As it is, he produced only two. The possible combinations of his gametes and those of his wife are such that only four genotypes are possible in the offspring, instead of the eight that independent assortment would produce.

Notice that in this couple's particular case, if a dystrophic child is born, he *must* be a nonsecretor. The physician has an easy task if the

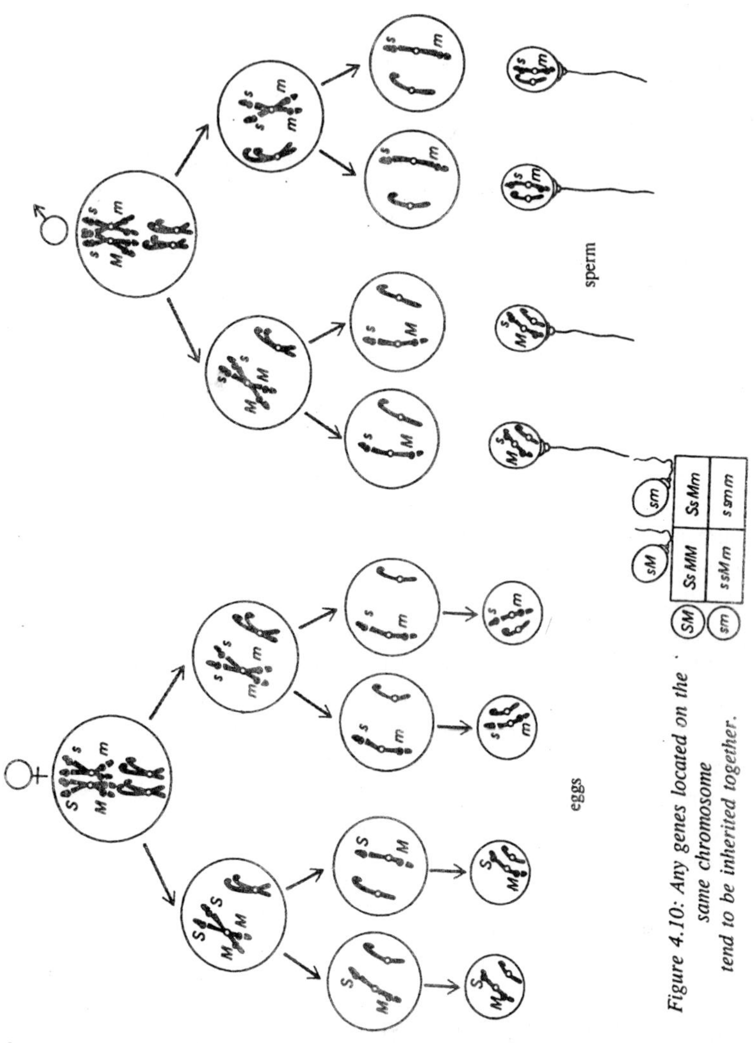

Figure 4.10: Any genes located on the same chromosome tend to be inherited together.

fetus is a secretor-the parents can rest reasonably assured that the child will be normal. But risk increases if the child is a nonsecretor. Thus far you may have gained the impression that linked genes *always* stay together.

As a matter of fact, though they usually do keep company, there are exceptions, and a few individuals (probably about 10% in the foregoing example) will not conform to what we would predict on the basis of genetic linkage. For example, some from the very cross we just studied might turn out to be dystrophic secretors, an "impossible" combination of traits. How can they be accounted for? The solution to this puzzle was determined with the microscope by watching the behaviour of chromosomes in meiosis.

Recall that when gametes are formed, homologous chromosomes come together during synapsis and crossing over occurs. As that happens, the chromosomes may exchange parts, as shown in Figure anywhere else in this chapter. Suppose that had occurred in the body of the female member of the couple whose case we have been considering.

In that particular case, it would turn out *opposite* to our original prediction and *only a* secretor baby would become dystrophic. By studying the re- sults of crossing over in a great many crosses, detailed chromosome maps of the location of specific genes in a number of species have been made.

BLOOD TYPES—A SPECIAL CASE

Although, as the saying has it, all blood is red, there is a surprisingly great diversity of other characteristics, one of which, *blood type*, is of enormous medical and legal importance. Through knowledge of blood types, one may transfuse blood safely, solve tangled inheritance disputes, and identify drops of blood left at the scene of a crime.

Blood type is determined by the kind or kinds of antigens (proteins) occurring on the surface of red blood cells. These have the potential for stimulating the production of antibodies (proteins that combine with specific antigens).

The antibodies are capable of reacting with the complementary antigens. Such a reaction can produce an abnormal clumping of blood cells called *agglutination*, or their complete breakdown by *hemolysis*.

The Rh Factors

The Rh series of blood types has been known only since the 1940s. There are several somewhat codominant varieties, but all may be thought of as producing either *a positive* or *a negative* phenotype. For our purposes we will lump the several alleles into two groups-R, which produces positive phenotypes, and r, which produces negative.

R is dominant. Thus a person with Rh-positive blood has the genotype RR or Rr. The negative phenotype can only be *rr*. About 85% of the population of the United States has Rh-positive blood.

A person with Rh-positive blood has Rh antigens associated with the blood-cell membranes, and *no* anti-Rh antibodies in the plasma. An Rh-negative person possesses no Rh antigens and no natural anti-Rh

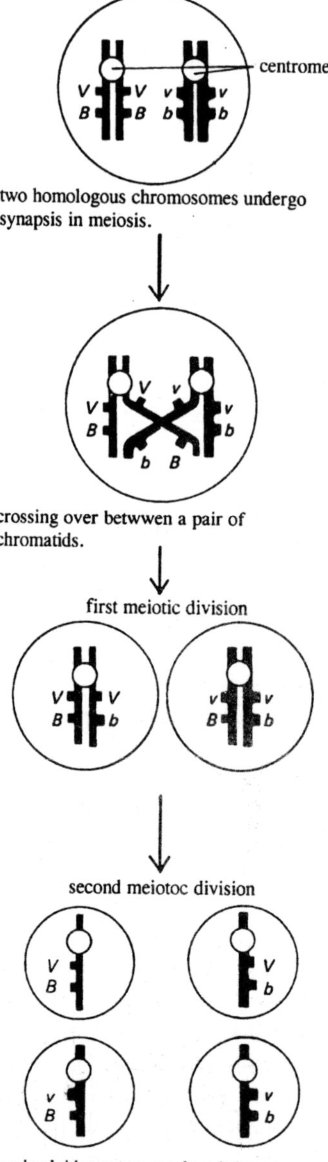

Figure 4.11: Crossing over and genetic recombination. Crossing over, the exchange of segments between chromatids of homologous chromosomes, permits recombination of genes- vB and Vb, for example.

antibodies.

But if he were to receive a transfusion of Rh-positive blood, he would quickly develop anti-Rh antibodies, which would then hemolyze the cells of the next transfusion of Rh-positive blood. The first such transfusion would, however, be relatively harmless in itself.

Although several kinds of maternal-fetal blood type incompatibilities are known, *Rh incompatibility* is probably the most important. If a woman is Rh-negative and her husband is Rh-positive, the fetus may be Rh-positive.

A small quantity of blood from the fetus may pass through some defect in the placenta (especially during the birth process) and into the mother's blood, sensitizing her white blood cells, which then produce antibodies to the Rh antigens. When this woman becomes pregnant again, sensitized white blood cells produce antibodies that may pass through the placenta into the fetal blood and cause clumping of the red blood cells.

Breakdown products of the hemoglobin released into the circulation damage many organs, including the brain. This disease is known as *erythroblastosis fetalis*. In extreme cases so many fetal red blood cells are destroyed that the fetus dies before birth.

When Rh-incompatibility problems are suspected, blood can be exchanged while the baby is still within the mother's uterus, but this is a risky procedure. Rh-negative women are now treated just after childbirth (or at termination of pregnancy by miscarriage or abortion) with an antiRh preparation.

This drug apparently clears the Rh-positive cells from the mother's blood very quickly, thus minimizing the chance of sensitizing her own white blood cells. As a result, her cells do not produce the antibodies that could harm her next baby.

The ABO System and Multiple Alleles

Multiple alleles exist when a particular gene, occupying one given locus, exists in more than two forms. Thus an organism can have no more than two of a given set of multiple alleles at a time, but more than two such alleles are known to exist.

An important example is afforded by the ABO series of blood types. This series of blood types was the first to be discovered-as a result of early experiments in blood transfusion, which were unpredictably but all too often fatal.

Landsteiner's Law

As we have seen, in the case of blood cells when complementary antibodies and antigens come into contact, the blood cells clump together (*agglutination*) or break open (*hemolysis*). Both these reactions can take

Table 4.3: ABO Blood Types.

Phenotype	*Genotype*	*Antigens*	*Antibodies*	*How inherited*
A	AA, AO	A	Anti-B	Dominant
B	B[3,130	B	Anti-A	Dominant
AB	AB	A and B	None	Codominant
O	OO	None	Anti-A and B	Recessive

place in laboratory glassware and presumably also in the body of a living person. For reasons not fully understood, the usual kinds of ABO antibodies develop normally even without known exposure to antigens capable of provoking them.

However, agglutination is the reaction most likely to occur in laboratory glassware, and hemolysis is the characteristic response *in vivo.* Hemolysis results in the release of hemoglobin in the plasma. This in turn can produce kidney damage that may lead to death.

Such reactions do not ordinarily take place in one's own blood because, as the hematologist Karl Landsteiner discovered, the *antibodies of the plasma are never complementary to the antigens of the cells* (*Landsteiner's law*). There is no such assurance when the bloods of two individuals are mixed, as in a transfusion.

If blood is transfused into a patient whose plasma contains complementary antibodies hostile to the cells of the donor, damage to these cells is bound to result. The reverse can also happen. If blood is transfused into a recipient and the donated *plasma* is incompatible with the recipient's cells, trouble will eventually result.

Initially, though, such transfusions may be harmless, since the half pint or so of potentially dangerous plasma is rapidly diluted in the recipient's blood volume to harmless levels.

The Genetics of the ABO Series

Table 10-1 gives the basic facts of inheritance for both the antibodies and the antigens of the ABO series. Three alleles are known for the ABO series, which by their interaction can produce blood types A, B, AB, and O-depending upon the exact combination of genes in the particular allelic pair possessed by an individual.

A normal person can possess no more than two of the ABO alleles. Type O gene is recessive to all other genes, and A and B exhibit codominance with respect to each other. Thus two genotypes can give rise to type A, and two to type B. AB and O each have only one possible genotype.

GENES AND DISEASE

More than 150 human disorders involving enzyme defects have been linked with genetic mutations. These disorders are sometimes referred to as inborn errors in metabolism. Most are inherited as autosomal recessive traits. Sickle-cell anemia, phenylketonuria (PKU), cystic fibrosis, and Tay-Sachs disease are well-known diseases that have been linked to gene defects.

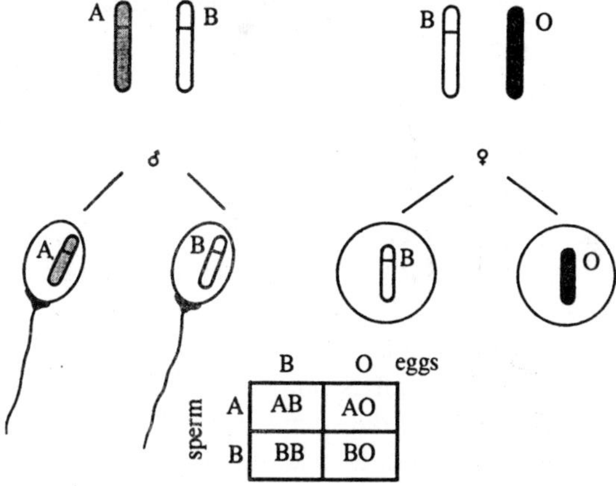

Figure 4.12: Multiple alleles for blood types. Three different alleles exist for ABO blood type. In this cross each parent produces only two kinds of gamete, but between them, there are three types of gametes with respect to ABO blood type. Four possible genotypes occur among their offspring.

Many recessive genetic diseases can now be detected in the heterozygous state by modern enzyme analysis and other advanced chemical techniques. It is also possible to detect abnormalities in fibroblasts (cells of connective tissue) found in the amniotic fluid, for these fibroblasts originate in the fetus.

Thus through genetic screening it can often be determined even before birth whether a fetus will suffer from a genetic disease.

CHROMOSOMES AND DISEASE

Chromosome abnormalities are called *aneuploidies*. An aneuploidy may involve an extra chromosome so that one of the person's homologous sets consists of three chromosomes instead of the normal two. (Having three of a kind is called *trisomy*.

These aneuploidies appear to arise through defects of meiosis, in which chromosomes fail to separate. This is called *nondisjunction*. In still other cases, a part of a chromosome may break off and attach to another chromosome. The gamete then may have chromosomes that are abnormally short or long. Such *translocations* may be functionally much the same as a trisomy if they result in the presence of too much genetic material in a zygote.

A trisomy might well produce a 50% increase in the activities of the products of most of the involved genes, and recent studies have con firmed this prediction in the case of some genes.

So it is little wonder that the body chemistry and development of its possessor will be unbalanced. People who have a trisomy of the No. 21 or 22 chromosomes or of the sex chromosomes may survive into adulthood.

Trisomies of the other chromosomes are much rarer because they are much more likely to be fatal. Quite possibly, trisomy of the No. 21 or 22 is less likely to be fatal because these chromosomes are the smallest and possess the fewest genes.

It is striking how little disorder is produced by abnormalities of the sex chromosomes, particularly by X-chromosome aneuploidy despite the relatively large size of the X chromosome.

The probable explanation is that even in normal females one of the X chromosomes in each cell is not functional, or at least not fully functional. This is known as the *Lyon hypothesis*. In early development one of the two chromosomes is inactivated. Which one is inactivated appears to be a random choice.

Thus for the most part a female possesses only the enzymes or other proteins produced by half of her X chromosomes, which in many cases will be the same as the amount produced by a male's single X chromosome.

Interestingly, in the majority of investigated cases, when a female is heterozygous for a sex-linked trait, half her cells display it and half her cells do not, showing that half her cells have inactivated the paternal X chromosome, and half have inactivated the maternal X chromosome.

The inactivated X chromosome even seems to be visible in certain female body cells. Thus female granulocytes (a type of white blood cell) often possess a nuclear "drumstick" projection never found in normal male granulocytes, and female epithelial cells (cells that line body cavities and cover body surfaces) display nuclear *Barr bodies* not found in normal male cells. These appear to be the condensed and inactivated second X chromosome.

CONSANGUINITY: MARRIAGE BETWEEN RELATIVES

Marriage between relatives is referred to as *consanguinity*, which is derived from a Latin word meaning "related," or "brother" or "sister." The risk of bearing a child with a major congenital abnormality of genetic origin is 70% greater if the parents are, for example, first cousins than if they are unrelated.

The death rate for children of such consanguineous matings is between three and four times higher than among a comparison population. Almost half the offspring of brother-sister unions are more or less grossly handicapped by genetic disease.

No mystery enshrouds the increased risk of malformed offspring from consanguineous matings. The problem can be traced to a greater chance of sharing harmful genes.

All of us no doubt shared the same ancestors, hence the same genes, in the distant past. But with time the pool of human genes became diverse as a result of mutations and evolutionary processes, so that today each of us is genetically unique.

Only identical twins have identical genes. Each of us carries an estimated eight harmful recessive genes. If you marry a nonrelative, the chance is remote that you will select someone who shares any of the same harmful genes.

There is little chance that any of your offspring will be unfortunate homozygotes, receiving a double dose of harmful recessive genes. However, if you selected your first cousin as your mate, you would have a common set of grandparents, and so in all probability one of every eight of your genes would be identical. Your offspring would be homozygous for one-sixteenth of all their gene traits. Second cousins share one thirtysecond of their genes.

5

PRINCIPLES OF TAXONOMY

In earlier chapters we have seen that many different kinds of animals exist. No one knows exactly how many kinds there are, but almost one million have already been described and more are being discovered every day. Some biologists estimate that when all the small, secretive worms, protozoans, and other invertebrates of the land and sea are thoroughly studied and understood, we may recognize as many as two or even three million different kinds of animals.

Taxonomy is the branch of zoology that is concerned with classifying and naming each of the different kinds of animals in such a way that related kinds are grouped together and separated from unrelated kinds. The taxonomist must do three things to insure that the name applied to a given kind of animal is meaningful.

First, he must determine that the name chosen has not already been applied to some other kind of animal. Second, he must describe the animal in such detail that another taxonomist can determine from his description exactly the kind of animal to which he has given the name.

Third, after a name is assigned to a specific kind of animal, he must so place the name in a classification that the known or suspected relationships are expressed.

THE BINOMINAL SYSTEM OF NMOMENCLATURE

The system of naming animals currently used by zoologists is based on a method developed progressively over a number of centuries and formalized in more or less its present form by the Swedish naturalist Carolus Linnaeus (1707-1788), in the tenth edition of his book *Systema Naturae,* published in 1758.

In this book Linnaeus applied a *scientific name* to each of the kinds of animals recognized by him. The scientific name consisted of two Latin or Latinized words, the first of which was the name of the genus to which the animal was assigned and the second the name of the species to which the animal belonged.

Linnaeus held that a species was a distinct kind of animal that had been created separately by some supernatural power and that it possessed some distinctive features that made it distinct from all other species. He recognized that some species resemble each other quite closely, and he grouped similar species together in a single genus.

For example, Linnaeus, recognizing the differences between dogs and wolves, assigned a species name of *familiaris* to 'the dogs and *lupus* to the wolves. Observing the similarities between the two animals, he thought that they must have been created as variants of a single pattern, and grouped them together in the single genus, *Canis.*

Thus, the scientific name of the dog *is Canis familiaris* and of the wolf *is Canis lupus.* In a similar way he named the house cat *Felis domesticus,* the lion *Felis leo,* the leopard *Felis pardalis,* and other cats as other species, all in the genus *Felis.*

Linnaeus, in his tenth edition of *Systema Naturae,* listed 4236 different scientific names for animals. Since these names represented a large spectrum of forms, shapes, and sizes of animals, he adopted a system of grouping similar genera together as orders, and groups of similar orders as classes. He grouped all of the classes of animals together as members of the animal kingdom, as distinct from the plant kingdom.

Common Names

Many beginning students wonder why the Latin names are used instead of common names. There are two good reasons.

(1) Common names have different meanings to various persons, even in the same part of the country. For example, "gopher" is used variously for several different species of ground squirrels, for rodents of the Family Geomyidae (pocket gophers), for moles (Order Insectivora) and, in the southeastern United States, for a turtle.

(2) Scientific names are uniform internationally, and, being Latin,

are always written in Latin script *(italics),* even if the accompanying text is in some unusual script such as Arabic or Chinese.

The bird that we know as the English sparrow is known by a variety of names in other countries: house sparrow in England, moineau domestique in France, Gorrion in Spain, Pardal in Portugal, Passera oltramontana in Italy, Haussperling in Germany, Musch in Holland and suzume in Japan; but to biologists in all these countries it is *Passer domesticus.*

THE MODERN TAXONOMIC HIERARCHY

As time went by and biologists learned more and more about the diversity of animal life and how this diversity may be transmitted to offspring through heredity, taxonomists realized that species are not the result of a series of separate creations, but rather are the result of differences in heredity in the various lines of descent from common ancestors.

To express more accurately this kinship resulting from the common ancestry of the various kinds of animals, taxonomists found it necessary to add more groupings to those used by Linnaeus. The major taxa (as these groups are called) in current use and their definitions in terms of kinship are as follows.

A *species* is a population or group of populations made up of individuals that, in their natural habitat, will actually, or can potentially, interbreed. The ability to interbreed is interpreted as evidence that such individuals are genetically closely related and thus demonstrate a high degree of kinship.

As we shall see later, the various individuals making up a species population may vary greatly as the result of differences in age, sex, or some other factor. The taxonomist must be familiar with the extent and meaning of such variations in a given population before he can be certain that his assignments of individuals to a given species is correct.

A *genus* is a group of species that have close ancestral relationships. In general, members of the various species of a given genus have more morphological and functional features in common than they have in common with species in a related genus. Since morphological and physiological features are assumed to be the result of gene action, it is generally assumed that more identical genes are present among members of a given genus than among members of different genera.

In a similar way, a family is a group of related genera; an order is a group of related families; a class is a group of related orders; and a phylum is a group of related classes. All of the different phyla of animals are grouped together as the animal kingdom.

These various taxonomic categories can be arranged in a hierarchy that expresses the various levels of kinship, as follows: Kingdom

Phylum (plural, phyla)

Class

Order

Family

Genus (plural, genera)

Species (plural is also species)

Taxonomists often find it convenient to recognize intermediate levels in the hierarchy. Many of these extra steps in the taxonomic hierarchy are indicated by adding the prefixes "super-," "infra-," and "sub-" to the names of the seven levels listed above.

In addition, the terms "cohort" and "tribe" are sometimes used to describe some additional steps in the hierarchy. Table 6-1 lists all the levels generally accepted by taxonomists and emphasizes the seven that are considered as necessary to define the relationships of a given organism.

RULES OF NOMENCLATURE

As we stated earlier, Linnaeus, in his tenth edition of *Systema Naturae,* listed 4236 different scientific names for animals. Today it is estimated that 952,000 different species of animals have been named. Some zoologists think that when all the little-known groups have been studied and the out-of-the-way parts of the world explored, the total may exceed 1.5 million.

With so many different kinds of animals being named by many different taxonomists, zoologists have recognized the need for a set of rules governing scientific nomenclature. To meet this need, in 1898 the International Congress of Zoologists created a permanent Commission on Nomenclature and assigned the Commission the responsibility for drawing up a set of rules governing nomenclature and serving in a judiciary capacity to render decisions concerning difficult cases.

The Commission prepared the International Code of Nomenclature that forms the basis of modern nomenclature. Some of the important rules in the code are:

1. The code deals with names for all taxonomic units from families to subspecies.

Table 5.1: Taxonomic Categories Currently in Use. Those Taxa in Bold Face are Usually Considered to be Necessary in Expressing the Relationships of a Given Animal.

Common name	*Man*	*House cat*	*Grass frog*	*Monarch butter fly*	*Ameba*
Kingdom	Animalia	Animalia	Animalia	Animalia	Animalia
Subkingdom	Metazoa	Metazoa	Metazoa	Metazoa	Protozoa
Infrakingdom	Bilateriata	Bilateriata	Bilateriata	Bilateriata	—
Cohort	Coelomata	Coelomata	Coelomata	Coelomata	—
Superphylum stomia	Deuterostoniia	Deuterostomia	Deutero-	Proterostomia	—
Phylum	Chordata	Chordata	Chordata	Arthropoda	Protozoa
Subphylum	Vertebrata	Vertebrata	Vertebrata	Mandibulata	Plasmodroma
Superclass	Tetrapoda	Tetrapoda	Tetrapoda	—	—
Class	Mammalia	Mammalia	Amphibia	Insecta	Sarcodina
Subclass	Theria	Theria	Brachomorpha	Neoptera	Rihizopoda
Infraclass	Eutheria	Eutheria	—	—	—
Cohort	Unguiculata	—	—	—	—
Superorder	—	—	Aneuromorpha	Exopterygota	—
Order	Primates	Carnivora	Salientia	Lepidoptera	Amoebida
Suborder	Anthropoidea	—	—	Rhopalocera	Ainobina

(Table Contd.)

(Table Contd.)

Common name	***Man***	***House cat***	***Grass frog***	***Monarch butter fly***	***Ameba***
Infraorder	—	—	—	—	—
Superfamily	Hominoidea	—	—	—	—
Family	Hominidae	Felidae	Ranidae	Nynlphalidae	Amoebidae
Subfamily	Homininae	—	—	—	Amoebinae
Genus	*Homo*	*Felis*	*Rune*	*Danaus*	*Amoeba*
Species	*sapiens*	*domcsticu.s*	*pipierrs*	*plexippus*	*protetts*

2. Zoological and botanical names are distinct, so that the same name can be applied to both a plant and an animal, although this practice is not recommended.
3. Within the animal kingdom no two genera can have the same name, and within a genus no two species can have the same name.
4. Scientific names must be either Latin or Latinized and preferably are to be printed in italics.
5. The name of a genus must be a single word in the nominative singular form and must begin with a capital letter.
6. The name of a species must be a single or compound word beginning with a small letter. It is usually an adjective and must agree grammatically with the generic name.
7. The generic or specific name to be applied to a given taxon is the one' first published in a generally acceptable book or periodical and in which the name is associated with a recognizable description of the animal.

   Any names that are later proposed for the same taxon are to be considered as synonyms and are not available for use with any other kind of animal or groups of animals.
8. No names are to be recognized which were published prior to the publication of *Systema Naturae,* tenth edition, 1758.
9. The name of a family is formed by adding "-idae" to the stem of the name of one of the genera in the group. This genus is to be considered as the type genus in the family. A subfamily name is formed by adding "-inae" to the stem of its type genus.

Difficulties in Taxonomy

Taxonomic zoologists, in attempting to fit animals in a classification, are faced with several problems, any one of which may cause great difficulty. To begin with, taxonomy attempts to group animals according to kinship; yet for most animals this kinship is unknown.

Usually all the taxonomist has to work with is a preserved specimen, and he seldom knows anything of its ancestry, genetics, physiology, or ecology. This lack of information forces the taxonomist to rely upon morphological and anatomical resemblances between various animals as a criterion for determining kinship.

But resemblances are not always the result of kinship. Furthermore, closely related animals that may even be members of the same species

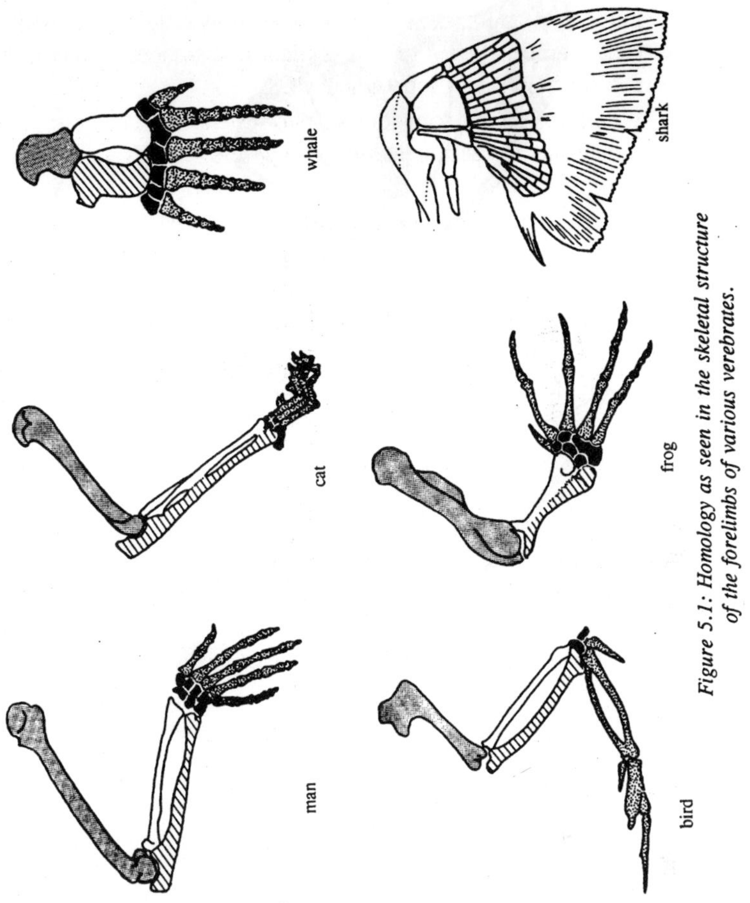

Figure 5.1: Homology as seen in the skeletal structure of the forelimbs of various verebrates.

sometimes vary greatly in their physical appearance. Let us examine these difficulties in more detail.

In the chapter on genetics we studied the mechanisms of inheritance. Offspring inherit most of the features of their parents. In other chapter of this book we shall see that unrelated organisms living in similar habitats may undergo convergent evolution and thus develop many superficial resemblances. Since the taxonomist is interested in expressing kinship and not merely resemblance in his classification, he must learn to distinguish between these two types of similarity.

Homology is the resemblance between two individuals or parts of two different individuals that results from common ancestry and therefore represents kinship. If we examine the structure of the forelimb of a man

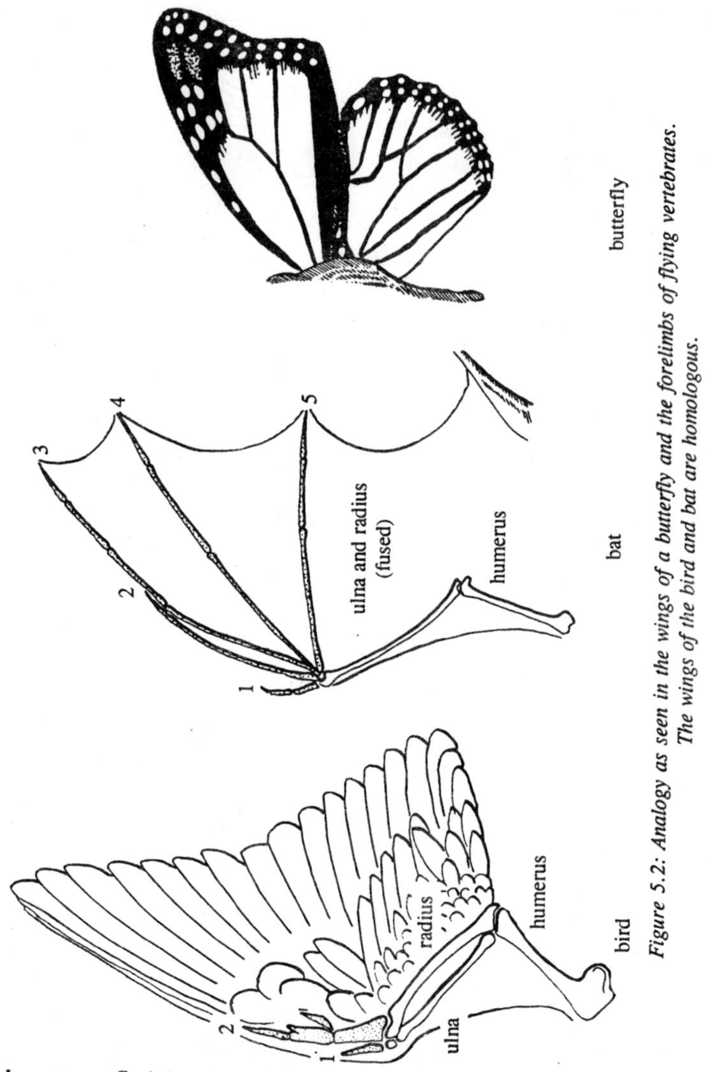

Figure 5.2: Analogy as seen in the wings of a butterfly and the forelimbs of flying vertebrates. The wings of the bird and bat are homologous.

and a cat, we find that the number, relative size, and relative arrangements of the bones are similar. Resemblances are also to be found in the embryonic origin of these forelimbs, and to a lesser extent in the muscles, nerves, and blood vessels present.

These resemblances demonstrate that the arm of a man and the foreleg of a cat are homologous structures, even though the functions of the two limbs are dissimilar. The foreleg of the cat is used primarily in locomotion, while the arm of the man is used for manipulating things and only rarely for locomotion. Similar homologies are to be seen in the bones of the foreleg of the whale, bird, frog, and shark, even though these limbs serve a variety of functions including walking, swimming, and flying. Homologies can be seen in many other vertebrate and invertebrate structures.

Analogy is the term applied to similarity in function when no common ancestry exists. Often, but not always, analogous structures have many superficial resemblances. For example, the wings of the butterfly are analogous, but not homologous, to the wings of a bird or the wings of a bat.

The forelegs of the praying mantis and the arms of a man show resemblances in gross structure and, since both are used to manipulate things, in function. Since limbs arose independently in the insects and in the vertebrates, these structures are analogous but not homologous.

We become aware of another problem, that closely related animals are not necessarily similar in structure, when we attempt to arrange all the members of an interbreeding population in a single species. We find that age, sexual, and genetic differences may result in great differences between members of the same species.

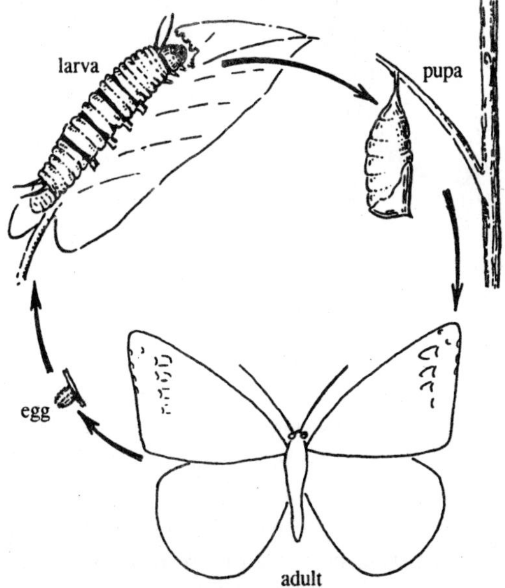

Figure 5.3: Life cycle of a butterfly. Differences in age resul in great morphological differences.

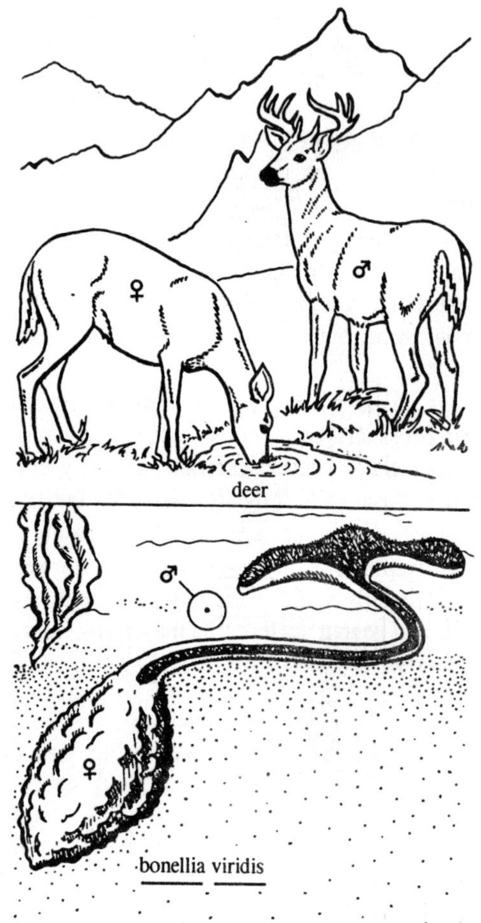

Figure 5.4: Sexual dimorphism in the deer and the peanut worm, Bonellia eiridis. The adult male peanut worm lives in the body of the adult female.

We are all aware that differences in age result in differences in the size and shape between young, adult, and old humans. In those kinds of animals that have complex life cycles, often few resemblances can be found between the various stages.

For example, without prior knowledge one would be hard pressed to see any relationship between the egg, larva, pupa, and adult monarch butterfly. The diversity in body form during the life cycle of the protozoan parasite that causes malaria is even more pronounced.

Sexual dimorphism, or differences between the physical appearance

Figure 5.5: Genetic polymorphism in the Cuban snail, Polymita.

of a male and a female, is well marked in humans, but such differences are much more extreme in certain other kinds of animals. For example, the presence of a large rack of antlers on a buck deer and its absence on a doe are well known.

Less well known is the fact that in certain marine worms (peanut worms, Phylum Echiurida) the males are so reduced as to be microscopic parasites living in the reproductive tract of the adult females.

Even within a group of animals of the same age and sex, a wide diversity of variation is often seen. Such genetic polymorphism within a given species can cause siblings to differ widely.

THE USE OF HOMOLOGY IN CLASSIFICATION

One of the major aims in classifying an animal is to express its relationship to other kinds. Since actual kinship is usually unknown, taxonomic zoologists use estimates of the number and kinds of homologies common to various individuals as the basis of arranging individuals into a species and species into higher groups.

No one knows exactly how many homologous features in common define any given taxonomic level or taxon. Simply as an example, let us assume that individuals in a species have 10,000 homologous features in common. The species in the genus might have 1500 homologies in common, families 700, orders 250, and the higher taxa progressively fewer homologies in common. For example, Persian cats have many homologies in common with Siamese cats and these will interbreed, so the two are members of a single species, *Felis domesticus.*

Felis domestic us has many homologies with the mountain lion but will not interbreed with it. Thus, both are arranged in the genus *Felis*, but the mountain lion is a different species, *Felis concolor*. Bobcats and cheetahs have fewer resemblances to *Felis* but are definitely "cats," belonging along with *Felis* to the Family Felidae.

Figure elsewhere in this chapter shows how a taxonomist uses homologies in classifying an animal. In this example individuals A and B have so many homologous features that they are judged to be part of an interbreeding population.

In other words they belong to the same species. Each individual C through I is judged as representing a different species. The distribution of homologous features among these permit the recognition of larger taxa such as genera, families, and orders.

PATTERNS OF HOMOLOGIES USED IN ANIMAL CLASSIFICATION

Several major types of body formation and organization occur within the animal kingdom. For example, the Phylum Protozoa includes animals made up of only a single cell, while those in all the other phyla are multicellular. In the following sections we will examine some of the patterns of the various phyla of multicellular animals, and in Table elsewhere in this chapter we will see how some of these patterns are actually used in classification.

PATTERNS IN CELLULAR SPECILIZATION

According to the degree of cellular complexity present in individuals, animals can be separated into groups. One large group, generally believed to include the most primitive living animals, includes the single-celled protozoans, such as the ameba and paramecium.

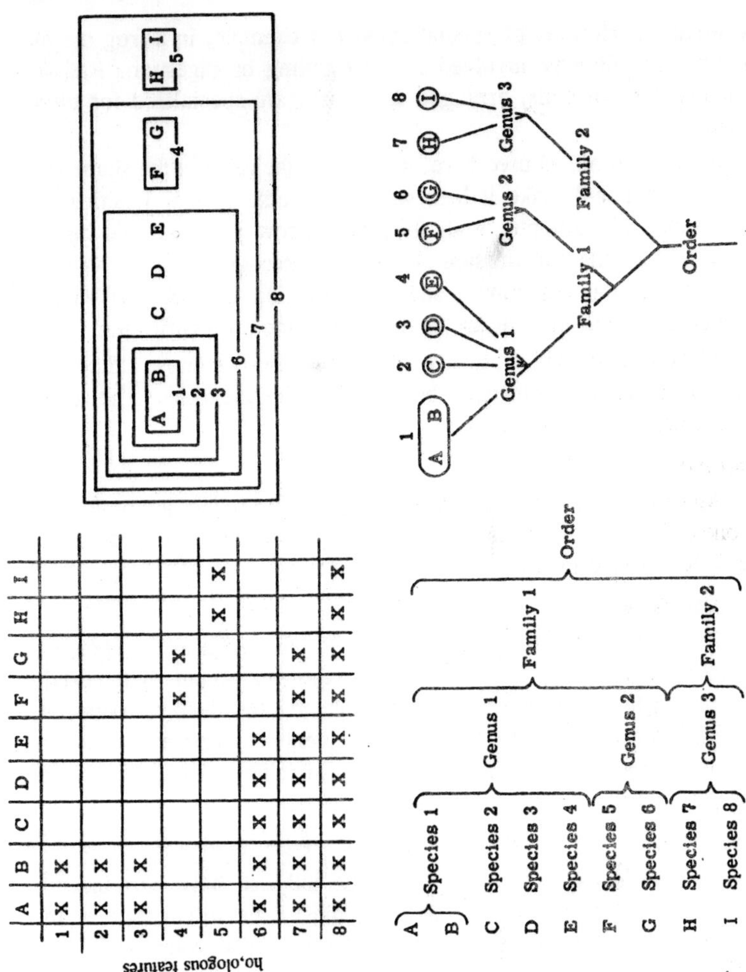

Figure 5.6: Steps used in estimating taxonomic hierarchies and phylogenetic relationships, based on the homologies in common.

These animals perform all the processes of living (food-getting, respiration, excretion, digestion, circulation, locomotion, and reproduction) within the physical limitations of the single cell. Within the cell, there is a division of labor, with certain parts being specialized to accomplish particular functions.

Other groups of animals consist of associations of several to large numbers of cells. In these multicellular animals the various special functions carried out in the individual cell of the singlecelled animal are usually performed by special cells. For example, in a frog not all the cells are directly involved in food-getting or digestion. Rather, certain groups of cells, arranged as organs, are specialized for these functions.

Specialization, as used here, means that the cell has the shape and structure that will make it best suited for some special function. A nerve cell, for example, with its long narrow processes, is highly specialized for the transmission of impulses. Recognition of the various levels of cellular association and specialization furnishes us with a number of categories that are useful in making a classification.

Most animals will fit neatly into one of these groups, although a few appear to be intermediate between certain categories. The levels of organization are as follows:

Protoplasmic Level

Animals such as the protozoans, in which all activities are performed by one cell, are in this group. Within this cell, portions of the protoplasm are differentiated to carry on specific functions.

Cellular Level

Animals that are loose associations of cells, such as the sponges, fall into this category. Some division of labor may occur, with certain cells primarily concerned with food capture and others with reproduction, but such specialized cells have little tendency to gather into layers (tissues). Certain colonial protozoans appear to have reached this level of organization.

Tissue Levelz

Animals such as the hydra and the jellyfish have certain cells grouped together as a tissue (although most cells still remain at the cellular level of organization) and are placed in this group. The nerve net, a group of interconnected cells specialized for transmitting impulses, is a good example of a tissue in a primitive animal. The tissues of higher animals are listed anywhere else in this chapter.

Organ Level

The flatworms, such as planaria, have many kinds of tissues, and some of these are grouped into distinct organs such as the proboscis and the gonads.

Organ-system Level

The higher animals have organs grouped together into functional systems, each primarily concerned with a specific function. This organ-system level of organization is first found in a group of marine worms known as the nemerteans. The organ systems of the higher animals are listed anywhere else in this chapter.

Patterns in Organ Systems

In animals of the organ-system level of development, various patterns of complexity of organ systems are often recognizable. Some of these patterns serve as useful criteria in classifying animals. The fact that not all organ systems appear in all groups also serves to identify various groups.

The digestive system may be absent, incomplete, or complete. An incomplete digestive tract has only a single opening to the outside of the body that serves as both a mouth and an anus. A complete digestive system has two openings, a mouth and an anus.

The circulatory system may be of the open type, with the blood being pumped out of the heart and flowing directly over cells and tissues, or it may be a closed system in which the blood remains in a series of tubes (arteries, capillaries, and veins).

The skeletal system may be absent or present and if present may be completely enclosed in the body (internal) or completely outside the body (external).

PATTERNS IN GROSS MORPHOLOGY

The gross external appearances of animals fall into a limited number of patterns. These include symmetry, arrangement of body parts in segments (metamerism), formation of a bead, and, internally, differences in celom (body cavity) formation.

Symmetry of some type is generally found in the arrangement of the parts of an animal. A few animals appear to be so highly irregular in shape as to lack symmetry of any kind. Such asymmetrical animals include the ameba and many sponges.

Certain colonial protozoans as well as the eggs and early embryos of some higher animals exhibit spherical symmetry. They have the shape of a sphere, and all planes that pass through the center will divide them into similar halves.

These animals have only floating or rolling movements, with almost all spots on the surface having an equal opportunity to be the first to encounter a stimulus. Slightly more complex animals, such as some sponges, the hydra, and the jellyfish, exhibit radial symmetry.

They have the shape of a flattened cylinder (a pie), with a number

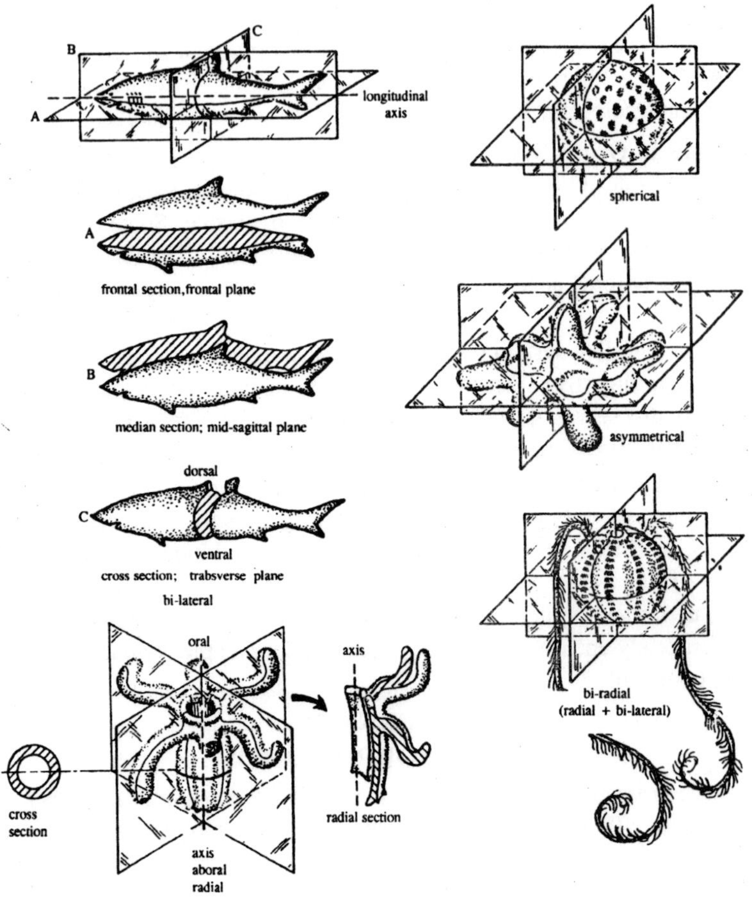

Figure 5.7: Types of symmetry in the animal kingdom.

of equivalent parts (called antimeres) arranged around a common central axis. The stirface on which the mouth appears is known as the oral surface, and the opposite surface is the aboral surface.

Many such animals are sessile, attached by the aboral surface. Since environmental stimuli may be met on any side, sensory receptors are found equally distributed all around the edge of the animal.

Most higher animals have a body form that can be divided into a right and a left half, one of which is a mirror image of the other. This is called bilateral symmetry. Since one end of such an animal is the first to encounter environmental stimuli as it moves forward, sense organs and nerve tissue are concentrated at that end.

This is known as cephalization, and it results in the development of a head. This concentration permits more rapid detection of and reaction to stimuli. In either the absence of or the development of a body cavity, animals show various patterns.

In the planaria and other primitive multicellular animals, the gut and other internal organs are completely surrounded, more or less solidly, by cells and tissues. No body cavity is evident. Such animals are acelomate.

In the higher animals where internal organ systems, especially the digestive system, become more complex, a cavity develops within the body, between the gut and the skin. We learned in our study of embryology that various parts and organ systems originate from specific layers of cells.

The digestive tract originates from the endoderm, the skin and associated nervous tissues from the ectoderm, and other systems, mainly muscle, circulatory, and skeletal, originate from the mesoderm. Mesoderm is physically located between the ectoderm (skin) and the endoderm (gut). In certain multicellular animals a body cavity, called a *pseudocelom*, develops because of the failure of the mesoderm to come into contact with the endoderm of the gut.

This arrangement is found in many worm-like animals, including the nematodes and the spiny-headed worms (Acanthocephala). In more highly developed animals the body cavity forms not by the separation of the mesoderm from the endoderm, but as a cavity within the mesoderm. Such animals are termed *eucelomate* or simply celomate.

In them, many tissues of mesodermal origin, such as muscles, connective tissue, and blood vessels, are in intimate association with the gut. The cavity that develops within the mesoderm is lined by a characteristic layer of flattened, mesodermal, epithelial cells known as the peritoneum.

The eucelomate animals are divided into two large groups, according to the origin of the cavities within the mesoderm. In one group, the *schizocelomates*, are most of the higher invertebrates such as mollusks, annelids, and arthropods. In these the celom originates as a split in a large mass of mesodermal cells.

In the other group, the *enterocelomates*, the celom originates from the fusion of a series of pouches that grow out into the mesoderm from the primitive gut. These are the echinoderms and chordates.

Another architectural pattern that occurs in several groups that otherwise do not appear to be closely related is that of metamerism.

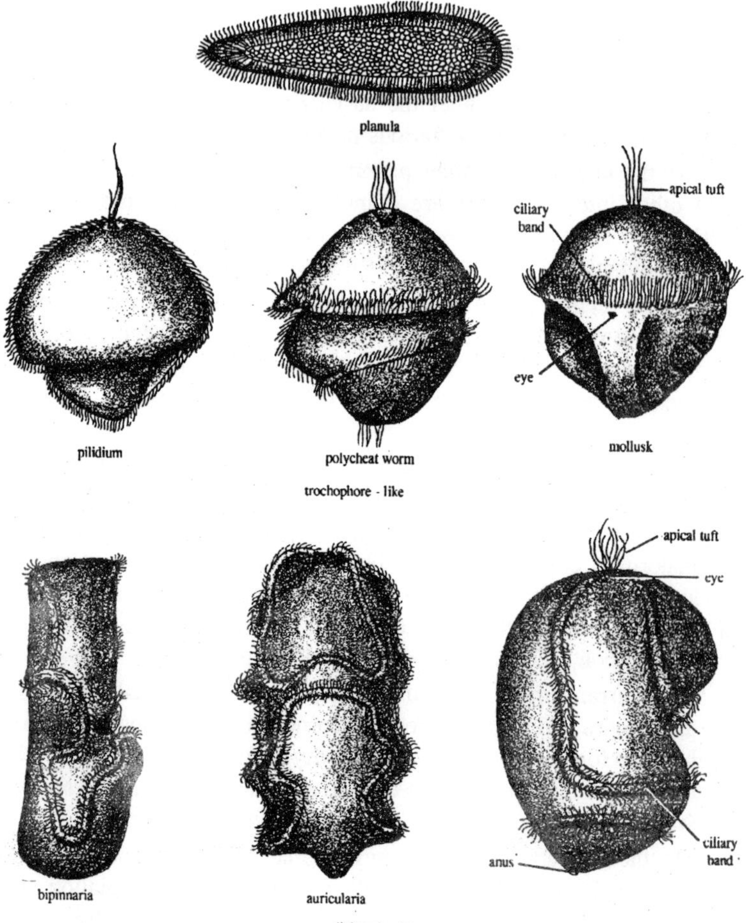

Figure 5.8: Types of invertebrate larvae.

In this pattern the body is made up of a series of linearly arranged metameres or somites, each of which is similar to the one in front of and behind it.

Such an arrangement is easily seen in the earthworm and other annelid worms. In the related arthropods, metameres are present but tend to be greatly dissimilar down the length of the animal.

In larval insects, such as the caterpillars, the metameres are more uniform. In the vertebrate animals metamerism is quite evident in embryonic stages but tends to disappear in adults. The ribs and vertebrae still reflect the primitive metamerism.

PATTERNS IN REPRODUCTIVE STAGES

In order to understand some of the evidence used in grouping animals in categories, it is necessary to review some of the basic conditions and concepts in the development of individuals. In the following review many aspects of embryology are oversimplified and others are ignored entirely.

More detailed information concerning embryology (the study of the development of a new individual from the fertilized egg to the formation of organs) is found in other chapter of this book. Several facts concerning basic relationships of animals have been noted in the study of embryology.

First, the amount of stored food (yolk) in the egg is varied, but this variation does not appear to be as closely related to an animal's ancestry as to its habits. However, the amount of yolk present certainly does influence the way in which the fertilized egg undergoes division in the formation of an embryo.

In brief, eggs with relatively little yolk (isolecithal) tend to have holoblastic cleavage (a complete division of the cell), while those with a great amount of yolk (telolecithal) have meroblastic cleavage (incomplete division), with only the cytoplasm and nucleoplasm being involved, leaving the yolk intact.

In a third type of egg (centrolecithal), the centrally located nucleus undergoes several divisions without corresponding divisions of the cytoplasm until after the nuclei have migrated to the surface of the zygote. Obviously, such differences in the form of the egg affect the type of cleavage and tend to obscure patterns.

Yet in spite of these handicaps, embryologists have distinguished several patterns that appear to reflect relationships. Most primitive multicellular animals produce isolecithal eggs that undergo holoblastic cleavage. Such cleavage continues until a hollow ball of cells (blastula stage) is formed. Cells budding off from the surface cells soon fill the hollow space, resulting in a stereoblastula.

The outer layer of cells (ectoderm) becomes the skin of the adult, while the inner cells (endoderm) become the gut. This stereoblastula, by elongation and development of cilia on the ectoderm, becomes a radially symmetrical, free-swimming larva that has recognizable anterior and posterior ends but no mouth or gut.

This planula larva, or rather some remote ancestor with similar morphological features, may well have been the ancestor of the radially symmetrical Coelenterates and Ctenophores as well as the bilaterally symmetrical Platyhelminthes. The higher multicellular animals are readily divisible into two groups, according to types of cleavage and fate of the blastopore. Recall that the blastula is a hollow ball, with the cells arranged around the outer edge. This develops into a gastrula by a process of invagination or one related to invagination.

To visualize this, assume the blastula to be an under-inflated basketball. Push your fist into one surface and the ball will fold in upon itself, resulting in a cavity communicating with the outside. This hole to the outside is the blastopore; the inner cavity corresponds to the primitive gut (archenteron), and its lining to the lining of the gut (endoderm), while the outer layer corresponds to the future skin (ectoderm).

Note that the blastopore is the communication between the primitive gut and the environment. In one large group of animals, including the round worms (Nematoda), annelids, mollusks, and arthropods, this blastopore either becomes the mouth or is closely associated with its future location. Members of this group are called *proterostomes*.

In the second group, which includes the echinoderms and chordates, the blastopore becomes or is closely associated with the location of the anus and a "new" mouth develops at the other end of the archenteron. These animals are termed deuterostomes. In the deuterostomes the division of cells in the formation of the embryo represents indeterminate cleavage, in that what a given cell in the early embryo will develop into is not fixed.

Thus, it is possible for experimental embryologists to trans plant cells in an early frog embryo (a chordate with indeterminate cleavage) from one site to another, and the cell will take on the characteristics and form the structure of those cells surrounding it in the new location. (Such transplants show different reaction when made in older embryos.)

In contrast, the proterostomes have determinate cleavage. In these the potential of a given cell in the embryo is fixed quite early. For example, if the zygotes of marine annelids are permitted to divide twice, thus resulting in four cells, and the four cells are separated, development will continue, but each cell will develop into only onefourth of an animal.

Finally, although the amount of yolk in the egg often obscures the pattern, most proterostomes have spiral cleavage, while the deuterostomes tend to have radial or bilateral but never spiral cleavage. The embryos of many animals, especially those that lay their eggs in marine waters, develop into motile larvae. Two major types of larvae, each with several sub-types, are recognized. The *trochophore-like* larva is found in the proterostomes.

This is a radially symmetrical top-shaped form with oral and aboral surfaces recognizable. The digestive tract is complete and, on the aboral surface, there is a sensory plate with a tuft of sensory cilia. The locomotor cilia may be scattered or arranged in one or more girdles around the larva.

In the deuterostomic group a dipleurula-like larva is common. Such a larva is bilaterally symmetrical and has a complete digestive system including a ciliated stomodeum; the ciliated locomotor hands are arranged in complex tracts. The various forms of larvae in each group are usually given separate names.

Furthermore, any given larval type may develop into a more complex form that is given a still different name. For example, the trochophore larva of the marine pelecypod mollusks develops into a veliger. In the holothuroidean echinoderms the dipleurula-like auricularia larva develops into a more complex doliotarian larva.

For our purposes, however, we are going to consider only three major types of invertebrate larvae-planula, trochophore-like, and dipleurula-like-in our survey of the animal kingdom.

MAJOR DIVISIONS OF THE ANIMAL KINGDOM

The animal kingdom is currently divided into 27 phyla. As seen in Table anywhere else in this chapter, they are defined in terms of the various patterns of homologies that were discussed in preceding sections. Since classifications are man-made interpretations of the available evidence concerning kinship, it is not surprising that they are subject to change.

As new evidence concerning kinship is secured from studies or morphology, embryology, physiology, and genetics, minor and occasionally major revisions in classifications are necessary. The following synoptic classification of the major groups of living animals is based on the works of Hyman, Barnes, and others.

KINGDOM ANIMALIA

Subkingdom 1. Protozoa
Phylum PROTOZOA

Subkingdom 2. Mesozoa
Phylum MESOZOA

Subkingdom 3. Parazoa

Phylum PORIFERA

Subkingdom 4. Metazoa

Infrakingdom A. Radiata

Phylum COELENTERATA

Phylum CTENOPHORA

Infrakingdom B. Bilateriata

Cohort A. Acoeloinata

Phylum PLATYHELMINTHES

Phylum RHYNCHOCOELA

Cohort B. Pseudocoelomata Phylum

ACANTHOCEPHALA

Phylum ASCHELMINTHES

Phylum ENTOPROCTA

Cohort C. Coelomata

Superphylum 1. Proterostomia

Phylum PRIAPULIDA

Phylum ECTOPROCTA

Phylum PHORNIDA

Phylum BRACHIOPODA

Phylum SIPUNCULIDA

Phylum ECHURIDA

Phylum MOLLUSCA

Phylum ANNELIDA

Phylum ONYCHOPHORA

Phylum TARDIGRADA

Phylum PENTASTOMIDA

Phylum ARTHROPODA

Superphylum 2. Deuterostomia

Phylum CHAETOGNATHA

Phylum ECHINODERMATA

Phylum POGONOPHORA

Phylum HEMICHORDATA

Phylum CHORDATA

6

Diversity of Animals

Animals are many-celled heterotrophs. They depend directly or indirectly for their nourishment on photosynthetic autotrophs-algae or plants. Most digest their food in an internal cavity, and most store food as glycogen or fat. Their cells do not have walls. Most move by means of contractile cells (muscle cells) containing characteristic proteins. Reproduction is usually sexual.

As adults, most are fixed in size and shape, in contrast to plants, in which growth often continues for the lifetime of the organism. The higher animals-the arthropods and the vertebrates—are the most complex of all organisms, with many kinds of specialised tissues, including elaborate sensory and neuromotor mechanisms not found in any of the other kingdoms.

For most of us, animal means mammal, and mammals are, in fact, the chief focus of attention in other section. However, the mammals, or even the vertebrates as a whole, represent only a small fraction of the animal kingdom. More than 90 percent of the different species of animals are invertebrates-that is, animals without backbones and most of these are insects. Indeed, the enormous variety displayed by the invertebrates is partly why they are so endlessly fascinating to study. They are, in addition, of great ecological importance; the insects, for example, have long challenged human dominance of the earth.

Finally, and perhaps most important, the invertebrates, confronted with the same biological problems that we face, demonstrate a spectrum of ingenious solutions. In this way, they illuminate the essential nature of these problems and so help us to understand and evaluate the solutions arrived at by mammals.

THE SOURCES OF DIVERSITY

In other chapter of this book, we commented upon the tremendous versatility of the prokaryotes, as exemplified by the wide range of environments they inhabit and the many ways in which they satisfy their energy requirements.

Among the invertebrates, we see, on a slightly different scale, this same pattern of adaptation to many different ways of life. Thus, for instance, on a single coral head, only a meter or two in diameter, one finds a dazzling array of different forms-sponges, jellyfish, starfish, sea urchins, anemones, and the coral animals themselves.

Similarly, to take terrestrial examples, a single spadeful of soil turns up earthworms, pillbugs, spiders, nematodes, and various other tiny animals; and the branch of a single tree may harbor a dozen different kinds of insects. Given the relentless force of natural selection, why do not the larger ones crowd out the smaller? Why are not the "lower" animals replaced by "higher' animals with superior strength or intelligence?

Darwin, again, offered the answer: The different organisms, he noted, "occupy different positions in the economy of nature." Each has been shaped by the long process of evolution to occupy a different niche in the environment. Natural selection has worked not to make one "superior" to the other but to continuously adapt the different forms to different ways of life.

This process of adaptation, of course, continues. Every species, including our own, is a traveler through time, caught for only an instant in the present.

THE SOURCES OF CONTINUITY

Through the patterns of diversity, there is a strong theme of continuity. One reason is simply that of "descent." We are all related; not only are we made of the same atoms and molecules and even macromolecules, but from *E. coli* to elephant, we even share many of the same enzymes.

Although the evolutionary relationships between us and the invertebrates are obscure, we can read into them traces of our own biological beginnings. In the twitch of a tiny segment of an earthworm's artery, we sense the echo of our own heartbeat.

Second, all organisms face the same set of problems. These problems can best be defined by recalling that an organism is a cell or group of cells. A primary need is to supply the cell or cells with, first of all, a source of energy. Also, most cells-on this planet, at least-require water, oxygen, a source of nitrogen, fixed carbon (in the case of heterotrophs), and a few ions.

Another requirement is to eliminate wastes, including excess carbon dioxide, nitrogenous wastes from the breakdown of amino acids, and, in some cases, excess water. Cells that live individual or colonial lives in a watery environment can solve these problems in relatively simple ways, but as organisms get larger, thicker, and more complex, the problem of servicing each individual cell becomes correspondingly more complicated.

Another set of problems that a multicellular organism must solve in order to exist arises from the fact that it is more than just a group of cells. It is, in fact, a complex society of cells, in which the needs of each individual cell are subordinated to the needs of the society. In a population of *Paramecium,* the organisms have common requirements, but each is in competition with the others.

In a society of even a few thousand cells—a small crustacean, for instance-the individual cells are dependent on the existence of the group and are organised in a system of mutual cooperation. The second group of problems faced by organisms, therefore, relates to the organisation or integration of activities.

Hormones are one of the chief means of integration in both plants and animals. In the animals, another, more rapid integrating mechanism has evolved: the nervous system, by which the organism keeps in touch with its environment and coordinates its own activities.

A QUESTION OF SIZE

At this point, one might well ask: Considering the problems faced by larger organisms, why did larger animals evolve? What selective advantages do the multicellular, more complex animals have as compared with the smaller ones? Some answers to these questions are obvious and simple.

Larger animals are, in general, more likely to eat than be eaten. Larger organisms, especially those that live underwater or on land, are generally able to travel faster and farther than small ones, and this is an advantage.

A small ciliate, for instance, might starve only a few centimeters from a food supply. On the other hand, its requirements are very modest.

Perhaps even more important, however, than mobility and edibility is what the French physiologist Claude Bernard called the *milieu interieur,* the internal environment of the animal, as distinct from the external environment that surrounds it.

A single-celled organism is as cold or as hot and as wet or as dry as its surroundings, whereas a larger animal is more independent and, to some extent, controls the environment in which its cellular society lives. Control of the internal environment is more readily achieved by the many-celled animal because of the simple surface-to-volume geometry we noted in other chapter.

Exchanges between a cell and its surroundings take place across a cell's available surface area. This is a principal reason why a cell, which depends for its existence on the exchange of substances with its environment, cannot be very large.

On the other hand, since it may be advantageous to conserve certain substances, such as water and heat, an organism may be better off, within limits of weight and mobility, if its relative surface area is reduced. One-celled animals can live successfully only in water or as parasites in the bodies of other organisms, which amounts to the same thing.

Many-celled animals can live not only in water but also on land, in the sky, and even, as we are now beginning to discover, in outer space-which is a logical extension of an old evolutionary trend. In this chapter, we shall discuss the so-called lower invertebrates and some that must clearly be considered higher, such as the clever and highly emotional octopus.

The chapter that follows deals with the insects and other arthropods and, briefly, with the vertebrates. There are almost 30 phyla of invertebrates. Of these, we are going to discuss relatively few, concentrating on the largest phyla and those of particular biological interest.

PHYLUM PORIFERA: SPONGES

Sponges seem to have had a different origin from other members of the animal kingdom and to have traveled a solitary evolutionary route. For this reason, they are often classified in a subkingdom of their own, the Parazoa ("alongside of animals").

In fact, until the eighteenth century, the sponges were classified as

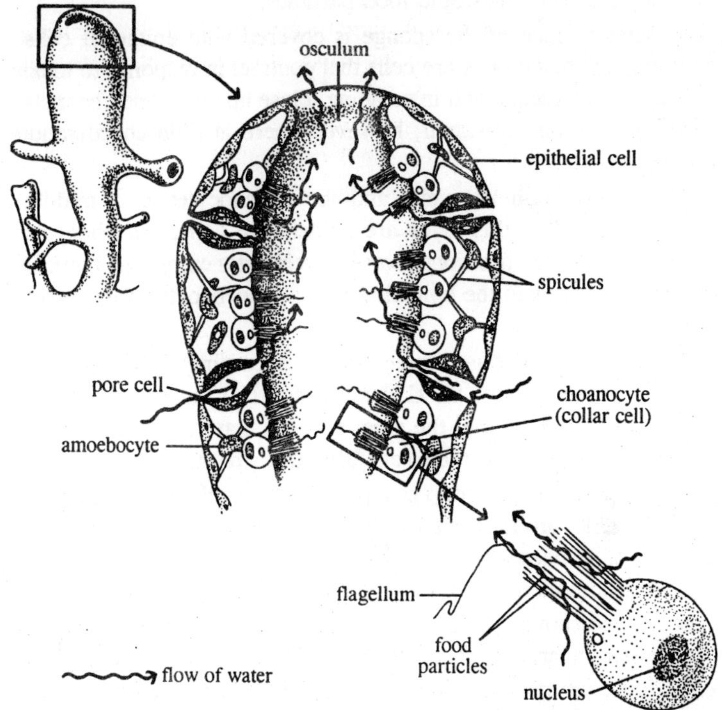

Figure 6.1 : The body of a" simple sponge is dotted with tiny pores, from which the phylum derives its name (Porifera, or "pore bearer"), Water containing food particles is drawn into the internal cavity of the sponge through these pores and is exhaled out the osculum.

plant-animals ("zoophytes") since they are all sessile (attached to a substrate) during their adult life. Sponges are found on ocean floors throughout the world. Most live along the coasts in shallow water, but some, such as the fragile glass sponges, are found at great depths, where the water is almost motionless. A few types are found in fresh water.

A sponge is essentially a water-filtering system, made up of one or more chambers through which water is driven by the action of numerous flagellated cells. Sponges are made up of a relatively few cell types, the most characteristic of which are the choanocytes, or collar cells, the flagellated cells that line the interior cavity of the sponge.

Similar cells, the choanoflagellates, are found among the ciliated protozoans, and it is possible that the sponges arose from such organisms. All of a sponge's digestive processes are carried out intracellularly; hence, even a giant sponge-and some stand taller than a person-can eat nothing larger than microscopic food particles.

The outer surface of the sponge is covered with epithelial cells. Among these epithelial cells are cells that contract in response to touch or to irritating chemicals, and in so doing, close up pores and channels. Each cell acts as an individual, however; there is little coordination among them.

Between the epithelial cells and the choanocytes is a middle, jellylike layer, and in this layer are amoebalike cells, amoebocytes, which carry out various functions. Some amoebocytes carry food particles from the choanocytes to the epithelial cells. Amoebocytes also secrete skeletal materials.

Sponges are grouped into three classes, according to their skeletal structure. In some species, the skeleton consists of individual spicules of calcium carbonate. Some, the glass sponges, have spicules of silica fused in a continuous and often very beautiful structure.

The third and largest group has unfused silica spicules, or a tough, fibrous keratinlike protein called spongin, or a combination of the two. The skeleton of sponges serves only for protection, stiffening, and support, but not for locomotion, since the adult forms are sessile.

The sponge shown in Figure elsewhere in this chapter is a small and simple one. In larger sponges, the body plan, although it is essentially the same, looks far more complex. These sponges have greatly increased feeding and filtering surfaces, owing to their highly folded body walls.

We have already encountered this evolutionary strategem for increasing biological work surfaces at the cellular level—as in the inner membrane of the mitochondrion-and we shall be encountering it again as we examine the structure of gills and lungs.

Sponges are somewhere between a colony of cells and a true multicellular organism. The cells are not organised into tissues or organs; each leads an independent existence. Yet there is a form of recognition among the cells that holds them together and organises them.

If the sponge Microciona prolifera is squeezed through a fine sieve or a piece of cheesecloth, the body of the sponge is separated into individual cells and small clumps of cells. Within an hour, the isolated sponge cells begin to reaggregate, and as these aggregations get larger, canals, flagellated chambers, and other characteristics of the body organisation of the sponge begin to appear.

This phenomenon has been used as a model for the analysis of cell adhesion, recognition, and differentiation, all of which are basic biological

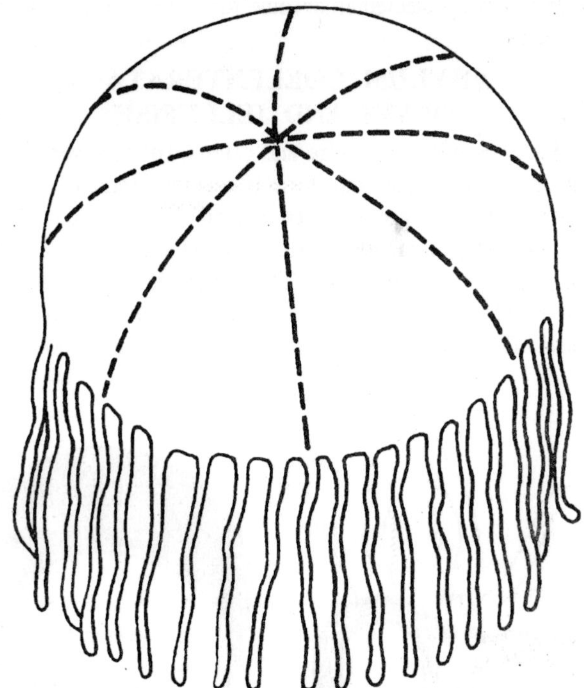

Figure 6.2 : In organisms with radial symmetry, any plane through the animal that passes through the central axis divides the body into halves that are mirror images of one another.

features of development in higher organisms.

Most kinds of sponges are hermaphroditic; that is, they have male and female reproductive organs in the same individual. Gametes appear to arise from an enlarged amoebocyte, but there are reports that choanocytes can also form gametes. A sperm enters another sponge in a current of water.

It is captured by a choanocyte and transferred to an amoebocyte, which then transfers it to a ripe egg (a method of fertilisation unique to the sponges). The fertilised egg develops into a ciliated, free-swimming larva. After a short life among the plankton, the larva settles and becomes sessile.

Sponges also reproduce asexually, either by fragments that break off from the parent animal, or by gemmules, aggregations of amoebalike cells within a hard, protective outer layer. Production of such resistant forms is found, in general, only among freshwater organisms.

In the ocean, conditions are relatively unchanging; but the freshwater environment is much harsher. Invertebrates that live in fresh water are more likely to have protected embryonic forms than even closely related marine species.

PHYLUM COELENTERATA: POLYPS AND JELLYFISH

The coelenterates are a large and often strikingly beautiful group of aquatic organisms. Their adult-form is generally radially symmetrical; that is, their body parts are arranged around a central axis, like spokes around a hub. As you can see in figure elsewhere in this chapter, the basic body plan is a simple one: The animal is essentially a hollow container, which may be either vase-shaped, the *polyp,* or bowl-shaped, the *medusa.* The polyp is usually sessile; the medusa, motile.

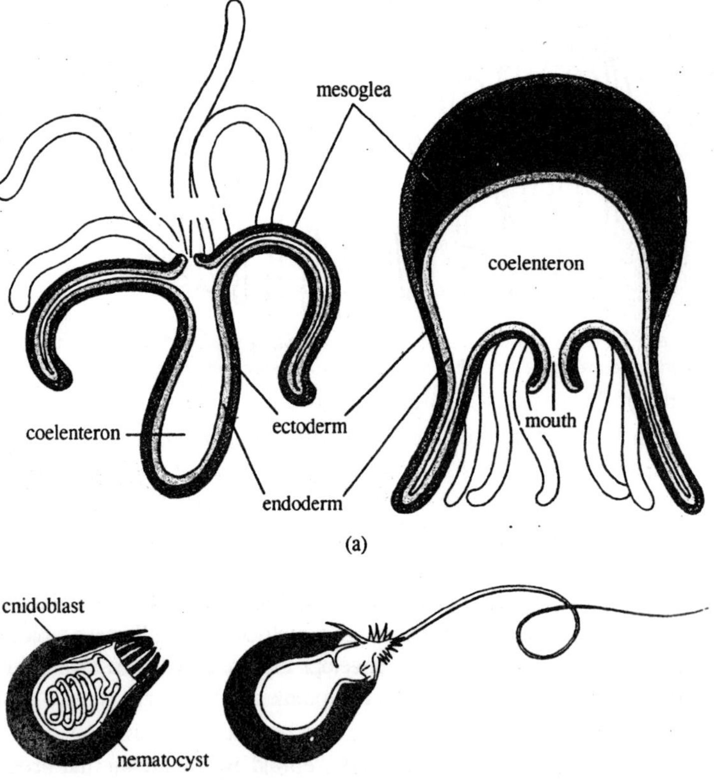

Figure 6.3 : (a) Among coelenterates, there are two basic body plans: the vase-shaped polyp (left) and the bowl-shaped medusa (right). (b) Cnidoblasts, specialised cells located in the tentacles and body wall, are a distinguishing feature of coelenterates.

Both consist of two layers of tissue: *ectoderm* and *endoderm* (from the Greek *ektos,* "outer," and *endon,* "inner," plus *derma,* "skin").

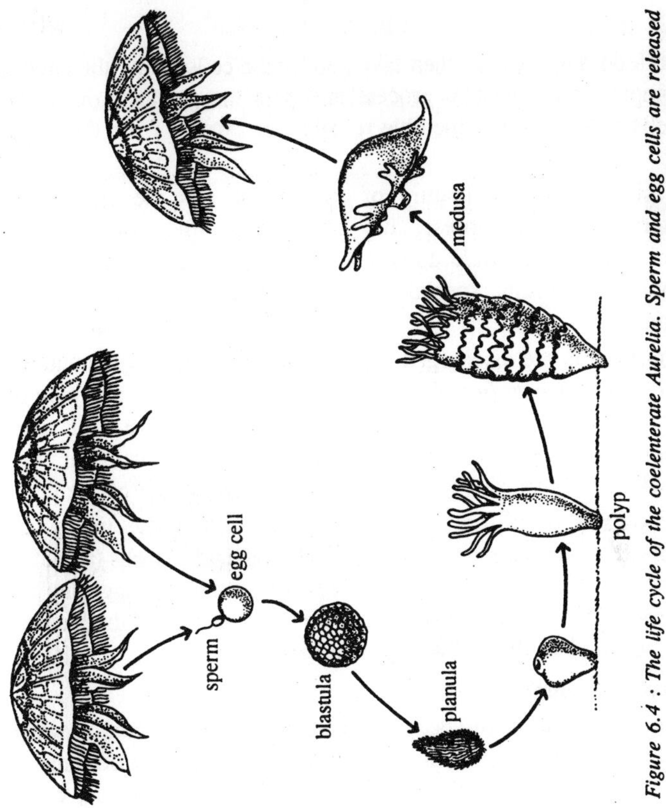

Figure 6.4 : The life cycle of the coelenterate Aurelia. Sperm and egg cells are released from adult medusas into the surrounding water. Fertilization takes place, and the resulting zygote develops first into a hollow sphere of cells, the blastula, and then elongates and becomes a ciliated larva called a planula.

Between the two layers is a gelatinous filling, the *mesoglea* ("middle jelly"), which is made of a collagenlike material. In the polyp form, the mesoglea is sometimes very thin, but in the medusa, it often accounts for the major portion of the body substance.

Most coelenterates go through both a polyp and a medusa stage in their life cycles. In such species, polyps reproduce asexually and medusas sexually. This sort of life cycle, in which the sexually reproductive form is distinctly different from the asexual form, superficially resembles alternation of generations in plants.

There is, however, no alternation between haploid and diploid forms as there is in plants; the only haploid forms are the gametes

Another distinctive feature of the animals in this phylum is the *coelenteron,* a digestive cavity with only one opening. Within this cavity, enzymes are released that break down food, partially digesting it extracellularly, as our own food is digested within the stomach and intestinal tract.

The food particles are then taken up by the cells lining the cavity; they complete the digestive process and pass the products on to the other cells of the animal. Inedible remains are ejected from the single opening.

A third distinctive feature of coelenterates is the *cnidoblast*. Coelenterates are carnivores. They capture their prey by means of tentacles that form a circle around the "mouth." These tentacles are armed with cnidoblasts, special cells that contain nematocysts (thread capsules).

Nematocysts are discharged in response to a chemical stimulus or touch. The nematocyst threads, which are often poisonous and may be sticky or barbed, can lasso prey, harpoon it, or paralyze it-or some useful combination of all three. The toxin apparently produces paralysis by attacking the lipoproteins of the nerve cell membrane of the prey.

Cnidoblasts occur only in this phylum, with some interesting exceptions. Certain other invertebrates, including nudibranchs (a kind of mollusk) and flatworms, can eat coelenterates without triggering the nematocysts. The nematocysts then migrate to the surface of the predator and can be fired in their new host's defense.

Classes of Coelenterates

There are three major classes of coelenterates: Hydrozoa, in which the polyp is usually the dominant form; Scyphozoa, predominantly medusoid, exemplified by the common jellyfish; and Anthozoa, which includes the sea anemones and the reef-building corals, and has only the polyp.

Class Hydrozoa: Hydra

One of the most thoroughly studied of the coelenterates is *Hydra,* which is a small, common freshwater form, convenient to keep in the laboratory. Figure elsewhere in this chapter shows a small section of the body wall of *Hydra*. The ectoderm is composed largely of epitheliomuscular cells, which perform a covering, protective function and also serve as muscle tissue.

Each cell has contractile fibers, myonemes, at its base and so can contract individually, like the contractile epithelial cells of the sponge. The endoderm is mostly made up of cells concerned with digestion; these cells also contain contractile fibers.

In *Hydra*, as in other polyps, the contractile fibrils of the ectoderm attach lengthwise to the mesoglea and the fibrils of the endoderm cells

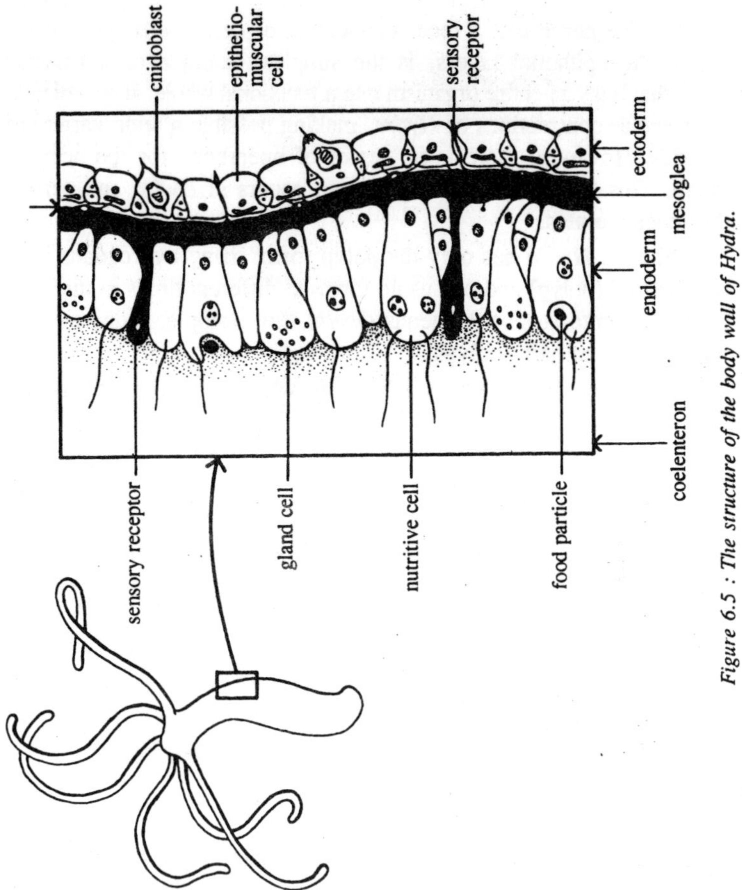

Figure 6.5 : The structure of the body wall of Hydra.

attach transversely, so the body walls can stretch or bulge, depending on which group is stimulated.

In addition to cnidoblasts and epitheliomuscular cells, which are independent effectors-cells that both receive and respond to stimuli-Hydra contain two other types of nerve cells: sensory receptor cells and cells connected into a network, the nerve net.

Sensory receptor cells are more sensitive than other epithelial cells to chemical and mechanical stimuli, and when stimulated they transmit their impulses to an adjacent cell or cells. The adjacent cell may be simply an epitheliomuscular cell, an effector, which then responds.

Note that this system is one step more complicated than the epitheliomuscular cell or cnidoblast, which acts as both receptor and effector. The nerve net, a loose connection of nerve cells lying at the base of the epithelial layers, is the simplest example of a nervous system that links an entire organism into a functional whole. It coordinates the muscular contractions of *Hydra,* making possible a wide variety of activities. However, there is no center of operations for the nervous system. This type of conducting system occurs in *Hydra* and certain other coelenterates.

Although *Hydra* has only the polyp form, many hydrozoans have both hydroid (polyp) and medusoid forms at different times in their life cycles. Coelenterates of the genus *Obelia,* for example, spend most of their lives as colonial polyps.

The colony arises from a single polyp, which multiplies by budding. The new polyps do not separate but remain interconnected so that their body cavities form a continuous channel, through which food particles are circulated.

Within the colony are two types of polyps: feeding polyps with tentacles and cnidoblasts, and reproductive polyps from which tiny medusas bud off. These medusas produce eggs or sperm that are released into the water and fuse to form zygotes.

Thus colonial polyps, with their division of labor between feeding and reproductive forms, are very like a single organism. Such a high degree of specialisation of structure and function among social organisms is seen in other phyla only among the social insects.

Class Scyphozoa: Jellyfish

A second major class of coelenterates is Scyphozoa, or "cup animals," in which the medusa form is dominant. Scyphozoans, more commonly known as jellyfish, range in size from less than 2 centimeters in diameter up to animals 4 meters across and trailing tentacles 10 meters long.

In the adult animal, the mesoglea is so firm that a large, freshly beached jellyfish can easily support the weight of a human being. The mesoglea of some jellyfish is filled with wandering, amoebalike cells, which serve to transport food from the nutritive cells of the endoderm. Unlike *Hydra,* scyphozoans have true muscle cells; these underlie the ectoderm, contracting rhythmically to propel the medusa through the water.

Nervous System of Medusa

In the medusa, there are concentrations of nerve cells in the margin of the bell. These nerve cells connect with fibers innervating (providing

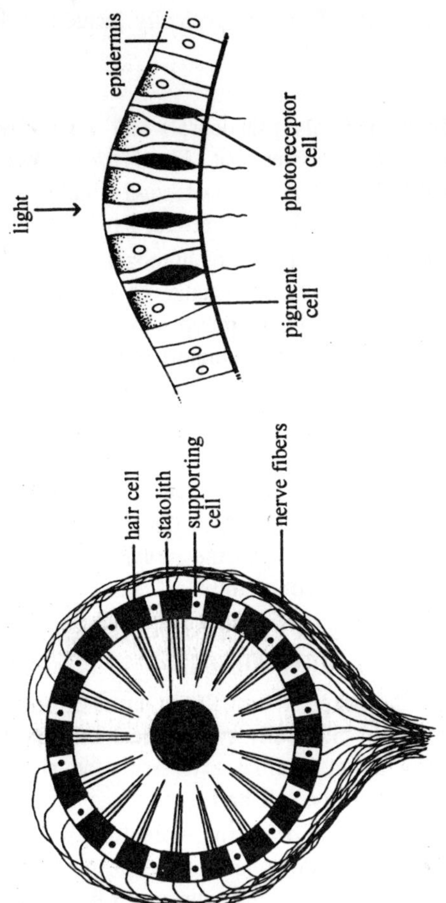

Figure 6.6 : (a) The statocyst is a specialised receptor organ that orients the jellyfish with respect to gravity. When the bell tilts, gravity pulls the statolith, a grain of hardened calcium salts, down against the hair cells. This stimulates the nerve fibers and signals the animal to right itself. (b) Eyespot (ocellus), the simplest type of photoreceptor organ. Ocelli of this sort are found among coelenterates.

the nerve supply for) the tentacles, the musculature, and the sense organs.

The bell margin is liberally supplied with sensory receptor cells sensitive to mechanical and chemical stimuli. In addition, the jellyfish has two types of true sense organs: statocysts and light-sensitive ocelli.

Statocysts are specialised receptor organs that provide information by which an animal can orient itself with respect to gravity. The statocyst, which seems to have been one of the first special sensory organs to have appeared in the course of evolution, has persisted apparently unchanged to the present day, appearing in many animal phyla.

Ocelli, which may have evolved even earlier, are groups of pigment cells and photoreceptor cells. They are typically located at the bases of the tentacles.

Class Anthozoa

Anthozoans ("flower animals")-the corals and sea anemones-are members of a class of coelenterates that, like *Hydra,* have lost the medusa stage. They differ from *Hydra* in having a gullet lined with epidermis and a coelenteron divided by vertical partitions.

In most corals, which are colonies of anthozoans, the epidermal cells secrete protective outer walls, usually of calcium carbonate (limestone), into which each delicate polyp can retreat. The coral-forming polyps are the most ecologically important of the coelenterates.

The 2,000-kilometer-long Great Barrier Reef off the northeast shores of Australia, and the Marshall Islands in the Pacific are examples of coral-created land masses.

A coral reef is composed primarily of the accumulated limestone skeletons of coral coelenterates, covered by a thin crust occupied by the living colonial animals. A reef is both the structural and nutritional basis of the complex coral reef community.

PHYLUM PLATYHELMINTHES: FLATWORMS

The flatworms are the simplest animals, in terms of body plan, to show bilateral symmetry. In bilaterally symmetrical animals, the body plan is organised along a longitudinal axis, with the right half an approximate mirror image of the left half.

It also has a top and a bottom or, in more precise terms (applicable even when it is turned upside down or, as in the case of humans, standing upright), a dorsal and a ventral surface. Like most bilateral organisms, the flatworm also has a distinct "*headness*" and "*tailness,*" anterior and posterior.

Having one end that goes first-cephalization-is characteristic of actively moving animals. In such animals, many of the sensory cells are also collected into the anterior end. With the aggregation of sensory cells, there came a concomitant gathering of nerve cells; this gathering is a forerunner of the brain.

Flatworms have three distinct tissue layers-ectoderm, mesoderm, and endoderm-characteristic of all animals above the coelenterate level of organisation.

Moreover, not only are their tissues specialised for various functions, but also two or more types of tissue cells may combine to form organs-for example, the muscular pharynx. Thus, while sponges are made up of aggregations of cells and coelenterates are largely limited to the tissue level of organisation, flatworms can be said to exemplify the organ level of complexity. There are three classes of flatworms: the free-living turbellaria and two parasitic forms, flukes and tapeworms.

The flatworms are believed by some zoologists to have evolved from the coelenterates (or, perhaps, vice versa), not by way of either adult form, however, but from the ciliated larval form.

Others are persuaded that the flatworms had independent origins among the ciliates. Still another group maintains that they are degenerate annelids. It is unlikely that this matter will soon be resolved.

The Planarian

The free-living flatworms form a large and varied group, and we shall single out just one for examination, the freshwater planarian. The ectoderm of the planarian is made up of cuboid epithelial cells, many of which are ciliated, particularly those on the ventral surface.

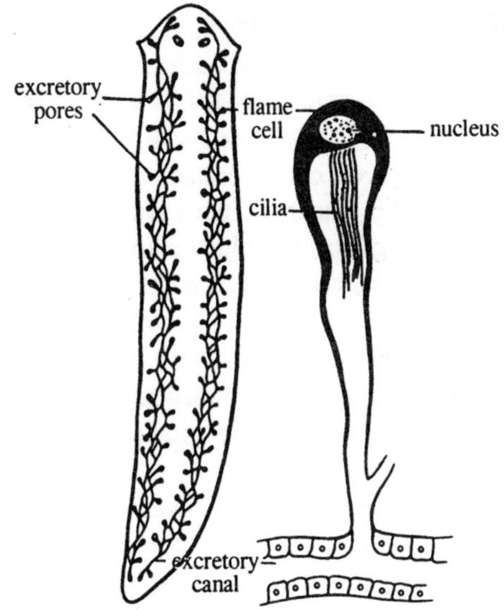

Figure 6.7 : Flatworms have a tubular excretory system. The system usually consists of two or more branching tubules running the length of the body.

Ventral ectodermal cells secrete mucus, which provides traction for the planarian as it moves by means of its cilia along its own slime trail. Planarians are among the largest animals that can use cilia for locomotion.

The cilia in larger species are usually employed for moving water or other substances along the surface of the animal, as in the human respiratory tract, rather than for propelling the animal.

The planarian has an endoderm composed largely of amoeboid cells, which, although they are phagocytic, are not wandering cells like the amoebocytes of the jellyfish. Between the ectoderm and the phagocytic endoderm is a *mesoderm,* or middle tissue layer.

In planarians, as in all other groups to follow, the muscle cells and the principal organ systems are of mesodermal origin.

The planarian, like the coelenterates, has a digestive cavity (gut) with only one opening, located on the ventral surface. This digestive cavity has three main branches, which is why planarians are placed in the order of flatworms known as Tricladida.

Like other flatworms, the planarian is carnivorous. It eats either dead meat or slow-moving animals it can fasten itself to or subdue by sitting on, such as smaller planarians. It feeds by means of a muscular tube, the pharynx, which is free at one end. The free end can be stretched out through the mouth opening.

Muscular contractions in the tube cause strong sucking movements, which tear the meat into microscopic bits and draw them into the internal cavity, where they are phagocytized by the endodermal cells.

Unlike the sponges or coelenterates, most flatworms have an excretory system. In the planarian, the system is a network of fine tubules that runs the length of the animal's body. Side branches of the tubules contain flame cells, each of which has a hollow center in which a tuft of cilia beats, flickering like a tongue of flame, moving water along the tubules to the exit pores between the epidermal cells.

The flame-cell system appears to function largely to regulate water balance; most of the metabolic waste products probably diffuse out through the ectoderm or the endoderm.

Planarians have a complicated reproductive system. The eggs are fertilised internally. At mating, each partner deposits sperm in the copulatory sac of the other partner. These sperm then travel along special tubes, the *oviducts*, to fertilise the eggs as they become ripe.

As we mentioned earlier, organisms like planarians, in which both types of gametes are produced by one individual, are known as hermaphrodites (from Hermes and Aphrodite).

Solitary, slow-moving animals, such as earthworms and snails, are often hermaphrodites; these animals may seldom encounter another adult member of the species, but every such encounter can result in a mating. Some types of hermaphroditic animals can fertilise themselves, although they do not usually do so if another individual is present.

The Planarian Nervous System

The evolution of bilateral symmetry brought with it marked changes in the organisation of the nervous system as well as of other systems. Even among primitive flatworms, the neurons (nerve cells) are not dispersed in a loose network, as in *Hydra,* but are instead condensed into longitudinal cords.

In the planarians, this condensation is carried further, and there are only two main conducting channels, one on each side of the flat, ribbonlike body. These channels carry impulses to and from the aggregation of nerve cells in the anterior end of the body. Such aggregations of nerve cell bodies are known as *ganglia* (singular, ganglion).

The ocelli of the planarian are usually inverted pigment cups. They have no lenses, and they cannot form an image. However, they can distinguish light from dark and can tell the direction from which the light is coming.

Planarians are photonegative; if you shine a light on a dish of planarians from the side, they will move steadily away from the source of light.

Among the epithelial cells are receptor cells sensitive to certain chemicals and to touch. The head region in particular is rich in *chemoreceptors.* If you place a small piece of fresh liver in the culture water so that its juices diffuse through the medium, the planarians will raise their heads off the bottom and, if they have not eaten recently, will lope directly and rapidly (on a planarian scale) toward the meat, to which they then attach themselves to feed.

The animal locates the food source by repeatedly turning toward the side on which it receives the stimulus more strongly until the stimulus is equal on both sides of its head. If the chemoreceptor cells are removed from one side of the head, the animal will turn constantly toward the intact side.

Planarians, with their simple nervous systems, their capacity to react to a variety of stimuli, and their powers of regeneration, have been the subject of a number of experiments. In one group, planarians trained to avoid electric shock were fed to untrained planarians.

The result, it was claimed, was that the untrained planarians that had eaten the trained ones behaved as if they had been trained. These experiments, still not verified, on the "transfer of training by cannibalism" led to a great deal of controversy in the 1960s and also, as you might expect, to a number of suggestions for more meaningful student-teacher relationships.

Tapeworms and Flukes

Phylum Platyhelminthes includes also the tapeworms and the trematodes (flukes), parasitic forms that can cause serious and sometimes fatal diseases among vertebrates. Members of both of these parasitic classes have a tough outer layer of cells that is resistant to digestive fluids and, usually, suckers or hooks on their anterior ends by which they fasten to their victims.

Trematodes feed through a mouth, but the tapeworms, which have no mouths, digestive cavities, or digestive enzymes, merely hang on and absorb predigested food molecules through their skin. Tapeworms are found in the intestines of many vertebrates, including humans, and may grow as long as 5 or 6 meters.

They cause illness not only by encroaching on the food supply but also by producing wastes and by obstructing the intestinal tract. The most common human tapeworm, the beef tapeworm, infects people who eat the undercooked flesh of cattle that have eaten fodder contaminated by human feces containing tapeworm segments.

All parasites, including parasitic flatworms, are believed to have originated as free-living forms and to have lost certain tissues and organs (such as the digestive tract) as a secondary effect of their parasitic existence, while developing adaptations of advantage to the parasitic way of life. Such adaptations also often include a complex life cycle.

PHYLUM RHYNCHOCOELA: RIBBON WORMS

The ribbon worms (sometimes called nemertines), although a small phylum, are of special interest to biologists attempting to reconstruct the evolution of the invertebrates. They appear to be closely related to the flatworms, but with an important difference: They have a one-way digestive tract beginning with a mouth and ending with an anus.

This is a far more efficient arrangement than the one-opening digestive system of the coelenterates and flatworms. In the one-way tract, food moves assembly-line fashion, with the consequent possibilities (1) that eating can be continuous and (2) that various segments of the tract can become specialised for different stages of digestion. The ribbon worms also have a circulatory system, usually consisting of one dorsal and two lateral blood vessels that carry the colourless blood.

This phylum is called Rhynchocoela ("beak" plus "hollow") because these worms are characterised by a long, retractile, slime-covered tube (proboscis). The proboscis, sometimes armed with a barb, seizes prey and draws it to the mouth where it is engulfed. Some inject a paralyzing poison into their prey.

PHYLUM NEMATODA: ROUNDWORMS

The number of species of roundworms (nematodes) has been variously estimated as low as 10,000 and as high as 400,000 to 500,000. Most are free-living, microscopic forms. It has been estimated that a spadeful of good garden soil usually contains about a million nematodes. Some are parasites; most species of plants and animals are parasitised by at least one species of nematodes.

Humans are hosts to about 50 species, including hookworms, pinworms, and *Trichinella.* The latter causes trichinosis, which is transmitted by eating uncooked or undercooked pork, a single gram of which may contain 3,000 cysts (resting forms) of *Trichinella.* Ingestion of only a few hundred of these cysts can be fatal to human beings.

Nematodes have a three-layered body plan and a tubular gut with a mouth and an anus. They are unsegmented and are covered by a thick, continuous cuticle, which is molted periodically as they grow.

An interesting, and unique, feature of nematode construction is the absence of circular muscles. The contraction of the longitudinal muscles acting against the tough, elastic cuticle gives the worm its characteristic whipping movement in water. The sexes are usually separate.

Nematodes may have evolved from early Platyhelminthes, possessing, as they do, a three-layered body plan without a true coelom. They have, however, what is known as a pseudocoelom, a body cavity that is between the endoderm and the mesoderm and lacks the epithelial lining of a true coelom.

Six other minor (in terms of species and numbers) phyla, mostly small, wormlike animals, have body plans based on the pseudocoelom, but Nematoda is the only major pseudocoelomate phylum.

PHYLUM ANNELIDA : SEGMENTED WORMS

This phylum includes almost 9,000 different species of marine, freshwater, and soil worms, including the familiar earthworm. The term annelid means "ringed" and refers to the most distinctive feature of this group, which is the division of the body into segments, visible as rings on the outside and with partitions on the inside.

This segmented pattern is found in a modified form in higher animals, too, such as dragonflies, millipedes, and lobsters, which are thought to have evolved from the same ancestors that gave rise to modern annelids.

The annelids have a three-layered body plan, a tubular gut, and a well-developed circulatory system that transports oxygen (diffused through the skin or through fleshy extensions of the skin) and food molecules (from the gut) to all parts of the body.

The excretory system is made up of specialised paired tubules, nephridia, which occur in each segment of the body except the head. Annelids have a nervous system and a number of special sense cells, including touch cells, taste receptors, light-sensitive cells, and cells concerned with the detection of moisture. Some also have well-developed eyes and sensory antennae.

In the flatworms and ribbon worms, the mesoderm is packed solid with muscle and other tissues, but in the annelids there is a fluid-filled cavity, the *coelom*, (pronounced see-loam) in this middle layer. (Note that the term coelom, although it sounds similar to coelenteron and comes from the same Greek root, meaning "cavity," refers quite specifically to a cavity *within* the mesoderm, whereas the coelenteron is a digestive cavity lined by endoderm.)

Within the coelom, the gut-lined with an epithelium-is suspended by double layers of mesoderm known as mesenteries. The fluid in the coelom constitutes a hydrostatic skeleton for the annelid, stiffening the body in somewhat the same way water pressure stiffens and distends a fire hose.

The muscles of the earthworm work against this hydrostatic skeleton much as our muscles work against our bony skeleton. Although the opening of a cavity within the mesoderm may seem less dramatic than other evolutionary innovations, it is extremely important.

Within such a space, organ systems can bend, twist, and fold back on themselves, increasing their functional surface areas and filling, emptying, and sliding past one another, surrounded by lubricating coelomic fluid. Consider the human lung, constantly expanding and contracting in the chest cavity, or the 6 or 7 meters of coiled human intestine; neither of these could have evolved until the coelom made room for them.

Earthworms

The earthworm is the most familiar of the annelids. Figure elsewhere

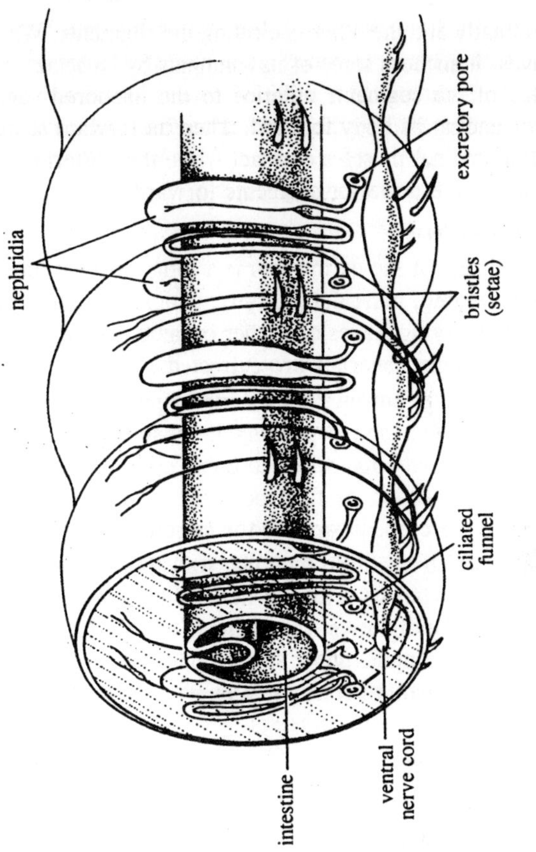

Figure 6.8 : Three segments of the earthworm, an annelid. On each segment are four pairs of bristles, which are extended and retracted by special muscles. These are used by the worm to anchor one part of its body while it moves another part forward.

in this chapter shows a portion of the body of an earthworm. Note how the body is compartmented into regular segments. Most of these segments, particularly the central and posterior ones, are identical, each exactly like the one before and the one after. Each identical segment contains four pairs of bristles, or *setae*; two *nephridia,* excretory tubules that pick up waste materials from the body fluids and excrete them through pores on the ventral surface of the worm; four sets of nerves branching off from the central nerve cord running along the ventral surface; a portion of digestive tract; and a left and right coelomic cavity.

The chief exceptions to this rule of segmented structure are found in the most forward segments. In these, sensory cells, a cluster of nerve cells (ganglia), and specialised areas of the digestive, circulatory, and reproductive systems are found.

The tubelike body is wrapped in two sets of muscles, one set running longitudinally and the other encircling the segments. When the earthworm moves, it anchors some of its segments by its setae, and the circular muscles of the segments anterior to the anchored segments contract, thus extending its body forward. Then its forward setae take hold, and the longitudinal muscles contract while the posterior anchor is released, drawing the posterior segments forward.

Digestion in Earthworms

The digestive tract of the earthworm is a long, straight tube. The mouth leads into a strong, muscular pharynx, which acts like a suction pump, drawing in decaying leaves and other organic matter, as well as dirt, from which organic materials are extracted.

The earthworm makes burrows in the earth by passing such material through its digestive tract and depositing it outside in the form of castings, a ceaseless activity that serves to break up, enrich, and aerate the soil. The narrow section of tube posterior to the pharynx, the *esophagus*, leads to the crop, where food is stored.

In the gizzard, which has thick, muscular walls lined with protective cuticle, the food is ground up with the help of the ever-present soil particles. The rest of the digestive tract is made up of a long intestine, which has a large fold along its upper surface that increases its surface area. The intestinal epithelium consists of enzyme-secreting cells and ciliated absorptive cells.

Circulation in Earthworms

In the protists and in the smaller and simpler animals, food molecules and oxygen are supplied to cells largely by diffusion, aided by the movement of external fluids and, sometimes, as we saw in coelenterates, by wandering, amoeboid cells.

A circulatory system that propels extracellular fluid around the body solves the problem of providing each cell with a more direct and rapid line of supply.

The circulatory system of the earthworm is composed of longitudinal vessels running the entire length of the worm, one dorsal and several ventral. The largest ventral vessel underlies the intestinal tract, collecting nutrients from it and distributing them by means of many small branches to all the tissues of the body and to the three smaller ventral vessels that surround the nerve cord and nourish it.

Numerous small capillaries in each segment carry blood from the ventral vessels through the tissues to the dorsal vessel. Also in each segment are larger parietal ("along the wall") vessels transporting blood from the subneural vessels to the dorsal vessel. Fluids collected in this way from all over the animal's body are fed into the muscular dorsal vessel, which propels the blood forward.

Connecting the dorsal and ventral vessels, and so completing the circuit, are five pairs of hearts, muscular pumping areas in the blood vessels. Their irregular contractions force the blood down to the ventral vessels and also forward to the vessels that supply the more anterior segments.

Both the hearts and the dorsal vessel have valves that prevent backflow. Note that the blood flows entirely through vessels. Such a system is known as a closed circulatory system. Evolution of a closed circulatory system, in effect, added a new compartment to the body plan and, in so doing, made possible a degree of control, not previously feasible, over the content of the circulating body fluid.

Excretory System of Earthworms

The excretory system consists of pairs of tubules, the nephridia; one pair for each segment. Each nephridium consists of a long, convoluted tubule that terminates in a ciliated funnel opening into the coelomic cavity of the anteriorly adjacent segment.

Coelomic fluid is carried into the funnel by the beating of the cilia and is excreted through an outer pore. As the fluid makes its way through the long tubule, water, sugar, salts, and other needed materials are returned to the coelomic fluid through the walls of the tubule, while other materials are absorbed into the tubule for excretion.

Thus the excretory system is concerned not only with the problem of water balance, as are the contractile vacuoles of *Paramecium* and the flame cells of planarians, but also with the homeostatic regulation of the chemical composition of the body fluids.

Thus, in effect, one segment monitors and regulates this aspect of the physiology of its neighboring segment-a neat trick for integrating the animal as a whole.

Respiration in Earthworms

The earthworm has no special respiratory organs; respiration takes place by simple diffusion through the body surface. The gases of the atmosphere dissolve in the liquid film on the surface of the earthworm's body, which is kept moist by secreted mucus and excreted water.

Oxygen travels inward by diffusion, since the surface film, exposed to the oxygen-rich atmosphere, contains more oxygen than does the blood in the network of capillaries just underlying the body surface. The oxygen is consumed by body cells as the blood circulates.

Carbon dioxide moves out to the surface film and then into the air by the same principle. In fact, all gas exchange in animals, whether the organism is land-dwelling or water-dwelling, takes place across moist membranes.

Nervous System in Earthworms

The earthworm has a variety of sensory cells. It has touch cells, or *mechanoreceptors*. These contain tactile hairs, which, when stimulated, trigger a nerve impulse. Patches of these hair cells are found on each segment of the earthworm. The hairs probably also respond to vibrations in the ground, to which the earthworm is very sensitive.

The earthworm does not have ocelli-as one might expect, since it lives most of its life in complete darkness-but it does have light-sensitive cells. Such cells are more abundant in its anterior and posterior segments, the parts of its body most likely to be outside of the burrow.

These cells are not responsive to light in the red portion of the spectrum, a fact exploited by anglers who search for worms in the dark using red-lensed flashlights.

Among the earthworm's most sensitive cells are those that detect moisture. The cells are located on its first few segments. If an earthworm emerging from its burrow encounters a dry spot, it swings from side to side until it finds dampness; failing that, it retreats.

However, when the anterior segments are anesthetised, the earthworm will crawl over dry ground. The animal also appears to have taste cells. In the laboratory, worms can bc shown to select, for example, celery in preference to cabbage leaves and cabbage leaves in preference to carrots.

Each segment of the worm is supplied by nerves that receive impulses from sensory cells and by nerves that cause muscles to contract. The cell bodies for these nerves are grouped together in clusters (ganglia). The movements of each segment are directed by a pair of ganglia.

Movement in each segment is triggered by movement in the adjacent anterior segment; thus a headless earthworm can move in a coordinated manner. However, an earthworm without its cerebral ganglia moves ceaselessly; in other words, cephalic ganglia modulate activity.

There are also, as in planarians, conducting channels made up of nerve fibers bound together in bundles, like cables, which run lengthwise through the body. These nerve fibers are gathered together in a double nerve cord that runs along the ventral surface of the body.

The nerve cords contain fast-conducting fibers that make it possible for the earthworm to contract its entire body very quickly, withdrawing into its burrow when disturbed.

Reproduction in Earthworms

Earthworms are hermaphrodites. Two earthworms, held together by mucous secretions from the clitellum (a special collection of glandular cells), exchange sperm and separate. Two or three days later, the clitellum forms a second mucous sheath surrounded by an outer, tougher protective layer of chitin.

This sheath is pushed forward along the animal by muscular movements of its body. As it passes over the female gonopores, it picks up a collection of mature eggs, and then, continuing forward, it picks up the sperm deposited in the spermathecas.

Once the mucous band is slipped over the head of the worm, its sides pinch together, enclosing the now fertilised eggs in a small capsule from which the infants hatch.

Other Annelids

Other annelids resemble the earthworm in that they are cylindrical worms divided into a series of similar segments, and they have a complex circulatory system of blood vessels, a main ventral nerve trunk, a complete digestive tube, and a coelom.

The phylum is usually divided into three principal classes: Oligochaeta, Polychaeta, and Hirudinea. Oligochaeta is the group that includes the earthworms and related freshwater species. The polychaetes, which are marine animals, differ from the earthworms and other oligochaetes in a number of ways.

The most striking difference is that they typically have a variety of appendages, including tentacles, antennae, and specialised mouthparts. Each segment contains two fleshy extensions, parapodia, which function in locomotion and also, because they contain many blood vessels, are important in gas exchange.

Many polychaetes live in elaborately fashioned tubes constructed in the mud or sand of the ocean bottom. Usually the sexes are separate, fertilization is external, and the larvae are freeswimming. Hirudinea are the leeches, which have flattened, often tapered, bodies with a sucker at each end.

Bloodsucking leeches attach themselves to their hosts by their posterior sucker, and then, with their anterior sucker, either slit the host's skin with their sharp jaws or digest an opening through the skin by means of enzymes. Finally, they secrete a special chemical (hirudin) into the host's blood to prevent it from coagulating.

PHYLUM MOLLUSCA: MOLLUSKS

The mollusks constitute one of the largest phyla of animals, both in numbers of species and in numbers of individuals. They are characterised by soft bodies within a hard, calcium-containing shell,

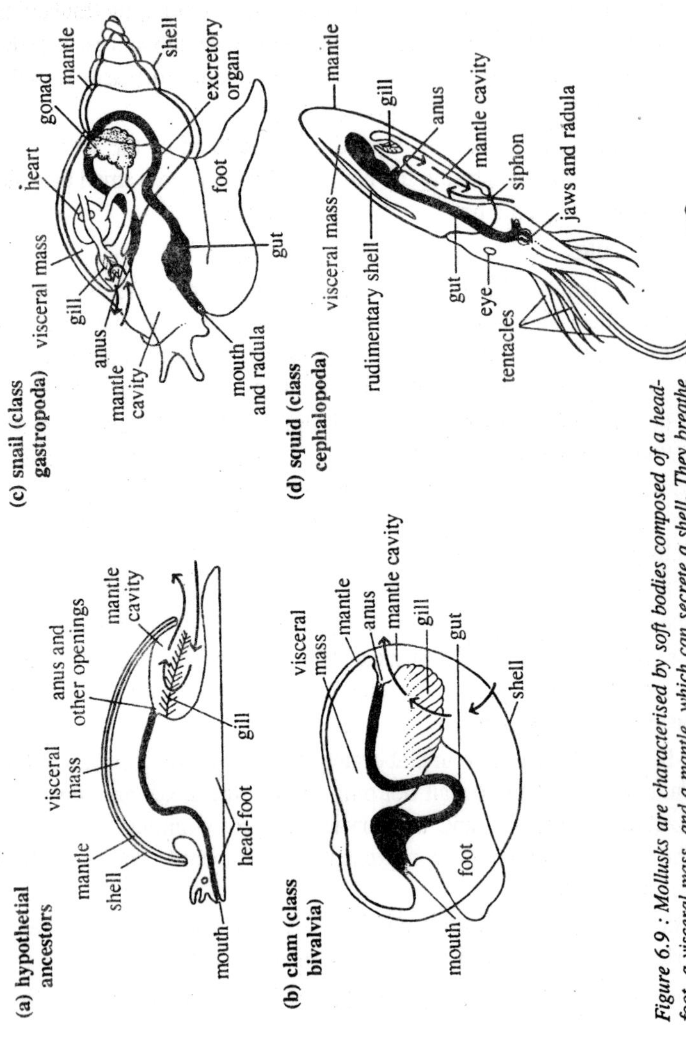

Figure 6.9 : Mollusks are characterised by soft bodies composed of a head-foot, a visceral mass, and a mantle, which can secrete a shell. They breathe by gills, except for the land snails, in which the mantle cavity has been modified for air breathing.

although in some forms the shell has been lost in the course of evolution, as in slugs and octopuses, or greatly reduced in size and internalised, as in squids.

There are three major classes of mollusks: (1) the gastropods, such as the snails, whose shells are generally in one piece; (2) the bivalves, including the clams, oysters, and mussels, which have two shells joined by a hinge ligament; and (3) the cephalopods, the most active and most intelligent of the mollusks, including the cuttlefish, squids, and octopuses.

The basic molluscan body plan is shown in figure elsewhere in this chpater. As you can see, this hypothetical animal was bilaterally symmetrical and segmented.

Among modern mollusks, only the chitons, a relatively small group, bear any obvious resemblance to the archetypal model, but modern mollusks, although diverse in size and shape, all have the same fundamental body plan.

There are three distinct body zones: a head-foot, which contains both the sensory and the motor organs; a visceral mass, which contains the organs of digestion, excretion, and reproduction; and a mantle, which hangs over and enfolds the visceral mass and which secretes the shell.

The mantle cavity, a space between the mantle and the visceral mass, houses the gills; the digestive, excretory, and reproductive systems discharge into it. Water sweeps into the mantle cavity (propelled in the bivalves by cilia on the gills), passing through the gills and aerating them. It then passes by the nephridia, gonopores, and rectum, which are always downstream from the gills.

Water leaving the mantle cavity carries excreta and, in season, gametes. The digestive tract is far more convoluted and so provides more working surface than that of the annelids.

In all mollusks, the digestive tract is extensively ciliated, with many different working areas. Food is taken up by the cells lining the digestive glands arising from the stomach and the anterior intestine, and then is passed into the blood.

A characteristic organ of the mollusk, found only in this phylum, and in all classes except the bivalves, is the radula, a tooth-bearing strap of movable pieces of chitinous tissue covering the tongue.

The radula apparatus, which operates with a rhythmic back-and-forth movement, serves both to scrape off algae and other food materials and also to convey them backward to the digestive tract. It is also used in combat.

Mollusks, as we noted previously, have gills. To understand the basic plan of gill structure and function, it is necessary only to recall the moist epidermis of the earthworm, through which oxygen diffuses, and the blood vessel lying close beneath it, which transports the oxygen to other parts of the body. A gill is a structure with an increased amount of surface area, through which gases can diffuse, and a rich blood supply for transport of these gases.

Oxygen diffuses inward, along the gradient, because the cells of the animal have removed oxygen from the bloodstream by cellular respiration. Carbon dioxide, produced by cellular respiration, diffuses outward.

Mollusks have three-chambered hearts; two of the chambers (atria) collect oxygenated blood from the gills, and the third (the ventricle) pumps it to the oxygen-depleted tissue.

Except for the cephalopods, mollusks have what is known as an open circulation; that is, the blood does not circulate entirely within vessels-as it does in the earthworm, for example-but is oxygenated, pumped through the heart, and released directly into spaces in the tissues from which it returns, deoxygenated, to the gills and then to the heart.

Such a blood-filled space is known as a hemocoel ("blood cavity"). Cephalopods, which are extremely active animals, have accessory hearts that propel blood into the gills, and a closed circulatory system.

Class Bivalvia

In the bivalves, the two-shelled mollusks, the body has become flattened between the two shells, and "*headness*" has generally disappeared. The bivalves are sometimes called Pelecypoda-"hatchet foot"—because the muscular foot is often highly developed in this group.

A clam, using its "*hatchet foot*," can dig itself into sand or mud with remarkable speed. However, the bivalves are largely sessile forms, and many of them secrete strong strands of protein by which they anchor themselves to rocks.

Most bivalves are filter-feeding herbivores; they live largely on microscopic algae. Their gills, which are large and elaborate, collect food particles.

Water is circulated through the sievelike gills by the beating of gill cilia. Small organisms and particles of food are trapped in mucus on the gill surface and swept toward the mouth by the cilia; the gills also sort particles by size, rejecting sand and other larger particles.

The shells are held together and opened at the hinge by a strong ligament and are drawn closed by one or two large muscles connecting the two shells.

Throughout the molluscan phylum, there is a wide range of development of the nervous system. The bivalves have three pairs of ganglia of approximately equal size-cerebral, visceral, and pedal (supplying the foot)-and two long pairs of nerve cords interconnecting them.

They have statocysts, usually located near the pedal ganglia, and sensory cells for discrimination of touch, chemical changes, and light. The scallop has quite complex eyes; a single individual may have a hundred or more eyes located among the tentacles on the fringe of the mantle.

The lens of this eye cannot focus on images, however, so it does not appear to serve for more than the detection of light and dark and movement.

Class Gastropoda

The gastropods, which include the snails, whelks, periwinkles, abalones, and slugs, are the largest group of mollusks. They have either a single shell or, as a secondary evolutionary development, no shell. Another feature common to all members of this group, as compared with the ancestral mollusk, is that all of them have undergone torsion.

In other words, the internal organs, the shell, and the mantle have been twisted 180° so that in the modern animal, the mouth and anus and also the gills share the same comparatively small mantle cavity, now pointing forward instead of toward the rear.

Third, the stomach and digestive gland have become twisted upward into a spirally coiled visceral mass. In response to this displacement and consequent crowding of the internal organs, the gill and nephridium of the right side have been lost in many species.

In some close relatives of the snails, such as the slugs, the digestive tract has become straightened out again by another course of evolutionary events, in which the shell was lost but the missing organs were not regained.

Land-dwelling snails do not have gills but the area in their mantle cavities once occupied by gills is rich in blood vessels, and the snail's blood is oxygenated there.

Some snails that were once land dwellers have returned to the water, but they have not regained gills. Instead, they must bob up to the surface at regular intervals to entrap a fresh bubble of air in their mantle cavities.

Thus the mantle cavity has, in effect, become a lung. Moreover, as with all lungs, the opening is reduced to retard evaporation. Gastropods, which lead a more mobile, active existence than bivalves, have a ganglionated nervous system with as many as six pairs of ganglia connected by nerve cords.

There is a concentration of nerve cells at the anterior end of the animal, where the tentacles, which have chemoreceptors and touch receptors, and the eyes are located. In some of the animals, the eyes are quite highly developed in structure; they appear, however, to function largely in the detection of changes in light intensity, like the eyes of the scallop.

Class Cephalopoda

The cephalopods (the "head-foots") are the most highly developed mollusks. The large head has conspicuous eyes and a central mouth surrounded by arms, some 70 or 80 in the chambered nautilus, 10 in the squid, and 8 in the octopus.

The nautilus, as the only modem shelled cephalopod, offers an indication of some of the steps by which this class disposed of the shell entirely. The animal occupies only the outermost portion of its elaborate and beautiful shell, the rest of which serves as a flotation chamber.

In the squid and its relative, the cuttlefish, the shell has become an internal stiffening support, and in the octopus, it is lacking entirely.

The octopus body seldom reaches more than 30 centimeters in diameter (except on the late late show), but giant squids sometimes attain sea-monster proportions. One caught in the Atlantic some hundred years ago was 15 meters long, not counting the tentacles, and was estimated to weigh 2 tons.

Freedom from the external shell has given the mantle more flexibility. The most obvious effect of this is the jet propulsion by which cephalopods dart through the water. Usually, water taken into the mantle cavity bathes the gills and is then expelled slowly through a tube-shaped structure, the siphon; but when the cephalopod is hunting or being hunted, it can contract the mantle cavity forcibly and suddenly, thereby squirting out a sudden jet of water.

Contraction of the mantlecavity muscles usually shoots the animal backward, head last, but the squid and the octopus can turn the siphon in almost any direction they choose. In addition to the siphon, cephalopods

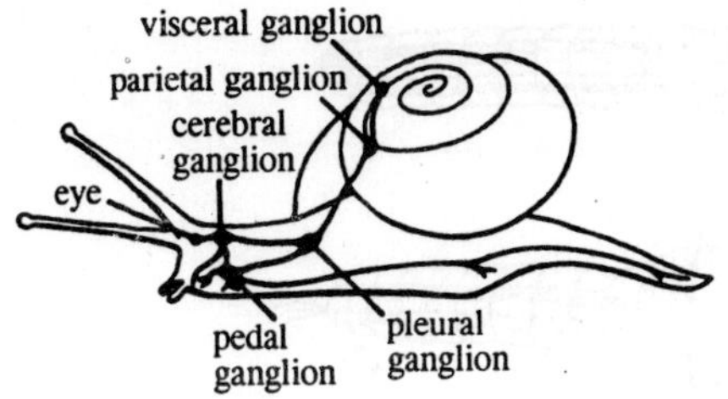

Figure 6.10 : The ganglionated nervous system of a gastropod. Each dot represents a pair of ganglia, each innervating a different segment of the body. The cerebral ganglia supply the tentacles and eyes; the pleural ganglia, the mantle; the pedal ganglia, the foot muscles; and so on.

have sacs from which they can release a dark fluid that forms a cloud, concealing their retreat and confusing their enemies.

These coloured fluids were at one time a chief source of commercial inks. *Sepia is* the name of the genus of cuttlefish from which a brown ink used to be obtained.

The cephalopods have well-developed brains, composed of many groups of ganglia, in keeping with their highly developed sensory systems and their lively, predatory behaviour. These large brains are covered with cartilaginous cases.

The rapid responses of the cephalopods are made possible by a bundle of giant nerve fibers that control the muscles of the mantle. Many of the studies on conduction of the nerve impulse are made with the giant axon of the squid, which is large enough to permit the insertion of an electrode.

Evolutionary Affinities of the Mollusks

Although the annelids and the mollusks are quite different in their basic body plans, there are some similarities between them that seem to suggest evolutionary links. One of these is the trochophore larva. Many of the annelids (the oligochaetes and hirudineans excepted) have this very distinct larval form.

Most marine mollusks (except the cephalopods) also pass through a trochophore stage in their development. Until fairly recently, the lack of unequivocal traces of segmentation in the mollusks seemed to argue against the evidence of close affinity provided by the trochophore.

In the 1950s, however, 10 living specimens of *Neopilina,* a genus of mollusks previously known only from Cambrian fossils, were dredged from a deep ocean trench off the coast of Costa Rica. *Neopilina,* which is little more than 2.5 centimeters long, resembles a combination of gastropod and chiton, with a single large shell but five pairs of gills,

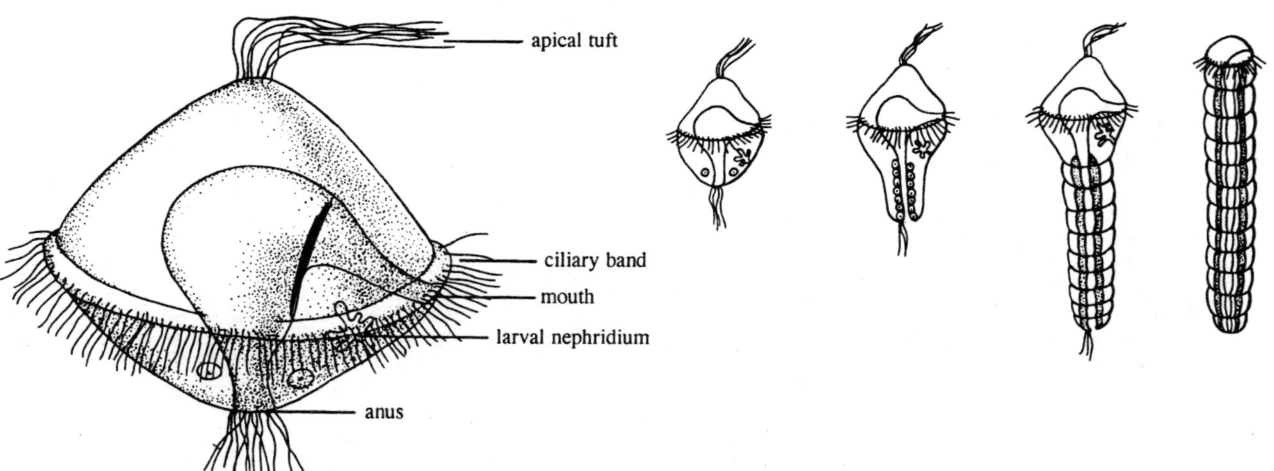

Figure 6.11 : How the annelid trochophore develops into a segmented worm. The process begins with the elongation of the lower part of the trochophore. The elongated region then becomes constricted into segments, which soon develop bristles. The apical tuft disappears, and the upper part of the trochophore becomes the head. The worm will continue to grow throughout its lifetime by adding new segments just in front of its rear segment.

five pairs of retractor muscles, and six pairs of nephridia, all arranged in what seems to be a distinctly segmental pattern.

A third link between mollusks and annelids is the pattern of embryonic development-protostomes vs. deuterostomes-which we shall discuss further at the end of this chapter.

PHYLUM ECHINODERMATA: STARFISH

The starfish and its relatives are known as echinoderms, or "spiny skins." Adult echinoderms are radially symmetrical, like most coelenterates, although the symmetry is imperfect with some traces of bilaterality in the adults and with bilaterally symmetrical larvae.

Starfish

The most familiar of the echinoderms is the starfish, whose body consists of a central disk from which radiate a number of arms. Most starfish have five arms, which was the ancestral number, but some have more.

A starfish has no head, and any arm may lead in its sluggish, creeping movements along the sea bottom. The central disk contains a mouth on the ventral surface, above which is the stomach. Like all echinoderms, the starfish has an interior skeleton that typically bears projecting spines, the characteristic from which the phylum derives its name.

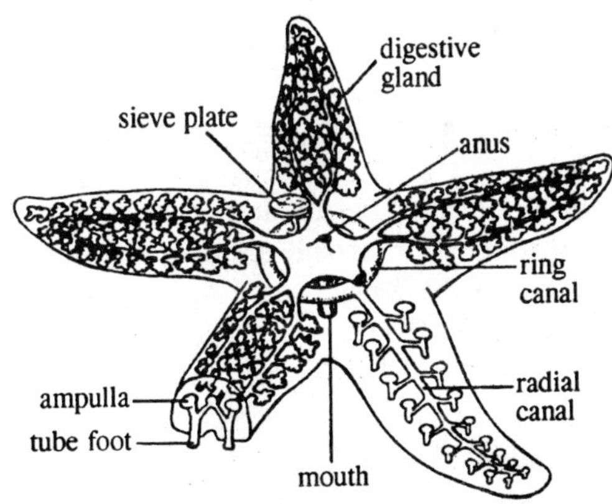

Figure 6.12 : The water vascular system of the starfish is its means of locomotion.

The skeleton is made up of tiny, separate calcium-containing plates held together by the skin tissues and-by muscles. Each arm contains a pair of digestive glands and also a nerve cord, with an eyespot at the end.

These latter are the only sensory organs, strictly speaking, of the starfish, but the epidermis contains thousands of neurosensory cells (as many as 70,000 per square millimeter) concerned with touch and chemoreception. Each arm also has its own pair of gonads, which open directly to the exterior through small pores.

The circulatory system consists of a series of channels within the coelomic cavity. Respiration is accomplished by many small fingerlike projections, the skin gills, which are protected by spines. Amoeboid cells circulate in the coelomic fluid, picking up the wastes and then escaping through the thin walls of the skin gills, where they are pinched off and ejected.

The water vascular, or hydraulic, system is a unique feature of the phylum. Each arm of a starfish contains two or more rows of water-filled tube feet. These tube feet are interconnected by a central ring and radial canals. Water filling the soft, hollow tubes makes them rigid enough to walk on.

Each tube foot connects with a rounded muscular sac, the ampulla. When the ampulla contracts, the water is forced under pressure through a valve into the tube foot; this extends the foot, which attaches to the substrate by its sucker. When the muscles at the base of the tube feet contract, the animal is pulled forward.

If the tube feet are planted on a hard surface, such as a rock or a clam shell, the collection of tubes will exert enough suction to pull the starfish forward or to pull apart a bivalve mollusk, a feat that will be appreciated by anyone who has ever tried to open an oyster or a clam.

When attacking bivalves, which are its staple diet, the starfish everts its stomach through its mouth opening and then squeezes the stomach tissue through the minute space that the starfish has made between the bivalve shells. The stomach tissues can insinuate themselves through a slit as narrow as 0.1 millimeter and begin to digest the soft tissue of the prey.

Echinoderm Evolution

The echinoderms are believed to have evolved from an ancestral, bilateral, mobile form that settled down to a sessile life, and then became radially symmetrical. The sea lilies represent this second hypothetical stage.

In the third evolutionary stage, some of the animals, as represented

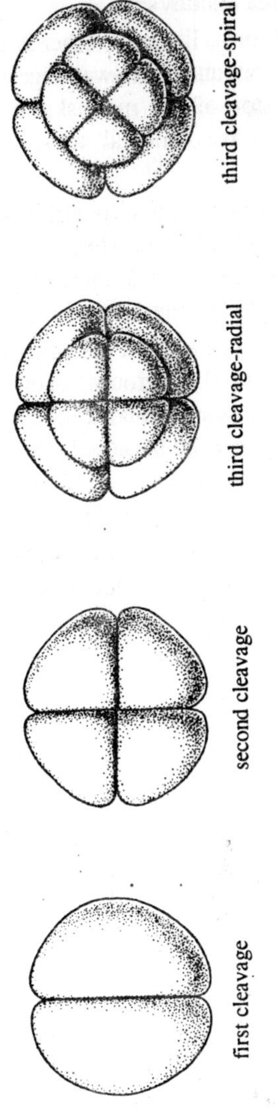

Figure 6.13 : Egg cleavages, showing radial and spiral patterns at the third cleavage. Radial cleavage occurs in deuterostomes (echinoderms and chordates); spiral cleavage occurs in protostomes (mollusks, annelids, and arthropods).

by the starfish and sea urchins, became mobile again. Following this line of reasoning, one might expect an eventual return to bilateral symmetry in this group, and, in fact, this is seen to some extent in the soft, elongated bodies of sea cucumbers.

The ancestral bilateral form, like most other hypothetical ancestors, was wormlike. It had a coelom and a one-way digestive tract. However, it differed from the ancestor of the mollusks and annelids in what zoologists consider a very fundamental way, its early embryonic development.

Among mollusks, annelids, and also arthropods, the early cell divisions of the zygote are spiral, occurring in a plane oblique to the long axis of the egg. In the echinoderms, the cleavage pattern is radial, parallel to and at right angles to the axis of the egg.

The second difference appears when the embryo becomes a hollow sphere of cells. In the embryos of both groups, an opening, the blastopore, appears. Among the mollusks, annelids, and arthropods, the mouth (stoma) of the animal develops at or near the blastopore, and this group is called the protostomes—"first the mouth."

In the echinoderms, which are called deuterostomes, the anus forms at or near the blastopore and the mouth forms secondarily. The chordates, the phylum to which we vertebrates belong, share these characteristics with the echinoderms.

7

EVOLUTION

Few people today would deny the proposition that living organisms are the descendants of organisms that lived in the past. Certainly the trees in a forest are the descendants of trees that lived in the past and produced seeds that gave rise to the present generation of trees.

Similar relationships are obvious in the animal kingdom. Most people who are at all observant will also readily admit that the offspring of a given organism is not always (and probably almost never) identical with its parents.

Organic evolution (from a Latin word, *evolutio,* meaning an unrolling), simply stated, is the concept that living organisms are the descendants, with modifications, of organisms that lived in the past. Evolution, as a division of zoology, is the study of the lines of development that the various groups of animals have taken from the remote past to the present.

In this chapter we are concerned with two aspects of evolution: the origin of life and the evidences for evolution. The next chapter will discuss the mechanisms of evolution.

ORIGIN OF LIFE

History of Concepts

The length of man's stay upon this planet has been, relatively speaking, but an hour of the time during which life in some form has been present. Only during the last few seconds of this hour has man been curious about the workings of nature. In this time he has recorded what he has seen about him and has sought a logical explanation for every physical event.

He has learned to un derstand the movements of the stars and planets, to dig into and to fly above his planet, and to breed animals and plants to provide more bountifully for his needs. He has learned to harness the power of the wind and water and of the atom itself.

While doing this he has also found time to learn many things merely for the sake of learning, things which do not contribute directly toward his own welfare, such as the fossil history of animals and plants, the chemical make-up of stars and planets, and the physical laws of the universe.

During much of this time, however, man accepted mystical explanations of life on his planet. In every culture traditions and legends have developed concerning the origin of life, and the scientific examination of these topics has been discouraged. In our own culture such legends are to some extent still with us.

There are many people, including some scientists, who still prefer to leave the topic outside the realm of scientific thought. It is not the purpose of this chapter to say that these people are wrong but merely to present for consideration the thoughts of others who have offered possible scientific explanations for the existence of life on our planet.

Even after the general acceptance of the concept of evolution, some scientists still thought that life was some mysterious force or vital spirit that set living things completely apart from the non-living. Furthermore, they thought that this force could not be studied scientifically but must be accepted on faith.

It was generally believed that life had originated at some remote period of earth's history as a sudden event, never to be repeated. Some believed that life was still being created by *spontaneous generation* in moist, dirty, or rotting areas.

Out of the failure of these ideas to stand up to scientific examination has arisen another idea-that the origin of life was not a sudden event but one that took millions of years of time and that the evolution of existing animals is merely the latest chapter of a long evolution of the earth, its elements, and its chemical compounds.

It is the development of this concept that we shall trace in this chapter. Since the history of science and scientists is really the history of scientific thought and ideas, and since the subject matter of this chapter is one of the more advanced ideas of science, let us approach it from the historical point of view.

Spontaneous Generation of Life

Today, in some rural areas, a common myth is that a hair from the tail of a white horse when dropped into water will transform into a living horsehair worm. The worm appears so suddenly and in its outward form is so much like the original white horse hair that the story seems almost plausible.

We know, of course, that there is no connection between the horse hair, which settles to the bottom of the water or drifts away, and the horsehair worm *(Gordius),* which spends the first stages of its life as a parasite in the muscles of grasshoppers and related insects. After it escapes, it is found in water. Everyone also knows that rotting animal material is soon filled with maggots, but educated people today are aware that these have hatched from the eggs of flies.

It has only been a short 200 years, however, since scientists were largely agreed that the appearance of such worms was a case of the spontaneous generation of life. Aristotle taught that insects develop from morning dew and rotting manure and that tapeworms generate from excreta from the intestinal tracts of animals.

He believed that even higher animals such as crabs and salamanders generated miraculously from wet earth and slime. He was joined in these beliefs by all the learned men of Greek civilization, and such was his authority that these ideas were accepted and expanded throughout the Middle Ages and even until comparatively recent times.

Van Helmont even wrote a recipe for the generation of mice from his dirty shirt and a few grains of wheat. He was amazed at the exact similarity between his artificially generated mice and those which he knew to have originated from the natural breeding of mice!

William Harvey, despite his brilliant and far-reaching ideas in physiology which make him one of the great men of science, and despite his important statement that all life comes from the egg, was not able to tear himself from the concept that lower forms of life, such as worms and insects, may also originate by spontaneous generation.

DISPROOF OF THE SPONTANEOUS GENERATION THEORY

Francisco Redi placed meat or fish under clean muslin coverings and demonstrated that while flies laid eggs on the muslin, maggots appeared only when those eggs were transferred to the meat and allowed to hatch. These experiments actually proved that spontaneous generation does not occur, but they failed to convince Redi, and he continued to believe that spontaneous generation was possible.

Van Leeuwenhoek's experiments demonstrating the appearance of microorganisms in various materials lent credit to the idea of spontaneous generation, although van Leeuwenhoek himself did not believe in it.

Abbe Spallanzani in 1765 (approximately 200 years ago) proved conclusively that microorganisms do not arise by spontaneous generation. He showed that boiled materials immediately sealed were never infested with such organisms, while those left open to the air were soon invaded.

Even this did not settle the issue, for the experiments of Gay-Lussac, showing that such boiled and sealed vessels contained no oxygen, were seized upon as evidence that the vital principle of life required oxygen. It was easy to say then, that spontaneous generation did in fact occur but required the presence of oxygen to do so.

Similar evidence against spontaneous generation continued to grow, but none of it was thoroughly convincing, and many scientists clung to the belief for another 100 years until Pasteur's irrefutable proofs of the fallacy.

SPONTANEOUS GENERATION IN THE DISTANT PAST

When the concept of spontaneous generation had to be abandoned, the scientific world turned to the theory that life must have existed forever, changing only in form. Those who did not accept this idea said that life must have been created at some remote period in the earth's history when conditions were different from what they are now; that is to say, if spontaneous generation is not possible now, perhaps it was at some other time in the past. Let us examine each of these views in more detail.

It was generally accepted, even long ago, that the earth had not always existed. Therefore, if life is eternal it must have existed before this planet. Such reasoning gave rise to theories of the spread of life throughout the universe. Some assumed that this planet was "seeded" from space-that primitive organisms arrived in meteorites or in other ways and, finding fertile soil here, grew and evolved to produce all the species now present.

Others thought that the "life principle" (that mysterious vital force present only in living things) was a part of the materials forming the earth and that somehow the living was separated from the non-living during the period of cooling of the newly formed earth. Most scientists were inclined toward the opinion that life on earth had originated as a sudden event, never to be repeated, at some time in the remote past when all conditions chanced to be exactly right.

This idea was advanced by A. Weisman and Haeckel and others during the late nineteenth century. Pfliiger differentiated between what he called dead or storage protein and live, protoplasmic protein, and he thought the difference was due to the presence of cyanogen groups (CN) in live protein.

He felt, therefore, that when cyanogen originated chemically, life also originated. His chemistry is no longer acceptable, but his thinking was a step in the right direction, since it suggested a pre-life evolution of chemical substances.

EARLY THEORIES OF CHEMICAL ORIGIN OF LIFE

By the beginning of the twentieth century a new type of attack was made on the problem of the nature and origin of life. Traube placed a crystal of copper sulfate in a water solution of potassium ferricyanide, causing the formation of an insoluble "membrane" of copper ferricyanide around the crystal.

This membrane is semipermeable, and, therefore, osmotic influence causes water to enter the membrane "bag" and swell it until it bursts. Fresh copper sulfate solutions streaming out through the opening in the ruptured membrane contact fresh potassium ferricyanide, and a new membrane is formed, sealing the opening.

This process continues, and as it does the membrane bag grows in size. Traube thought he had created a model of a growing cell. O. Butschli placed a drop of olive oil in a solution of potassium carbonate and observed that the droplet developed "pseudopodia" and moved about in imitation of the movements of an ameba.

Others produced models which seemed to imitate many of the properties of life; Ludac even managed to "create" things which looked much like algae and fungi. Many people felt they were creating crude living things and that the mysteries of life would soon be solved. At the same time there was growing discontent with the concepts of a sudden appearance of life on earth.

Preyer pointed out that if the earlier condition had to be different from modern conditions for spontaneous generation to have occurred, then the organisms just produced would have quickly perished, since life requires the conditions now existing.

Others pointed out that even the simplest organisms are extremely complex and that it is unlikely that such complexity could have by chance appeared suddenly under any conceivable set of conditions.

Modern Concept of Chemical Origin of Life

Because scientists did not give, up thinking about it, new concepts gradually have arisen which envision a long evolution of chemical substances before life actually originated.

These ideas have been well summarized by A. I. Oparin in his book "The Origin of Life," published in an English edition in 1938. The following discussion is based on Oparin's book.

ORIGIN OF EARTH

A number of theories attempting to explain the origin of the earth and the other planets have been suggested, but that of Sir James jeans has found the widest acceptance and is supported most thoroughly by established facts. According to his theory, some two billion years ago another star passed very close to our sun.

As that star approached, its attraction drew out a tongue of material from the gaseous atmosphere of the sun, many thousands of miles into space. As the visiting star swept past, the material became a long, cigar-shaped strand held at one end by the attraction of the sun and drawn out at the other end by the attraction of the passing star.

With time, this star drew farther away and its influence became negligible. Then the drawn-out material broke into segments which assumed orbits about the sun. Supporting this thesis is the fact that the composition of the planets closely resembles that of the atmosphere of the sun, not only with respect to the elements but also as to the proportion in which each is found.

Moreover, those planets nearest the sun and those farthest removed from the sun are small, while the intermediate planets are large, reflecting the original cigar-shape of the mass from which they condensed.

Primordial earth, composed of vaporized material from the sun's atmosphere, had a very high temperature. As it cooled the heavier materials naturally settled toward the center of the mass, thus establishing a molten core of iron, nickel, and similar heavy materials.

Most of the carbon was carried into this core, where it existed largely as C_2 rather than in the form of compounds. Similarly most of the oxygen was carried into the core in the form of oxides of metals. Nitrogen was similarly combined with the metals as nitrogen compounds.

Helium and hydrogen, being very hot and very light, were largely lost to space, thus accounting for the lesser abundance of these elements in the atmosphere of the earth than in that of the sun. Probably the little hydrogen retained by the earth was in combination with the metals of the core. Over the molten core a layer of solidifying lava rock formed, separating the core from the primitive atmosphere of the earth. This atmosphere consisted of little but superheated water vapor.

Origin of Simple Organic Chemicals

Some astronomers believe that after the earth had somewhat solidified the moon was spun off and that the Pacific Ocean basin marks the wound from which this mass of material originally came. Others have alternate theories. In any case, the moon undoubtedly was exerting its effects on the earth while the core was still thoroughly molten and covered by only a rather thin rocky crust.

The tides produced in the molten core must frequently have resulted in ruptures of the lava crust and allowed the molten materials inside to spill out over the surface of the planet. There the metal carbides and nitrides of the core material were exposed to super-heated atmosphere, and chemical reactions occurred producing hydrocarbons and ammonia respectively.

These hydrocarbons were probably of the simple aliphatic types: methane, ethane, and unsaturated, short-chain compounds. The atmospheres of some other planets of our solar system are rich in hydrocarbons and ammonia, and the atmosphere of the earth probably would have remained in this state had it not been for the subsequent appearance of life.

Secondary reactions between hydrocarbons, ammonia, and water vapor led to the formation in time of most of the other simple organic molecules, such as ketones, aldehydes, alcohols, organic acids, amides, and amines.

Evolution of Complex Organic Molecules

With further cooling, the water condensed and rained down in torrents, eventually forming oceans. The falling water, with its organic compounds, formed seas that were dilute solutions of organic compounds. If life then existed these compounds would have been quickly consumed and altered by microorganisms, but since the planet was still sterile, they continued to react with each other and with the water of the sea.

It must be remembered that all the organic reactions which occur in living things are speeded by the action of enzymes, but these same reactions can all occur, though far more slowly, in the absence of enzymes. We need only grant enough time, and every compound known in living things may appear under the conditions we have outlined.

Laboratory demonstrations of the formation of complex organic molecules under similar conditions have been carried out.

Sugars, amino acids, and other important components of protoplasm have been formed experimentally this way. It is also known that amino acids, under appropriate conditions, will polymerize to form long chains which by definition are proteins. Furthermore, these proteins have a tendency to align together, forming larger particles.

The particles formed are of a size range which classify them as colloids. Colloids have a number of interesting and unique properties. Colloidal particles tend to attract water molecules and "bind" these molecules closely.

This is not a chemical combination but merely a close physical association. When colloids of opposite electrical charge bump into each other they sometimes combine their water "shells," as shown in Figure anywhere else in this chapter. Such combinations of colloidal particles are called coacervates.

The formation of coacervate results in an even tighter "binding" of the surrounding water molecules, so that there is a definite membrane-like border between the bound water molecules and those outside the influence of the coacervate.

colloid particle with loosely bound water of hydration

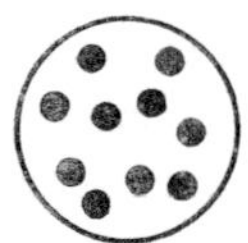

coacervate composed of a number of colloidal particles surrounded by more tightly bound water of hydration

Figure 7.1: Coacervate formation.

Moreover, the contained colloidal particles tend to orient in a definite kind of structure. Both these characteristics are necessary preliminaries to the formation of a living organism. The membranelike barrier tends to adsorb or bind on to itself various molecules that come in contact with it, and if these molecules are passed into the coacervate, they can react chemically with the contained colloids.

Such incorporation can result in growth in the size of the coacervate, as well as in increased internal complexity. It has been shown that, for purely physical reasons, if a droplet, cell, or coacervate continues to grow as a result of materials entering it, the internal forces will be greatest along the longest axis of the structure. It is hard to imagine any droplet being perfectly spherical at all times, so ultimately this factor must come into play, and the droplet will enlarge more rapidly in the direction of its greatest dimension, drawing out into a cylindrical shape.

Again under the influence of purely physical laws, when a coacervate reaches some particular length, depending upon the viscosity of its contents, it will break into two droplets. Our primitive coacervate, in attaining growth, would undoubtedly have behaved in a similar fashion and divided when it reached some critical size.

Thus, even before life existed, there was a situation very much like natural selection. Certainly the coacervate that grew most rapidly would "reproduce" its kind most often and receive the lion's share of available organic materials from the environment.

To grow most rapidly it would need the best internal structure-one which was capable of reacting efficiently with materials adsorbed in ways that increased the quantity of the colloidal materials and led to growth.

The vast majority of, if not all, substances can react as catalysts in chemical reactions. In general, impurities or combinations of substances are more efficient catalysts than are pure substances. It is not only possible but probable, therefore, that catalysts (or simple enzymes) were included in the primitive coacervates, and because competition for survival (on purely physical-chemical grounds) already existed, there would be selection for the more efficient enzymes which could most rapidly process materials adsorbed.

Further changes depended upon both the conditions in the surrounding environment and the physical-chemical makeup of the complex coacervates. Within a coacervate probably both synthetic (growth and increased stability) and degradatory (breakdown and decreased stability) reactions occurred simultaneously.

In other words the coacervate was in a state of dynamic equilibrium, as is the living cell, and required, for its further existence, the constant intake of new materials to replace the unavoidable constant outflow of degraded, breakdown materials. Until this time all the coacervates were heterotrophic, requiring preformed organic materials as "food." Probably a time came when the supply of preformed organic molecules (food) was so reduced as a result of incorporation into coacervates (feeding) that further growth and reproduction was restricted.

Perhaps at this time some coacervates, because of unique internal structure and contents, were able to use light energy in utilizing more simple molecules as "food." Thus arose the autotrophic forms. The appearance of autotrophs replenished the supply of organic materials, so that the surviving heterotrophs were again able to continue their evolution.

Prior to the appearance of autotrophs "metabolism" must have been entirely anaerobic, since elemental oxygen did not exist in the atmosphere. Autotrophic forms, however, resulted in the breakdown of oxides, releasing oxygen into the atmosphere.

This provided the opportunity for more efficient utilization of food materials by the heterotrophs in which, by chance, the mechanisms for oxidation of simple organic materials existed. Again, a primitive kind of natural selection might well account for the universal ability of animals to utilize oxygen today.

ORIGIN OF LIVING ORGANISMS

It is true that the most advanced "organism" so far postulated is still far simpler than the simplest known living organism. There was a long evolution between the complex coacervate and the simplest virus, protozoan, or algae; yet the coacervate has all the basic properties and abilities required and lacks only the complexity of structure.

The progressive stages from coacervate to organism are easier to imagine than are the earlier pre-protoplasmic stages of evolution, since they must have been much like the evolution of species after the appearance of life.

Again it should be emphasized that life did not suddenly appear at a moment when all was exactly right for its appearance, as the scientists of the last century believed. Rather, life appeared slowly over many millions of years, and if we had all of the stages spread out before us it would be impossible to put a finger on any one coacervate or organism and say, "Here is the first living thing."

Rather, as we learned in other chapter of this book, there is an indefinite boundary between the living and nonliving things that exist even today. The appearance of life undoubtedly required more time than has the evolution of the various species of living things since then.

EVIDENCE OF EVOLUTION

Since our concept of organic evolution is descent with modification, it might be well to look around us and observe many cases in which the offspring differ from the parents. We know, for example, that it is possible for dark-headed, darkeyed parents to have blond, blue-eyed offspring. While this is not evolution, it certainly suggests a mechanism that might contribute to evolution.

In a similar way observations of the structure, function, and action of various organisms and their component parts reveal a number of patterns that suggest, if they do not prove, descent with modification from some remote ancestral common parents.

The fact that large numbers of different examples have been observed and are still being observed in all kinds of biological material, lends great support to the suggestion that evolution has taken place. A huge mass of circumstantial evidence of evolution, plus the almost complete absence of observations to support any other concept, makes evolution the most logical concept so far formulated.

Some selected examples that support the concept of evolution are outlined in the following sections under the general headings of morphology, embryology, physiology, genetics, ecology, paleontology, taxonomy, and distribution.

Comparative Morphology

One of the first and most important sources of evidence for evolution comes from a comparison of the structure of various animals. Almost all living things are made up of units of structure known as cells. We have seen the basic unity of structure and processes within these cells.

We can study the cells of almost any given living organism and then generalize from these studies the characteristics of cells of other living organisms. Furthermore, we know that cells become specialized for accomplishing specific functions, that groups of like cells congregate as tissues, groups of tissues form organs, and groups of organs form organ systems.

Of course, different patterns of organization occur (a tree, a rosebush, a grasshopper, a snail, a fish), but the basic units and systems are present in all. The fact that, having similar organization patterns, organisms can be arranged in groups (e. g., dogs, wolves, coyotes, foxes) and that such groups can be gathered together in larger groups (e. g., dog group, cat group, and rat group as mammals; chickens, ducks, and hawks as birds) further implies descent from common ancestors.

We have already seen the need to distinguish between features that have resulted from common descent (homology) and those that have common functions but not common origins (analogy). For example, the vertebrates and the cephalopods are related only very distantly through ancestors that did not possess eyes.

Figure 7.2: Some vestigial structures in man.

However, the eyes of the two have many morphological features in common. If studies should reveal that these similarities have resulted from common origin (homology), then we would have to rearrange our classification in such a way that the two would be represented as being more closely related. But detailed studies of the anatomy and embryology of these eyes reveal several striking differences.

Tissues forming the nervous portion of the vertebrate eye originate as an outpocketing of the embryonic brain, while in the cephalopod all of the eye originates as a modification of the skin. The lens in both originates from the skin, but in the vertebrate the eye is made up of modified skin cells, while in the cephalopod the lens is composed of a non-cellular crystalline secretion from skin cells.

These and other major differences have led to the conclusion that the eyes of the cephalopod are analogous but not homologous to the eyes of the vertebrate. Each evolved, from separate ancestral populations, as a means of more efficient utilization of light as a source of information concerning the environment. The resemblances, then, are the result of convergent evolution in two distantly related groups.

Many examples of morphological homologies of vertebrates have been documented. Recall, for example, the similarities in the skeletal system, including the cranium with its associated parts, the vertebral column, and the appendages. Figure elsewhere in this chapter shows some of the various radial adaptations that have occurred in the homologous forelimb skeletal elements of vertebrates.

Figure elsewhere in this chapter shows how radial adaptation in one group (mammals) forms one of the bases of recognizing larger taxonomic units. Such similarities exist also in the nervous system (the brain and its parts, cranial nerves, sense organs), digestive system, circulatory system, and reproductive system, to mention but a few. All such homologies appear to be the result of descent with modification.

Vestigial Structures

A study of comparative morphology also reveals the presence, in some organisms, of structures that appear to have no purpose, and are in fact, greatly reduced in size. Such reduced and apparently useless structures, called vestigial organs, include the small external ears on whales, moles, and other aquatic and fossorial animals; the presence of eyes in cave fish and other cavedwelling vertebrates; the presence of a pelvic girdle in the boa and certain other snakes; the presence of embryonic tooth buds in birds and in the toothless whales; and the rudimentary wingbones in the flightless kiwi bird of New Zealand. All of these and a host of others are examples of vestigial organs.

For man alone over 100 vestigial structures have been listed. The semilunar fold in the inner corner of the eye is a vestigial nictitating membrane or "third eyelid," a structure that occurs widely in frogs, lizards, and birds. Muscles to move the ears (as in a dog or cat) and others to move the skin are present but are usually not well developed.

Ancestral placental mammals have three molar teeth above and three below on each side. In man, the most posterior of these teeth, the "wisdom teeth," are variable as to size, shape, and time of eruption, often never appearing at all.

At the junction of the small and large intestine is the small, finger-like vermiform appendix, a vestige of the large cecum so well developed in many herbivorous mammals such as the cow, rabbit, and rodent. The coccyx, already vestigial in six-week-old embryos, is the remnant of a tail. It consists of five poorly developed caudal vertebrae.

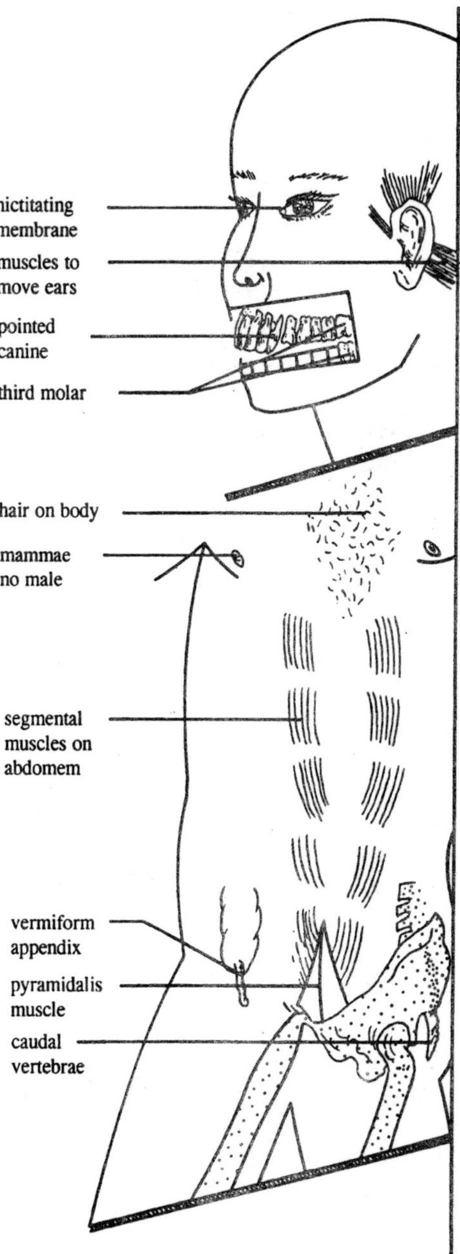

Figure 7.3: Some vestigial structures in man.

All such vestigial structures appear to be the result of descent with modifications from ancestors in which the vestigial structures were well developed.

COMPARATIVE EMBRYOLOGY

Many homologies are to be found in the comparative study of the embryonic stages of animals. We have already seen basic homologies in such features as cell multiplication by division (mitosis and meiosis), patterns of cleavage, and fate of the blastopore.

Figure elsewhere in this chapter illustrates the basic similarities that exist, especially in the younger stages, in the embryos of vertebrates. Such observations led the German embryologist, von Baer, to formulate some general "laws" of embryology.

The detailed study of embryology reveals that in a generalized way morphological stages characteristic of adults of distantly related ancestral groups occur in early embryonic stages of the mammal. Figure elsewhere in this chapter shows similarities in the circulatory system of an adult shark and a human embryo only 3 mm. in length. The embryonic mammal develops branchial arches, but the adult fate of these arches differs greatly in the shark and the mammal.

In addition to furnishing masses of data relating to probable homologies of various structures in animals, comparative embryology often furnishes the only available clues as to the relations of various highly modified organisms. For example, only embryological studies demonstrate that the tunicates (sea-squirts) are clearly chordates.

Earlier taxonomists, without the benefit of embryological studies, had the tunicates variously classified as worms and mollusks, and certain parasitic barnacles which show features characteristic of other crustaceans only during their larval stages.

COMPARATIVE PHYSIOLOGY AND BIOCHEMISTRY

In othe part of this book we considered the organs and organ systems of animals, and we saw how these structures have varied morphologically and functionally as evolutionary adaptations to specific environmental situations. Progressive functional changes accompany and parallel the structural changes we have observed, providing still further support for the concepts we have been considering.

Moreover, they show that evolution occurs on various levels simultaneously. The internal chemistry of animals evolves, just as do their appearance and behaviour. This does not surprise us, of course, since we know that the outward appearance of animals and much of their behaviour is under the influence of the gene-directed chemistry of individual cells within the organism. Lasting modification of appearance and behaviour (evolution), therefore, can only come about through changes in the genetic makeup via consequent changes in cell chemistry.

In other chapter of this book, we learned that the proteins of one animal are often "foreign" to another, so that tissue grafts taken from a donor animal are likely to be rejected by a recipient animal. In fact, in the cases we considered (rats) this was certain to happen unless the individual animals both belonged to the same carefully inbred strain.

In lower animals, however, individuals differ from each other much less, and transplanted tissues often "take" well on any individual of the same species. Sometimes grafts to other species of the same genus are possible. The possession of the same or similar proteins by two species can also be demonstrated by developing antibodies to one protein in a third species and then testing the other protein with that antibody.

Laboratory instruments are available which will characterize proteins in still other ways, and thus permit us to compare them. An example is the electrophoresis apparatus which separates proteins on the basis of differences in their electrical charges. All these techniques provide us with tools for investigating organic chemical relationships of animals-relationships which have presumably resulted from evolutionary divergence.

ECOLOGY

The various aspects of the relationships of individual organisms to their surroundings (= ecology), if now re-examined by the student, will be seen to be arranged in various levels that suggest evolution, just as do the various features of comparative morphology.

Certainly, the progression from stereotyped to learned behaviour appears to reflect an evolution of behaviour. In a similar way, the results of evolution can be seen in the development of complex intraspecific (within a species) interactions, such as in the case of social organizations.

Even in interspecific (between different species) interactions, evolution is evident in the development of complex positive relationships such as mutualism and negative relationships such as parasitism.

Taxonomy and Distribution

As we saw in other chapter of this book, one of the aims of taxonomy as a discipline is to arrange organisms in groups that will

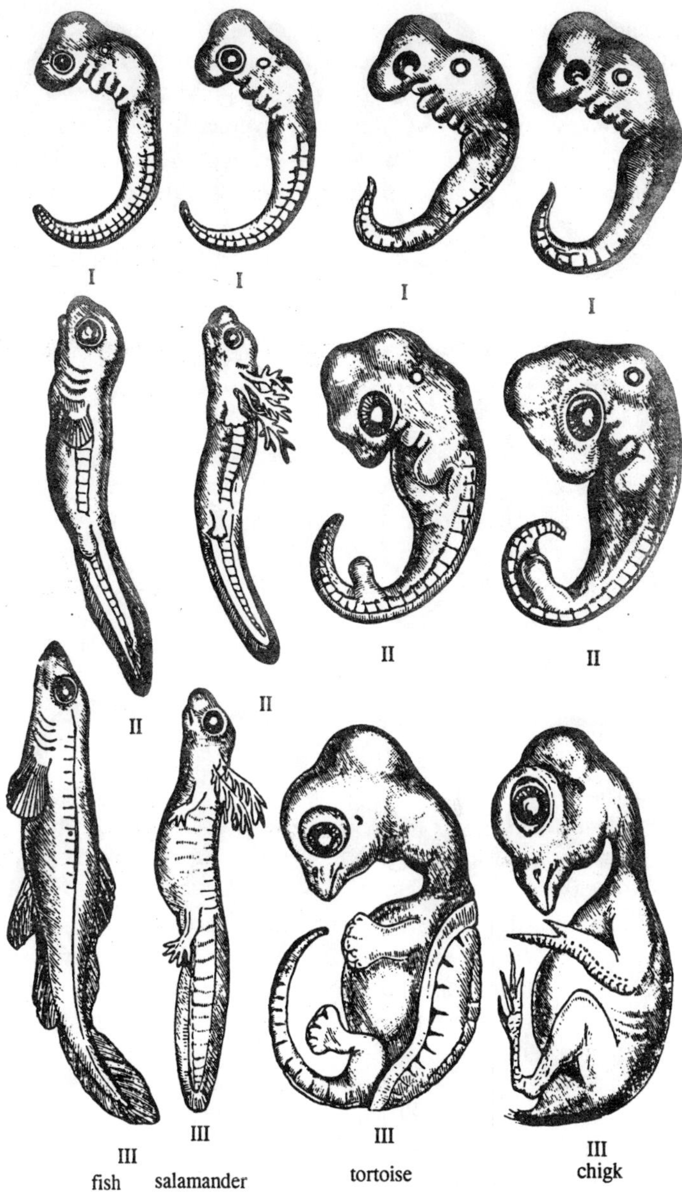

Figure 7.4: (a). Figure continue on next page.

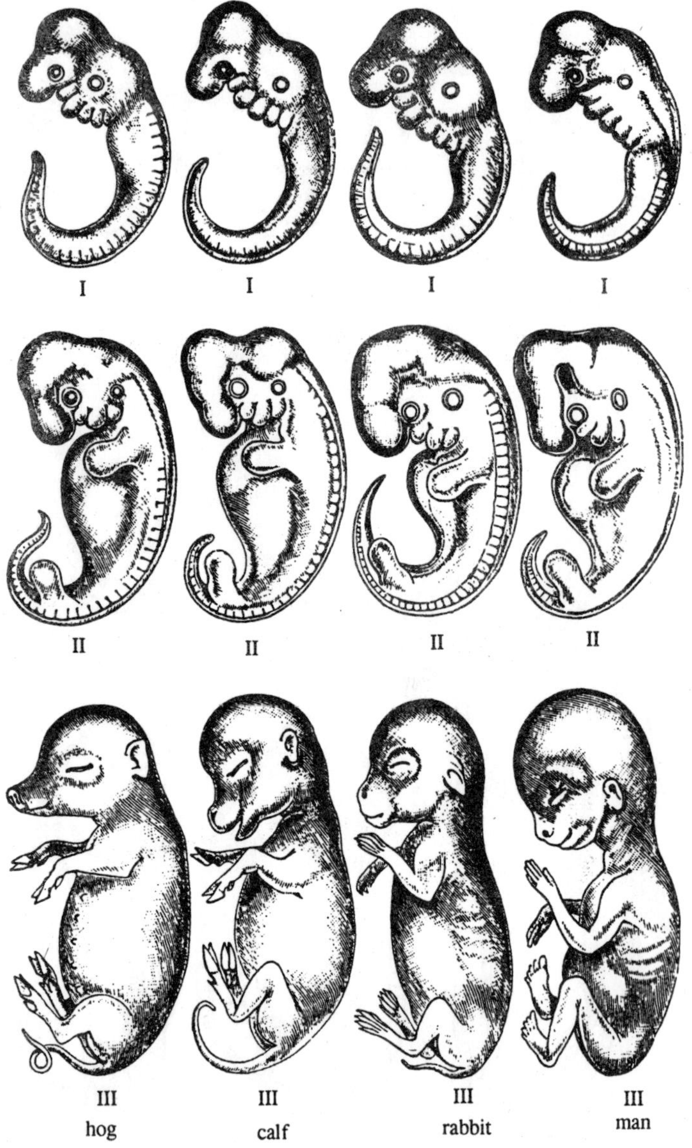

Figure 7.4 (b) : Three successive stages of a number of different vertebrates illustrating that early stages are very similar and that the closer the relation between the groups, the later specific differences develop. All embryos are drawn so as to eliminate differences due to size.

express their homologous inter-relationships. From this viewpoint, it is not logical to use taxonomy as evidence for evolution. On the other hand, the fact that organisms are usually classifiable on this basis implies that evolution has occurred.

Geographic distribution offers fairly convincing evidence for the concept of evolution. Similar areas separated widely and by large geographic barriers, as South America and Africa are, usually possess biotas that are quite different (although some, by convergent evolution, may have features in common).

Furthermore, fossils from each region indicate that the differences have been present for some time, and that the separated regions have each developed (by evolution) their own characteristic biotas. Such differences are expressed in the biogeographical realms.

Discontinuous geographical distribution of morphologically similar or even identical organisms often occurs. Alpine species on the tops of isolated mountains often are identical with species usually found great distances to the north in arctic or subarctic situations. Considering the fact that there have been climatic shifts in the past (such as glaciation), it appears that these discontinuous distributions represent formerly continuous ones.

No more complicated natural or mystical explanation is required. Living organisms on islands also represent discontinuous distribution that supports the concept of evolution. In general, islands have fewer kinds of organisms in their biotas than do adjacent mainland areas.

The species present on the island are usually those that have great powers of dispersal (i.e., probability of successful movement over adverse habitats). Organisms that have stages in their life cycle that can pass undigested through the intestine of a bird (such as many kinds of seeds) or cling in mud to the feet of flying birds (such as many aquatic invertebrates) are commonly found on islands as are birds and, to some extent, bats.

Organisms with wind-borne dispersal stages, such as seeds, spores, and air-borne insects and spiders, are usually common, especially if the island is in the path of prevailing winds from the nearest adjacent mainland. The farther an oceanic island lies from the mainland, the fewer the species present. Amphibians and terrestrial mammals are rarely present on such islands.

Of course since man became such a traveler across the oceans, many kinds of plants and animals have been accidentally or deliberately introduced on most oceanic islands. When insular species show differences,

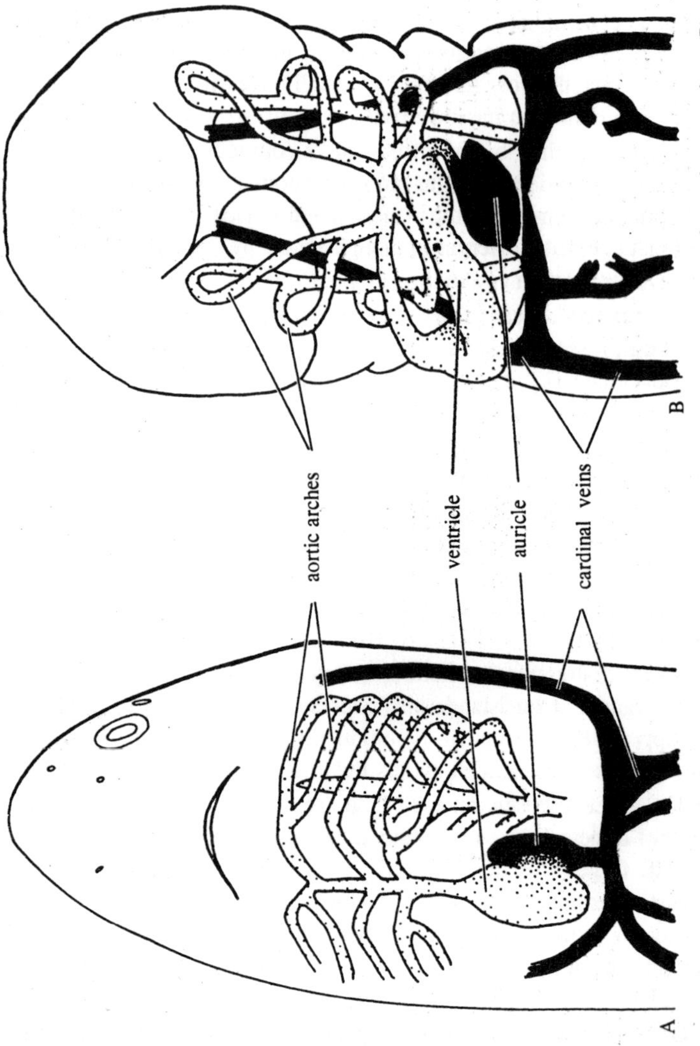

Figure 7.5: Morphological similarities in the circulatory system of an adult shark (A) and a 3 mm. human embryo (B). Note the presence of aortic arches, a two-chambered heart, and the presence of pre- and postcardinal veins.

their nearest relatives morphologically are those that are nearest geographically-on adjacent islands or the adjacent mainland. The obvious conclusion is that they have evolved from common ancestors on the mainland after being geographically isolated.

PALEONTOLOGY

The information given above strongly suggests that evolution has occurred, but on grounds of pure logic other interpretations are also possible. After all, evolution involves change over long periods of time, while all the evidence we have presented concerns organisms studied only for a short time span. Paleontology, however, gives us a very special tool for the study of evolution, for it gives us glimpses into the morphology of the plants and animals that lived in the more remote past.

If our interpretation of the data from living organisms is correct (that living organisms are the descendants, with modifications, of organisms that lived in the past), then paleontology should offer the final proof or disproof. The general evidence from the study of distribution of life in the past supports the concept that evolution has occurred.

The oldest deposits containing fossils have only the remains of very simple organisms. Progressively more recent deposits contain progressively more complex organisms (as well as simpler forms). As later and later deposits are examined, the fossils encountered resemble more and more closely the living species of our own time.

Let us examine the comparative morphology and the fossil record of a specific organism as an example. The modern horse and its relatives the zebras and asses are known as natives from the Old World (Eurasia and Africa). All the horses of the New World, including the "wild horses" and wild burros of the western United States are the descendants of horses brought from the Old World by man.

An examination of the morphology of living horses reveals that many features of their structure are highly specialized as adaptations for their particular ecological niche-that of a herbivore feeding on grasses. Since the fossil record will not show anything but features of the skeleton, adaptations of the soft tissues, of anatomy, and of behaviour can not be compared.

Several features of the skeletal system of living horses show obvious adaptation. The limbs are modified for fast running (an adaptation for escaping predators in the relatively open grasslands normally inhabited by horses) in several ways; (a) the individual bones are elongated; (b) the joints of the hip, knee, and ankle can move only in one plane and cannot be rotated; (c) many bones of the forelimbs are fused; (d) the ankle is raised high above the ground and the toes are elongate; and (e) the number of functional toes is reduced to one. This toe (the third) is enlarged, and its claw is thickened and enlarged as a hoof.

Signs of second and fourth toes persist as "dew claws" and splints of small bones. The neck is elongate and mobile, permitting the reaching down to secure grass. The teeth are adapted for nipping grass (the incisors) and grinding it up (the premolars and molars). The cheek teeth (molars and premolars) are especially modified; the teeth are rootless, so that growth can continue for a longer time; the crowns of the individual teeth are high (thus permitting a tooth that will wear for a long time on a diet of harsh grass); and the enamel cutting edges of the teeth are greatly increased by a complicated folding of the tooth.

If the assumption that modern horses evolved from more generalized ancestral parents is correct, then the fossil record should provide a series of fossils, from progressively older deposits, that show stages intermediate between the specialized living horse and the hypothetical generalized ancestors.

Figure anywhere else in this chapter illustrates some features of living horses and shows that progressively older fossils do, in fact, provide evidence to confirm our concept of evolution. Note that beginning with the oldest form shown, *Hyracotherium (= Eohippus),* there is a progressive change from a threetoed form walking on pads (such as those of the dog) to the modern one-toed, hoof-bearing horse.

Progressively the ankle is higher, the bones more elongate, the second and fourth toes further reduced, and the cheek teeth enlarged and more complex. Even the portion of the skull which is anterior to the eyes is increased (associated with an increase in size of the teeth). Figure elsewhere in this chapter shows that when all the fossil evidence is considered, horse evolution is not a case of orthogenesis (straight line evolution from A to B to C), rather horse evolution has been a complex, branch-like process (even more complex than indicated here).

Furthermore, additional paleontological study reveals that at the time *Orohippus* lived, worldwide climates were of a tropical-subtropical nature, and large grasslands did not exist. These ancestral horses were not grass-feeders (grazers) but fed on leaves and twigs of the woody shrubs characteristic of the Eocene Epoch.

From Eocene to Recent times there has been a climatic shift to cooler, drier situations, and by Miocene times the large grasslands of western North America had developed. During this time ancestors of our modern horses became modified for their modern grazing habits, moving into the newly created habitat where there were relatively few competitors.

The evolution of the horse is not the only welldocumented example that the study of paleontology has revealed. On the contrary, every college textbook of vertebrate paleontology presents hundreds of such cases illustrating the evolution of amphibians, reptiles, birds, and mammals, and textbooks of invertebrate paleontology present still more

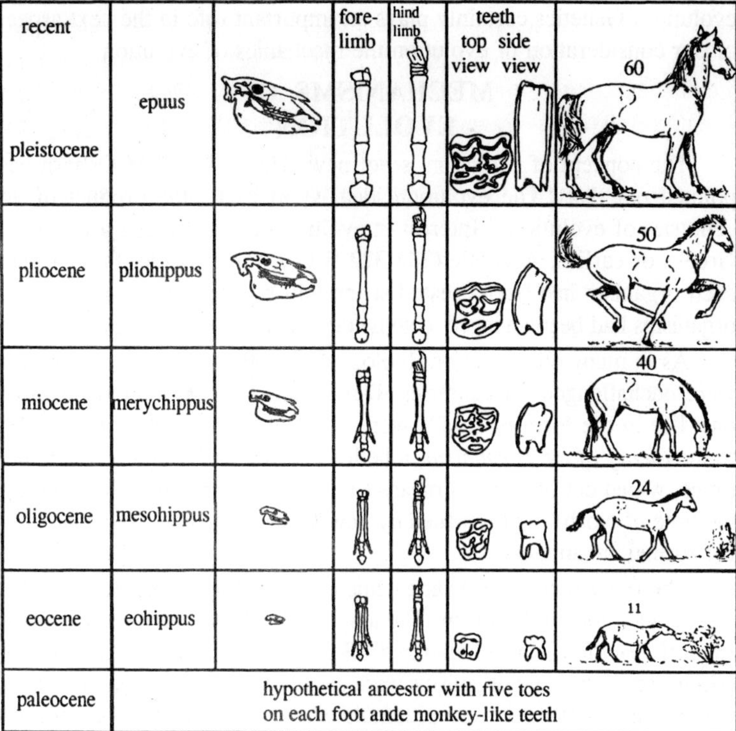

Figure 7.6: Evolution of the horse, evidence.

examples of the evolution of invertebrates.

GENETICS

Just as paleontology holds a special place in the discussion of evolution because it furnishes us with a series of time-oriented samples of past life, genetics assumes a special place because it shows a method by which evolution has come about. The field of genetics is a relative newcomer among the biological sciences.

Morphological studies have been carried on for centuries, and both physiology and embryology have been studied since the fifteenth and sixteenth centuries. Genetics, however, is just about 100 years old, and most of its contributions to knowledge have been made in the twentieth century. Genetics has done much to explain the data on evolution drawn from other fields.

Practically everything we studied in other chapter of this book (genetics) could well be reviewed here as further evidence for organic evolution. Genetics certainly plays an important role in the next aspect of our consideration of evolution-the mechanics of evolution.

MECHANISMS OF EVOLUTION

The concept of evolution is not new. Henry Fairfield Osborn has pointed out that "The evolution idea is, in itself, the product of 24 centuries of evolution." Interest in evolution can be traced back to the Greeks or earlier. Aristotle (384-322 B.C.), for example, thought that each organism had been created separately but that, once created, the organisms had been changed to some degree by a "perfecting principle."

As in many other areas of biology, Aristotle's ideas on this subject were unchallenged for centuries. During this long period evidences of past life in the form of fossils were observed. These observations led to the *theory of catastrophism*, a belief that life had been created many times, wiped out by various means (including a worldwide flood during the time of Noah), and replaced by new forms differing somewhat from the former inhabitants.

The renaissance of learning came to the biological sciences slowly, and it was not until Buffon (French, 1707-1788) that the concept of *special creation* was challenged. Buffon's studies led him to the conclusions that living organisms were easily changed by the environment, that any small changes were accumulated from generation to generation to make larger changes, and that each animal in an ascending series resulted from changes accumulated by the successive ancestors.

Erasmus Darwin added the concept that functional responses to external stimuli (such as enlarged muscles resulting from much exercise) were inherited.

Inheritance of Acquired Characteristics

The first general theory of evolution was outlined in 1802 and fully reported in 1809 by a Frenchman, Jean Baptiste de Lamarck. Lamarck was originally a botanist but is most noted for his work with the comparative anatomy of the invertebrates.

He was the first to divide the animal kingdom into the invertebrate and vertebrate portions. Lamarck's work in morphology and taxonomy led him to the conclusion that species are not constant but that they are derived from pre-existing species.

Lamarck's theory of evolution, now generally known as the *theory of inheritance of acquired characteristics*, embodied the following ideas. (1) Living organisms and their component parts tend to increase continually in size. (2) If an organ is used constantly, it tends to become enlarged, whereas lack of use results in degeneration. (3) Production of a new organ results from a new need and from the new movements which this need starts and maintains. (4) Modification produced by the above principles during the lifetime of an individual will be inherited by its offspring, with the result that changes are cumulative over a period of time.

Two of Lamarck's examples will illustrate his viewpoint. The ancestral birds were land dwellers. If such a bird were to wade about in the water in search of food, it would spread its toes in striking the water.

This continued stretching of the skin at the base of the toes and the muscular movements of the legs would force additional blood to the toes and result in the skin becoming enlarged into a web, such as is found in ducks, geese, and other water-dwelling birds. In the snake, on the other hand, Lamarck thought that continued crawling through grass would result in the body being elongate to pass through narrow spaces.

Long legs would be a handicap by interfering with crawling and would have to be folded back and not used, while short legs would be of no use in moving a long body. Thus, lack of use resulted in the disappearance of legs in snakes.

Almost from the first Lamarck's theories were challenged. The first idea, the tendency to increase in size, is correct for several known lines of descent but is not universally true. In the second idea, use may well cause enlargement of structure, as, for example, the muscles of a weight-lifting athlete becoming strengthened and enlarged, but such enlargement usually decreases when the activity is ceased, and certainly children never inherit acquired characteristics from their fathers.

The third idea, that new organs result from new needs, appears to have no foundation in fact. Lamarck thought the environment acted directly on the plants, causing the production of new features that would adapt the plant to the environment. In animals, on the other hand, he thought that the environment acted through the nervous system.

The long neck of the giraffe, he thought, resulted from generation after generation of neck stretching. Every serious attempt to test Lamarck's idea of the inheritance of acquired characteristics has yielded inconclusive results or has proven it false. Pavlov trained mice to come for food at the sound of a bell and claimed that fewer and fewer training trials were necessary in succeeding generations of mice.

MacDougall claimed similar results for rats. However, others who have analysed these data find them inconclusive, and similar tests conducted by other workers have failed to confirm Pavlov's and MacDougall's findings. One classic experiment consisted of severing the tails of successive generations of mice at birth (thus insuring lack of use throughout their lives). Even after more than 50 generations, not only did the newly born mice have tails, but the tails were just as long as those of their remote ancestors.

THE BIOGENETIC LAW

In 1821, Meckel pointed out that the embryos of higher animals pass through stages that resemble lower animals. In 1834, Karl Ernst von Baer changed the comparison to point out that the embryos of high and low types are more similar than are their adult stages. Von Baer states his beliefs as four principles. (1) General characters appear in development before special characters. (2) From more general the less general and finally the special characters of an individual appear successively. (3) An animal, during its development, departs progressively from the form of other animals. (4) Young stages of an animal are like the young or embryonic stages of lower animals but not like the adults of those animals.

It is a curious quirk of fate that von Baer was an ardent antievolutionist and that while he did not interpret his findings as supporting evolution, others did.

Theroy of Natural Selection

In 1858, two Englishmen published jointly, in the Proceedings of the Linnaen Society, papers on a new concept of evolution. This concept, the theory of natural *selection*, was destined to greatly influence the thinking of modern man in many different fields and to become the basis of most modern biological concepts of evolution.

One of these men, Alfred Russel Wallace was a naturalist who had traveled widely in tropical South America and southeastern Asia. In early 1858 Wallace was working on the island of Ternate in the Dutch East Indies (now Indonesia), when in February, he became ill with a fever.

During an attack of the fever he happened to think of an "Essay on Population" by Malthus and the large diversity of plants and animals that he had been observing, when, as he said, "Suddenly there flashed upon me the idea of the survival of the fittest." He thought about the theory throughout the fever and wrote a rough draft of the concept that same evening. Soon afterward he finished his short essay, "On the Tendency of Varieties to Depart Indefinitely from the Original Type," and sent it to Charles Darwin in England.

Charles Darwin (1809-1882) was independently wealthy. The son of a physician, he hay spent a number of years in private schools any two years in medical school. Darwin, too, had traveled widely in the tropics. He had spent almost five years, December 27, 1831, to October 2, 1836, on a voyage around the world and had written books about his observations on nature, including Journal of Researches, The Structure and Distribution of Coral Reefs, Geological Observations on Volcanic Islands, Geological Observations on South America, and A Monograph on the Cirripedia [Barnacles, living and fossil].

Darwin had already arrived independently at the concept of natural selection, and as early as 1844 had written out a summary of the theory but did not publish it. Rather, Darwin had proceeded to gather evidence, both from original research and from the writings of others, to support the concept. Perhaps he was well aware of how Lamarck's earlier theory had been received and wanted all possible supporting evidence before publishing his own new theory.

In any case, we can easily imagine Darwin's consternation upon receiving Wallace's essay. Upon the insistence of the geologist Charles Lyell and the botanist Joseph Hooker, Darwin prepared an abstract of his conclusions for joint publication with Wallace's essay. These papers were published in 1858.

The following year, 1859, Darwin published his findings in full in a book, The Origin of Species by Natural Selection, or the Preservation of Favoured Races in the Struggle for Life. This book has been judged by many as the most important book of the nineteenth century, since it contained overwhelming evidence of the fact that evolution has and does occur, and presented a logical theory regarding the major mechanism of evolution-natural selection.

The concept of evolution was nothing new, but unlike earlier writers, including Lamarck, Darwin presented such a well-marshaled mass of evidence that most learned men and many laymen were convinced for the first time of the fact of evolution.

Darwin's theory to account for evolution, natural selection, was not quite so generally accepted but did stimulate much research devoted to investigating it.

According to Darwin's theory, there are in brief three major steps in natural selection. (1) More plants and animals are produced than survive. (2) Variations of all grades exist in these plants and animals. (3) A struggle occurs for mere existence, and as a result of this natural selection there is a "preservation of the favoured races."

Pangenesis

Just after the appearance of Darwin's books a few biologists were critical of the theory on the ground that Darwin could *not point* out *a single* example of evolution in progress or explain how variations were passed on to the offspring. To help correct this obvious deficiency, Darwin, in 1868, presented his "provisional hypothesis of pangenesis."

This theory assumed that all the organs, and perhaps all the cells, in the body of an animal produced miniatures of themselves. These miniatures, called gemmules or pangenes, were shed into the blood stream and carried to the sex glands, where they were assembled to form sex cells.

In this manner, environmental changes would produce modified organs, which in turn would produce modified gemmules that would transmit the change to the next generation.

The pangenesis hypothesis was easy to check. Galton, in 1875, and others at later times made a series of experiments involving blood transfusions and, later, transplants of ovaries between black and white varieties of rabbits and chickens.

Gametes produced by the transplanted ovaries were consistent with the phenotype of the individual in which the ovary originated-and not with the animal currently carrying the ovary. Blood transfusions had no effect on the gametes produced. These experiments readily demonstrated that the pangenesis hypothesis was incorrect.

The Romantic Period

"Darwinism," as the theory of natural selection came to be called, was subjected to a series of unscientific attacks which have continued for years. Even today we hear occasional criticisms by some individual or small group attempting to ridicule the Darwinian concepts and even the fact of evolution.

In general, among biologists and other scientists, there was an enthusiastic acclaim for Darwinism and an uncritical acceptance of anything that was claimed to support the theory. In England, T. H. Huxley and Herbert Spencer were active proponents of "Darwinism." In fact, it appears to have been Spencer who coined the phrase "the survival of the fittest."

In the United States, David Starr Jordan, an ichthyologist, and Asa Gray, a botanist, saw adaptive significance in every organic structure. In Germany, Ernst Haeckel, a taxonomist, and August Weismann, an embryologist, were great supporters of Darwinism. In 1866, Haeckel

Table 7.1: The Gastrea Theory of the Origin of the Metazoan Animals.

Phylogenetic Stage, According to Gas tree Theory	*Supposed Equivalent Embryological Stage*
Arneboid ancestor, perhaps *Amoeba*	Amneboid ova of sponges and some coelenterates (other ova specialized modifications)
Synarnoeha-a hypothetical colony	Morula (solid ball of cells)
Blastea-a hypothetical volvox-like colony of ameboid (and not flagellated) cells	Blastula
Gastrea-a hypothetical animal of two cell layers, the inner layer digestive in function, the outer layer flagellated	Gastrula
Development of third germ layer and elongation into worms much like living *Turbellaria*	Advanced embryonic stages
Origin of advanced, celomate invertebrates and chordates by diversification	Adult organism

restated von Baer's biogenetic law as, "Ontogeny is a brief and rapid recapitulation of phylogeny."

His gastrea theory is a literal interpretation of the biogenetic law-the life cycle of an individual is a brief and rapid review of the evolutionary ancestry of that individual. Table anywhere else in this chapter summarizes the early stages that are part of the gastrea theory.

The Agnostic Period

Because of a number of factors, the Romantic Period was followed by a period of time during which evolution was recognized as a fact but natural selection was largely discounted as a mechanism of evolution. One factor casting doubt on natural selection was the publishing of many papers giving "evidences" of it that were not evidences at all but merely overly enthusiastic interpretations and even false statements.

The discovery (or actually, the rediscovery) of Mendel's laws of heredity in 1900, together with an incomplete understanding of genes (genes were thought to be permanent, unchanging structures), evoked still further doubts about natural selection. A Danish botanist, Johannsen

(18571927), in 1909 published results of experiments with pure-line inheritance of size in beans.

The beans used by Johannsen, like the sweet peas used by Mendel, reproduce mostly by self-pollination. The beans produced by a single self-fertilizing bean plant were assumed to be pure-line. When large beans were picked from a random sample, their descendants averaged larger than pure-line descendants from small beans.

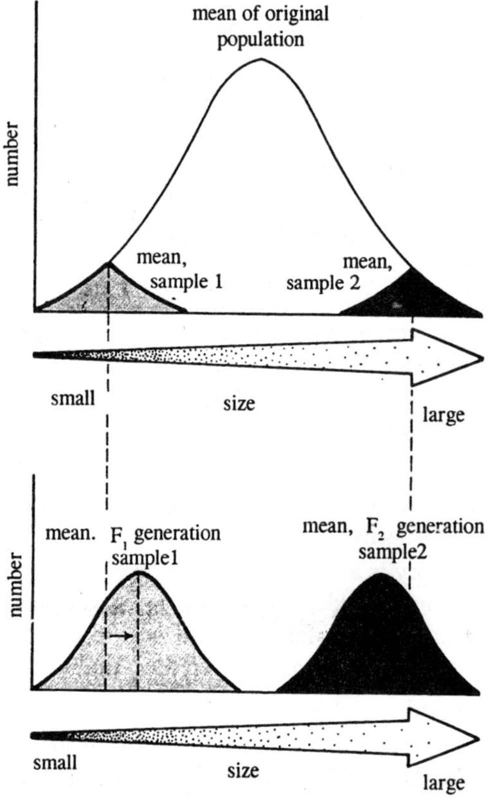

Figure 7.7: The selection as seed stock of small beans and large beans from a large random sample of beans results in the production of offspring of two different size groups.

Within each pure-line, however, there was always a range of variation in size resulting from variations in the environment (including nutrition, sunlight, temperature, soil, moisture, and other such factors). When large and small beans were planted from a single pure-line stock, the range of size in the beans produced was almost identical.

From this Johannsen concluded that selection is effective only in

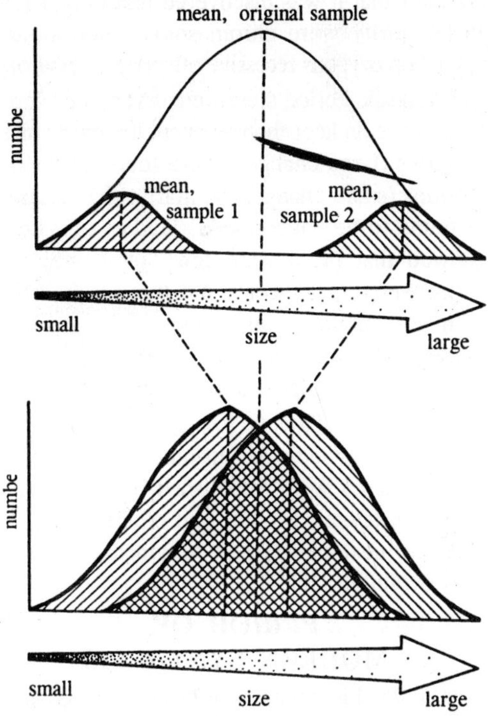

Figure 7.8: The selection as seed stock of small beans and large beans from the beans produced by a pure-line stock results in offspring that are little if any different in average size.

stocks that contain genetic variability and that variability produced by the environment was unimportant in evolution. From this view, all selection could do was isolate some of the genotypes already in the population.

As early as 1901, H. De Vries developed the mutation theory of evolution that was based on the sudden appearance of "sports" or freaks among domestic plants and animals, such as the sudden appearance of a short-legged sheep from normal parents. Darwin had been aware of such "sports," but considered them so rare as to be of little importance in evolution.

De Vries, however, took the position that evolution regularly proceeded by large, sudden, and distinct changes which he called mutations. He supported the mutation theory with examples of changes in the evening primrose that grew in his garden.

These mutations De Vries considered to be new species, and it was not until years later that it was discovered that only a few were actual mutations; the majority were chromosomal aberrations (triploids or tetraploids) or the homozygous recessive offspring of heterozygous parents.

During the Agnostic Period there were several developments destined to have great influence on later thought about the mechanics of evolution. (1) Macromutations (large changes) were found to be extremely rare. (2) Micromutations (small changes) similar to the variations studied by Darwin were found to be common. (3) Studies of wild species in the laboratory showed that there were few "pure-lines" in nature. (4) Taxonomists discovered that species in nature rarely differed by only a single trait or macromutation; rather, most differed in a large number of smaller, genetically controlled traits. (5) Statistical methods were applied to the genetics of populations of wild species.

During this period, relatively few studies were made concerning evolution as such, but as indicated in other chapter of this book, the bases of modern genetics were established by such men as McClung, Castle, Morgan, Sturtevant, Muller, and others. Such studies laid the foundations for the next period and provided a background for the genetic basis of evolution.

PERIOD OF MODERN SYNTHESIS

Since about 1925, biologists have become increasingly aware that evolution is a complex process that results from mutations and selection. The modern interpretation of the evolutionary process has come to be known as Neo-Darwinism. Responsible for the rise and understanding of Neo-Darwinism are such brilliant biologists as the Englishmen J. S. Huxley, R. A. Fisher, and J. B. S. Haldane and the Americans Sewall Wright, H. J. Muller, T. Dobzhansky, and R. B. Goldschmidt.

To help us understand Neo-Darwinism let us restate Darwin's original thesis in modern terms, adding at the appropriate places pertinent concepts that have been formalized since the theory of natural selection was first proposed.

(1) Biotic potential is high. This is Darwin's "more plants and animals are produced than survive."

(2) Genetic and non-genetic variations exist in plants and animals. This is Darwin's variations "of all grades."

(3) Evolution is a population phenomenon. In a medium to large-sized population of sexually reproducing biparental organisms, the genetic variation present usually persists at some given

level in a state of equilibrium; shifts in environmental conditions may exert selection pressures for or against a given genotype (Darwin's natural selection) and cause a shift in the equilibrium; and new variations in the form of genetic mutations are constantly being produced at a low rate within a given population. In small, sexually reproducing populations random recombinations of genes may shift the genetic equilibrium of the population in the absence of any change in the environment.

(4) Various levels of evolution can be recognized.

(5) Some generalized trends in evolution have been recognized.

In the following sections each of these points is considered in more detail.

Biotic Potenital

We have already seen that the biotic potential of living organisms is extremely great and that it is not possible for all the offspring produced to survive. Further examples of this large biotic potential are the oysters, which can produce 114,000,000 eggs at a single spawning, and the *Ascaris,* which has produced in the laboratory more than 700,000 eggs in 24 hours. We have already seen that most individuals of necessity do not survive, in order that the energy cycle be maintained.

Genetic and Non-Genetic Variations

That variations exist among living organisms is also well known. In fact, the chapter on genetics is almost entirely concerned with variations and with the mechanics of transmission of these variations to the next generation. Today we recognize that variations are of several different types (Darwin's "of all grades"). One classification of types of variations follows.

Non-genetic Variations

This group includes the sorts of differences that might exist between identical twins and are generally the result of differences in environment. For example, one twin might have been sick, underfed, too cold, or otherwise exposed to a different environment and as a result possess slight differences in shape, function, or behaviour. Such variations are generally conceded to be non-transmittable to the offspring. Johannsen's experiments with pure-lines of beans involved variations of this sort and adequately demonstrated that such variations are not inherited.

Genetically Controlled Variations

Geographic variations are variations associated with differences in the geographic location of the individual. Rabbits in a cold, damp climate tend to have shorter ears (thus conserving body heat) and darker colours (absorbing more heat and blending with the darker background colours) than do rabbits of the same species living in warm, dry climates. Within a given population several types of non-geographic variations may occur.

In other chatper of this book we have seen how these variations may be expressed phenotypically (phenotypic variation) or may be present only genotypically (genotypic variation) in heterozygous organisms. Some of the variations may be associated with differences in age (age variation) or sex (sexual variation).

Since more individuals are produced than can possibly survive and since variations "of all grades" do exist, it is only logical that an individual possessing some variation that gives that individual some survival advantage over others of the same species (such as getting to food first or escaping from an enemy) would in fact survive when others would not. In essence, then, this is the survival of the fittest under natural selection.

Genetic Equilibrium in Populations

Students often get the idea that dominant genes soon replace recessive genes in a population. In a large population, however, no matter how rare a recessive gene may be, it may remain (unexpressed perhaps) in a population for generations.

Recall Mendel's first law of genetics, the law of segregation, stating that whenever two different allelomorphic genes are brought together in a hybrid (in other words, a heterozygous individual), the two genes segregate into separate gametes, and each gamete is pure with respect to the character.

To see how this law works, let us assume that a population of organisms exists on an oceanicisland far removed from other individuals of the same species, thus eliminating the possibility of other genotypes entering the population under study; that the organisms being studied reproduce sexually and zygote formation is entirely at random, with any one ovum being just as apt to be fertilized by one male gamete as another; and that at the time of the beginning of our observations 25 per cent of the total population were males that were homozygous dominant for tallness (TT), 25 per cent were homozygous dominant females, 25 per cent were homozygous recessive males (tt, short), and 25 per cent were homozygous recessive females. The F_1 generation could then be determined from the chart in Table anywhere else in this chapter.

Table 7.2: Chart Showing the Percentages of the Various Genotypes in an F_1 Generation Resulting from an Equal Number of Homozygous Dominant and Homozygous Recessive Parents of Each Sex (See Text).

Sex of Parents	***Males***			
	Genotypes and percent ages of total population		TT 25%	tt 25%
		Gametes produced	T	t
Females	TT 25%	T	TT 25%	Tt 25%
	tt 25%	t	tT 25 %	tt 25%

The F1 generation will consist of 25 per cent homozygous dominant individuals (TT), 50 per cent heterozygous (Tt), and 25 per cent homozygous recessive individuals. Assuming equal sex distribution in these three groups, the frequency of genotypes in the F_2 generation will be as shown in Figure and Table anywhere else in this chapter.

Thus, we see that the F_2 proportions are exactly the same as those in the F_1. Furthermore, these proportions will be retained in all subsequent generations as long as the assumptions that we have made are true: (1) There is an equal sex distribution in the various genotype classes. (2) There is equal fertility and survival of the TT, Tt, and tt individuals. (3) Selection of mates is completely random. (4) Either mutations do not occur or the rate of mutation from T to t is the same as that from t to T.

In 1908, G. H. Hardy (an English mathematitian) and W. Weinberg (a German physician) independently developed a mathematical method of expressing this genetic equilibrium. As presently conceived, the Hardy-Weinberg law (as their findings came to be known) states that: If alternate forms of a gene (alleles) are present in a population in a given proportion, and if random mating and equal survival of offspring exists, then the original proportion will be retained in all subsequent generations, unless it is upset by some other factor such as mutation or selection pressure.

In the Hardy-Weinberg system, p is equal to the frequency of one allele in the population (T in our example) and q is equal to frequency

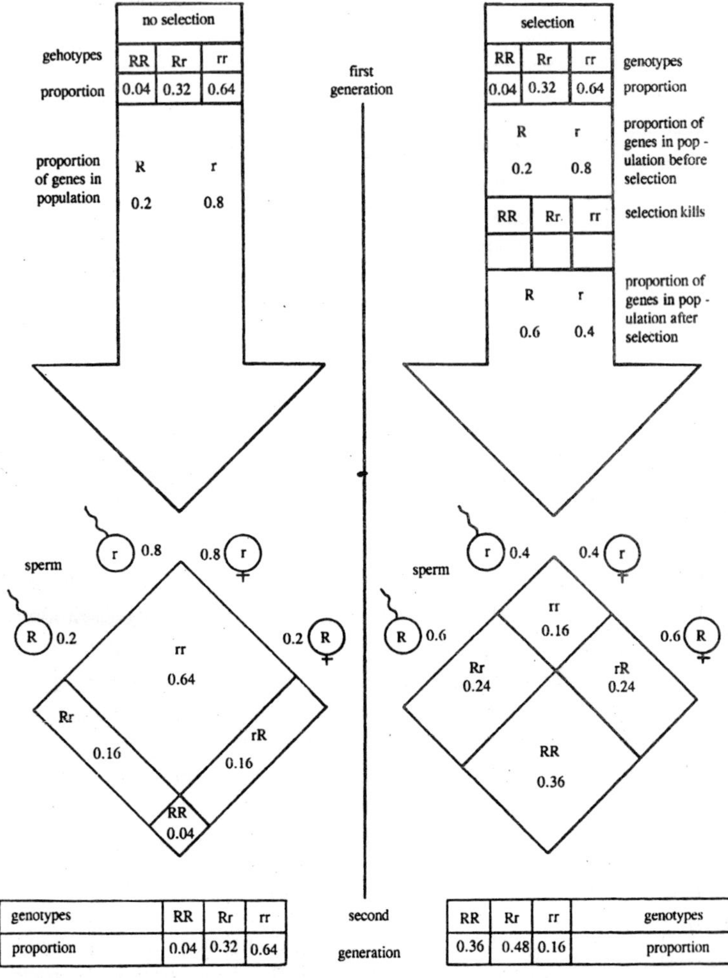

genotypes	RR	Rr	rr
proportion	0.04	0.32	0.64

RR	Rr	rr	genotypes
0.36	0.48	0.16	proportion

Figure 7.9: Effectiveness of environmental selection on a phenotype. The hypothetical situation assumes that resistance to hydrocyanic gas fumigant in scale insects results from an incompletely dominant gene.

of the second allele (t in our example). Thus, p + q would equal 100 per cent. We could then express the F_1 chart in terms of p and q, as shown in Table anywhere else in this chapter.

In other words, there would be p^2 homozygous dominants, q^2 homozygous recessives, and 2pq heterozygotes. Still using our example, we can now substitute values for p and q, for we had assumed a 50:50 ratio in our original population.

p = frequency of T (50% or 0.5)

q = frequency of t (50% or 0.5)

Substituting these values in the Hardy-Weinberg equation we find the following:

$$p^2 + 2pq + q^2 = 100\% \text{ (or } 1.0)$$

$$(0.5 \times 0.5) + 2(0.5 \times 0.5) + (0.5 \times 0.5) = 1.0$$

$$0.25 + 0.50 + 0.25 = 1.0$$

TT Tt tt

These are the exact values that we arrived at using the checkerboard method. The advantage of the Hardy-Weinberg formula is that it is not restricted in application to the sorts of problems that can be solved simply by using the checkerboard.

Consider the problems you would encounter with the use of the checkerboard method for determining the population composition of the F_1 generation if 60 per cent had been dominant and 40 per cent recessive. Using the Hardy-Weinberg formula this is simple.

$$p^2 + 2pq + g^2 = 1.0$$

$$(0.6 \times 0.6) + 2(0.6 \times 0.4) + (0.4 \times 0.4) = 1.0$$

$$0.36 + 0.48 + 0.16 = 1.0$$

TT Tt tt

The Hardy-Weinberg formula has still further applications. Assume that you find in a large population that 9 per cent of the individuals are homozygous recessive for a given trait. What percentage of the genes in the population are recessive? Using this formula, we find:

$$q^2 = 9\% \quad \underline{\text{or}}\ 0.09$$

$$q = \sqrt{0.09} = 0.3 \text{ or } 30\%$$

From this it is obvious that even though a homozygous recessive phenotype may be rare in a population, the recessive gene may be fairly common. For example, it has been estimated that only one person of each 20,000 is an albino, yet this recessive trait occurs in a heterozygous condition in about one person of each 150.

$$q^2 = 0.005\% \text{ or } 0.00005$$

$$q = 0.00005 = 0.007 \text{ or } 0.7\%$$

ENVIRONMENTAL SELECTION PRESSURES

We have already indicated that the genetic equilibrium in a population may be upset by selection pressures operating for or against given phenotypes. Let us now look for actual situations in nature where we can see this selection pressure in operation. We soon discover that such situations are rare, primarily for two reasons. (1) Most living organisms are fairly well adapted for survival in the specific environment in which they live, so that most variations in a population offer little advantage or disadvantage to the possessor. (2) Natural selection is operative over a period of generations, and studies of natural selection have been made only in the past 100 years.

Several pertinent experiments have been performed. One is based on the known fact that in many cases small rodents of a given species living in regions of light-coloured soils have light-coloured pelages (even almost white in places like White Sands National Monument, New Mexico), while those of the same or closely related species living on dark soils tend to have dark coat colours (even black on some black lava flows).

Presumably predators such as owls would cause a selection pressure favouring mice possessing coat colours matching the background. Lee R. Dice of the University of Michigan set up an experiment to test this hypothesis. Two varieties of mice were chosen that differed mainly in colour of fur. One variety was pale, almost white, in colour; the other was a dark gray.

Two open-topped cages were also prepared, one with a white sand floor that matched the colour of the light-coloured mice, the other with a gray soil floor that matched the coat colour of the gray mice. Equal numbers of light and dark mice were placed in each cage and exposed to hungry owls. In one experiment, a total of 192 mice were captured by owls, 65 per cent of which did not match the background colour.

The remaining of the captures were individuals that did match the background. Thus it is obvious that, at least in this case, coat colours contrasting with the background were selected against. It takes little imagination to visualize that in only a few generations phenotypes matching background colour might well replace phenotypes contrasting with background colour (assuming that all other selection pressures remained constant for both types).

Other examples of what appears to be selection in operation are the results of sudden major, manmade changes in the environment. A classic example occurred in the citrus orchards of California where the scale insects (Family Coccidae) were controlled by fumigating the trees with hydrocyanic gas.

A few individuals survived each treatment, but the number was so small as to be economically unimportant. By 1914, however, the usual concentrations of hydrocyanic gas failed to kill scale insects at one locality in California, and during the next few years the resistant varieties gradually spread to other regions. Genetic studies have revealed that this resistance is the result of a single incompletely dominant gene carried on the X-chromosome.

At a certain concentration of the fumigant, 96 per cent of the non-resistant insects are killed, while the same concentration kills only 55 per cent of the resistant variety. In other words, ten times as many resistant insects survived. For the sake of simplicity, let us ignore the fact that the gene is on the X-chromosome. Then we can diagram the effectiveness of selection on a phenotype.

Similar resistance to insecticides has developed in houseflies, bedbugs, and other insects. Even disease-producing bacteria develop mutant strains that are resistant to such germicides as the sulfa drugs, penicillin, and antibiotics in general. In fact, by gradually increasing the amount of penicillin in the growth media, varieties of the bacterium, *Staphylococcus aureus,* have been developed in the laboratory that can live in 250 times the concentrations that are normally fatal.

The method involves the progressive selection of mutant genotypes that add increments of resistance to the population. Fortunately for man such penicillin-resistant strains become penicillindependent and cannot survive in its absence. Some more natural experiments in selection are known. A classic case is the shift within the past 100 years of the incidence of melanism (dark colour) that has occurred in two species of moths *(Amphidasys beturaria* and *Odontoptera bidentata)* in industrial areas of England and elsewhere in western Europe.

This industrial melanism has come about as follows. The "normal" light-coloured moths are homozygous recessive for a dominant gene causing melanism. Further, the "normal" light-coloured moths are less vigorous (pliotrophic effect) than are the melanistic phenotypes.

However, in pre-industrial England and Europe the light-coloured phenotype has a great selective advantage in that it matched the background colours and usually escaped detection by the insectivorous birds. Any melanistic mutants, on the other hand, were readily detected and eliminated in spite of their increased vigor.

At that time, melanistic individuals were so rare as to be generally unknown. However, with the development of industry, much soot and other dark waste products contaminated the surrounding countryside, making the background colour much darker. Under these conditions, decade by decade melanistic moths have become more numerous, until at present certain industrial regions have only the melanistic phenotype present. Perhaps with the recent anti-smoke ordinances and the probable development of atomic radiation energy sources, the next 100 years will see a shift back to the light-coloured phenotype in these same areas.

Even such environmental factors as wind can result in selection. For example, although beetles are generally strong fliers, those on the windswept island of Madeira in the North Atlantic Ocean (600 miles from Portugal and 400 miles from Africa) are for the most part either wingless or possess wings that are useless for flight.

It is generally assumed that those kinds of beetles that fly were soon blown from the island and that any beetles possessing mutations resulting in poor flight or loss of wings had a high selective advantage; thus, the present beetle fauna consists mainly of flightless forms.

Mutations and Mutation Rates

We have already seen in our discussion of the gene theory that many genetic mutations are the result of small changes in the molecular structure of the genetic material, DNA, in the chromosome. (Large changes of this kind in genes usually result in the destruction of the gene; thus, they have little or no bearing on the problem of evolution).

Table else where in this chapter lists the estimated frequency with which some mutations arise in various organisms under normal environmental conditions. Under the influence of various stimulants, known as mutagens, mutation rates are much higher.

Such mutagens include x-rays, atomic radiation, and other types of hard radiation; heat (mutation rates in *Drosophila* are doubled or trebled for each 10° C. rise in environmental temperatures); mustard gas [one of the "war gases" $(Cl \bullet CH_2 \bullet CH2)_2S$]; formalin; urethane; and many others. Even certain genes in *Drosophila* have been discovered to increase mutation rate in other genes on the same and other chromosomes.

Not all gene mutations result in changes from a "normal" to a "mutant" gene. Many examples from laboratory experiments with *Drosophila, Neurospora* (bread mold), and bacteria demonstrate conclusively that reverse mutations occur, changing the "mutant" gene back into a "normal" gene.

GENETIC DRIFT

In the two preceding sections we explored the behaviour of genes in populations of infinitely large size. In extremely large populations, chance may result in some slight deviation from the ratios of gene frequencies predictable for a given generation by the Hardy-Weinberg

Table 7.3: Rates at which Various Mutations Have Been Estimated to Arise.

	Trait	*Action*	*Approximate Mutation Rate per 1,000,000 Gametes*
Man	Hemophilia	Recessive; on X-chromosome	20 to 30
	Chondrodystrophy	Recessive; dwarfism resulting in short legs and arms but normal head and body	40
	Epiloia	Recessive; tuberous sclerosis	6
	Amaurotic idiocy		6
	Aniridia		8
	Retinoblastoma		14
	Thalassemia		400
	Sickle-cell anemia		1000 in American Negroes
Corn	B	Color factor	492
	I	Color inhibitor	106
	P_2	Purple color	11
	Su	Sugary seeds	2.4
	Y	Yellow color	2.2
	Sh	Shrunken seeds	1.2
	WX	Waxy seeds	Less than 0.5

formula ($p^2 + 2pq + q^2 = 1$), but such deviations normally will be so small as to be negligible.

It is obvious that most populations are not infinitely large. When the nonbreeding individuals (the aged, sick, and sexually immature) are considered, the effective breeding size of most populations is probably quite small.

Consider, however, the possible effects of chance in a small population of 100 individuals. If a given allele were to occur only once in the population, then chance alone could easily eliminate it in a single generation. Conversely, chance might increase the allele many times, even to 10 per cent of the population.

This genetic drift or Sewall *Wright effect* occurs without respect to the selective advantages or disadvantages (as long as it does not cause immediate death) to the possessor of the allele. In small populations, genetic drift supersedes the action of selection pressure. Many alleles are lost and most small populations are more homozygous than are large populations. Furthermore, many small populations are relatively poorly adapted to their environment. Such situations may well develop into evolutionary blind alleys.

R. C. Stebbens has pointed out the "*bottleneck*" effect, a corollary of the Sewall Wright effect that is often overlooked by biologists. In other chapter of this book we saw that there tends to be a balance of nature and that any given species of organism tends to maintain a characteristic population level year after year.

Every field biologist is aware, however, that among organisms having short life spans, populations actually fluctuate drastically from year to year, while organisms having longer life spans show similar large fluctuations over longer periods of time.

In terms of the evolution process these "bottlenecks" assume great importance, for only the reproductively active survivors in the low populations can pass on genetic material to the later, larger populations. Genetic drift during the time of a bottleneck may well result in the wide distribution in a large population of one or more non-adaptive phenotypes.

The Evolution Process

We have seen that we can describe mathematically the genetic stability in a hypothetical population existing under assumed conditions. If we let p be the frequency of one allele and q the frequency of a second allele, the genes in a population can be described by the Hardy-Weinberg formula as: $p + q = 1$, and the phenotypes in a population as: $p^2 + 2pq + q^2 = 1$.

We saw that there are various factors operating in most populations that change this formula. One of the simplest possible changes would be a mutation of some of the p alleles to form q alleles. This we can represent as $p \rightarrow q$. Furthermore, we have discovered the q alleles may mutate back into p alleles. This we can represent as $p \leftarrow q$ and the two simultaneous processes (in terms of the whole population) as $p \rightleftarrows q$. We also found that for certain traits mutation rates have been estimated.

Let us assume that we have a population of corn homozygous for gene R controlling seed colour. The mutations rate of $R \rightarrow r$ has been found to be 492 per million gametes. If we let Op equal the rate of change in gene frequency for R as a result of this mutation and r represent the mutation rate, then the gene frequency in the population would change from one generation to the next, as follows:

$\Delta p = -\mu p$

In the first generation, we find the following:

$\Delta p = -(0.492 \times 10^{-4})\ 1.0$

$\Delta p = -0.0000492$

$p = 1.0 - 0.0000492 = 0.9999508$

$q = 0.0000492$

If this mutation rate were not opposed by other forces (such as reverse mutation rates, $Oq = -\mu q$, and selection pressures) an equilibrium would be reached only when the entire population became homozygous for q.

Selection pressure is another factor influencing the gene frequency in a population. Now let us assume a hypothetical situation in which p is dominant to its allele q, and at a given time the gene frequencies are as follows: $p = 0.9$, $q = 0.1$.

Furthermore, let us assume that the homozygous recessive phenotype is selected against in such a way that one of each 100 individuals did not survive until sexual maturity. We can express this mathematically as s (selection pressure) = 0.1. Since selection in our example operates only on the homozygous recessive genotypes, the change in gene frequencies would be as shown in Table elsewhere in this chapter.

Table 7.4: The Effect of Selection of a Given Level on Changes in Frequencies of Genes in a Population.

Genotypes	*pp*	*pq*	*qq*	*Total*
Adaptive value of genotype	1	1	I - s	
Initial gene frequency	$p^2 = 0.81$	$2pq = 0.18$	$q^2 = 0.01$	1.0
Frequency after selection	$p^2(0.81)$	$2pq(0.18)$	$(1 - s)g^2(0.009)$	0.999

The frequency of p and q in the next generation would be:

$$\frac{p}{p=(1-s)q^2}0.901$$

$q = 1 - p$

Table anywhere else in this chapter shows the effects of various levels of selection pressure on a hypothetical population wherein p and q were equally distributed when the selection pressure was first applied. Note that the negative value of s implies that selection favours the phenotype.

Since mutation rates and selection pressures usually operate simultaneously, we are now ready to incorporate both into a single formula.

Table 7.5: Changes in Gene Frequency Resulting from Various Levels of Selection Pressure.

s	*1.0*	*0.6*	*0.1*	*0.01*	*– 0.5*
W = adaptive values of genotype	0	0.4	0.9	0.99	1.5
Frequency of p before selection	0.5	0.5	0.5	0.5	0.5
Frequency of p after selection	0.67	0.58	0.5128	0.5012	0.444
Increment of change in frequency of p	+0.17	+0.08	+0.0128	+0.0012	-0.056

The result is:

$$Aq = \mu p - sq^2 (p)$$

wherein Aq is the rate of change in the frequency of gene q in the population (in other words, evolution); pp is the measure of the rate of mutation of p → q minus the rate of mutation of p ← q; and sq^2 is the gain or loss of q alleles through selection pressures. Since still other factors influence changes in frequencies of alleles, the whole process is best indicated by a diagram.

LEVELS OF EVOLUTIONARY CHANGE

Biologists have long recognized two basic patterns in evolution-sequential evolution and divergent evolution. The mere recognition of the two may tend to overemphasize their differences in the minds of some students, for divergent evolution is dependent upon the same processes as is sequential evolution.

The major difference between the two is the reproductive isolation, by one or more of the several means to be discussed below, of segments of the original population in a divergent evolution group, and isolation by time in sequential evolution.

Sequential evolution is the modification from generation to generation of the one or more alleles in a population. One of the many available examples of sequential evolution in operation is to be found in a study performed by a group of British geneticists between 1939 and 1952.

The object of their study was the phenotypic expression of a pair of alleles in the scarlet tiger moth, *Panaxia dominula.* An incompletely dominant gene in the homozygous condition results in a tiger moth having many white spots on the anterior black wings. The heterozygous

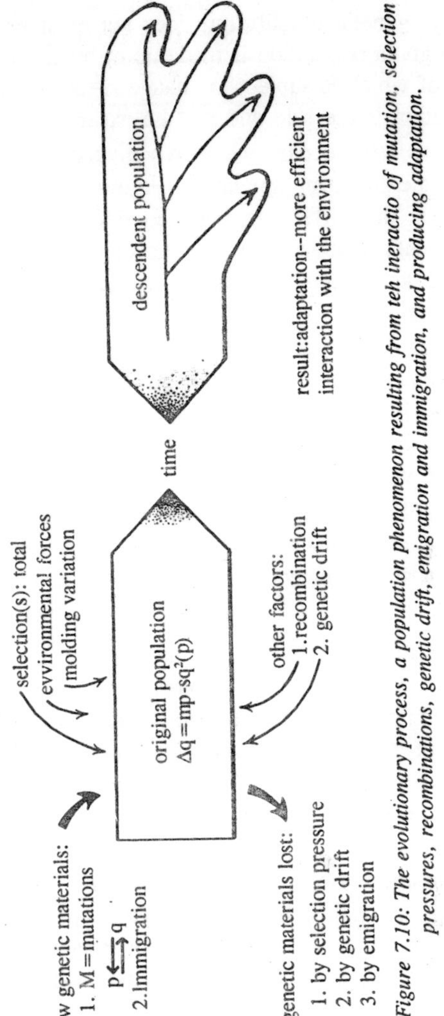

Figure 7.10: The evolutionary process, a population phenomenon resulting from teh ineractio of mutation, selection pressures, recombinations, genetic drift, emigration and immigration, and producing adaptation.

condition results in several (but not many) light spots, and the homozygous recessive condition results in only two light spots being present on the anterior black wing. Figure elsewhere in this chapter summarizes the findings. The scarlet tiger moth is ideal for such a study, since no adults live over winter.

Any changes noted would be the result of differences in the genetic make-up of the various seasonal generations. Note that some show highly significant differences, while others show relatively little differences. Obviously, genetic equilibrium does not exist here. When we realize that any given population is made up of hundreds of thousands of genes, each of which is subject to change, it becomes obvious that sequential evolution is the rule and not the exception.

Divergent evolution occurs when two divergent population lines result from a single ancestral population. Figure any where else in this chapter illustrates the difference between divergent and sequential evolution. Divergent evolution is the type of evolution usually encountered by paleontologists and results in the information that makes construction of phylogenetic trees.

Jay M. Savage of the University of Southern California has recently devised an extremely useful classification of levels of evolutionary change. We have already seen how microevolution operates. Speciation, macroevolution, and megaevolution have been the subject of many recent studies, many of which have not entirely separated the various types.

This is probably not at all surprising, since the mechanism in each case is identical and only the result is different. Furthermore, all result in organisms that are better equipped to live in a given environment.

Speciation

Speciation is the process by which new species of organisms are evolved in nature. Like all evolution, speciation is generally conceded to be a population phenomenon. We have already seen that populations of organisms are rarely if ever cosmopolitan in distribution and furthermore, that even within a given region populations are rarely uniformly distributed.

To illustrate this aspect of distribution, let us examine in some detail the distribution of the western pocket gopher, *Thomomys bottae*. Figure anywhere else in this chapter indicates the general limits of the species and illustrates how a species population may be fragmented into a number of subgroups, *subspecies*, or geographic races, each of which possess morphological traits that seem to better equip the individual to live in that specific environment.

Even within the range of a single subspecies, the populations are far from being evenly distributed. Rather, local situations result in small areas, such as an alfalfa field or a metdow, where small segments of the population are concentrated.

These groups, usually genetically quite similar, are called demes. Each deme is separated, to some extent, from adjacent demes, and much gene exchange occurs within the limits of the population making up the deme.

There is always, however, the actual or potential exchange of genetic materials (including new materials) with adjacent *demes*, and in a chain or net-like manner with all other demes making up the subspecies populations and eventually even the whole species population.

Often demes differ one from another in a series of very gradual changes, so that if we were to take a series of samples from along the route of this gradual shift in characteristics, for any one genetically controlled trait the result would be a character *cline*. Many such clines have been reported in nature.

A species, then, consists of a series of actually or potentially interbreeding populations. Surrounding and, in some cases, in the same area and habitat of the western pocket gopher are populations of related species of pocket gophers (*Thomomys talpoides, Thomomys umbrinus,* and others).

Gene exchange does not occur between any two of these distinct species. The factors that prohibit the exchange of genetic materials between related species are known as *isolating mechanisms*. The various types of isolating mechanisms operating to keep species separate in nature are outlined in Table elsewhere in this chapter.

From a consideration of these isolating mechanisms and from our knowledge of microevolution, it is obvious that whenever segments of a population (even members of a deme) become isolated geographically over a period of a number of generations, the two isolated segments of the population might well accumulate enough genetic differences to result in a lack of genetic exchange, even if the original barrier be removed. Such *allopatric speciation* is thought to have been the mechanism by which many modern species arose.

Furthermore, within a given population or even within a given deme, a single mutation could possibly result in one segment of the population being reproductively isolated. Several examples of presumed sympatric speciation have been found in nature, especially among insects and plants. Once such genetic isolation occurs each population (now species) would, through normal microevolution or genetic drift, follow its own evolutionary course.

Macroevolution

Evolution of groups above the species level is generally assumed to employ the same mechanisms as microevolution and speciation. The rate and amount of change, however, are generally assumed to be much greater. George Gaylord Simpson, a noted vertebrate paleontologist and evolutionist, has developed a convenient technique for expressing evolution

Table 7.6: Types of Isolating Mechanisms that Prevent Gene Exchange Between Populations of Related Species of Organisms.

Barrier	Example
EXTERNAL BARRIERS-Operate to prevent mating from occurring	
1. Geographic isolation	Populations live iii different regions (allopatric) with no common borders between their distributional areas, as land snails on different islands.
2. Genetic isolation	Situations of various types that would prevent mating if allopatric species were together and do prevent those living together (sympatric) from mating.
a. Ecologic	Differences in minor habitat requirements of preferences such that individuals of the two related groups rarely if ever actually meet.
b. Ethologic	Differences in mating behavior prevent mating, such as differences in courtship patterns in some birds and turtles.
c. Morphologic	Differences in structure prevent mating, such as gross size differences.
INTERNAL BARRIERS-Operate to prevent mating from occurring, or if occurring from being successful	
d. Physiologic	Differences in physiology resulting in different mating seasons, egg sizes, and other situations that prevent mating, fertilization, or development.
e. Cytologic	Differences in cell structure or mitosis prevent fertilization or mating.
3. hybrid barriers	Even if mating does successfully occur, several factors may influence the resulting hybrids in such a way as to make the gene exchange entirely unsuccessful.
a. Non-viability or weakness	The resulting hybrids either do not develop properly or are so poorly developed that they have little chance of survival to adulthood.
b. Failure to reach sexual maturity	Some hybrids fail to become sexually mature, thus having no way of passing on the successful gene exchange.

c. Sterility	Often hybrids, such as the well-known mule, reach apparent sexual maturity, but the resulting gametes are incapable of forming zygotes.
d. Sterility in later generation	In a few cases, the hybrid sterility does not show up until later generations, thus resulting in loss of genetic exchange at this time.

of the larger type. We are well aware that the total environment consists of an extremely large variety of habitats. Furthermore, such habitats can be grouped into a series of major adaptive zones.

As time progresses such major adaptive zones may persist or may terminate in a given region, while other major adaptive zones arise to replace them. A series of such major adaptive zones and their interrelationships is known as an adaptive grid. Figure elsewhere in this chapter is an extremely simplified illustration of this concept.

Within a given major adaptive zone *macroevolution* or *adaptive radiation* results in attempts to invade and occupy (by selection pressures operating on mutations and not through conscious thought or desire on the part of the organisms) all other habitats not already occupied. Many examples of adaptive radiation are known. In fact the whole section on animal diversity illustrates this repeatedly.

Megaevolution

Megaevolution results when a population (= gene pool) successfully shifts from one major adaptive zone to another. Obviously not all gene pools (=populations) that contain genes permitting such shifts are successful in making the shift.

In fact most such attempts are probably unsuccessful. Living frogs demonstrate clearly and concisely how various species have independently attempted to shift from one major adaptive zone (one in which the eggs must be deposited in water for the life cycle to be completed) into a second major adaptive zone (one in which the life cycle does not require a developmental stage in water).

These various attempts are all best classified as part of the process of adaptive radiation. In terms of the total number of theoretically possible different combinations of traits (=major adaptive type), we find that only a relative few have occurred in the living world. Once a given major adaptive type has evolved, it usually persists over long periods of time.

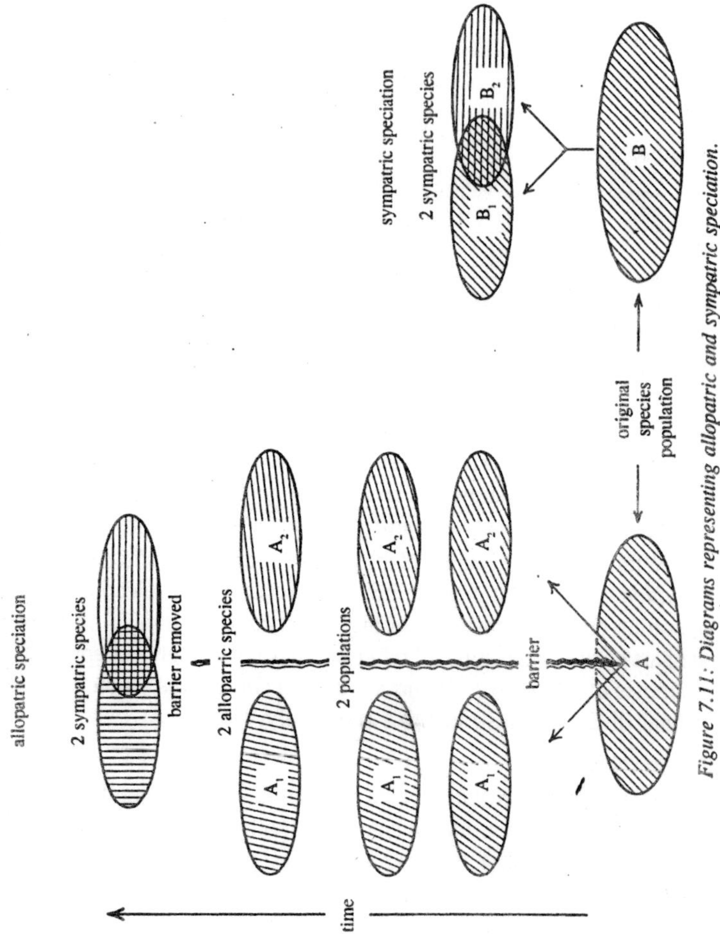

Figure 7.11: Diagrams representing allopatric and sympatric speciation.

Each of the phyla and most of the classes of living organisms (microorganisms, plants, and animals) represents a major adaptive type, so there are something less than 200 different ones known. Within a given major adaptive type is a large range of subtypes (adaptive radiation), permitting the major adaptive type to survive in a number of characteristic adaptive zones.

Macroevolution has four major characteristics. (1) A new major adaptive type is the result of evolutionary experimentation and exploration by divergent ancestral stocks wherein one crosses the ecologic barrier into the new adaptive zone. (2) Such breakthroughs and shifts are always rapid; otherwise they fail. (3) The new major adaptive zone is always devoid of competition (otherwise the newcomer does not survive), is ecologically available, and always requires a new major adaptive zone for successful invasion and occupation. (4) Once a new major adaptive type has become established, it undergoes adaptive radiation, again "challenging" the limits of its major adaptive zone.

SOME GENERALIZED TRENDS IN EVOLUTION

We have seen that the various aspects of evolution are all interrelated. Figure 28-11 expresses these relationships in a diagrammatic

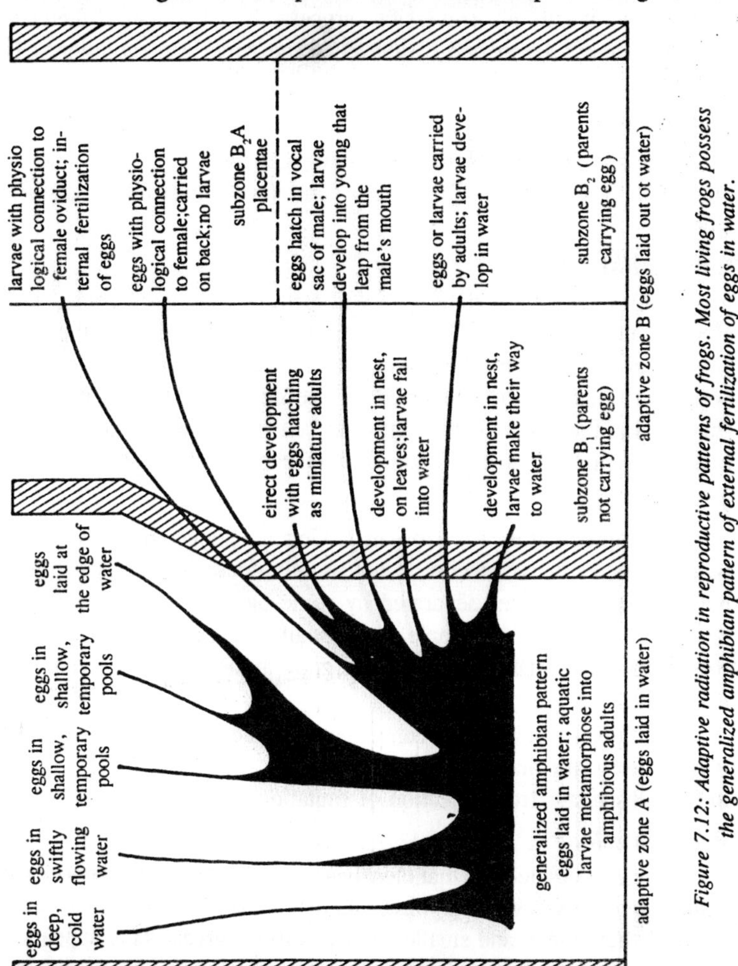

Figure 7.12: Adaptive radiation in reproductive patterns of frogs. Most living frogs possess the generalized amphibian pattern of external fertilization of eggs in water.

way and illustrates a further concept that, in general, when a given group is started on a given adaptive path, reverse evolution against the direction of selection pressure is usually impossible.

This factor, then, results in generalized trends in evolution. Several of these have been formalized as laws or rules, and some have fairly general application to evolution, although some exceptions can be pointed out for each rule.

Dalla's Law

This law, first proposed by the paleontologist, Dollo, points out that evolution is usually an irreversible process. It is the central theme of the book *Time's Arrow and Evolution* by the American evolutionist H. F. Blum.

Cope's Law

This law, proposed by the American paleontologist Cope, points out the tendency for increase in size so common in most major adaptive types.

Gause's Rule

As first emphasized by an ecologist, Gause, two species with identical ecological requirements cannot indefinitely occupy the same ecological niche. While both populations are small in relation to the population that can be supported by the ecological niche, both will survive, but under competition one will be exterminated or by selection pressure become adapted for some other ecological nichc.

Jordan's Rule

As pointed out by Karl Jordan, a German zoogeographer, closely related species or subspecies do not usually occur in identical regions but in adjacent regions separated by some barrier. There are several known exceptions (for example, ecologically separated groups), but the rule emphasizes the importance of geographic isolation in species formation.

The three following rules concern geographic clines in warm-blooded vertebrate species and subspecies. Obviously, the conditions covered by these rules result from selection of mutations.

Bergman's Rule

Bergman pointed out that closely related species and subspecies of endothermic (warm-blooded) birds and mammals are larger in the colder parts of their range and smaller in the warmer areas. This appears to be an application of the volume-mass ratio effect in that larger size has less relative surface for heat loss.

Allen's Rule

J. A. Allen, an American mammalogist, states that birds and mammals living in cold regions have shorter extremities (ears, toes, legs) than related forms living in warm regions. Some experiments have shown that mice raised at high temperatures have longer ears and longer feet than those raised at lower temperatures.

If this be true, it implies that length of extremities is not controlled entirely by fixed genetic traits; rather, physiological conditions have a remarkable control over size of body parts. Many exceptions to this rule are known.

Gloger's Rule

First pointed out by Gloger, in the Northern Hemisphere most species of birds and mammals that have a fairly extensive northsouth range have lighter-coloured (less melanin) subspecies than those living in humid, moist climates. Furthermore, lighter colours are also associated with low humidities (such as the semiarid Southwest). Thus, both humidity and temperature may be operative selection pressures for coat colour.

8

Behaviour

Suppose that your instructor were to arm you with a hypodermic syringe full of poison and demand that you find a particular type of insect (which you have never seen and which can fight back) and that you inject the ganglia of its nervous system (about which you have been taught nothing) with just enough poison to paralyze your victim, but not enough poison to kill it.

You would be hard put to accomplish these tasks, but a solitary wasp no longer than the first joint of your thumb does it all with elegance and surgical precision, and without instruction. The bee-killer wasp *Philanthus* captures bees, stings them, and places the paralyzed insects in burrows excavated in the sand.

She then lays an egg on her victims, which are devoured alive by the larva that hatches from that egg. From time to time the *Philanthus* returns to her hidden nest to reprovision it until the larva becomes a hibernating pupa in the fall. Her offspring will repeat this, doing it to perfection without ever having seen it done.

When *a Philanthus* covers a nest with sand, she takes precise bearings on the location of the burrow before flying off again to hunt. There is no way in which knowledge of the location of the burrow could be genetically programmed in the wasp.

How to dig it, how to cover it, how to kill the bees-these behaviours appear to be genetically programmed. But since a burrow can be dug only in a suitable spot, its location must be learned after it is dug. That this is so was determined by the Dutch investigator Nikko Tinbergen.

Tinbergen surrounded the wasp's burrow with a circle of pine cones, on which the wasp took her bearings. Before she returned with

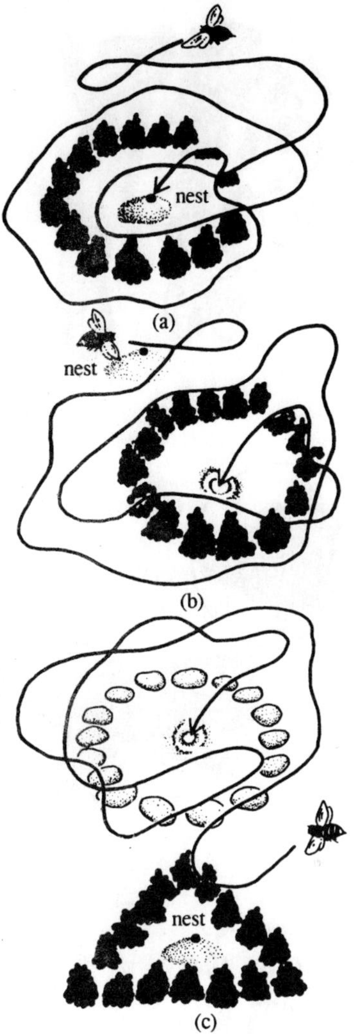

Figure 8.1: Tinbergen's sand wasp experiment.

another moribund bee, Tinbergen moved the circle of pine cones. The wasp could not find her burrow-the cones no longer surrounded it. Only when the experimenter restored the cones to their original location could the wasp find her burrow.

WHAT IS BEHAVIOUR?

Behaviour refers to the responses of an organism to signals from its environment. Notice how efficiently the wasp carried out a complex,

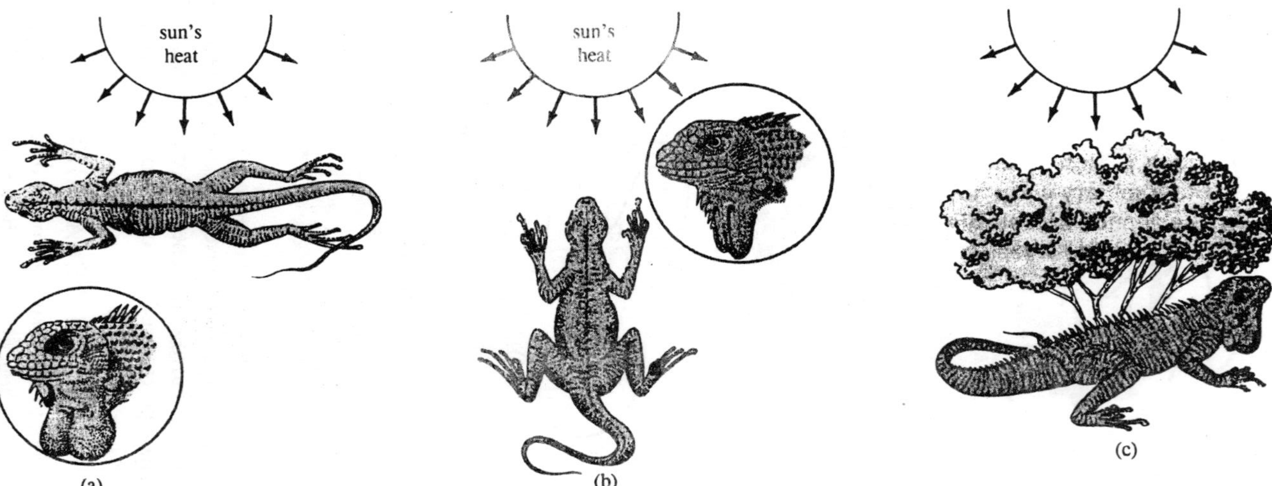

Figure 8.2: Behavioural thermoregulation in a lizard. The cold lizard (a) lies at right angles to the sunlight, puffing up its body to increase the surface area available for heat absorption. When too warm (b), the lizard orients itself parallel to the sun's rays and deflates its body. Eventually (c), it seeks shade.

though largely genetically programmed, sequence of behaviours. Very little of her behaviour had to be learned.

In contrast, the existence of programmed behaviour is hard to demonstrate in human beings. We owe the complexity of our behaviour to a *generalized* ability to learn. The *Philanthus* wasp's intelligence is as narrowly specialized as her stinger.

Much of what organisms do can be analyzed in terms of specific behaviour patterns that occur in response to stimuli (changes) in the environment.

A dog may wag its tail, a bird may sing, or a butterfly may release a volatile sex attractant. Behaviour is just as diverse as biological structure and is just as characteristic of a given species as its structure and biochemistry.

Behaviour as Adaptation

Animal behaviour used to be studied in isolation from the physical characteristics of animals. Perhaps few people stopped to think that behavioural patterns are as much adaptations as an animal's wings, legs, shell, or stinger.

In fact, the physical traits of an animal make little sense without reference to its behaviour. Animal behaviour also used to be studied almost exclusively under artificial laboratory conditions. This was partly due to a movement in psychology to make the behavioural sciences more objective by studying behaviour in a simplified environment where controls were easier to maintain.

The restoration of behaviour studies to their proper place in natural history was the contribution of such scholars as Nikko Tinbergen and Konrad Lorenz, who with others founded the science of ethology in the 1920s and 1930s.

Ethology is the study of behaviour in natural environments from the point of view of adaptation. Since behaviour is *adaptive,* ethologists believe it is best studied in the field or under conditions reflecting the natural life of the organism that exhibits it.

A particular behaviour may help an organism obtain food or water, acquire and maintain territory in which to live, protect itself, or reproduce. Certain behavioural responses may lead to the death of the individual but increase the chance of survival of the population or species through the survival of the offspring.

Behaviour tends to be *homeostatic* as well as adaptive. The body of a homeothermic organism has a collection of physiological responses that help to keep body temperature constant. For example, a human may shiver to generate more heat or perspire when too hot. A dog may pant, cooling the blood in the blood vessels of its respiratory tract.

Many poikilotherms (cold-blooded animals) can regulate their body temperature by behavioural adaptations. Lizards, for example, may warm their bodies by basking in the sunlight. To absorb the maximum amount of heat, the lizard places its body at right angles to the sun's rays, puffs itself up and spreads out all body membranes. If the lizard becomes too warm, it may first orient the body parallel to the rays of sunlight, decreasing the area exposed directly to sunlight.

It may also retract its body membranes and shrink its body as much as possible. If that proves insufficient, the lizard will seek shade, spreading out all body membranes and the body itself to the maximum to radiate excess heat. This behavioural mechanism of thermoregulation is surprisingly effective.

It has been shown that lizards infected with dangerous bacteria can maintain their temperatures several degrees above normal. In effect, these cold-blooded creatures run a fever. The fever and behaviour responsible for it can even be abolished with aspirin.

Simple Behaviour

Even bacteria "make decisions": whether to move toward food or away from a toxic substance; toward a place with a certain temperature, or away from it if it is too hot or too cold. Some bacteria are sensitive to other stimuli, such as the earth's magnetic field. But no bacterium has a nervous system, specialized sense organs, or muscles.

How does it sense stimuli and make an appropriate response? Evidence is accumulating that some proteins, such as those responsible for transporting food materials into a bacterium through its cell membrane, also function as receptors capable of detecting food substances.

Bacteria respond to many stimuli by moving toward or away from them. When the flagella rotate counterclockwise, they rotate together and the bacterium travels in a fairly straight line. Clockwise rotation pulls the bundle of flagella apart and makes the bacterium dance in place. Such microscopic dances are known as *twiddles*.

Resumption of the counterclockwise movement sends the bacterium in a straight line again, but not necessarily in the original direction. The bacterium is able to respond to gradients in a stimulating substance in the surrounding water. In the presence of a stimulus to which it responds positively, the bacterium employs less twiddling (random motion), so on the whole the bacterium tends to approach the source of

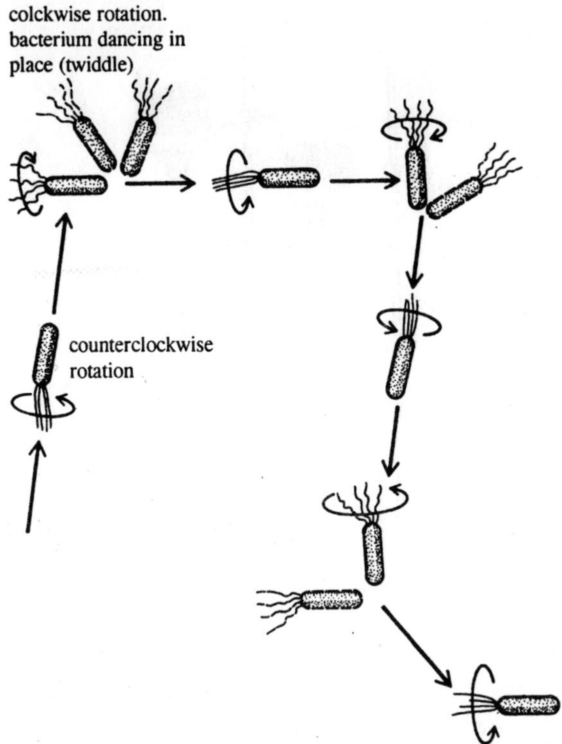

Figure 8.3: Bacteria swim in straight lines when their flagella rotate counterclockwise but twiddle briefly when the rotation is reversed, for flagellar rotation cannot be coordinated when it is clockwise.

the stimulus. Negative stimuli cause the bacterium to reverse this, so the organism tends to move away from the source of the noxious material or situation.

Such simple behaviour appears to be basically a matter of physics and chemistry, little more complicated, perhaps, than the guidance systems of a military missile. But the physics and chemistry are so organized as to adapt the bacterium actively to the changes that are constantly occurring in its environment.

Comparable mechanisms probably govern the phagocytosis of food by amebas or of bacteria by white blood cells. And even multicellular organisms display simple behaviour, some of which can be simply explained.

Tropisms

Plants have neither muscles nor a nervous system, so how can they

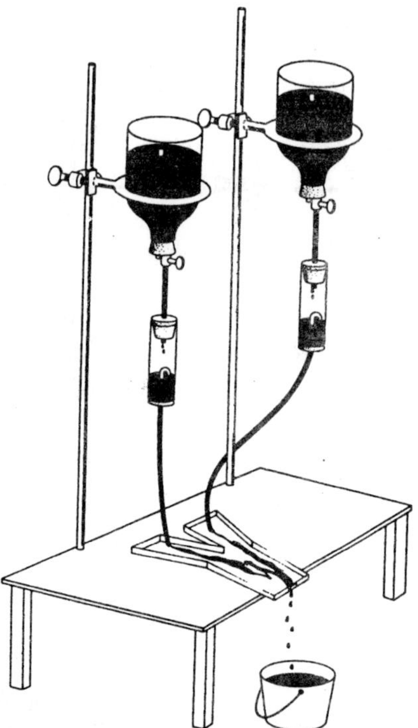

Figure 8.4: A simple maze for studying chemotaxis in a flatworm. The worm will turn left or right depending on the location of a source of an attractive chemical.

be said to behave? Yet plants certainly do grow, and time-lapse motion pictures demonstrate stimulus-oriented growth. Growth responses toward or away from a stimulus are known as *tropisms*.

As discussed in other chapter of this book, plant tropisms depend upon hormones; *phototropisms* occur in response to light, *geotropisms* in response to gravity, and *thigmotropisms* in response to a solid object. Plant behaviour is not limited to tropisms. We have already seen in previous chapters that a fair number of plants employ effectors-such as traplike leaves with which they can even capture insect prey.

Taxes

Many animals far more complex than bacteria or plants respond to stimuli in much the same way, with simple orientational behaviours known as *taxes*. A taxis generally involves the reception of a stimulus and a movement toward or away from that stimulus. Thus, a positive geotaxis is a movement downward in response to gravity, and a negative phototaxis is a movement away from a light source.

Flatworms, exhibiting positive chemotaxis, congregate on a piece of raw meat left overnight in a stream. They need no other stimulus than the chemical cues given off by the meat. If a flatworm is placed in the apparatus shown in Figure elsewhere in this chapter and meat extract is placed in one of the bottles, the flatworm will swim into the arm of the trough that receives water from the bottle containing meat extract.

By adjusting the lighting and the rate of flow from both bottles so that all other stimuli to which the worms might possibly respond are equal on both sides of the animal, it is possible to show that it is responding to the meat extract alone. Even such complex animals as insects and mammals have a large collection of simple orientational behaviours in their repertoires.

BIOLOGIOCAL RHYTHMS AND CLOCKS

It is to an organism's advantage that its metabolic processes and behaviour be synchronized with the cyclic changes in the external environment. Cyclic control mechanisms change these processes at repetitive intervals, giving rise to daily rhythms, monthly cycles, or annual rhythms.

Even some plant behaviour, such as "sleep" movements in which the leaves fold to conserve water and heat at night, lacks such obvious triggers as physiological imbalance or external cues and follows a regular daily or longer cycle. In human beings, also, physiological processes seem to follow an intrinsic rhythm.

Human body temperature, for example, follows a typical daily curve. The activities of many marine animals that live along the shore are linked to the cycle of the tides. Fiddler crabs on the eastern coast of the United States emerge from their burrows to feed at each low tide (twice every 24 hours).

Lunar Cycles

Some biological rhythms of animals, and perhaps plants, reflect the *lunar (moon) cycle*. The most striking ones are those in marine organisms that are tuned to the changes in the tides due to the phases of the moon.

For instance, the swarming of the Pacific palolo worm at a particular time of year is governed by a combination of tidal, lunar, and annual rhythms. The Atlantic fireworm swarms in the surface waters surrounding Bermuda for 55 minutes after sunset on days of the full moon during the three summer months.

The grunion, a small fish of the Pacific coast of the United States, swarms from April through June on those three or four nights when the spring tide occurs. At precisely the high point of the tide the fish squirm onto the beach, deposit eggs and sperm in the sand and return to the sea in the next wave. By the time the next tide reaches that portion of the beach 15 days later, the young fish have hatched and are ready to enter the sea.

Circadian Rhythms

Periods of activity and sleep, feeding and drinking, body temperature, and many other processes have a cycle approximately 24 hours long. Hence they are called *circadian rhythms* (from the Latin words circa, approximately, and *dies,* day). Some animals are *diurnal*, exhibiting their greatest activity during the day, whereas others are *nocturnal* and most active during the hours of darkness.

Still others are *crepuscular*, having their greatest activity during the twilight hours, at dawn, or both. If an animal's food is most plentiful in the early morning, for example, its cycle of activity must be regulated so that it becomes active shortly before dawn, even though dawn changes slightly from day to day. As the adage goes, "The early bird catches the worm."

What Controls the Biological Clock?

Current evidence seems to indicate that there is no single biological clock in most organisms. Instead, the interaction of a number of biochemical processes may produce the timed accumulation of certain substances to critical levels.

These substances, whatever they may be, might be responsible for governing behavioural and physiological rhythms. The pineal gland is thought to play a role in the timing system of rats, birds, and some other vertebrates. Regions of the hypothalamus have been shown to be a part of the biological clock in mammals. In many organisms the biological clock appears to have a genetic basis.

Normal fruit flies, *Drosophila,* have a clock that has a running period of 24.2 hours. The running period is the clock's repetitive cycle when the animals are isolated from environmental cycles and kept under constant conditions. Mutant fruit flies have been discovered with free running periods of 19 and 28 hours. Each mutation has been traced to the same locus on the X chromosome.

Some investigators hold that biological rhythms are *endogenous*; that is, they are regulated internally by a biological clock capable of detecting the passage of time. According to this theory, no regular environmental stimulus is needed to keep the clock running.

Snails and some other marine organisms whose activities vary with the tide continue to show the cyclic variations in activity when removed to an aquarium and protected from changes in light, temperature, and other factors. This persistence of rhythmic changes in activity, coordinated with the cyclic changes in the environment from which the animal was removed, is strong evidence for the endogenous explanation of biological clocks.

Other investigators argue that biological rhythms are *exogenous*; that is, they are controlled by environmental stimuli. It has been shown that biological clocks often interact to some extent with external and internal stimuli and often can be reset by such environmental cues.

If animals that breed in the spring are transported from the Northern to the Southern Hemisphere, their cycle eventually shifts to coincide with the occurrence of spring in their new home.

THE GENETIC BASIS OF BEHAVIOUR

An insect such as a bee can maintain an elaborate society because the instructions for that society are genetically inherited and programmed. A bee is capable of only the most limited learning-that which is required by the immediate demands of its environment. The complexity of some genetically programmed behaviour is wondrous, but no more so than the genetically determined complexity of the anatomy and physiology of any organism.

Although the distinction is not always clear, ethologists recognize two sorts of behaviour, innate and learned. *Instinctive*, or *innate*, *behaviour* is genetic; genes control the development of the programmed neural and motor patterns.

In contrast, learned behaviours develop as a result of experience. Some innate behaviour appears to be functional from the moment that the neural circuitry is in place, and does not seem to be modified by environmental factors. The first web of the orb-weaving spider, for example, is complete in all detail and repeatedly built in the same manner throughout the life of the spider.

Sign stimuli, also called *releasers*, often serve as triggers for fixedaction patterns of behaviour. When quick action is essential, as in escaping from a predator, a danger sign is more useful than a detailed description of the danger. Alarm signs, whether they are sights or

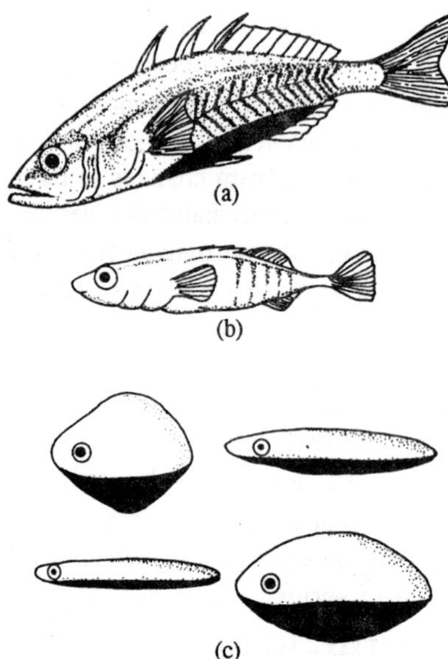

Figure 8.5: A sign stimulus is a particular feature that triggers an innate response. A male stickleback fish (a) will not attack a realistic model of another male stickleback if it lacks a red belly (b), but it will attack another model, however unrealistic, that has a red "belly" (c). Therefore, it is the specific red stimulus, rather than the recognition based on a combination of features, that triggers the aggressive behaviour.

sounds, are usually simple and contrast sharply to the environment. Small birds typically show an immediate flight reaction to animals with large eyesunderstandably, considering that their major predators, owls and hawks, have large eyes.

In the spring male stickleback fish establish territories from which they drive other males. Investigators found that very simple model fish with red undersides were more effective in releasing defense behaviour than more realistic models lacking the red underside. Apparently, the red belly of the male is the important sign stimulus responsible for releasing territorial defense behaviour in sticklebacks.

In many species innate behaviour is capable of modification as a result of interaction with the environment. Herring gull chicks peck the beaks of the parents, which regurgitate partially digested food for them. The chicks are attracted by two sign stimuli: a red spot on the beak and the beak's shape and downward movement.

This "begging behaviour" is sufficiently functional to get the chicks their first meal, but much energy is wasted in pecking. Some pecks are off target and fail to reach the parent's beak. However, the begging behaviour becomes more efficient over time, and in experiments with models of the parent's beak, the chicks become increasingly selective of the shape necessary to evoke the begging response. Thus, the initial functional instinct is perfected by environmental interaction.

Behaviour is essentially a property of the coordinating mechanisms of the body (that is, of the nervous and endocrine systems). The capacity for behaviour is therefore subject to whatever genetic characteristics govern the development and *range of function* of these systems.

One may think of a continuous scale of behaviours, ranging from the most rigidly programmed, genetically inherited types, through those that are somewhat modifiable, to those that, though containing a genetic component, are extensively developed through experience.

LEARNING

Learned behaviour can be defined as behaviour that is modified as a result of interaction with the environment. The simplest form of learning is *habituation*, learning to ignore repeated stimuli that are not followed by either benefit or obvious cost. Learning capabilities reflect the specialized mode of life of an animal.

The same rat that has difficulty learning the artificial task of pushing a lever to get an immediate reward learns in *a single* trial to avoid a food that has made it ill as long as six hours after the food was eaten.

Those who poison rats to get rid of them can readily appreciate the adaptive value of this learning talent to the rat. Such quick aversive learning forms the basis of warning colouration, found in many poisonous insects and brilliantly coloured but distasteful bird eggs. Once made ill by such an egg, the predators learn to avoid them.

The most complex learning is *insight learning*, the ability to remember past experiences that may involve different stimuli and to adapt these recalled events to solve a new problem. Insight learning is most easily demonstrated in primates.

A dog can be placed in a blind alley that it must *circumvent* in order to reach a reward. The difficulty of the problem appears to be that the animal must move away from the reward in order to get to it. At first the dog typically flings itself at the barrier nearest the food. Eventually, by trial and error, the frustrated dog may find its way around the barrier and reach the reward.

A baboon placed in the same kind of situation is likely to see the solution immediately. Learning is widely believed to depend upon changes in the readiness of individual neurons to form circuit relationships with one another and to transmit impulses in specific directions. In order to learn, an organism's neurons must have a large number of potential interactions with one another, and hence there must be many, not just the few required by programmed behaviour.

Since innate behaviour is really a consequence of the biophysical properties of individual neurons and of their interconnections, the more narrowly stereotyped a system of behaviour is, the more obvious is its genetic control. Yet without the necessary preexistence of the proper neural circuitry, even learned behaviour would be impossible.

Moreover, the kind of learned behaviour that the organism typically and most easily develops also depends upon the layout of that circuitry.

PHYSIOLOGICAL READINESS

Before any pattern of behaviour can be exhibited, an organism must be physiologically ready to produce it. Breeding behaviour does not ordinarily occur among birds or most mammals unless steroid sex hormones are present in their blood at certain concentrations.

A human baby cannot walk unless its reflex and muscular development permits it. Yet these states of physiological readiness are themselves produced by a continuous interaction with the environment. The level of sex hormones in a bird's blood may be determined by seasonal variations in day length. The baby's muscles develop in response to exercise.

Without the trial and error involved in learning how to walk, walking would be retarded. Perhaps the best example of such interaction between readiness and environment is afforded by the white-crowned sparrow, which exhibits considerable regional variation in its song.'

This bird, even if kept in isolation, eventually will sing a very poorly developed but recognizable white-crowned sparrow song. However, if it is allowed to grow up under the care of its parents for the first three months of life, when it matures, it will sing in the local "dialect" characteristic of its parents or foster parents.

If such learning does not take place in those three months, it never will, and if the sparrow consorts with birds of other species, it will not learn their songs.

IMPRINTING

Anyone who has watched a mother duck with a swarm of ducklings must have wondered how she can keep track of such a horde of almost

Figure 8.7: Insight learning and in this case, simple tool use. confronted with the problem of reaching food hanging fromteh celiling, the chimpanzee stacks boxes until it can climb and reach the food.

identical little creatures, tumbling about in the weeds and grass, let alone tell them from those belonging to another hen. Though she is capable of recognizing her offspring to an extent, basically it is they that have the responsibility of keeping track of her-a far simpler chore.

Each duckling follows her about, like a nail attracted to a magnet. Even if it gets into trouble, the duckling usually must take the initiative. It emits distress cries, and in response the mother will rescue it if she can. Clearly, the survival of the duckling requires an extremely rapid establishment of the behavioural bond between it and its parent.

In fact, such a behavioural bond is usual between parent and offspring, especially if the offspring are able to follow the parent about. This form of learning—in which a young animal forms a strong attachment to an individual, usually one of the parents, within a few hours of birth (or hatching)- is known as *imprinting*.

An early investigator of imprinting, ethologist Konrad Lorenz, discovered that a newly hatched bird may imprint on a human, or even an inanimate object, if its parent is not present. Though the behaviour itself is genetically determined, the bird learns the object.

Among many kinds of birds, especially ducks and geese, imprinting is established even before hatching. The older embryos of these birds are able to exchange calls with their nest mates and parents right through the porous eggshell.

When they hatch, at least one parent is normally on hand, emitting the characteristic vocalizations that the hatchlings have already learned. During a brief critical period after hatching, the chicks learn to associate these vocalizations with the appearance of the parent.

Imprinting establishes the bond between mother and offspring among many mammals, as well as among birds. In many species the mother establishes a bond with her offspring while the offspring is imprinting upon her.

The mother in some species of hoofed mammals will accept her offspring for only a few hours after its birth. If they are kept apart past that time, the young are thereafter rejected. Normally, this behaviour enables the mother to distinguish her own offspring from those of others, evidently by olfactory cues.

MIGRATION

The dramatic seasonal migrations of birds have long excited human curiosity, but it is only recently that even their rudiments have been properly understood. Until Renaissance times, for instance, the winter disappearance of many migratory birds from Europe was attributed to hibernation in such unlikely places as the muddy bottoms of ponds.

Widespread human travel and communication over long distances has led to our modern view that even without any obvious immediate motivation (such as hunger), many animals regularly travel long distances to breed or just to spend certain seasons of the year. Some migrations involve astonishing feats of endurance and navigation.

Ruby-throated hummingbirds cross the vast reaches of the Gulf of Mexico twice each year, and the sooty tern travels across the entire South Atlantic from Africa to reach its tiny island breeding grounds south of Florida.

Though there is no reason to think that migration is purposeful, it can seem carefully planned. Birds may feed heavily weeks before those food reserves will be needed, and often fly south even *before* the weather turns cold or food becomes scarce.

Salmon swim into fresh water toward the end of their life cycles.

Monarch butterflies fly southward, and the *next generation* flies north in the spring. The propensity for this behaviour must be inherited and maintained by natural selection.

Migration, in other words, must be a specific adaptation in the life-styles of many organisms. Yet the adaptive significance of migratory behaviour is not always clear. It is obviously to the advantage of birds to fly south in the winter, but why certain eels migrate to the Sargasso Sea to spawn is a mystery.

The behavioural trigger that sets off migratory behaviour varies. Some animals migrate upon maturation. In others explicit environmental cues trigger the process. In migratory birds, for example, changes in day length are sensed by the pineal gland.

These trigger characteristic rest less behaviour called *Zugunruhe*—migratory restlessness. The bird evinces increased readiness to fly and flies for longer periods of time. The *direction* of travel is also important, and this raises the general problem of animal navigation. Birds appear to navigate by a combination of celestial (sun and star) plus geographic and climatic cues.

Honeybees (perhaps) and some birds are sensitive to the earth's magnetic field. However, the cues employed by many animals to negotiate their migratory journeys are not understood. One of the organisms in which migration is fairly well understood is the whitethroat, a small European warbler.

Working in the 1950s, Franz and Eleonore Sauer hand-reared a number of these birds (presumably to rule out any possibility of transmission of information from parent to offspring). When (and only when) the birds could see the star patterns of the night sky, they attempted to fly in the normal direction of migration for this species, a direction that they had no opportunity to learn.

When the birds were brought into a planetarium and the night sky of a different locale was simulated on the planetarium dome, they attempted to fly in a direction that would have taken them to their normal wintering grounds from that locality.

The conclusion seemed inescapable: Though the direction of migration was unlearned, the birds were able to find it by means of celestial navigation. The "need" to migrate and the direction of migration are unlearned. The star patterns that make navigation possible are learned. But how to learn them is innate.

The entire mechanism is so constructed, though, that the learned behaviour is dependent upon the unlearned, so under normal circumstances all birds of the same population learn the same thing and behave, for the most part, identically during migration.

This intricate interaction of learned and unlearned behaviour does have one common theme: that of adaptation. If any component were to fail, the birds would not reach their destination.

WHAT IS SOCIAL BEHAVIOUR?

In a pioneering work, *The Social Life of Animals,* W.C. Allee[1] showed that many animals are far more resistant to noxious environments in groups than alone. Schools of fish are less vulnerable to predators than single fish because large numbers tend to confuse their predators.

Many fish have elaborate evasive maneuvers that are workable only when large numbers of individuals perform them together. Flocks of birds may be able to find food better than single individuals. Insects are able to construct elaborate nests and raise young by mass-production methods when they cooperate.

A pack of wolves and a pride of lions have greater success in hunting than the individual animals hunting alone. Animals that are hunted may be better able to detect or discourage predators when some individuals in the group are always on watch.

It seems clear that social behaviour offers definite benefits. The mere presence of more than one individual does not mean that the behaviour is social. Many factors of the physical environment bring animals together in *aggregations*, but whatever interaction they experience is circumstantial.

A light shining in the dark is a stimulus that causes large numbers of moths to aggregate around it. The high humidity under a log may attract aggregations of wood lice. Although it may be adaptive for these organisms to aggregate, their behaviour is not social. Ethologists generally define *social behaviour* as adaptive *conspecific* (among members of the same species) interactions.

Many species that engage in social behaviour form societies. A *society* is a group of individuals belonging to the same species that cooperate in an adaptive manner. A hive of bees, a flock of birds, a pack of wolves, and a school of fish are examples of societies.

Some societies are loosely organized, whereas others have a complex structure. In a well-organized society there is cooperation and a division of labor among animals of different sexes, age groups, or castes.

A complex system of communication reinforces the organization of the society. The members of a society tend to remain together and to resist attempts by outsiders to enter the group.

COMMUNICATION

The ability to communicate is an essential ingredient of social behaviour, for only by exchanging mutually recognizable signals can one animal influence the behaviour of another. *Communication* occurs when an animal performs an act that changes the behaviour of another organism.

Communication may facilitate finding food, as in the elaborate dances of the bees. It may hold a group together, warn a group of danger, indicate social status, solicit or indicate willingness to provide care, identify members of the same species, or indicate sexual maturity.

Modes of Communication

Animal communication differs significantly from most human communication in that it is not symbolic. As you read, information is conveyed to your mind by words; yet the words themselves are not the information. They stand for it.

The relationship between the word "cat" and the animal itself is a learned one; a person who could read only Japanese would not recognize it. This is not to say that *signals* in some sense are not employed by animals. In a way, all releasers are signals. However, releasers are not necessarily learned, whereas true symbols are.

Although in humans some body communication is culturally determined learned behaviour, a large part of it (such as smiling) is truly universal and appears to be physiologically determined. The pupil of the human eye dilates in certain emotional situations, such as sexual interest or excitement.

Without realizing it, people respond to such subtle cues. In experiments, a photograph of a woman's face with the pupils retouched to appear greatly dilated was far more attractive to male subjects than one in which they were shown as pinpoints.

Signals are often transmitted involuntarily as an accompaniment of the physiological state of the organism. Information about an animal's emotional or mental state may be transmitted even if no other members of the species are nearby. For example, a bird automatically gives an alarm call when it sights a predator.

Certainly there are times when human beings would rather not communicate their true feelings-yet there may be instances in which we do not really have any choice, as with pupil dilation. And who has not blushed at a time when he would have given almost anything not to have done so?

Do animals ever employ symbols, or are animal signals totally restricted to the equivalent of gasps of alarm? The matter is controversial. Many ethologists think that even dogs do not respond to spoken language as we do, but deduce the behaviour we command from an astute reading of human facial expression, vocal intonation, and bodily attitude.

On the other hand, chimpanzees have been taught to speak a very few words meaningfully, and to a limited extent can use sign language appropriately. Whether apes employ symbolic language in nature is unlikely, although the potential seems to exist.

The singing of birds is an obvious example of auditory communication, serving to announce the presence of a territorial male. Some animals communicate by scent rather than sound. Antelopes rub the secretions of facial glands on conspicuous objects in their vicinity.

Dogs mark territory by frequent urination. Certain fish, the gymnotids, use electric pulses for navigation and communication, including territorial threat, in a fashion similar to bird vocalization. As E.O. Wilson has said, "The fish, in effect, sing electrical songs." Who would have guessed it?

Pheromones

Pheromones are chemical signals that convey information between members of a species. They are a simple, widespread means of communication. Secretion of pheromones is the only communication mechanism available to unicellular organisms and to many simple invertebrates because other communication channels require rather complex sending and receiving mechanisms.

Pheromone communication has been discovered in nearly all organisms studied, including plants. Many types of signals can be conveyed by pheromones. Most act as releasers eliciting a very specific, immediate, but transitory type of behaviour. Others act as primers triggering hormonal activities that may result in slow but longlasting responses. Some may act in both ways.

An advantage to pheromone communication is that little energy must be expended to synthesize the simple but distinctive organic compounds involved. Conspecific individuals have receptors attuned to the molecular configuration of the pheromone; other species ignore it. Pheromones are effective in the dark, they can pass around obstacles, and they last for several hours or longer.

Major disadvantages of pheromone communication are slow transmission and limited information content. Some animals compensate for the latter disadvantage by secreting different pheromones with different meanings.

Pheromones are important in attracting the opposite sex and in sex recognition in many species. Many female insects produce pheromones that attract males of the appropriate species. We have taken advantage of some sex attractant pheromones to help control such pests as gypsy moths by luring the males to traps baited with synthetic analogs of the female pheromone.

Some aspects of the sexual cycle of vertebrates are affected by pheromones. The odor of a male mouse introduced among a group of females causes their estrous cycles to become synchronized. In some species of mice the odor of a strange male, a sign of high population density, causes a newly impregnated female to abort.

DOMINANCE HIERARCHIES

In the spring a paper-wasp nest may be founded cooperatively by females that have survived their winter hibernation. During the early course of construction a series of squabbles among the females takes place, in which the combatants bite one another's bodies or legs and (rarely) sting.

In the end one of the young potential queens gets the upper hand over all the rest, and thereafter she is hardly ever challenged. The queen spends more and more time on the nest, and less and less time out foraging for herself. She takes the food she needs from the others as they return, and if they do not like it, they can leave; some do.

The queen then begins to take an interest in raising a family-her family. Since she is almost always at hand, she is able to prevent other wasps from laying eggs in the brood cells by rushing at them, jaws agape. At the same time, she cannot be stopped from laying all the eggs she wants, since she has already demonstrated that she cannot be successfully challenged.

Furthermore, if any of the other females do manage to lay, she eats their eggs. Her eggs are undisturbed. Those subordinates that stay experience a definite regression of the ovaries, and eventually become sterile workers. The young that have been raised in the nest grow up as sterile workers from the outset, although they retain the potential of becoming reproductively competent in the event that the queen dies.

A careful analysis of this aggressive behaviour discloses that the queen can bite any other wasp without serious fear of retaliation. There is usually another wasp, however, that can bite any wasp she chooses (other than the queen) without fear of retaliation.

Thus, though the queen can bite any wasp in the nest, the other wasps are not equal in their relationships with one another. One can arrange the wasps into a definite *dominance hierarchy*, an arrangement of status that regulates aggressive behaviour within the society:

Queen → Wasp A → Wasp B → ... Wasp J → Wasp K

Suppression of Aggression

Once a dominance hierarchy is established, little or no time is wasted in fighting. Subordinate wasps, upon challenge, generally exhibit submissive poses that inhibit the aggressive behaviour of the queen toward them. Consequently, few or no colony members are lost through wounds sustained in fighting.

Physiological Determinants

In some animals dominance is a simple function of aggressiveness, which is itself often influenced directly by sex hormones. Among chickens the cock is the most dominant. If a hen receives testosterone injections, her place in the dominance hierarchy shifts upward.

If she is spayed, the reverse takes place. Recent tests on rhesus monkeys have shown that when males are dominant, their testosterone levels are much higher than when they have been defeated. Not only can estrogen reduce dominance and testosterone increase dominance, but dominance may even increase testosterone.

It is not always easy to unscramble the situation! In many species males and females have separate dominance systems, but in many monogamous animals, especially birds, the female takes on the dominance status of her mate by virtue of their relationship.

However, this is not always the case. Like many fishes, labrid coral reef fishes are capable of sex reversal. What is odd is that the most dominant individual is always male, and the remaining fishes within his territory are always female.

If the male dies or is removed, the most dominant female will become the new male. Should anything new happen to "him," the next ranking female will become the new sultan of the harem. Still other fishes exhibit the reverse behaviour. In them the most dominant fish becomes a female.

TERRITORIALITY

Virtually all animals, and even some plants, maintain a minimum personal distance from their neighbors, as one can observe in the even spacing among the members of a flock of birds resting on a telephone line. Most animals have a geographical area that they seldom or never leave. Such an area is called a *home range*.

Since the animal has the opportunity to become familiar with everything in that range, it has an advantage over both its predators and its prey in negotiating cover and finding food. Some, but not all, animals defend a portion of the home range against other individuals of the same species and even against individuals of other species. Such a defended area is called a *territory*. The tendency to defend such a territory is known as *territoriality*.

Territoriality is easily studied in birds. Typically, the male chooses a territory at the beginning of the breeding season. This behaviour results from high concentrations of sex hormones in the blood. The males of adjacent territories fight until territorial boundaries become fixed.

Generally, the dominance of a cock varies directly with his nearness to the center of his territory. Thus, close to "home" he is a lion. When invading some other bird's territory, he is likely to be a lamb. The interplay of dominance values among territorial cocks eventually produces a neutral line at which neither is dominant. That line is the territorial boundary.

Bird songs announce the existence of a territory and often serve as a substitute for violence. Furthermore, they announce to eligible females that a propertied male resides in the territory. Typically, male birds take up a conspicuous station, sing, and sometimes display striking patterns of colouration to their neighbors and rivals.

Territoriality among animals may be adaptive in that it tends to reduce conflict, control population growth, and ensure the most efficient use of environmental resources by encouraging dispersion and spacing organisms more or less evenly throughout a habitat.

Usually, territorial behaviour is related to the specific life-style of the organism that displays it, and to whatever aspect of its ecology is most critical to its reproductive success.

For instance, sea birds may range over hundreds of square miles of open water but exhibit territorial behaviour that is restricted to nesting sites on a rock or island, their resource that is in the shortest supply and for which competition is keenest.

SEXUAL BEHAVIOUR AND REPRODUCTION

The minimum social contact, and for some species of animals (for example, many species of spiders) the only social contact, is the sex act. Fertilization and perhaps the rearing of young are some animals' only forms of social behaviour. Let us consider the sex act as a basic example of social behaviour, for the elements to which it can be reduced are also the least common denominators of most social behaviour.

Like other social relationships, the sex act is adaptive in that it promotes the welfare of the species. It requires *cooperation,* the *temporary suppression of aggressive behaviour,* and *a system of communication.* Among some jumping spiders, for example, mating is preceded by a ritual courtship on the part of the male, the effect of which is to produce temporary paralysis in the female.

While she is thus enthralled, the male inseminates her. Should she recover before he makes his escape, he becomes the main course at his own wedding feast. Whether he appreciates the opportunity or not, he is thus able to make the ultimate in material contributions to the eggs the female will presently produce.

She would otherwise have to bear the metabolic burden of their production all by herself. Since an individual that reproduces perpetuates its genes, it is not surprising that natural selection has favoured mechanisms, including behaviour, that promote successful reproduction. To fertilize as many females as possible, the males often compete intensely with one another.

Sexual competition among males of the same species often has contributed to the evolution of large male size, brilliant breeding colours, ornaments, antlers, and other features that give a male an advantage in establishing dominance among his peers and attracting females. Since the female usually chooses the mate, selection has favoured those male characteristics that make a male most attractive.

Selection has also favoured those female attributes that enable her to determine that the male is worthy of her investment. Success of a male in dominance encounters with other males indicates his fitness to the female. Although the female of some species accepts the first male that attempts to court her, in other species the female tests the males by provoking encounters.

Female baboons and chimpanzees in estrus have enlarged, brilliantly coloured genital swellings that attract all males and incite competition among them. The victorious male courts the female. An important function of courtship is to ensure that the male is a member of the same species, but it also provides the female further opportunity to evaluate the quality of the male.

Courtship may also be necessary as a signal to trigger nest building or ovulation. Courtship rituals may be long and complex. The first display of the male releases a counter behaviour of a conspecific female.

This, in turn, releases additional male behaviour, and so on until the pair are ready for copulation. Certain male spiders make an offering of food to the female during courtship.

This inhibits any aggressive tendencies that the female may have on being approached and also provides the female with some of the food needed for egg production. Sexual selection has also led to strategies whereby a successful male protects an inseminated female from copulation with other males.

After copulation a male damselfly continues to grasp and fly with the female until she has deposited her eggs. A successful drone honeybee discharges much of his genital apparatus into the virgin queen's genital passages, thereby blocking them against insemination by another male.

Pair Bonds

A *pair bond* is a stable relationship between animals of the opposite sex that ensures cooperative behaviour in mating and the rearing of the young. In some species a newly arrived female is initially treated as a rival male. Then, through the use of instinctive appeasement postures and gestures by both male and female, the initial hostility is dissipated and mating takes place.

Such sexual appeasement behaviour may be very elaborate and gives rise to mating dances in some birds. The releaser mechanisms involved in the establishment and maintenance of the pair bond are often remarkably detailed. A male flicker possesses a black, mustache-like marking under the beak.

This is lacking in the female. If a "happily married" female flicker is captured and such a mustache is painted on her, her mate will vigorously attack her as if she were a rival male. He will accept her again if it is removed. Such cues enable courtship rituals to function as behavioural genetic isolating mechanisms among species.

Care of the Young

Care of the young is an additional component of successful reproduction in many species, and it, too, requires a parental investment. The benefit of parental care is the increased likelihood of the survival of the offspring, but the cost is a reduction in the number of offspring that can be produced. Because of the time spent carrying the developing embryo, the female has more to lose than the male if the young do not develop.

Thus, females are more likely to brood eggs and young than males, and usually the females invest more in parental care. Investing time and effort in care of the young is usually less advantageous to a male, for time spent in parenting is time lost in inseminating other females. Even worse, it may not be certain who fathered the offspring.

Raising some other male's offspring is a definite genetic disadvantage. In some situations, however, it may be to the male's advantage to help rear his own young, or those of a genetic relative. Receptive females may be scarce.

And gathering sufficient food may require more effort than one parent can provide. In some habitats the young may need protection against predators.

PLAY

Play is an important aspect of the development of behaviour in many species, especially young mammals. It serves as a means of practicing adult patterns of behaviour and perfecting means of escape, prey killing, and even sexual conduct. In true play the behaviour may not be actually consummated.

Thus a kitten pounces upon a dead leaf but of course does not kill it, even though the kitten administers a typical carnivore neck bite. When playing with a littermate, the same kitten may practice the disemboweling stroke with its hind claws, but the littermate is not intentionally injured in the process.

HIGHLY ORGANIZED SOCIETIES

Some animal societies exhibit elaborate and complex patterns of social interactions. In these societies there is considerable division of labor not directly connected with the care of the young.

Insect Societies

Although many insects cooperate socially, such as tent caterpillars, which spin a communal nest, the most elaborate insect societies are found among the ants, wasps, and termites. Insect societies are held together by an elaborate system of releasers, and as a result they tend to be quite rigid.

The social insects secrete pheromones that accomplish such tasks as suppressing the ovaries of worker honeybees or alerting an ant hill to the presence of an enemy ("alarm substance" is given off from a special abdominal gland of an excited worker).

Virtually all the intercommunication within insect societies is comparable to the hormonal communication within a single organism. The social coordination achieved approaches the behaviour of the cells

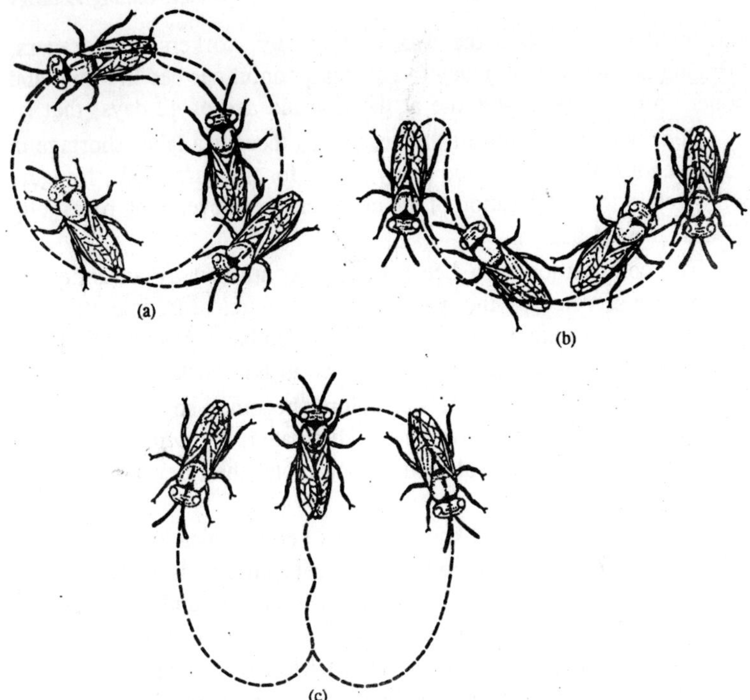

Figure 8.8: Three kinds of communication dances performed by honeybees, as observed by Karl von Frisch. (a) The round dance. (b) The sickle dance. (c) The waggle dance.

of a loosely organized individual of about the level of a sponge. The social organization of honeybees has been studied more extensively than that of any social insect.

A honeybee society generally consists of a single adult queen, up to 80,000 worker bees (all female), and at certain times, a few males called drones that fertilize newly developed queens. The queen deposits about 1000 fertilized eggs per day in the wax cells of a comb. Each fertilized egg develops into a larva that is fed by worker bees.

After about 6 days the workers seal the cell off with wax and the larva develops into a pupa. About 12 days later an adult worker bee emerges from the wax cell. Division of labor in the bee society is mostly determined by age.

The youngest hive bees serve as nurse bees. They have special glands on the head that secrete *royal jelly* essential for the nutrition of all larval bees, and which, in larger quantities, produces queens.

After about a week as nurse bees, workers begin to produce wax and build and maintain the wax cells. Older workers are foragers, bringing home the vital honey (a half-teaspoonful per bee lifetime) and pollen. Most worker bees die at the ripe old age of 42-days, that is.

Behavioural cues tip off the bees when there is a labor shortage in any category. If there are too many larvae for the nurse bees, foragers will pitch in for the duration of the emergency, redeveloping royal-jelly glands, if need be.

The composition of a bee society is controlled by an antiqueen pheromone secreted by the queen. It acts as a releaser, inhibiting the workers from raising a new queen, and it also has a primer effect, for it inhibits the development of the ovaries in the workers.

If the queen dies, or if the colony becomes so large that the inhibiting effect of the pheromone is dissipated, the workers begin to feed some larvae the special food that promotes their development into new queens.

The most sophisticated known mode of communication among bees is a stereotyped series of body movements known as a *dance*. If a worker runs across a rich source of nectar, it can communicate this fact to the other bees within the hive by dancing on a vertical comb surface.

If the food supply is nearby, the bee performs a *round dance*, which generally excites the other bees and causes them to fly about in all directions till they have found the nectar. But if the source is distant, the bee performs a *waggle dance*. This "step" has a figure-eight configuration.

As the bee treads the long axis of the figure-eight, she emits a series of distinctive sounds and waggles her abdomen from side to side. The angle between the long axis and the force of gravity is the same as the angle between the sun's rays and the shortest flight direction to the food source.

Vertebrate Societies

Among vertebrate societies we find a far greater range and plasticity of potential behaviour than among insect societies. Vertebrate societies are far less rigid and much more adaptable to changing needs. In some ways they are also less complex.

Vertebrate societies usually contain nothing comparable to the physically and behaviourally specialized castes of termites or ants. What is more, except for human beings, individual members of vertebrate societies are not as specialized in their tasks as are the social insects. A beehive may be considered collectively a kind of superorganism, but

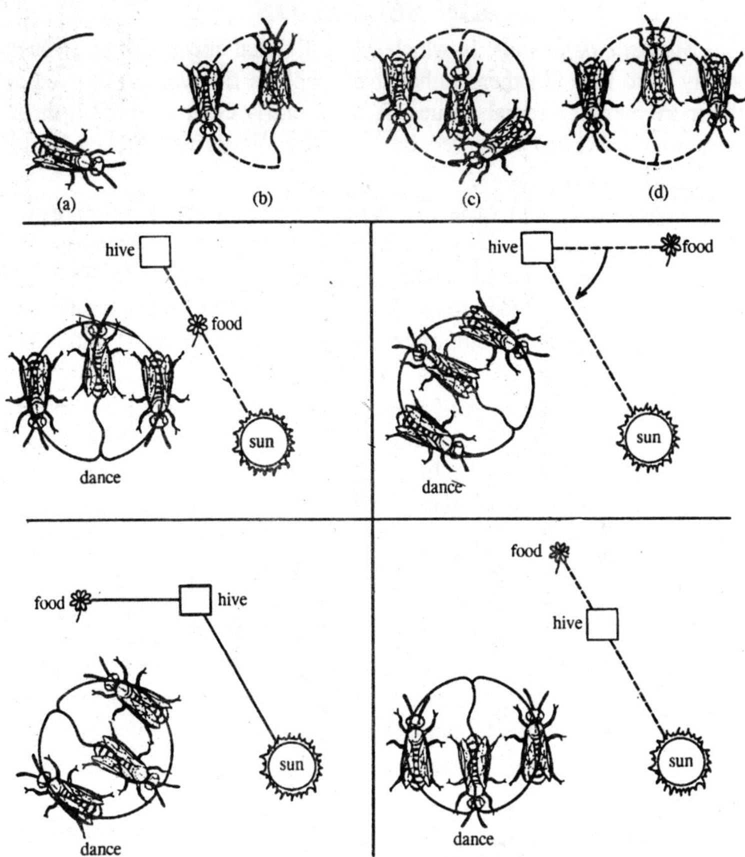

Figure 8.9: Indication of direction by the waggle dance.

it is hard to interpret a wolf pack or a herd of red deer in that fashion. Whereas the elaborate societies of social insects result from genetic programming of their behaviour, the complexity of human society results from culture, behaviour that is symbolically transmitted from generation to generation. It is true that human behaviour is not wholly determined by culture.

We even have a genetically determined capacity for acquiring and transmitting culture itself. However, the medium for cultural transmission is not the information contained in DNA but the information contained in language. Because of language and the culture it makes possible, the principal distinguishing characteristic of human societies is their great reliance upon *use of tools,* by which we have transformed the face of our planet.

KIN SELECTION

Altruistic behaviour, in which one individual appears to act in such a way as to benefit others rather than itself, is frequently observed in the more complex social groups. A particularly clear case of altruistic behaviour has been observed by biologists Watts and Stokes in the mating of wild turkeys.

Several groups of males, in each of which there is a dominance hierarchy, gather in a special mating territory and go through their displays of tail spreading, wing dragging, and gobbling in front of females who come to the area to copulate. One group attains dominance over other groups as a result of cooperation among the males within the group.

The dominant member of the dominant group is the one to copulate most frequently with the females. Seemingly, the males that helped establish the dominant group but have low status within it gain nothing. Close analysis has shown that members of a group are brothers from the same brood. Since they share many genes with the successful male, they are indirectly perpetuating many of their genes.

In this case altruism is closely related to *kin selection*, vicarious gene propagation among closely related individuals. Kin selection may account for the evolution of the complex societies of social insects, in which some individuals specialize for reproduction and other close relatives do the chores of the colony.

In the bee society the workers are sterile females, and the queen functions vicariously as their reproductive organ. If the queen produces offspring, at least a large portion of the genes shared by the queen and worker will have been passed on to the next generation, even though the worker herself has not reproduced.

This is particularly true of bees, wasps, and ants. Since the males are haploid, each male passes on his *entire* complement of genes to his offspring without the intervention of meiosis, and all sperm are genetically identical. Thus, each female bee has three-fourths of her genes in common with her sisters, instead of the more usual half.

In fact, since the queen bee mates infrequently during her lifetime (she can store sperm for long periods between copulations), every bee alive in a hive at the same time may well have the same father. Expressed more exactly, any given worker bee will probably have half of her genes derived meiotically from the same father and therefore identical to half of the genes possessed by any other worker in the hive-plus half of the *remaining* half in common with any other worker in the hive that had, as it probably did, the same mother. That gives all workers a *coefficient of relatedness* of 75%, that is, 0.75.

Organisms in which both sexes are diploid, such as ourselves, have only a 0.50 coefficient of relatedness with our own children. To be sure, it is not important how closely related worker bees may be to one another, since they never have offspring in the normal course of events.

However, sooner or later some of those sibling larvae being reared so assiduously by the worker bees will become drones or a new queen and will pass on those genes to the next generation. Apparently, therefore, it is more efficient for the worker to propagate her genes by proxy and the mass production of larvae than to lay her own eggs and go through the complete process of raising them to maturity herself.

Kin selection is not limited to social insects. Among some birds (Florida jays and others), nonreproducing individuals aid in the rearing of the young. Nests tended by these additional helpers as well as parents produce more young than nests with the same number of eggs overseen only by parents.

The nonreproducing helpers, siblings of the parents, are apparently increasing their own biological success by ensuring the successful propagation of their genes through their siblings offspring.

SOCIOBIOLOGY

Sociobiology is the school of ethology that focuses upon the evolution of behaviour through natural selection. It represents a synthesis of population genetics, evolution, and ethology. Like many biologists of the past (such as Darwin), Edward O. Wilson and other sociobiologists emphasize the animal roots of human behaviour, but they have attempted to inform their discipline with population genetics, with particular emphasis on the effect of kin selection on patterns of inheritance.

Many of the concepts discussed in this chapter, such as altruism and paternal investment in care of the young, are based on contributions made by sociobiologists. For the sociobiologist, the organism and its adaptationsincluding its behaviour-are ways its genes have of making more copies of themselves. The cells and tissues of the body support the functions of the reproductive system.

The reproductive system's job is the transmission of genetic information to succeeding generations. There are unique pitfalls in attempting to reconstruct the evolution of behaviour, since behaviour rarely leaves an explicit fossil record. Additionally, by applying human social terms to behaviour in animals that may be only superficially similar, we create the perhaps entirely false impression that it is the *same* behaviour. It is an easy step from that to the assumption that the causes and utility of these behaviours are the same as those of corresponding human behaviour.

Consider, for instance, the question of whether humans are territorial. We do tend to preserve space between us as individuals, to defend our homes, and as groups to defend larger, political areas. However, do these behaviours have the same genetic and adaptive value in humans as in animals? And is human territoriality homologous with that of other animals, or is it merely analogous?

Also, problems of objectivity can exist. Any assumptions we may have about our own territoriality can cause us to look at the behaviour of animals as a mirror of our own. Among closely related species of primates, social organization and the degree of territoriality and aggressive behaviour vary widely. Which of these species should we choose as models for studying human behaviour?

Most of the controversy that has been triggered by sociobiology seems related to its possible ethical implications. Sociobiology is often taken as denying that human behaviour is flexible enough to permit substantial improvements in the quality of our social lives.

Yet sociobiologists do not disagree with their critics that human behaviour is flexible. The debate therefore seems to rest on the *degree* to which human behaviour is genetic and the *extent* to which it can be modified.

As sociobiologists acknowledge, people through culture possess the ability to change their way of life far more profoundly in a few years than a hive of bees or a troop of baboons could accomplish in hundreds of generations of genetic evolution.

This ability is indeed genetically determined, and that is a very great gift. How we use it and what we accomplish with it is not a gift but a responsibility upon which our own wellbeing and the well-being of other species depend.

9

ECOLOGY

A decade or two ago one might have thought that ecology was invented by politicians. The concept seemed new to many people who heard for the first time (often in political speeches) about such issues as strip-mining, undrinkable water, all-but-unbreathable air, and vanishing wildlife.

Today, despite the continued importance of environmental issues, many politicians have taken up new issues, and some look upon ecology as a passing fad, no longer a major problem of the 1980s. Unfortunately, the problems have not gone away, and our global life support system continues to deteriorate.

How could this have happened? The facts have not changed. Perhaps the explanation is that they were not perceived as facts but as doctrines of a social and political movement. Somehow in the heady excitement of the ecology movement we failed to communicate that ecology itself is not a movement. Ecology is a science.

If that can be made clear, perhaps the facts can be approached once again in a new spirit. Dismantled programs can be reassembled, obscured goals rediscovered, jaded minds re-educated, and perhaps this time, priorities permanently reordered.

The first formal statement of the concept of ecology is attributed to the 19th-century German biologist, Ernst Haeckel. As proposed by him, the term embodies two Greek roots, oikos, house or habitat, and *logos,* study of. *Ecology* is, then, the branch of biology that examines the interactions between organisms and their environment, as well as with one another.

ECOLOGICAL ORGANIZATION

Groups of organisms may be associated in three main levels of ecological organization-populations, communities, and ecosystems. A *population* is a group of individuals of the same species that occupy a particular area at the same time. All the populations that occupy a particular area at a given time make up a *community*.

A community and its physical, nonliving environment constitute an *ecosystem*. As discussed in other chapter of this book, an ecosystem may be as small as an aquarium containing fish, plants, and decomposers or as large as an ocean or forest. The largest, most self-sufficient ecosystem known is the *ecosphere* our planet Earth and all of its inhabitants.

HABITAT AND ECOLOGICAL NICHE

No organism is distributed evenly over the face of the earth. Rather, each population occupies a particular habitat, a specific type of environmenta burrow in a prairie, the muddy bottom of a lake, or a treetop. Even the water trapped in the leaves of a pitcher plant may contain protozoa and mosquito larvae that somehow escape digestion.

One thinks of habitat as horizontal-an area on a map. Yet communities generally show a variety of different vertical habitats that vary in physical factors, such as temperature, light, and oxygen. In a forest, for example, there is a vertical stratification of plant life, from mosses and herbs on the ground to shrubs, low trees, and tall trees.

Each of these strata has a distinctive animal population. Even such highly mobile animals as birds are more or less restricted to certain layers. Some species of birds are found only in shrubs, others only in the tops of tall trees.

There may be daily and seasonal changes in the populations found in each stratum, and some animals are found first in one, then in another habitat as they pass through their life histories. An *ecological niche* is the role of a species in an ecosystem.

To describe an organism's ecological niche, we must know what it eats, when it is active, where it goes, and how it affects other organisms and its nonliving environment. Ecological niche helps determine habitat. One would not expect to find a polar bear in an Amazon rain forest.

It may be helpful to think of an organism's habitat as its address (where it lives) and of its ecological niche as its profession (how it functions in its community). What determines where an organism can live and its ecological niche? Among the most important determinants are the organism's structural, functional, and behavioural adaptations. Also important are the competition of other organisms and the stage of development of the community.

POPULATION DYNAMICS

In a stable population there is a balance between biotic potential and environmental resistance. *Biotic potential* is the capacity of a population to increase its numbers. This capacity is kept in check by *environmental resistance*, a combination of factors that limit the survival of the individuals of the population and prevent the population from increasing indefinitely.

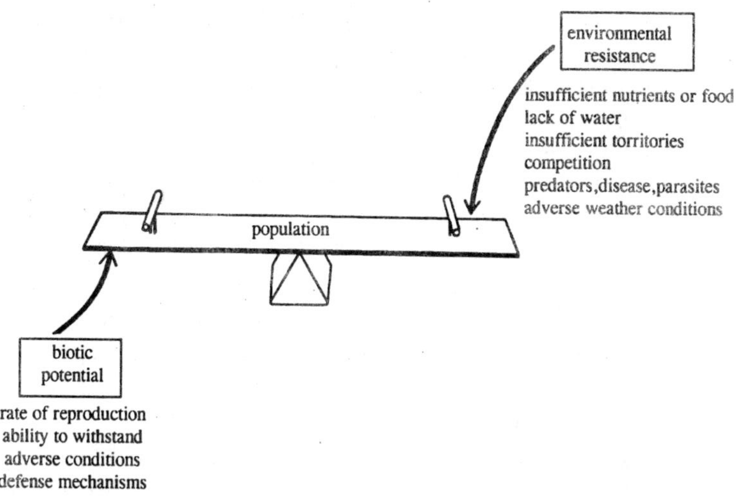

Figure 9.1: In a stable population there is a balance between the factors that increase numbers and those that limit population size.

Environmental resistance includes such obvious limiting factors as lack of nutrients or water, adverse weather conditions, and lack of appropriate habitats. Less obvious factors, such as competition, predation, and disease, also limit the growth of a population. If the environmental resistance for a population is less than its biotic potential, its numbers will increase.

However, if environmental resistance is greater than biotic potential, its numbers will decrease. As population size approaches the *carrying capacity*, the maximum population that the area can support without being damaged, the environmental resistance increases.

Adaptations and Biotic Potential

The environment includes *nonbiotic factors*, such as climate and the availability of light, water, and oxygen. Equally important are such *biotic factors* as competitors, predators, and parasites. To survive and to propagate its genes, an organism must be adapted to both biotic and nonbiotic factors. It must be able to withstand harmful factors and take advantage of life-sustaining factors.

The better adapted an organism is to its environment, the greater its biotic potential-its ability to reproduce and increase its population. A cactus, for instance, must be able to withstand drought and so has no leaves but does have a very extensive root system and much tissue in which water may be stored.

It must also be able to withstand predation from animals that might take advantage of its water stores or accumulated food in an area where few plants of any kind are able to grow. Its spines certainly do discourage most grazers. As a primary producer, it is also adapted to the abundance of sunlight it receives and so has a green, often flattened stem provided with chlorenchyma and stomata for photosynthesis.

Its biotic potential depends upon these adaptations and the extent to which they are appropriate for its environment and life-style.

Limiting Factors

Certain requirements must be met for an organism to survive and reproduce-an equable temperature range, adequate oxygen, an appropriate mixture of inorganic nutrients in the soil, sufficient food, adequate nesting sites, and so on.

If some factor is essential, then it has the potential of posing a limit for the organism, or for growth of the population. A *limiting factor*, then, is whatever essential factor is in the shortest (or most excessive) supply.

Were one to provide the optimum amounts of a former limiting factor, then something else would become limiting in turn. If a population of rats were supplied with a superabundance of food, for instance, the availability of water might nebertheless limit population growth.

Were that supplied in large amounts, the availability of nesting sites might become limiting. If those were supplied, the stress engendered by excessive interaction among the animals might produce disease, or the crowding might permit disease organisms and parasites to pass from one to another so efficiently that epizootics (animal epidemics) would result. Indeed, we often do not realize what really is essential either

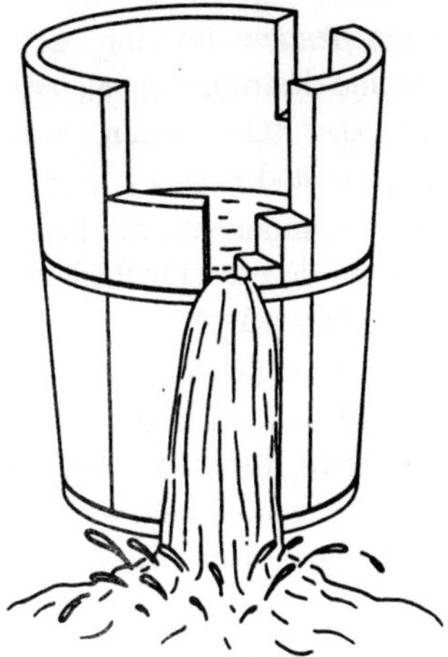

Figure 9.2: How agricultural chemist Justus von Liebig, a 19th century pioneer, viewed limiting factors. The capacity of the bucket depends on the length of the shortest stave. So, too, the welfare of an organism depends on the specific environmental factor that is least optimal for it.

to ourselves or to other organisms until it gets to be in short supply! Limiting factors do more than limit potential populations.

They also govern distribution and occurrence of populations within a community. As we will see in the next chapter, climatic limiting factors are primarily responsible for the differential distribution of major biotic communities on the earth.

What is or is not an effective limiting factor depends on the adaptations of each type of organism. That is why one environment will give a particular species a competitive advantage over another, while another environment may see this reversed. It is also why organisms tend to remain in their ecological niches.

All known organisms produce more offspring than the number of individuals in the parental generation. One does not usually think of cactus plants as being capable of overrunning the earth, but ordinary North American prickly pear almost overran the continent of Australia earlier in this century.

In the absence of natural enemies, the cactus spread without seeming limit, crowding out other vegetation and rendering vast tracts of land useless for grazing or agriculture. Only when one of the cactus's natural enemies, the *Cactoblastis* insect, was deliberately introduced did the prickly pear menace subside.

In this case, the major component of the environmental resistance to the growth of the cactus population was a natural enemy. It was largely a *population-independent* limiting factor because the insects were able to search out and destroy most specimens of the cactus, even those isolated from one another. (Other examples of population-independent limiting factors are drought and frost.)

But there are other components of the cactus's environmental resistance. Considering the desert habitat of the cactus, one necessity that is bound to be in short supply is water. Water is a potential limiting factor for all desert organisms.

Since the cactus requires a vast root system to collect whatever water does become available, there is a limit to how closely spaced cacti and other desert plants can be before their root systems compete to their mutual disadvantage. Water is therefore also a *population-dependent* limiting factor for them.

In actual practice many potential limiting factors may interact with one another, especially when one or more of them is near its tolerable extreme. Trees, for example, are less likely to be killed by frost when they are also abundantly watered.

Thus, it has become fashionable to view the growth, population density, and geographic distribution of an organism as determined by a complex of factors, which *together* constitute the environmental resistance that a given species must tolerate.

The environmental resistance of a habitat, then, determines whether a particular organism can be a member of a specific community. A habitat's environmental resistance for one organism is far different from its resistance for another. The desert has much less environmental resistance for a plant like a cactus, which is adapted to it, than it has for one like a water lily, which is not.

Competition

One of the more important potential limiting factors in the life of any organism is competition. Competition can take many forms. Since two organisms of the same species have essentially identical ecological niches and much the same set of adaptations, *intraspecific competition* for the always limited resources of the environment can be expected to be acute.

For instance, in the spring common North American gray squirrels are very much in evidence. Often they attract attention with risky antics as they pursue one another through the treetops, over lawns, and across roadways. One is observing here, in most cases, young male squirrels being driven away from the nest by older, established territorial animals.

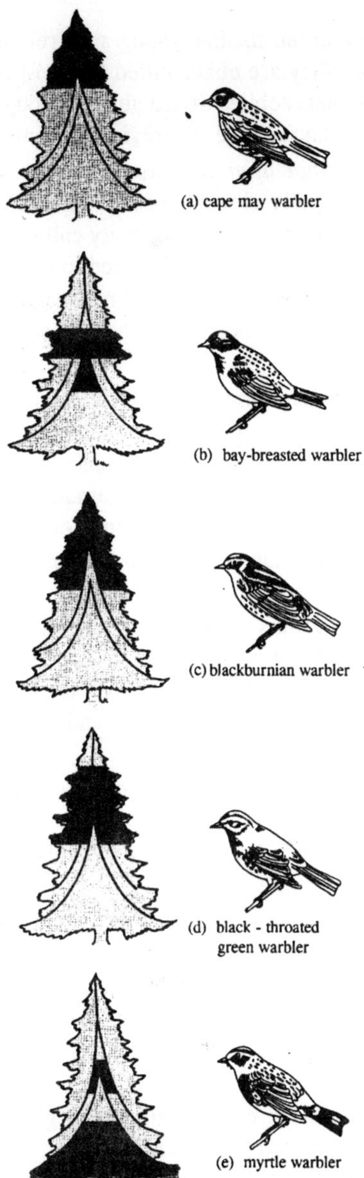

Figure 9.3: Interspecific competition is reduced among warblers in the genus Qendroica as a result of vertical stratification. Each species forages for insects in different parts of the same spruce trees. The coloured regions indicate where each species spends at least half its feeding time.

Even in a densely urban habitat young squirrels have been shown to travel miles before they are either killed (as most of them are) by such hazards as cats or automobiles or are able to occupy territories vacated by the death or advancing age of previous tenants.

Interspecific competition can also be sharp among members of different but ecologically similar species. A classic instance involves two species of anole (sometimes incorrectly called "chameleon") lizards in Florida. The native American anole used to occur almost everywhere in the lower southeastern states, but when Florida was colonized by the imported and larger Cuban anole, the American anole largely disappeared from urban habitats.

Interspecific competition among songbirds affords another example, more easily studied in most parts of the country. One need only observe events at a winter bird feeder to see intense interspecific competition and interspecific dominance relationships among grackles, blue jays and song sparrows. Yet almost no competition is observable among birds of radically differing ecological niches. Song sparrows do not normally compete with buzzards, for instance.

According to Gause's law, often referred to as the principle of competitive exclusion, two species that compete in every way cannot coexist, at least not indefinitely. One of them is bound to have a superior set of adaptations to its life-style and sooner or later will force its competitor into local extinction.

Competition certainly helps determine whether an organism can live in a given area. In Florida, for example, many native coastal mangrove forests have been displaced by imported Brazilian pepper trees.

The mangroves have grown there for millennia, and although other environmental disturbances (to which pepper trees are more resistant) have certainly played a part, it is the competitive superiority of the pepper trees in this habitat that has produced the demise of the mangroves. A well-tended lawn is a different kind of case.

As long as it is properly fertilized and watered, it will have few weeds, since under those circumstances the grass has a competitive advantage. If it is neglected, however, the advantage goes to the weeds, which promptly overgrow the lawn.

When organisms possess specialized adaptations, they must usually give up something in return. Take the cactus we have been discussing. Most grass cannot grow where the cactus will survive, but the cactus *could* grow almost anywhere grass can grow.

Why don't cacti take over the world? The answer probably is that where grass and other less specialized plants can grow, water is not normally an important limiting factor. Their stomata can remain open all day, and they can have welldeveloped leaves or blades with much surface area for gas exchange and light absorption.

They can tolerate the accompanying water loss because water is available in relative abundance. The cactus, however, has no leaves and must rely on the small surface area of its stem for photosynthesis. Moreover, it stores carbon dioxide for photosynthesis during the *night,* keeping its stomata closed during the day.

So the sacrifice that the cactus makes to the demands of its harsh environment is photosynthetic inefficiency. This puts it at such a competitive disadvantage in areas of water abundance that it usually occurs only where the soil will not retain water.

Predation

Predation is nothing more than one living organism killing and eating another. By this definition, even herbivores can be predators upon plants, as in the case of tent caterpillars feeding upon the leaves of trees, possibly killing the trees by complete defoliation. However, we tend to think of predation as having an animal victim.

Unlike plants, animals can usually respond actively to attack. Large ruminants in vigorous health are formidable antagonists for wolves, and if they are alert, difficult to approach as well. Among smaller organisms defenses against predation rely less upon brute force.

Aposematic, or warning, behaviour or colouration warns predators of some nasty defense possessed by a potential victim. Doesn't the loud buzz and striking yellow-and-black colour scheme of a hornet convey a clear message to you? It evidently makes a lasting impression on birds who have tried to eat such insects.

In some forms of mimicry an animal presents the aposematic behaviour without anything to back it up; a predator with experience with (or in some cases an innate aversion to) the model will avoid the mimic also. Other strategies of predator avoidance include rapid escape or withdrawal to inaccessible location, as one can observe in a cockroach under hot pursuit.

A nocturnal pattern of activity keeps some organisms, again like cockroaches, out of the way of diurnal organisms such as ourselves, although there are many predators adapted for night hunting. Camouflage and protective colouration also tend to conceal potential prey organisms from possible predators.

Predators also have many adaptational strategies for overcoming the defenses of their prey: Wolves hunt in packs, thereby saturating the prey's defenses; lions ambush their prey; African hunting dogs tire the prey by chasing in relays; and coyotes attack vulnerable parts of the prey, like the soft bellies of armadillos.

The prey-predator relationship is sometimes viewed as a kind of evolutionary arms race, in which predators must counter increasingly efficient defensive adaptations on the part of their prey with increasingly efficient methods of predation. On the other hand, a too—efficient predator might render its prey-and therefore itself—extinct.

Why this does not happen more often probably results from: (1) habitat complexity and (2) prey population reduction. When simplified prey-predator systems have been studied in the laboratory, the extinction of prey (and ultimately, predator) populations was much less likely to occur when habitat diversity was great.

The more nooks and crannies where prey organisms can hide, or the more out-of-the-way places where they can live, the less likely it is that even the most efficient predator can find them all. Prey population reduction is related to this. If the predator is indeed very efficient, it will succeed in reducing the population density of the prey.

The rarer the prey organisms become, the harder they are to find, especially in a diverse habitat. The predators starve, or at least raise fewer young successfully, and the predator population then also declines. The reduction in predators may permit the prey population to recover to some extent, which in turn produces an upswing in the density of predators, and so on.

This negative feedback mechanism therefore tends to regulate the populations of both predator and prey, often in cyclic fashion. To be sure, nature is rarely so simple. When predator populations are subsidized from some other food source, the predators can become numerous enough to wipe out local populations of prey completely.

Rats living in a garbage dump can become so numerous that one cannot find nestling birds within a quarter of a mile-yet normally, rats would never be so numerous as to have a substantial impact on the bird population. Predators are only one of the several components of environmental resistance, and not necessarily the most important.

The impact of predators upon prey populations seems to vary with the particular prey-predator relationship. In some cases, such as the wolf-moose interaction, the predators seem able to take only old and sick prey. Since these probably do not have the potential to reproduce

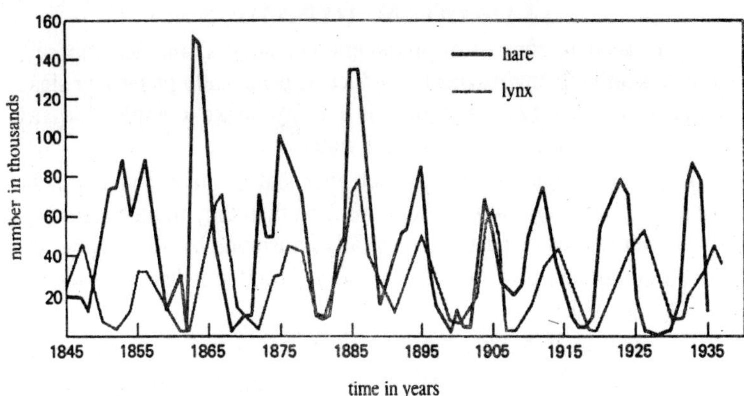

Figure 9.4: Changes in the abundance of the lynx and the snowshoe hare, as indicated by the number of pelts received by the Hudson's Bay Company. This is a classic case of cyclic oscillation in population density and of dependence of predator upon prey.

anyway, the wolves could influence moose population density only if they were able to take many young moose. An even better example is afforded by the interaction of houseflies and robber flies.

It is unlikely that robber flies reduce the housefly population even as well as a flyswatter does. Acting together, however, the *many* housefly predators may have an important influence on housefly population density. Actually, the effect of prey population density upon that of predators is better understood.

In a classic instance, the Hudson Bay Company has kept careful records of all pelts brought to their Canadian agents in trade since colonial times. Their records seem to indicate that as the populations of hares vary, so, too, do the much smaller populations of the fur-bearing predators, like the lynx, that live largely on the hares.

The most efficient predator of all is doubtless *Homo sapiens.* Few strategies can protect prey organisms from the attacks of this predator. Its ability to seek out and destroy every last specimen of a prey species or to destroy habitat has rendered many species extinct.

The island of Mauritius once harbored a kind of giant flightless pigeon that became extinct in the 1700s because European sailors hunted and killed every one of them. Yet the dodo was neither the first nor the last.

When the human population has encountered the combination of limiting factors that must ultimately stabilize it, one wonders how many other species of organisms will remain in what is bound then to be a biotically impoverished world.

ECOSYSTEM DYNAMICS

An ecosystem consists of producers, consumers, and decomposers, and their nonliving environment. Producers, principally plants and algae, capture solar energy and with this energy make complex organic compounds from carbon dioxide and water.

This food is both an energy-rich fuel and a building material for tissues. Producers typically make more food than they immediately need and can themselves be partially or totally consumed by consumers. The consumers-animals or protists-then use the food for their own energy and tissue growth.

They consume this food in their own tissues and store the excess. Consumers both eat the food and breathe the oxygen that producers have made. Decomposers are microbes, principally fungi and bacteria, which metabolize dead material and body wastes.

Nutritional Life-Styles

There are really only two ways to obtain food. Producers are *autotrophs* (self-nourishers) and make their own food from simple inorganic materials. All other organisms are *heterotrophs*, organisms unable to synthesize their own foodstuffs from inorganic materials. Heterotrophs *must* live at the expense of autotrophs or upon decaying organic matter. All consumers and decomposers are heterotrophs.

Producers

The producers, or autotrophs, include plants, algal protists, and autotrophic bacteria. Autotrophs require only water, carbon dioxide, inorganic salts, and a source of energy. It is the source of energy that varies. Plants and certain bacteria are *photosynthetic autotrophs*, deriving the energy needed for biosynthetic processes from sunlight.

A few bacteria are *chemosynthetic autotrophs* and obtain energy by oxidizing certain inorganic substances, such as ammonia or hydrogen sulfide. These bacteria have special enzyme systems that catalyze the oxidation of these substances and couple the oxidation with the generation of energy-rich phosphates.

For example, nitrite bacteria *(Nitrosomonas)* oxidize ammonia to nitrites; nitrate bacteria *(Nitrobacter)* oxidize nitrites to nitrates; iron bacteria oxidize ferrous to ferric iron; and still other bacteria oxidize hydrogen sulfide to sulfates. The energy derived from these oxidations is used to synthesize all the organic materials necessary to maintain life and growth.

The nitrite and nitrate bacteria are important in the cyclic use of nitrogen, for together they convert ammonia to nitrate, a form more readily used by many plants.

Consumers

All consumers are heterotrophs. Most obtain food as solid particles that must be eaten, digested, and absorbed (holozoic nutrition). They must constantly locate, catch, and eat other organisms.

To do this, animals possess a variety of sensory, nervous, and muscular structures to find and catch food, and digestive systems that convert food into molecules small enough to be absorbed.

Herbivores are animals that eat plants and obtain energy-rich compounds from the contents of the plant cells, compounds made by the plant using energy derived from sunlight. *Carnivores* eat other animals; *omnivores* eat either plants or animals.

Many *symbionts*, such as parasites, commensals, and mutualistic partners, are consumers. Parasites may obtain their nutrients by ingesting and digesting solid particles or by absorbing organic molecules through their cell walls from the body fluids or tissues of the host.

Detritus feeders, usually known as *scavengers*, have some of the characteristics of decomposers. Many detritus feeders, like earthworms, prepare material for attack by decomposers. Others, like fly maggots, eat the decomposers themselves.

Decomposers

Fungi and most bacteria can neither make their nutrients by autotrophic processes nor ingest solid food. They absorb their required organic nutrients directly through a cell membrane. This type of heterotrophic nutrition is known as *saprobic* nutrition.

Saprobes grow wherever there are decomposing bodies of animals or plants, or masses of plant and animal by-products. The humus of the uppermost layers of the forest floor, for instance, or the bottom ooze of some aquatic habitats is largely composed of decaying matter.

Yeasts are good examples of saprobes. They need only inorganic salts, oxygen, and some kind of sugar. From sugar they derive the energy to make all the other substances needed for life-proteins, fats, nucleic acids, vitamins, and so on.

When plenty of oxygen is available, yeasts obtain energy by oxidizing glucose completely to carbon dioxide and water via the citric acid cycle. When the supply of oxygen is limited, they ferment glucose and form alcohol and carbon dioxide. This, as we have seen, yields only about one-twentieth as much energy as the complete oxidation of glucose, and therefore yeasts and other organisms that are capable of both aerobic and anaerobic metabolism grow very slowly in the absence of oxygen.

Food Chains and Food Webs

A series of organisms that eat and in turn are eaten by others is called a *food chain*. The position of an organism in a food chain is called its *trophic* (feeding) *level*. Producers are found at the first trophic level, herbivores at the second, and carnivores at the third and higher levels. A very simple food chain might consist of grass eaten by a cow, which in turn is eaten by a human being.

As in all food chains, the producer, in this case the grass, occupies the first trophic level. When the cow, a *primary consumer*, eats the grass, some of the chemical energy stored in the grass's organic molecules is transferred to the second trophic level. The cow now enjoys the benefits of the photosynthetic activities of the grass.

The human being in this case is a *secondary consumer*, who by eating the cow gains some of the chemical energy originally captured by the producer but now stored in the bonds of the cow's own organic compounds. Thus, in a food chain, energy is transferred from the eaten to the eater.

An animal may be a member of several food chains and may occupy different trophic levels in those food chains. For example, a human may bc a primary consumer in one food chain, eating plant foods, but a secondary or tertiary consumer in other chains, eating herbivores or carnivores.

In most communities there are many food chains that interconnect at various levels, forming a *food web*. A food web may be extremely complex, involving thousands of types of organisms. This produces many alternative pathways of energy flow, which contribute to the stability of the community.

Organic waste products and corpses of producers and consumers support decomposers. In turn, decomposers serve as the basis of subsidiary food chains that support such organisms as detritus feeders. For example, a food chain might begin with plants whose dead leaves are decomposed by fungi and bacteria.

The microorganisms are eaten by detritus feeders, perhaps maggots. Then, chickens might consume the maggots. Finally, the chicken or its eggs might be eaten by human beings.

If we were to count the number of organisms in each trophic level,

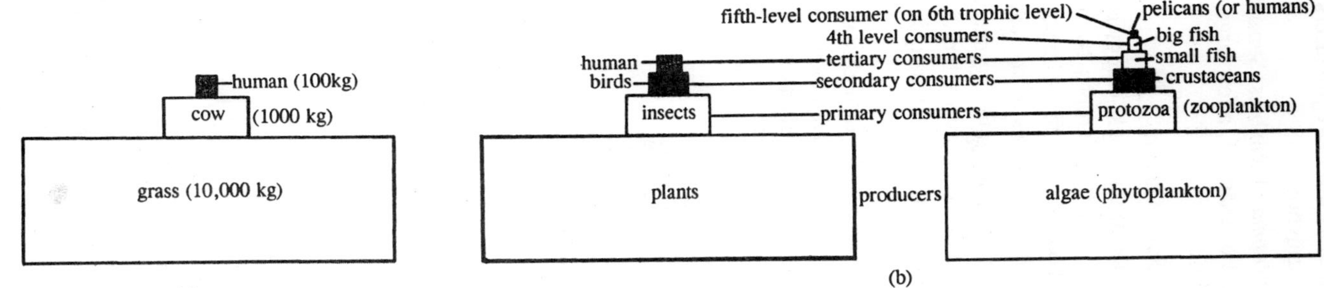

Figure 9.5: (a) A simple food chain. Note that over a given period 10,000 kilograms of grass can support only 1000 kilograms of cow, which in turn can support only 100 kilograms of human being (if that person ate only beef). (b) Comparison of a terrestrial (left) with an aquatic (right) food chain. Draw several food chains of your own design.

we would typically find that there are more producers than herbivores, and more herbivores than carnivores.

This can depicted by a *pyramid* of numbers. Sometimes, the pyramid of numbers can be inverted. For example, a few large trees can support many insects and small birds.

Energy Transfer Through Food Chains

As we saw in other chapter of this book, energy is transferred from autotrophs, principally plants, to heterotrophs by means of organic compounds. One of the functions of these food compounds is to provide energy that is liberated by such processes as the citric acid cycle.

Another function is to provide the building materials for bodies. Virtually any chemical element that is necessary for life is first absorbed from the environment by some plant, which initially incorporates it into food molecules.

These then pass into the metabolisms of herbivores and carnivores and ultimately organisms of decay. Eventually, those organisms of decay liberate all the elements put into food by plants in the form of simple, inorganic substances.

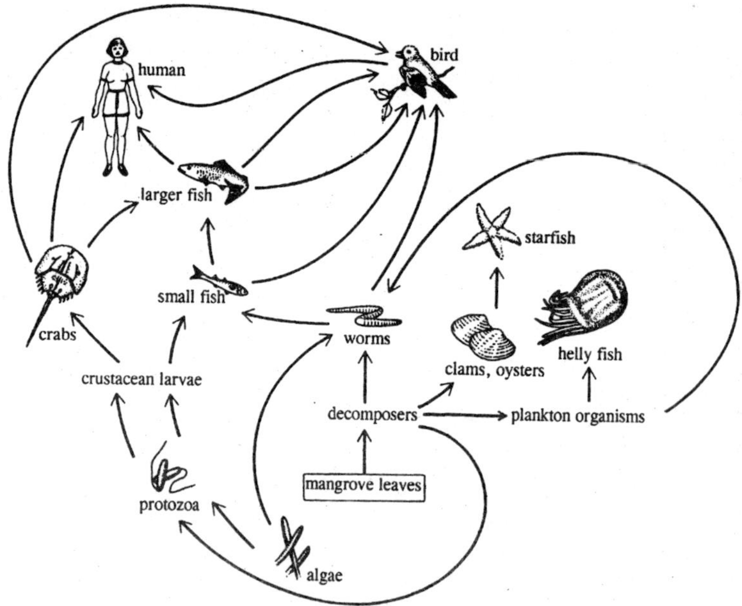

Figure 9.6: A marine food web. Arrows point from each organism to its consumer. Note that even this web is simplified. Human beings, for example, could eat algae, thereby acting as primary consumers.

Only a small portion of the energy captured by a producer can be transferred to the herbivore that eats it. This is because the producer uses a great deal of energy for its own biological activities. Energy must be used for synthesis of needed compounds, growth, transport of materials, and many other processes within the plant.

Then, also, for every energy process that the plant carries on, a great deal of energy is lost as heat, as explained by the second law of thermodynamics. Similar energy consumption occurs within the herbivore. Additional energy is lost when undigested food passes out of the body in feces or when the organism dies.

Some of that energy is captured by decomposers and detritus feeders. Decomposing organisms also produce heat. A manure pile can be seen to steam on a cold day, and curing hay produces enough heat to be a fire hazard.

On average, the energy transfers from one trophic level to the next are only about 10% efficient. This means that only about 10% of the energy captured by the producers can be passed on to the primary consumers. Then, only about 10% of the energy within the primary consumers can be passed on to the secondary consumers, and so on.

In studying energy transfer it is convenient to think of a food chain as a food pyramid that shows the relative size decrease of each level.

Biomass and Trophic Levels

A number of studies of communities have indicated that the primary producers are typically the most numerous and, collectively, weigh the most. The *biomass*, weight of living material, decreases with increase in trophic level, and there are usually also fewer carnivores in any ecosystem than there are herbivores.

In many cases the herbivorous animals have a biomass about 10% that of the plants. In turn, highly specialized carnivores may together weigh only 10% of the collective weight of the herbivores. Thus, there could be a 1000-fold reduction of biomass from primary producers, such as grass, to ultimate predators (those that have no natural predators), such as hawks.

Predators, especially large ones, are never common, for it takes many square miles of habitat to support each one. The biomass ratio varies considerably among communities and even within the same community at different times. The reason is that producers and primary consumers may be eaten at different rates so that, at least temporarily, predators might eat so many herbivores that they outnumber their prey. However, over a period of time the rate of production of primary producer biomass cannot be outpaced by the rate of production of any of the consumers dependent upon it. Productivity studies over a period of time always yield progressive reductions with each trophic level.

One might wonder why it is advantageous for an organism to be a consumer at all, let alone a carnivore. But consider how little energy is obtainable from most kinds of plant food relative to its bulk; it is no accident that many reducing diets emphasize lettuce.

Indeed, most herbivores spend most of their time just eating, as one can readily observe by watching a cow spend her day chewing cud. The consumer of the cow, however, eats energy that is far more concentrated. Carnivores can often go for days between meals. Their population densities may be low, but individually, they live well.

Herbivores may be thought of as rather inefficient transformers of energy, taking energy from a large source of low concentration and transforming it to a small product of high concentration. This suggests a possible reason why there are seldom four links in a typical food chain.

The ultimate predators of such a chain would be specialized for eating carnivores, but there would be nothing to be gained by always eating carnivores rather than herbivores (the energy concentration of their tissues would be about the same). In a long food chain the total biomass of the ultimate predators would be very small indeed; they would be rare and vulnerable to extinction.

Productivity

In most ecosystems all energy input is via the producers. The rate of total energy storage by producers in an ecosystem over a certain period of time is referred to as *gross productivity*. However, much of the energy stored by producers is used in cellular respiration and other activities.

The rate of energy storage in the biomass of the producers, after their rate of energy use has been subtracted, is *net productivity*. This energy may be stored in the form of new biomass (growth and new producers), stored organic compounds, or even in seeds and fruit.

Net community productivity is the rate at which energy is stored in the community as a whole. To compute it, respiration in producers, consumers, and decomposers is subtracted from gross productivity.

Different kinds of ecosystems have different characteristic productivities. Over most temperate regions annual net production is about 500 to 2000 grams per square meter. Productivity depends upon environmental conditions favourable to growth of the producers. Fertile soil, sufficient sunlight and moisture, and a long growing season contribute to high productivity.

This is why estuaries, marshes, and many tropical ecosystems are very productive, whereas desert areas have low productivity. Except near the coasts, oceans are not very productive, owing mainly to a lack of sufficient nutrients. Dead plants and animals sink to the ocean bottom, where they are decomposed.

However, the nutrients released are not readily used because there is not enough light to support photosynthesis. About 60% of the earth's surface is covered by open ocean, where the annual net productivity is only about 500 grams per square meter or less. On agricultural land measurements of productivity reflect crop yields.

Nutrient Cycling

Simple inorganic substances can be recycled indefinitely, being built up into organic materials and broken down again into simple components any number of times (at least in theory). By their action decomposers usually prevent the permanent accumulation of corpses and wastes, and more important, liberate recyclable materials not liberated by the metabolism of consumers.

These include not only carbon, hydrogen, and oxygen, but also nitrogen, sulfur, potassium, phosphorus, iron, and other elements. Some may be lost by runoff from precipitation, but in undisturbed ecosystems most find their way back to the roots of the primary producers. Detritus feeders, such as maggots, lobsters, and earthworms, play an auxiliary role to decomposers.

Both decomposers and detritus feeders are themselves eaten by

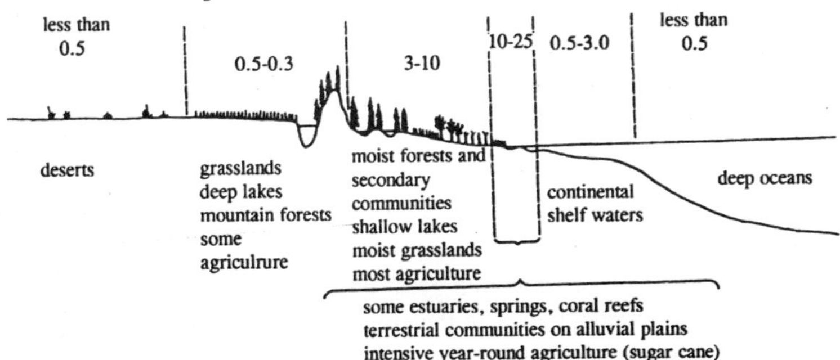

Figure 9.7: The world distribution of primary production in grams of dry matter per square meter per day, as indicated by average daily rates of gross production in major ecosystems.

consumers and are also decomposed by other decomposers. Ultimately, the entire biomass produced by the primary producers is reconverted to inorganic materials by the action of decomposers.

Both biological and geological activities are involved in nutrient cycling. Appropriately, such pathways are referred to as *biogeochemical cycles*. The phosphorus cycle is shown in Figure elsewhere in this chaper.

STRESS AND ECOSYSTEMS

Stress may prove a limiting factor for some organisms; it may also become a limiting factor sooner for some organisms than for others. If stress is applied to a community, it will reduce species diversity and complexity by eliminating or reducing the population of those organisms least well adapted to it.

On the other hand, those organisms well adapted to the stress (and thereby freed from competition) may prosper greatly as long as the stress persists.

The earliest studies of community stress were performed at Brook haven National Laboratories on Long Island to determine what effect large doses of ionizing radiation might have on natural communities. The researchers discovered that the sparse oak woodland exposed to the radiation was completely destroyed at the highest intensities, with progressively less destruction in areas farther from the radiation source, until at a considerable distance there was no obvious effect.

The important thing was that the number of species, or more exactly, the species diversity increased with the distance from the radiation source. In other words, small amounts of radiation killed rather few species, larger amounts killed more, and the very largest amounts killed all.

Though this may seem obvious in retrospect, a less than obvious implication of the study, and one that has been repeatedly confirmed with many stressing agents, is that stress simplifies communities. This is because the stressing agent leaves only those organisms that are resistant to it.

These may, however, attain great numbers of biomass, since they are freed from competition with the stress-sensitive species. The nature of the stressing agent makes a difference in the exact species composition of the community; two such agents might simplify the same community comparably but in different ways, for each would leave a different assemblage of organisms unscathed.

An excellent example is a lawn. As long as it is regularly mowed, all the plants in it (not only grass but also chickweed, plantain, dandelion, portulaca, and other pests) must be resistant to the mowing. The grass is resistant by virtue of its basal meristem. Most of the others are resistant as a result of their low, spreading growth habit, which enables them to miss the blades.

Should the mowing stop, a much greater variety of plants could and would live there-shrubs and tall weeds, for instance. In time the diversity of the lawn would become very great and by then it would, in fact, have ceased to be a lawn and would have begun the successional process (soon to be discussed) that would perhaps ultimately produce woodland.

Stress renders a community more susceptible to further stress because it reduces its diversity. A disease that kills a particular species of grass would be of little consequence in a woodland or even a prairie but could be a disaster in your front lawn.

Since the pollution and other stress that we place on natural communities around us tends to simplify them in just this way, we approach ever nearer the point at which they can absorb no further punishment and some random factor causes their collapse.

SUCCESSION

Communities of organisms do not spring into existence in final form but typically pass through a series of stages, beginning with a *pioneer community* and ending with a *climax community*, which as far as one can tell is ultimately stable and undergoes little further change.

The whole sequence of communities leading to the climax is known as a *sere*. The progressive series of changes in the kinds and numbers of organisms leading to a climax community is known as *ecological succession*.

Generally, the earliest stages of ecological successions are the most highly stressed, since habitats unmodified by living things are usually harsh. Therefore, early stages of successions tend to have low species diversity. As they proceed, however, they tend to ameliorate the environment, which produces new ecological niches that can be occupied by other, more diverse organisms.

Stress may even produce conditions to which newcomers are better adapted than are the members of the pioneer community, so the pioneers are succeeded by interlopers that could not have existed under the original conditions.

A climax is reached when a community is established that contains no potential ecological niches that could be filled by, or better filled by, any organisms not already present in the community. Stress tends to delay succession, or rather to produce a kind of climax community that will persist as long as the stress is applied. In the absence of the stress, succession will continue.

A Typical Succession

In theory, soil nutrients originate from the parent rocky material that, when weathered, gave rise to the soil. This is such a slow process that the mineral needs of mature plant communities cannot be sustained solely by continued weathering of the rock.

The very earliest plant communities to colonize a habitat, however, may indeed have obtained their mineral nutrients from the rocky materials upon which they grew. A succession that begins in such an initially lifeless habitat is said to be a *primary succession*. This is different from a *secondary succession* (as might take place in a neglected lawn) which begins with a pre-existing community.

Imagine a bare rock surface on a moderately tall mountain in a warm climate. Few organisms could do more than rest briefly on its surface, for it would provide almost none of the conditions needed for life. One form of life could exist and even thrive there, however: lichens.

The very first lichens might form a layer growing among the grains of a rock surface, or even a millimeter or two inside the rock itself, but soon they would be visible on the rock surface. As has already been discussed, a lichen is not a plant; it is a compound organism consisting of one of several species of a fungus in association with one or another species of algae or cyanobacteria.

Lichens are amazingly hardy, tolerating extremes of dehydration that would kill any true plant. This obviously suits them to the harsh, bare-rock habitat. Equally important, lichens have an incredible ability to digest or solubilize that rock and to concentrate nutrients from it and from the surrounding air, probably via rainfall.

Lichens are not immortal, however, and when they die and decay, the minerals they have accumulated in their bodies are released by decomposers and taken up by living lichens, in addition to whatever the new generation of lichens can liberate afresh from the rock.

Thus, the lichen community gradually accumulates an ever-increasing capital of minerals. These minerals are stored in the bodies of living lichens, in the organisms that are now living on them, and to a lesser extent, in the organic detritus that is beginning to accumulate under and around them. By now, fine particles of rock have weathered away from the surface but have been trapped by the lichen community and cannot be washed away as before.

Eventually, the mineral particles and organic detritus form a thin layer of true soil capable of briefly holding some moisture. This soil contains a substantial part of the accumulating mineral capital of the developing community of organisms.

As its thickness increases and more minerals accumulate in it, the soil becomes suited to the requirements of some real plants-mosses. They now take hold among the lichens and grow vigorously. In fact, these mosses are better adapted to the less rigorous conditions the lichens have created than are the lichens themselves.

Gradually they crowd the lichens out, going through many cycles of life and decay themselves in the process. Minerals continue to weather out of the parent rock, now buried, after perhaps a thousand years, beneath as much as an inch of soil.

These minerals are added over the course of years to the accumulating capital of the now radically changed community. Few or no minerals leave the community, for as soon as they are released from the dead organisms by decay bacteria and fungi, they are either reincorporated into young organisms or held in the soil temporarily in absorbed form.

Eventually, the moss may produce enough soil, especially in the deeper crevices, so that grass and even small trees can take root. Even later these successor forms may so dominate the community that the lichens and moss that preceded them may be almost impossible to find.

Why Successions Occur

Why does ecological succession take place at all? Why must a sere occur to prepare the habitat for the climax community? Each community modifies the habitat, so it becomes less harsh and stressful. That permits the establishment of another community that is more complex and more exacting in its requirements.

The reason for this becomes evident when one considers the effects of stress upon communities. What environment could be more stressful than that of a pioneer community? The extremes of temperature often are almost outside the range that most living organisms can tolerate.

Water is usually in very short supply, and mineral nutrients can be almost unavailable. Only a few of the very toughest organisms can withstand a pioneer environment in a primary succession.

In succession, the actions of pioneer organisms on the habitat may make it more tolerable, but the very pioneer organisms that have made the habitat less harsh are bound to lose in the competition that will likely ensue with less specialized organisms.

These, in turn, modify the habitat further and are replaced by still other organisms until, finally, no more efficiently productive organisms are to be found and a climax community results. Since a stressed community is also a simple community, as conditions moderate in the course of succession, the community becomes steadily more diverse until in the near-climax state diversity and complexity are at a maximum.

HUMAN ECOLOGY

Human beings have an ecology quite as much as do prairie dogs or ivy plants. And although one rarely speaks of a species as a geological or ecological disaster, that is the category in which *Homo Sapiens* surely belongs. No organism in the history of life has had a greater impact on the planet than we have had.

In a few short generations we have utterly transformed the face of the earth and greatly accelerated the rate of extinctions of species. One might be able to take a neutral position at this point; after all, who cares what happens to snail darter fish or the furbish lousewort plant, or even the chimpanzee?

Yet what we face is not merely the absence of a few species of interest to bird watchers, or the destruction of forests of concern only to those who have time to enjoy them. What we face is the real possibility of the heedless disassembly of our planet's life support system, for as you must understand by now, the cycling of nutrients and gases, and the flow and storage of biologically useful energy, depend on the interaction of a variety of living things.

In other words, the conditions required by living things, ourselves included, have been produced by other living things,' and the life support system of life is life itself.

THE ECOLOGY OF AGRICULTURE

In large measure the ecological impact of humanity varies widely with the kinds of human societies and their specific technologies. Of these, perhaps no technology has had more direct and indirect ecological impact than agriculture.

Such techniques as scientific crop rotation, use of chemical fertilizers and pesticides, mechanical tillage, and sophisticated irrigation systems did not exist 200 years ago. What has made most of them widespread and practical is the ready availability of energy. Energy of one kind or another chemically fixes nitrogen in fertilizer factories, turns the wheels of tractors, and mines water from the ground.

Agricultural Communities

An agricultural community, such as a field of corn or cabbages, usually has characteristics that set it apart from the community it displaced. First, *an agricultural community* is unstable because it can be maintained only by human intervention and energy input. Maize (corn), for example, can reproduce only with human aid. Another way of looking at the matter is that humans are essential for the continuance of agricultural communities.

Second, an agricultural community is simpler than any natural ecosystem. The plants of an agricultural community may be of only a single species. This *monoculture* greatly simplifies the community, and since the plant that is being monocultured can be consumed by human beings, the community that results is highly and desirably productive from a human viewpoint.

However, that very monoculture renders the agricultural community unstable and highly susceptible to insect pests or diseases, which can spread from one host organism to another with little hindrance.

In the natural state host plants (those attacked by pests) are interspersed with others that a particular pest species will not eat. Moreover, wild plants are usually genetically diverse and often possess natural pest-control adaptations, such as poisonous alkaloids.

Plant breeders usually develop strains without the alkaloids, but that makes the varieties they produce much more susceptible to insect attack. Furthermore, plant breeders try to produce varieties with increased yield, improved marketability, greater ease of shipping or harvesting, and resistance to particular diseases.

At any one time agriculture tends to be dominated by the latest varieties, so any threat to that single variety is potentially able to wipe out an entire major crop for one or more years. (This actually happened several years ago with a dominant variety of corn, which was uniquely susceptible to a new strain of fungus disease.)

In modern monocultural agriculture, therefore, unnatural pest-control methods and other practices have become necessary. Inevitably, these methods have substantial ecological impact, often extending far outside the boundaries of the areas where they are applied.

Third, the chemical cycles of an agricultural community are often incomplete. The cultivated species are consumed at a spot remote from where they are grown, and their substance is not usually returned to the soil but escapes from the terrestrial ecosystem through a sewage disposal plant or garbage dump.

This interruption of nutrient cycles causes the soil to deteriorate unless artificially fertilized-which brings with it problems of its own (such as increased eutrophication of adjacent bodies of water).

Fourth, *competition among species is greatly reduced.* Farmers go to great lengths to suppress species considered undesirable (called *weeds*) that compete with cultivated varieties or interfere with their harvest.

It should be obvious that an agricultural community is not and cannot be the same as the natural community it has replaced. The demands of agriculture simply do not permit this, and this realization has led to the development of game parks and preserves in many countries.

Yet even on farmland itself some compromise is possible, and with enlightened management, agricultural lands can be made to yield a modest return of wild game, or merely to serve as homes for wild species. However, even in the better-educated nations of the West, a knowledge of ecology sufficient to induce most farmers and other citizens to sacrifice even a small part of the potential food production of their land for seemingly impractical purposes is lacking.

In the heavily populated and economically less developed countries, the situation is even worse. Hungry peasants encroach continually on wild game preserves and expunge most surviving large wild animals from the land they have already acquired. (This is sometimes abetted by money supplied by Westerners for illegal trophies.)

Forestry

The deforestation of all countries has proceeded with alarming speed since the Industrial Revolution and, in some localities, since ancient times. One reads, for instance, of the Biblical cedars of Lebanon, and the modern Lebanese flag even depicts one.

Yet there is practically nothing left of the great forests whose timber was used in the construction of the palace and temple of King Solomon. This deforestation resulted not only from simply cutting the trees down, but also from heavy grazing by sheep and goats that prevented the growth of seedlings.

More recently, firewood and wood charcoal fueled the early Industrial Revolution. To this day the greatest use of forest products worldwide is for fuel. In countries that have limited or no fossil fuel resources, this often leads to dramatic deforestation. So acute is deforestation in modern India, for example, that the major fuel used over vast areas is dried cattle dung.

However, there are many other uses for timber as well. In the 19th century forests were extensively and wantonly cut to provide wood for construction timber and paper pulp, with fires often completing the destruction that the logging had begun. To some extent such practices continue today.

Many nations have embarked on extensive reforestation programs. However, the trees planted often are not native and do not fit in well with the local ecology. In any case they are usually managed as a crop, so ecologically, this *silviculture*, as it is called, resembles agriculture.

Tree farms are not forest communities; usually they are single-species aggregations with little wildlife, and usually they do not contain climax species. Douglas fir seedlings, for instance, will not grow well in the shade of mature trees and must be planted in clear-cut areas from which all mature trees have been removed.

PESTICIDES

The *first-generation pesticides*-inorganic chemicals, such as sulfur, lead, arsenic, and mercury-have been used to repel or kill pests for hundreds of years. Many of these substances are quite toxic, and they sometimes accumulated in the soil in amounts that inhibited plant growth. Pests also became resistant to them (a case of natural selection), so over time they lost their effectiveness.

The era of *second-generation pesticides* began about 1940 with the discovery of DDT. These pesticides are synthetic organic compounds that can be classified into three groups: (1) DDT and related *chlorinated hydrocarbons* (Chlordane, Dieldrin, Mirex), (2) *organophosphates* (malathion, parathion), and (3) *carbamates* (Sevin, Temik).

These highly effective organic pesticides have been developed and put into widespread use by everyone from farmers and health departments to suburban homeowners.

The chlorinated hydrocarbons interfere with nerve action by antagonizing the sodium pumps in nerve cell membranes. Most other organic pesticides are anticholinesterases that render the enzyme cholinesterase incompetent. Anticholinesterases are, in general, more toxic than chlorinated hydrocarbons.

Human beings are less susceptible to the action of both classes of pesticides than insects, partly because of their large body size and partly because of differences in physiology.

Problems With Using Pesticides

Most widely used pesticides are broad-spectrum poisons that kill nonpest species as well as pests. Another major problem with using pesticides is that many insects become resistant to them. Although initially the pesticide may cause a rapid decline in the pest population, resistant mutants gradually replace the susceptible insects.

By 1980 more than 200 DDT-resistant species were known. Often, a pesticide-resistant population evolves, while the natural predators of these insects do not become resistant. With their natural enemies devastated, the pest population increases in numbers and may become a greater threat than before the pesticides were used.

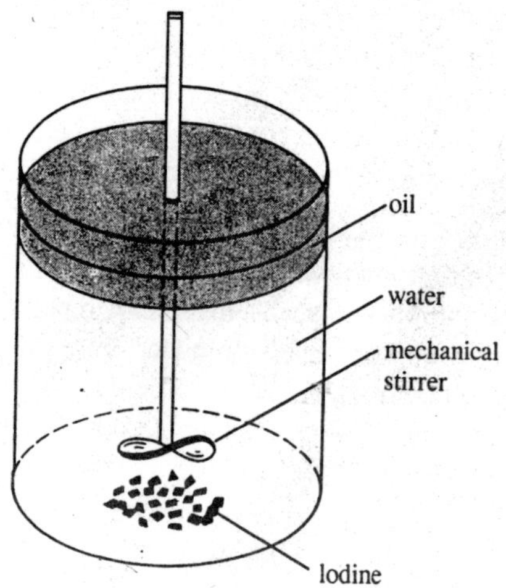

Figure 9.8: How a substance almost insoluble in water can become concentrated in another medium. Imagine a simple experiment with iodine, water, and mineral oil.

Predators do not develop resistance as quickly as pests because they are often larger and reproduce at a slower rate. They are also fewer in number because they are at a higher level on the food chain. Thus, the probability that resistant individuals are present or that resistant strains will be selected is lower.

DDT and Other Chlorinated Hydrocarbons

The organophosphate and carbamate pesticides are *biodegradable*, which means they decompose several weeks or months after being sprayed. DDT and other chlorinated hydrocarbons are *persistent pesticides*. They are not biodegradable.

Another problem with the chlorinated hydrocarbon pesticides is that they do not remain confined to the areas where they are sprayed. Food chains, air movements, and to a lesser extent, water currents distribute persistent pesticides globally, so there is now probably no organism on land or in the sea whose tissues are completely free from them. Traces of DDT have even been found in the fat of penguins in Antarctica, thousands of miles from where it was sprayed.

The chlorinated hydrocarbon pesticides are insoluble in water. For this reason they are neither readily broken down metabolically nor easily excreted. When an animal eats food containing DDT, wastes from the food are eventually excreted, but a large portion of the DDT remains in the body and accumulates in body fat.

This leads to the process known as *biological magnification*, in which chlorinated hydrocarbons (and some other substances, including certain radioactive elements) are concentrated in ecosystems. Thus, in a sprayed lawn the cricket that eats a little grass each day eventually accumulates more pesticide than the grass did.

The toad that eats these crickets soon has a greater DDT content than the crickets, and so on. In this way an ultimate predator, such as a hawk or human, concentrates in its body an appreciable portion of the pesticides absorbed by many acres of vegetation. Milk of nursing mothers has been found to contain concentrations of DDT higher than acceptable limits set by the Food and Drug Administration for cows' milk.

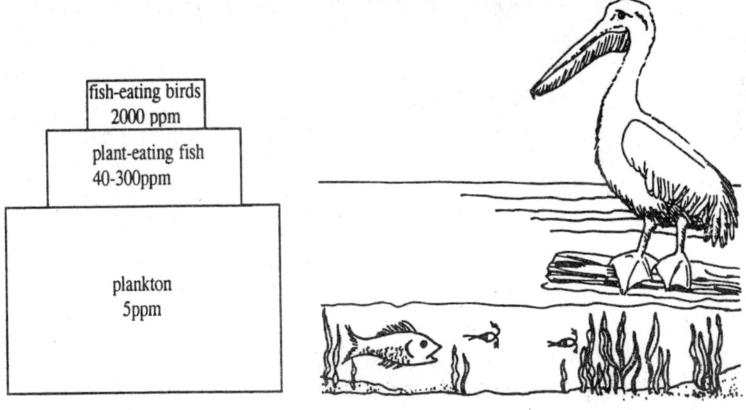

Figure 9.9: A toxicant pyramid, which provides further stages of concentration. Most of the biomass consumed on each level is excreted, but DDT and similar fat-soluble pesticides are not excreted to anywhere near the same extent and therefore tend to become progressively concentrated in the higher members of the food chain.

Reducing Pesticide Use

Because DDT poses a serious threat to ecosystems, its use in the United States was banned in 1973. However, in the early 1980s it was still being manufactured in the United States for export to the many other countries that still use it. Several closely related chlorinated hydrocarbon pesticides have also been banned, but others continue to be used widely.

Although the problems connected with pesticide use are reduced to some extent when biodegradable compounds, such as the carbamates or organophosphates, are substituted, there is no known pesticide that is free from undesirable ecological consequences.

The carbamate Sevin, for instance, is almost completely harmless to mammals but it is instant death for bees, and bees are vital for pollination of food and wild plants. Since all pesticides kill more than the pests against which they are directed, in the end our pesticide problems can be solved only if we can avoid them.

Yet this seems less likely to happen than ever. In fact, we now use twice the amount of pesticides used in 1962, the year Rachel Carson's *Silent Spring* was published. Why are pesticides still used so widely? The reasons are not hard to find. The World Health Organization contends that an international ban of DDT would be a disaster to world health.

The agricultural production of the United States might decrease by 30% if all pesticides were banned, and poorer nations would suffer even more from decreased food supplies and increased incidences of insect-borne diseases, especially malaria. Ironically, however, the mosquitoes that carry malaria have in recent years developed behavioural and other resistance to DDT, so although DDT remains damaging to everything else, it is steadily less effective against the pests for which it is intended.

Moreover, the consequences of population growth made possible by malaria control may well outweigh the good that has been accomplished. We can avoid using pesticides, to be realistic, only if we are content to produce less food. We can produce less food only if we have fewer mouths to feed. With fewer mouths to feed, we could, perhaps, confine human settlement to the parts of the globe ecologically suited to us-for example, by avoiding malarial swamps.

Alternatives to Pesticides

There are alternatives to the use of pesticides short of complete abandonment of our crops to the insect world, although none permit as high a level of agricultural production as our overpopulated world demands. Some are effective by themselves; others help reduce the need for pesticides.

Among these alternatives are the use of natural enemies, the release of sterile males, and such practices as careful crop rotation to break pest life cycles by depriving them regularly of their preferred food plant.

WASTE DISPOSAL AND POLLUTION

Waste may be defined as any product of our civilization that is usually discarded rather than used, or a formerly useful product no longer used for its original purpose or for any other. *Pollution* is a reduction in the quality of the environment by the addition of materials (or heat) not normally found there.

Pollution exists when wastes or other substances have a significantly damaging effect upon public health, property, ecosystems, or aesthetic values.

Polluting costs us a great deal. Why do we do it? Most of the reasons are economic.

1. By avoiding the costs of waste disposal, the polluter compels society to bear either the costs of his pollution or the costs of correcting it.
2. By passing on-as in the case of dumps of toxic chemicals-the cost of cleanup to future generations, we avoid having to pay for it ourselves. The unborn have no effective recourse against us for despoiling their heritage.
3. By providing convenience of use through disposable packaging, we increase sales of many goods, while compelling the public to bear the costs, ecological and otherwise, of that disposal. (What would your garbage collection bill amount to if the 60% to 80% of it that is packaging did not need to be thrown out?)
4. By deliberately designing goods to wear out or become unstylish, and by otherwise encouraging wasteful consumption, we increase the flow of goods and services through the economy.

Waste, of course, results in the need for waste disposal, plus the depletion of virgin resources that future generations will need.

WATER POLLUTION

At present, the two major sources of water pollution are industrial wastes and municipal sewage. How do they produce their effects?

Organic wastes provide a rich source of nutrients for decay bacteria and fungi. Hence feces, blood from slaughterhouses, oxygen-demanding wastes from paper mills, and peelings from vegetable-processing plants (among many other things) stimulate the growth of bacteria whose metabolism rapidly removes oxygen from the water.

Industrial wastes may also contain large amounts of sediment, chemically combined nitrogen, phosphorus, carbon dioxide, methane, hydrogen sulfide, and smaller amounts of miscellaneous chemicals, heavy-metal ions, and even pesticides.

Industry accounts for most water pollution in the United States. Usually far more concentrated than municipal sewage, industrial waste produces up to 12 times the amount of pollution per gallon of effluent that municipal wastes do.

But what they lack in concentration municipal wastes somewhat make up in volume, especially with street drainage and surface runoff after rain and snow. A polluted environment is a demanding one. Not surprisingly, few organisms can tolerate it. Yet those able to exist in it often attain astronomical numbers and very large biomass.

Most aquatic organisms, including, unfortunately, those we hold most desirable, are sensitive to the effects of pollution and are destroyed by it. When organic wastes are dumped into a stream, a predictable sequence of events occurs. Near the source of pollution, surprisingly, numbers of fish and other organisms may persist because the organic wastes have not had time to decay, and the dissolved oxygen level is high.

In severe instances, somewhat farther away, conditions worsen, with bacteria and fungi that degrade organic sewage using up so much oxygen that anaerobic conditions exist. Still farther away, the polluted water has begun to purify itself: Organic materials start to disappear, oxygen diffuses into the water from the air, and except for cultural eutrophication, something like a normal ecology is established.

About half the population of the United States depends upon rivers for drinking water (the rest of us use groundwater). Although legislation requires industries and municipalities to treat their wastes before dumping them in the nearest stream or river, the purification process is never 100% effective.

Thus, many pollutants, including suspected carcinogens, are present

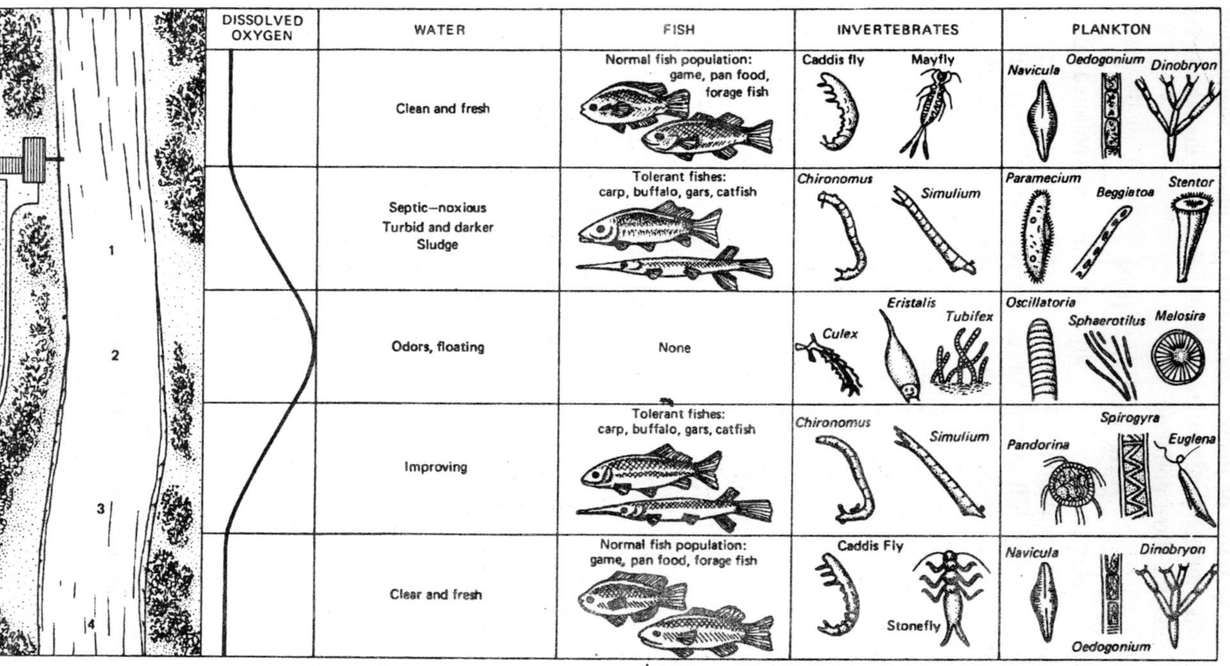

Figure 9.10: Zonation of pollution ecology in a stream receiving untreated sewage. As the amount of oxygen dissolved in the water decreases, fishes disappear.

in the drinking water of many communities. Eventually, many river pollutants (like air and land pollutants) find their way to the oceans-the ultimate *sinks* for most pollution.

AIR POLLUTION

Have you ever considered the plight of a fish in a polluted lake? It is exposed to a continuous dose of toxic substances every moment, every day, from which it usually has no escape. Air pollution puts us in the position of the fish, for each of us must breathe about 20,000 times every day.

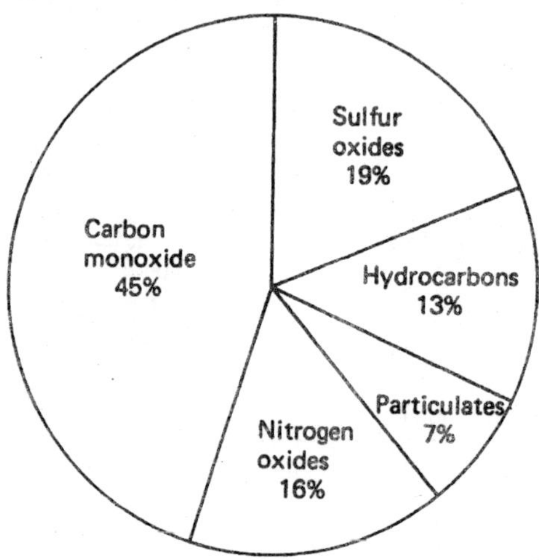

Figure 9.11: The average makeup of air pollution.

With each breath we inhale a wide variety of toxic gases and particles spewed into the air by automobiles, power plants, industries, and cigarette smokers. The United States alone dumps more than 220 million tons of pollutants into the air annually. The pollutants that account for most air pollution are carbon monoxide, sulfur oxides, nitrogen oxides, hydrocarbons, and particulates.

Their relative contributions to air pollution are indicated in Figure elsewhere in this chapter. These pollutants interact to form secondary pollutants and smog. Cigarette smoke is also an important indoor air pollutant. It contains several other pollutants and represents a highly concentrated source of pollution.

Although the total volume of polluted air produced by smokers does not begin to compete with the amount spewed forth by industry, the health consequences are more severe, for the air polluted by the smoker is the air closest to us-the very air we must breathe.

Industrial pollution is generally somewhat diluted by the time it wafts our way. Nevertheless, the effects of industrial and other gross pollution on public health and the ecology are substantial.

Ecological Effects of Air Pollution

Air pollution has many sources, ranging from the smokestacks of power plants to the exhaust pipe of the family car. Our consumptive life-style ensures a multitude of sources of such air pollution, especially in manufacturing areas and in the vicinity of cities.

In Chicago, air pollution at times reduces the amount of sunlight about 40%, and in New York City, 25%. When sunlight is reduced, photosynthesis is also diminished. In addition, trees and other plants absorb great quantities of pollutants directly from the air.

For the most part damage occurs in the photosynthetic tissue (mesophyll) of the leaf. The surfaces of mesophyll cells, which are moist to facilitate gas exchange in photosynthesis, are vulnerable to attack by toxic substances in the air. Fluoride particulates, photochemical smog (generated from automobile emissions by a chemically complex atmospheric process), sulfur dioxide, and perhaps even very fine soot can kill vegetation.

Some species of plants are more susceptible to certain pollutants than other species. At a concentration of less than one part per million, the common pollutant nitrogen dioxide reduces the growth of tomato plants by 30%. In Los Angeles County and areas up to 60 miles away, forests are being damaged by photochemical smog.

Photosynthesis is reduced by 66% when smog concentrations are 0.25 part per million. Such decreases in photosynthesis slow the flow of resins under the bark, in turn rendering the trees susceptible to plant disease and insect pests. With the increase in air pollution that present trends are producing, vast damage to vegetation may occur in North America and even the world. This damage is caused not only by the direct means already mentioned, but also by acid rain.

Meteorology of Air Pollution

Atmospheric inversion is the cause of most air pollution episodes. In such cases weather conditions form a lid of warm air above cooler, polluted air. Though inversions do not actually increase pollution, they seal the pollutants below and prevent them from being dispersed.

In Los Angeles County, where conditions favour them, inversion layers form when warm air moves in from the deserts to the east and lies over the mountains that surround Los Angeles. Beneath this warm air is a layer of cooler air that has moved in from the sea. Such inversions also form, though less regularly, in virtually every area of the country.

Simple air stagnation, which can occur anywhere, is almost as bad, for then pollution is not dispersed by normal wind action. It is that very wind action, helpful in moving polluted air, that unfortunately results in acid rain perhaps hundreds of miles from where the pollutants originated.

It is common for acid rain to be caused by air pollution in other nations, and this has caused international disputes among such countries as Great Britain and Sweden, and the United States and Canada.

Acid rain can add sulfur to crops that need this element (not always present in fertilizer). But in comparison to the ecological harm that is done, this benefit is trivial. Acid rain damages trees and other vegetation directly, probably leaches far more nutrients from the soil than it could possibly add, and where the surface waters are soft (that is, where they lack natural buffering capacity) kills fish and other aquatic life over vast areas, reaching into wilderness lakes and ponds seldom visited by people but despoiled by them nonetheless.

Air pollution probably also affects climate on a global scale. Some scientists fear that if we continue to inject great quantities of particulates into the atmosphere, we may bring on another ice age. Particulate matter could serve as nuclei for the condensation of high clouds, which would reflect sunlight away from the earth.

One scientist has calculated that the addition of only 50 million tons of pollutant particles to the atmosphere could reduce the average surface temperature of our planet from its present 60°F (15°C) to about 40°F (7°C). Most forms of plant life could not survive in such a cold climate.

Other scientists fear that the vast amounts of carbon dioxide we are producing may have a *greenhouse effect*, holding heat in so that average temperatures will rise. The really upsetting aspect of global air pollution is our ignorance of its probable effects and our inability to predict them with certainty.

Whatever the long-term effects on climate, pollutants are likely to affect the delicate balance of the ecosphere. It seems foolish to await a practical demonstration of just which prediction turns out to be correct.

RADIOACTIVE POLLUTION

Radioactive strontium has been released into the atmosphere mostly by the atmospheric testing of strategic nuclear weapons, a practice forsworn in 1963 by those countries that signed the Nuclear Test Ban Treaty.

In the event of even limited nuclear war, however, not only radioactive strontium but also radioactive iodine and many other such substances would find their way into the food chain, producing a harvest of disease for generations after the acute deaths from the nuclear exchange.

Even during peace, widespread generation of nuclear wastes by power plants could have a similar effect, particularly in the event of accidents encountered in transporting those wastes, destruction of a nuclear power plant by sabotage or warfare, or diversion of nuclear fuel.

The radioactive isotope of strontium is chemically similar to calcium and so travels in ecosystems much as calcium does. Like calcium, it becomes incorporated into bones and teeth and can produce such damage as bone cancer.

It has a half-life of 28 years-that is, in 28 years half of it will still remain, the other half having decayed into nonradioactive products. In another 28 years the remaining half will not have declined to zero but will itself have been halved, so one might say the quarter life of radioactive strontium is 56 years. That is a long time to carry such a substance in one's bones.

This is not idle speculation. Reindeer "moss," the arctic lichen mentioned in other chapter of this book, has, like other lichens, the ability to greatly concentrate substances from precipitation and perhaps from atmospheric dust as well.

It greatly concentrates radioactive strontium, which is further concentrated, somewhat like persistent pesticides, when reindeer eat the lichens. When Laplanders or Eskimos milk the reindeer, the radioactive strontium is still further concentrated and may end up in the body of a child. Less marked but similar biological magnification takes place in the grass-cow-human food chain.

The indirect ecological effects of widespread nuclear war are beyond calculation, but it is likely that a large nuclear exchange involving only two nations would ultimately destroy all or almost all the earth's major ecosystems as radioactive fallout was carried around the globe by atmospheric circulation.

SOLID WASTE DISPOSAL

Each of us accounts for about 3.6 kilograms (almost 10 pounds) of garbage, trash, and other solid wastes per day, and the amount is rising steadily. Until quite recently there was little thought of doing anything other than picking solid wastes up from one place and putting them down in another. But we are rapidly running out of rugs under which to sweep the debris of modern society.

Solid waste disposal is a relatively recent problem. Through colonial times the principal household waste other than excrement was organic garbage, and not much of that. Disposable containers were unknown. A bottle or a pot would ordinarily be discarded only if it were broken and unsalvageable.

Bones were gnawed clean or boiled down for soup, or both. The little that found its way out into the yard was rapidly consumed by the traditional garbage disposal of primitive communitiespigs, dogs, and

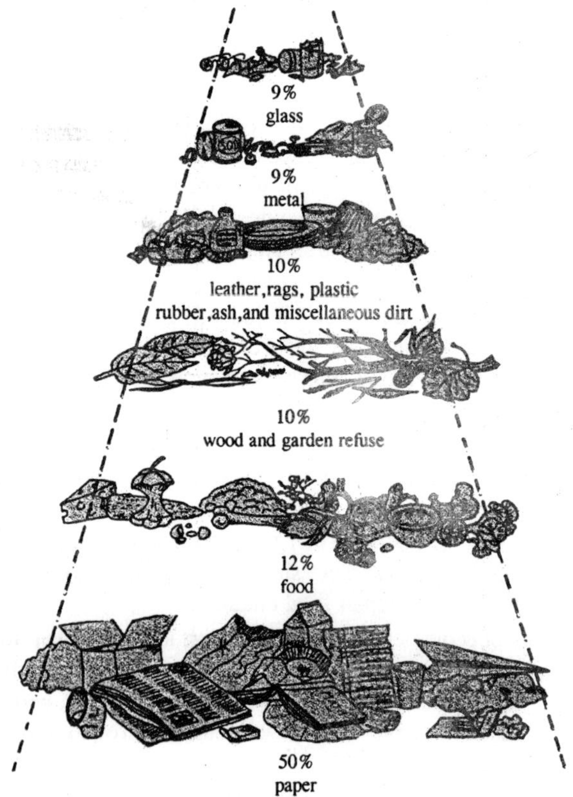

Figure 9.12: Composition of municipal trash in the U.S.

chickens. In turn, such animals were often slaughtered and eaten-a good example of the recycling of wastes.

Today's American consumer discards large quantities of paper (newspapers, paper bags, cups, plates, cartons, and other packaging materials) and substantial amounts of edible food scraps, as well as nonreturnable glass and plastic bottles, steel and aluminum cans, and wood and garden refuse, little of which is recycled.

In addition to these municipal wastes, agricultural activities generate more than 1.8 billion metric tons (a metric ton is about 2205 pounds) of wastes each year, mainly manure. Mining and industrial wastes add to the problem.

Although some rural communities still dispose of their solid wastes in open dumps, and many coastal cities practice ocean dumping, the two principal means of solid waste disposal today are the *sanitary landfill* and incineration. After waste is dumped in a sanitary landfill, it may be further compacted by bulldozers.

Each day a layer of soil is pushed over the garbage to discourage flies and rats. Using the sanitary landfill method, abandoned strip mines have been filled and eventually reclaimed, and artificial mountains have been constructed for skiing in the Midwestern plains.

Not all land should be filled, however. Marshes and even lakes are favourite sites for landfills, despite the ecological value of these wetlands.

Landfills, like dumps, can pollute groundwater as contaminants leak into the ground. Another problem with sanitary landfills is that filled land has a limited number of suitable uses. If used as a building site, settling may cause walls and foundations to crack.

Methane gas resulting from anaerobic decomposition in the depths of the fill may seep into buildings and constitute an explosion hazard. For these reasons filled land is best used for parks and other recreational purposes.

Many communities burn their garbage rather than dump it. In a modern incinerator the trash is burned in a carefully engineered furnace but some air pollution does result. The heat produced by the fire may be used to boil water and generate steam, which can be sold for industrial use.

RECYCLING

Many pollutants may be thought of as resources out of place. Solid wastes can be recycled and reused, and recycling can also be applied to sewage. After all, the minerals and organic matter that originate in

Midwestern prairies end up flowing into New York Harbor, where they are only a dangerous nuisance. This sewage could be reclaimed, and so could solid wastes.

Technology is available for recycling most solid wastes. Yet less than 10% of consumer goods are recycled. About 20% of the paper used in the United States each year is recycled. If we increased this to 50%, the amount recycled in Japan, we could save about 100 million trees. Enough energy would be saved to supply 750,000 homes with electricity. Why don't we practice recycling to a greater extent?

Perhaps the main reason recycling has not become more popular is that it is generally thought to be expensive. Manufacturers consider it cheaper to consume the energy needed to produce goods from virgin materials than to hire the labor necessary to recycle.

An aluminum can is worth about 1 cent in the United States. For that penny, many people would rather throw the can in the trash than worry about recycling it. However, it takes about 20 times more energy to manufacture a can from raw ore than from recycled scrap metal.

If the costs of manufacturing and then disposing of the can were considered, the value of recycling would be more readily appreciated. Changes in tax laws, which now encourage use of virgin materials over recycling, and other legislative incentives might be useful in promoting recycling.

ENERGY OPTIONS

Just as there could be no life on earth without the energy from the sun, there could be no modern society without the energy harnessed by human beings. Yet as population has increased and technology has expanded, we have come to realize that we have an energy problem.

This problem has resulted from too many people consuming too much energy, both directly and indirectly, by consuming too many goods that required energy input for manufacture. During the past several years it has become increasingly evident that we are depleting oil and natural gas resources at an alarming rate, and that the amount of coal available is also limited.

New technologies are being developed that will enable us to replace traditional energy sources with new ones, but at present we still depend on fossil fuels (mainly petroleum) for about 90% of our energy needs.

Two important energy options being developed are nuclear power and solar power. Thirty years ago nuclear experts heralded the age of nuclear power with the claim that nuclear power would be "too cheap

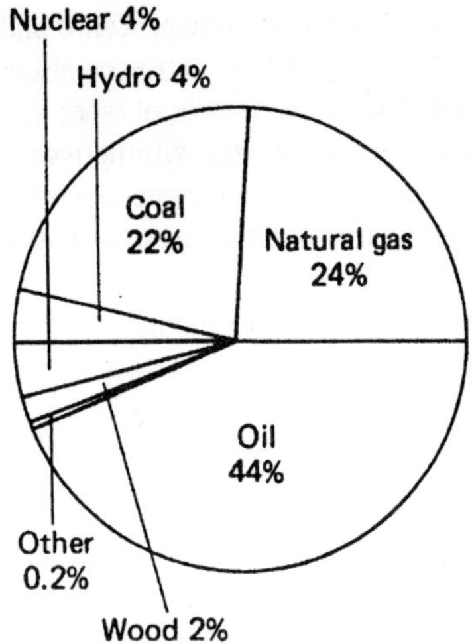

Figure 9.13: Composition of fossil fuels depended on for 90% of our energy needs.

to meter." These words could not have been less true. With changes in the economy and massive cost overruns, nuclear power has become very expensive.

Questions about environmental impact, availability of uranium ore, and safety have seriously threatened the nuclear power industry. (Only two nuclear plants ordered to be built in the United States during the past 9 years have not been later canceled, and these two are unlikely to ever be completed.)

An average of 12 mishaps per day occur in nuclear plants, mainly due to equipment problems or failures, and the problem of safe disposal of nuclear wastes has never been solved. The nuclear power plants currently in use are fission plants.

A controlled chain reaction is established in some suitable material, usually a uranium isotope of plutonium. The heat that is produced boils water or some other fluid, producing steam that drives a turbine and generator. *Fusion-type* nuclear power depends on the fusion of atoms of light elements, such as deuterium, tritium, and lithium, to produce the heat.

Nuclear fusion may prove less harmful than fission, but the technology is still in its developmental stages and no one knows when this energy option will become a reality. Meanwhile, it is probable that fission-type nuclear power plants will continue to account for a small percentage (perhaps 5%) of the world energy budget.

Many experts consider solar power a safe and viable alternative to nuclear power. The energy is free and very abundant, it causes no air pollution and few environmental hazards of other kinds, and the technology promises to be less expensive than alternatives. Solar energy can be used in buildings through passive designs maximizing the use of natural sunlight and through the installation of solar collectors, which trap and store heat.

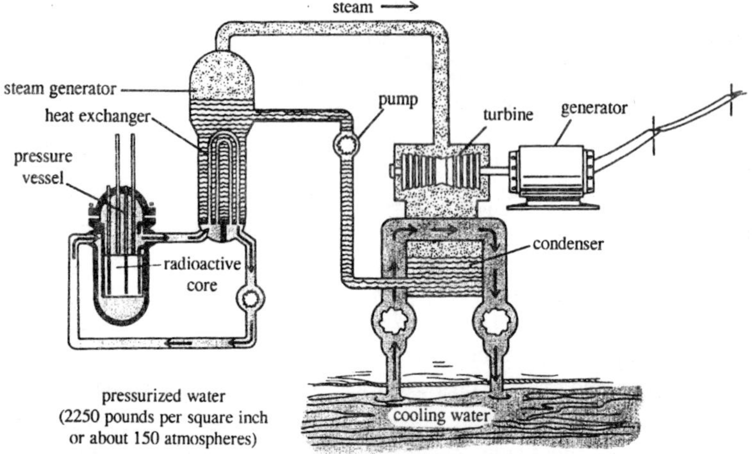

Figure 9.14: Schematic illustration of a nuclear fission plant powered by a pressurized water reactor.

Technology is available for converting sunlight into direct-current electricity, but thus far it is expensive. Photovoltaic cells, tiny cells similar to the silicon semiconductor chips used in calculators, can convert up to 20% of the sunlight striking their surface into electricity. Another solar technology is the brine pond that traps heat at high temperatures; that heat can be converted to electricity.

Other energy options include hydropower and wind, tide, and geothermal and ocean thermal power. With the exception of hydropower, these sources are not economically feasible at present and are not expected to contribute more than about 1 % of the annual energy budget by the year 2000.

Energy experts project that we will still be tightly locked in to the fossil fuels for our energy needs as we enter the 21st century. In their 800-page report on the energy situation from 1985 to 2010, the Committee on Nuclear and Alternative Energy Systems concluded that the highest priority of the United States' national energy policy should be reducing the growth of energy demand.

EXTINCTION

Although extinctions have always occurred, human beings directly or indirectly have raised the rate at which they occur perhaps 1000-fold. The species most vulnerable to extinction appear to be large, predatory, and migratory, such as the polar bear.

However, extinction also pursues animals with other combinations of characteristics: those that require large tracts of wilderness or solitude, live in very specialized or restricted habitats, compete with human beings in any respect, or yield economically valuable products. Extinctions also result from importing alien species against which an endangered organism has no effective defense.

Recently, environmental pollution has also been involved in some extinctions. Although it is difficult to be sure, the destruction of *habitat* appears to account, at least in part, for the bulk of extinctions and endangerments of species. The extinction of the passenger pigeon probably resulted from the destruction of the beech forests in which it nested as much as from the market hunting that is usually blamed.

Another extinct species, the ivory-billed woodpecker, required large virgin tracts of cypress forest. Today little of that habitat is left. In large measure extinction-whether from hunting, habitat destruction, or other cause-results from the tendency of our species, like any other species, to multiply to the limits of environmental resistance.

The resultant conversion of as much other life as possible to human biomass, plus our formidable technology-aided competition with them for resources or space assures the destruction of any species that is not directly and obviously valuable to us. Much of the destruction has resulted more from thoughtlessness than from any need.

But how can we prevent the extinction of most species with which we come in contact if our population continues to increase? Surely we may yet discover that species long considered useless have potential for domestication or play some vital role in the ecosystem to which we ourselves belong. Let us hope that when that time comes, it will not be too late.

OVERPOPULATION

Fifty years ago many communities dumped their raw sewage into the nearest river or bay. They could depend on natural bacterial decomposition to break it down with little negative effect upon the ecology of the waterway. As communities grew, however, additional numbers of people produced more sewage than nature could handle.

As water became more and more polluted, communities had to invest in expensive sewage treatment systems. Technology, in other words, had to take over nature's functions.

More people means more than just increased sewage, however. More people need more food, clothing, houses, schools, roads, automobiles, television sets, energy, and all the material goods our society holds so dear.

Each of these can be translated into increased pressure on the environment. For example, the need for more food results in the use of more pesticides and more chemical fertilizers, which results in damage to the soil and increased land and water pollution. Production of chemical fertilizers requires the use of more petroleum, contributing to energy shortages.

At the same time, more people need housing, stores, schools, and roads, so more land is taken out of agricultural production, leaving farmers to try to raise more food on less land. The one-third of the world's population that lives in the developed countries consumes 85% of the earth's resources and is responsible for most of the stress placed on the environment.

The other two-thirds of humanity strive to consume at our level. It has been estimated that the maximum world population that could be supported at the United States' level of affluence is less than *1 billion.* The environmental impact of enriching even this billion to current United States norms would involve increased industrial pollution, increased erosion of agricultural land, further depletion of natural resources, and much more.

Such a goal is totally unrealistic, however, because at the current growth rate world population will reach 8 billion by the year 2100. And inevitably most human beings living then will subsist in unprecedented conditions of poverty.

Overpopulation is thus one of the most pressing problems of our time-a problem from which we in the United States are *not* insulated. Aside from the moral issues involved, the National Security Council has described population increases around the world as a threat to our national security. How much greater a threat it must be to the Third World nations in which population growth is now the greatest-and to their neighbors.

How Population Grows

Early in this century the Russian ecologist G.F. Gause studied the growth of populations of *Paramecium,* the ciliate protist. Given optimal conditions, the population increased slowly at first, in what is sometimes called the *lag phase* of population growth. Soon, however, the population entered a rapid exponential growth phase, the *logarithmic phase*. Ultimately, population growth slowed and stopped in the *equilibrium phase*. The overall curve is S-shaped.

Gause's observations have since been extended to cover a multitude of different organisms, including mammals. When the biotic potential of an organism initially greatly exceeds the resistance of its environment, its population growth closely resembles that of Gause's microorganisms.

When the population becomes sufficiently dense, competition for food and other resources limits further growth. Population stabilizes at the *carrying capacity*, the maximum population that the environment can sustain indefinitely.

If, in achieving population growth, the organisms have consumed essential nonrenewable resources, or have consumed renewable resources so excessively that they lose their ability for renewal, there is little or no equilibrium phase. In such a case the essentials for supporting even a small population are lacking and the population enters a phase *of decline,* itself often logarithmic. In this way even very dense populations can "crash" and may suffer almost instant extinction.

It is instructive to view human population growth in this light. Beginning with 14,000 years ago up through the middle ages the human species was essentially in its lag phase of population growth. Disease and food shortages served as powerful environmental resistance.

But around the time of the Industrial Revolution our population entered the logarithmic phase of its growth, and is now increasing by about 200,000 persons per day. Today, in some nations, human population is *doubling* every 15 years, or even more rapidly.

At any one time population depends upon a balance between two factors, *birth rate* and *death rate*. Different organisms have different ways of balancing the two. A very high death rate could be compensated for by a high birth rate, for example, but if the death rate were low, high populations could be maintained by a much lower birth rate.

The populational, or demographic, events of the past 250 years are shown in Figure elsewhere in this chapter. Notice that among developed countries, birth rate has declined over the long run. Death rate has also declined, mostly due to the control of infectious disease. Since birth rate and death rate have mostly marched in step, the population of such countries as Sweden has increased only modestly, and in some, such as West Germany, it appears to be in a state of slight decline.

The birth rate in less developed countries has also fallen dramatically, but modern medicine has brought mortality down even faster, so that their population has increased greatly despite the decline in birth rate. Current and past population growth affects age distribution in a nation's population. In the graph of the United States population shown in Figure elsewhere in this chapter, notice that there are very few individuals in the uppermost age ranges.

Mostly because of the post World War II baby boom, there is a bulge in the population profile at around the teen and young adult ages. Sweden, shown in the second graph, has a stable population history. Due to widespread use of birth control methods and ready availability of excellent medical care for the entire population, about as many Swedes are born each year as die.

Thus, Sweden has achieved *zero population growth.* However, the average Swede lives to quite an advanced age so that the numbers of people in all age ranges are about the same up to about age seventy. Mexico, shown in the third graph, typifies heavy population growth in the third world.

In such a nation, children have always been perceived as an economic asset-extra hands to work subsistence farms, and eventually, providers of care to aged parents. Since, until recently, many children died early from infectious disease, powerful economic motivation has caused widespread resistance to population control.

But here there is a conflict of economic interest between individuals and their society. In all three graphs we have stippled the age ranges in which people consume resources without, on the whole, making substantial economic contributions. A demand for schooling, pediatric care, nursery care, and much else is generated by the children of Mexico. Yet the resources of Mexican society are largely insufficient to meet this demand.

Moreover, the growth rates of the Mexican population result in the doubling of the need for *all* of society's services every 15 years. Even an affluent country like Sweden or the United States could not readily double all its roads, schools, hospitals, sewage disposal plants, fire departments, apartment buildings, and more every 15 years. And if it did, think of the ecological consequences.

However, the developing countries cannot even run fast enough to stay where they are, yet understandably, they aspire to the same standards of affluence that the developed nations enjoy.

What has produced the demographic differences between the

developed and less-developed nations? Evidently, the citizens of the developed nations ceased some time ago to regard children as an economic asset.

In the United States, for example, it costs in excess of $60,000 to raise a child to economic independence (not counting the cost of a college education), almost none of which is returned to the parent. Upwardly mobile people therefore tend to limit their family size.

Most developed countries went through a difficult time of social transition in the 19th and early 20th centuries, when they accumulated the capital necessary to establish the industrial economies in which children are no longer an economic asset.

Not so the less-developed nations: With all capital consumed as fast as it is generated by the urgent needs of their populations, they are not likely to achieve industrial economies or undergo the kind of demographic transition that has placed the developed countries in their present enviable position.

When Is a Nation Overpopulated?

It is commonly held in the United States that *other* countries, especially less developed nations, are overpopulated, but surely not the United States itself. However, as suburban sprawl stretches out, merging one city into another, as farms are sold and the cost of food rises, as resources dwindle and we experience fuel and other shortages, as water pollution and air pollution produce increasing blight, many individuals no longer need to be convinced that overpopulation is a reality, a present reality, in this country.

In the long run the ideal population for a nation, continent, or planet is one that can be sustained indefinitely. Higher population densities than this generally result from temporary expansion of the carrying capacity of the habitat by technological means. These expansions thus far have always depended on the consumption of nonrenewable resources and our passing some of the costs to the ecosystem.

Since nonrenewable resources will dwindle and finally cease, and since the ability of the ecosystem to absorb pollution is limited, expansion cannot continue indefinitely. Populations dependent on present-day mechanical technology will eventually be drastically reduced.

Since more resources will by that time have been consumed, the resulting population is likely to be both poorer materially and fewer in number.

INDEX

F

G

H

I